Keeping Out the Other

KEEPING OUT THE OTHER

A Critical Introduction to
Immigration Enforcement Today

David C. Brotherton and
Philip Kretsedemas, Editors

COLUMBIA UNIVERSITY PRESS

NEW YORK

Columbia University Press
Publishers Since 1893
New York   Chichester, West Sussex
Copyright © 2008 Columbia University Press

Mark Dow, "What We Believe They Deserve: Guantanamo, 9/11, Haitians, Mariel Cubans,
and 'National Security' as a Pretext for Unchecked Power," 12 Tulsa J. Comp. & Int'l L. 61.
Copyright © 2004 Tulsa Journal of Comparative and International Law. Reprinted by
permission of Tulsa Journal of Comparative and International Law.

Detention of asylum seekers in the US and UK: Deciphering noisy and quiet constructions by
Michael Welch and Liza Schuster. Copyright © 2005 Sage Publications. Reprinted by
permission of Sage Publications Ltd.

Library of Congress Cataloging-in-Publication Data
Keeping out the other : a critical introduction to immigration enforcement today / David C.
Brotherton and Philip Kretsedemas, editors.
    p. cm.
    Includes bibliographical references and index.
    ISBN 978-0-231-14128-4 (cloth : alk. paper)—ISBN 978-0-231-14129-1 (pbk. : alk. paper)
    1. United States—Emigration and immigration—Government policy.   2. Emigration
and immigration law—United States.   3. Illegal aliens—United States.   I. Brotherton,
David.   II. Kretsedemas, Philip, 1967–   III. Title.
JV6483.K44 2008
325.73—dc22   2007046568

Columbia University Press books are printed on permanent and durable acid-free paper.
This book was printed on paper with recycled content.

Printed in the United States of America
c 10 9 8 7 6 5 4 3 2
p 10 9 8 7 6 5 4 3 2

References to Internet Web sites (URLs) were accurate at the time of writing. Neither the
author nor Columbia University Press is responsible for URLs that may have expired or
changed since the manuscript was prepared.

CONTENTS

Justice and the Outsider

DAVID COLE

SOLON, THE GREAT ATHENIAN JURIST, once predicted that "justice will not come until those who are not hurt feel just as indignant as those who are." Nowhere is that maxim more true than with respect to the immigrant. Foreign nationals, at least until they become citizens, occupy a necessarily compromised position in our community. They live and work among us. They are our friends, neighbors, colleagues, and fellow students and teachers. They pay taxes, provide expertise that we lack, often take jobs that others will not take, and contribute immeasurably to the diversity of our local and national communities. But at the same time, immigrants are denied a political voice in the federal system; they may not vote or run for federal elective office. Their very presence here is qualified by the sovereign prerogative to send them "home"—even when for all practical purposes their true home has become the United States and they have not been back to their country of birth since infancy. And immigrants are very often convenient scapegoats for Americans' fears—the ones first targeted in times of crisis as "the enemy." As such, immigrants experience a vulnerability that many of those of us who are citizens do not. Their experiences are not our experiences, in the main. To understand their situation requires an empathic leap.

But as Solon's remark suggests, it is in the possibility of that empathic leap that justice lies. Hermann Cohen, an eighteenth-century Jewish philosopher, put it similarly in a commentary on the Bible: "The alien was to be protected, not because he was a member of one's family, clan, or religious community; but because he was a human being. In the alien, therefore, man discovered the idea of humanity."[1] This volume seeks to build a bridge of empathy toward the idea of humanity—to generate in those of us who are citizens the indignation that is necessary before justice will be done to the foreign nationals among us, or who are under our sovereign control.

The problem of justice for immigrants has been especially acute since September 11, 2001, when nineteen foreign nationals hijacked jet planes and used them as suicide bombs, prompting the United States to respond with a "war on terror." But as several of the contributors to this book demonstrate, anti-immigrant sentiment and repression is not a recent phenomenon in this (or indeed, any other) country. Political repression in times of crisis nearly always begins by targeting the foreign national as outsider. This allows politicians to cheat on the trade-offs between liberty and security by assuring the public that their own rights are not being sacrificed, because foreigners are the targets, and foreigners do not deserve the same legal guarantees as citizens. The most infamous federal laws of political repression in U.S. history advertised their antialien character in their very titles—the Alien and Sedition Acts of 1798, and the Alien Registration Act of 1940 (also known as the Smith Act). Nor is the problem of disregard for the treatment of immigrants limited to times of crisis. Indeed, the legal term of art for a foreign national, the "alien," captures all too perfectly the sense of absolute Otherness that we assign to those formally outside our political community—as if their presence is always at least potentially an invasion.

The problem of justice for the immigrant is both political and legal. On the political side, the issue is how to protect those who are denied a voice in the political process. The failure of immigration reform in the spring of 2007, even when it was backed by a coalition featuring President George W. Bush and Senators John McCain and Ted Kennedy, and particularly the intensity of opposition to any notion of "amnesty" for so-called illegal aliens, dramatically illustrated the difficulty of a political solution. Two years earlier, immigrants had staged massive rallies across the country, prompting talk of a new civil rights movement for immigrants. But in the end, most of those who demonstrated do not vote, while their opponents most certainly do. How does one organize political pressure for a group of people who cannot speak for themselves?

One response is to appeal to the interests of those who can vote. Immigrants are our ancestors, our fellow employees, our friends and neighbors. In that sense, the "us-them" dichotomy is a false one, often perpetrated by those who would exploit division for demagogic goals. We are in a very real sense a nation of immigrants. Economists have shown that immigration generally results in a net gain for the American economy as a whole—even if in the short term some immigrants impose additional costs on those regions most likely to attract new immigrants. Individuals who are willing to leave their home and country of origin for a foreign land where they may know no one and not speak the language often tend to be self-starters, willing to work hard to succeed once they are here. Immigrants add to the cultural diversity of our communities, our schools, and our lives in ways that are difficult to measure but impossible to deny. Finally, as Hermann Cohen reminds us, immigrants, like us, are "human beings" and deserve equal respect simply by virtue of that shared humanity.

The last point is also crucial to the legal argument for immigrants' rights. There is no denying that citizens and foreign nationals have different statuses in our society. Citizens cannot be expelled, no matter how heinously they act; foreign nationals are always at least potentially subject to expulsion. But it does not follow, in the broad sense often asserted, that foreign nationals do not deserve the rights that citizens do. While the Constitution does speak specifically of citizens' rights in some instances, such as the right to vote and to run for federal elective office, most of the rights it recognizes are extended to "persons" or "people" or "the accused," terms that do not distinguish between citizen and foreign national, and that would appear to encompass both. There is no reason, for example, that a foreign national facing trial for murder should be accorded any fewer rights than his citizen codefendant. Moreover, international human rights treaties, many of which the United States was central in helping to draft and propagate, are predicated on the notion that rights stem from human dignity, and dignity is in no way limited to citizens.

The Bush administration has since 9/11 repeatedly rejected such thinking. When it authorized military tribunals for "terrorist" crimes, it made them applicable only to foreign nationals, not citizens accused of the same crimes, and argued that foreigners do not deserve the same rights as Americans. When it was searching for ways to free up Central Intelligence Agency interrogators to use cruel and inhuman tactics to coerce information from suspects, it came up with the novel—and fundamentally immoral—notion that the right to be free of cruel, inhuman, and degrading treatment, a right that stems from an international human rights treaty that the United States signed and ratified, simply does not apply to foreign nationals held outside our borders. And administration lawyers have applied that same thinking to the men held without trial at Guantánamo Bay, Cuba, consistently arguing that they have no constitutional rights.

There is a different approach. In 2004 the Law Lords in the United Kingdom, the equivalent of the U.S. Supreme Court, declared a post–9/11 law enacted by Parliament to be incompatible with the European Convention on Human Rights precisely because it impermissibly discriminated between foreign nationals and citizens.[2] The law in question authorized indefinite detention of foreign nationals who were suspected of terrorist involvement but could not be deported (often because they would face torture if returned to their country of origin). The Law Lords reasoned that if a person poses a threat to national security, the nature of that threat is not affected by whether the person is a citizen or a foreign national. And of course, the burden of incarceration on individual freedom is the same whether one has a British or a Jordanian passport. Accordingly, the Law Lords ruled, the law violated the convention because it discriminated against foreign nationals.

The Law Lords' ruling did not suggest that all distinctions between foreign nationals and citizens were illegitimate. Far from it. But rather than rest in an unthinking fashion on assertions that foreign nationals are not entitled to the same rights as citizens, the Law Lords analyzed the particular right in question, and the particular government interest at stake, and asked whether the citizen/foreign national distinction made any sense *in that setting*. We would do well to do the same—to ask, at each point, whether an individual's nationality is a relevant consideration in his or her treatment by the government, or whether the shared humanity of us all demands equal regard.

The essays in this volume pose these questions from a variety of different perspectives. But in the end, they are all directed to Solon's goal of bringing justice to those who are hurt by making the rest of us feel just as indignant.

Notes

1. H. Freedman, ed., *Jeremiah: Hebrew Text and English Translation with an Introduction and Commentary* (London: Soncino Press, 1949), 52.

2. *A (FC) and others (FC) v Secretary of State for the Home Department*, 56 (HL 2004) (UK).

ACKNOWLEDGMENTS

THIS BOOK WOULD NEVER HAVE COME TOGETHER without the encouragement of a number of people who share a deep commitment to immigrants' rights. We are especially indebted to Mark Dow and the National Immigration Project of the National Lawyers Guild for helping us connect with many of the contributors whose essays are included herein. We also express our gratitude to the sponsors of the conference "Criminal Justice and Deportation: The Invisible Crisis," which was held at John Jay College of Criminal Justice on October 22 and 23, 2003; in particular, the JEHT Foundation, the President's Office of John Jay College, and the New York City Legal Aid Society.

Our main goal has been to pull together a timely compilation of essays that document some of the most worrisome features of immigration enforcement today and that address the diverse social justice concerns raised by these issues. As with any anthology, the strength of this book rests on the experiences and critical insights of its contributors. We feel that, in this area, we have been very fortunate. Our contributors represent an impressively diverse cross section of scholars, activists, journalists, and lawyers who have many years of experience working on the front lines of the immigrants' rights movement. We strongly encourage the reader to review the About the Contributors section before delving into the chapters, since it may help to underscore the significance and experiential context of many of the contributors' observations.

Finally, we hope this book demonstrates how theory, political strategy, and policy critique can be informed by the experiences of noncitizens who have been directly affected by enforcement practices—shedding new light on the situation of noncitizens in the United States today and illustrating what these trends portend for U.S. society as a whole.

AEDPA	Antiterrorism and Effective Death Penalty Act
BIA	Board of Immigration Appeals
BJS	Bureau of Justice Statistics
CAT	Convention Against Torture
CPB	Customs and Border Protection
DHS	Department of Homeland Security
DOJ	Department of Justice
EOIR	Executive Office of Immigration Review
EWI	Entered Without Inspection
FOIA	Freedom of Information Act
ICE	Immigration and Customs Enforcement
IIRAIRA	Illegal Immigration Reform and Immigrant Responsibility Act
INA	Immigration and Nationality Act
INS	Immigration and Naturalization Service
IRCA	Immigration Reform and Control Act
LPR	Legal Permanent Resident
MDC	Metropolitan Detention Center (New York, Brooklyn)
NAFTA	North American Free Trade Agreement
NCIC	National Crime Information Center
NSEERS	National Security Entry-Exit Registration System
OIG	Office of the Inspector General
OIS	Office of Immigration Statistics
PRWORA	Personal Responsibility and Work Opportunity Reconciliation Act
RIDA	Real ID Act

TPS	Temporary Protected Status
UNHCR	United Nations High Commission for Refugees
USA PATRIOT	Uniting and Strengthening America by Providing Appropriate Tools Required to Intercept and Obstruct Terrorism
USMS	U.S. Marshals Service

CHAPTER I

Open Markets, Militarized Borders?
Immigration Enforcement Today

PHILIP KRETSEDEMAS AND DAVID C. BROTHERTON

THE UNITED STATES has often been portrayed as remarkably liberal in its openness to migration flows, but the history of its immigration enforcement practices tells a somewhat different story. Among other things, it demonstrates how the desire for new immigrants has always been accompanied by practices aimed at removing or discouraging the migration of so-called undesirables. This was no less true during the open-borders era of U.S. immigration (illustrated most prominently by the Chinese exclusion laws) than it was of the national origins quotas of the 1920s or recent policy measures that have restricted immigrant rights and expanded the sorts of violations that can trigger deportation proceedings.[1]

These tendencies can be viewed as an unresolved contradiction that lies at the heart of an otherwise impressive history of proimmigration policy. However, it is also possible to see how the liberal and the reactionary features of U.S. immigration policy work in tandem with each other. In this regard, it is too limiting to view get-tough enforcement *only* through the lens of an immigration control agenda. It can just as easily be argued that tougher enforcement measures follow from policies and labor market recruitment strategies that are geared toward sustaining (and even increasing) current immigration levels.[2] It is also rather telling that there has been no decrease in immigration levels since the terrorist attacks of September 11, 2001, despite the crackdown on immigrant rights that occurred shortly thereafter.[3] There was not even a decrease in immigration flows among Arab-Muslim populations, which were the primary target of post–9/11 antiterrorist operations—even though the United States has become more reluctant in processing Iraqi and other Middle Eastern asylum seekers.[4] There *has* been a steady increase in deportations since this time, but this is part of a broader trend that began in the mid-1990s, during the peak years of the latest immigration boom.[5]

This book provides a critical introduction to the various forms of immigration enforcement that have taken shape in this environment, which is composed of a rather ambiguous mix of pro- and anti-immigrant sentiments. The chapters herein illustrate how the antagonism and conflicting priorities within U.S. immigration policy are translated "on the ground" for different groups of immigrants and noncitizens. And as the contributors demonstrate, very little ambiguity exists at that level. Regardless of whether deportation and detention are being used to scare immigrants out of the United States, to separate "good" immigrants from "bad" immigrants, or to manage a growing low-wage immigrant workforce, it is clear that these practices have given rise to new forms of inequality that are tied to immigrant legal status.

But before we head deeper into the U.S. context, it should be noted that these trends are by no means unique to the United States. Moral panic over unauthorized migration and immigration in general has surfaced not only in advanced industrialized nations like France, England, and Japan but in the middle-tier and developing economies of Malaysia, Indonesia, and South Korea.[6] This illustrates the scope of global anti-immigrant sentiment and demonstrates that the politics of immigration control is not just about wealthy, industrialized nations seeking to exploit and exclude migration flows coming from the global south. Although this is a large part of the story, the intensification of immigration control at the global level is also tied to anti-immigrant sentiments, ways of imagining national identity, and views on social and economic policy that span a range of national cultures. Furthermore, struggles over immigration policy and immigration control often blur the lines between the political right and left.

For example, progrowth, neoconservatives (most notably the 2000–2008 Bush White House) have constituted one of the most influential proimmigration forces in the recent debate over immigration in the United States. But proimmigration conservatives also support most of the get-tough enforcement measures being advocated by immigration restrictionists. Meanwhile, the immigration restrictionist movement—although typically associated with far-right, blue collar constituencies—also has a foothold among conservative Democrats and some racial minority populations, even though it is also rife with antagonism among economic restrictionists, cultural conservatives, and more extreme segments that have ties to the white nationalist movement.[7]

Four decades ago, the visibility and popular-political coordinates of the illegal immigration debate were very different from what they are now. At the level of national policy discourse, illegal immigration was a nonissue. Business interests and laissez-faire conservatives were openly tolerant of unauthorized Mexican migration as something that was in the pragmatic interest of the agricultural industry. As Kitty Calavita explains, immigration enforcement was typically used during this period to regulate labor flows. Enforcement measures eased when farmers were in need of labor and intensified when there appeared to be an unmanageable "glut" of unauthorized migrant labor.[8] These practices were pushed to their extreme limits with Operation Wetback, which was used in the early 1950s to deport several hundred thousand unauthorized migrants and thus compel farmers to start using the government's guest worker program. Meanwhile, worker justice and immigrant rights coalitions (as well as large segments of the Mexican American population) opposed illegal immigration as something that was being used to undermine the organizing efforts of Mexican farmworkers and the U.S. working class in general.[9] Today, in contrast, the U.S. labor movement has shifted in favor of legalizing unauthorized migrant workers, instead of restricting the flow of these workers. It is ironic, however, that the last mass-scale legalization program was initiated by the Immigration Reform and Control Act of 1986, under the watch of the Reagan administration. Meanwhile, most supporters of aggressive free-market expansion today (who also favor a business-friendly immigration policy) are openly critical of illegal immigration and favor a "sensible" increase in immigration enforcement.

It is necessary to keep these complexities in mind when coming to terms with the driving influences and practical outcomes of immigration enforcement. This complexity also extends to the immigrant experience itself. For example, the recent crackdown on immigrant rights has occurred alongside several trends that would appear to bode well for immigrant integration into the U.S. mainstream. Immigrants are playing a vital role in U.S. labor markets, accounting for over 100 percent of workforce replenishment in some regions.[10] Most of these immigrant workers are low income, but a significant minority are entrepreneurs and highly skilled professionals. Further, even low-income immigrants tend to have higher rates of workforce attachment than equivalent segments of the native-born population,[11] and over the past decade, the incomes of low-income immigrant households have risen faster than the incomes of low-income native-born households, although this has occurred alongside a growing gap between the wages of immigrants and native-born persons.[12] Immigrant populations are also becoming more involved in electoral politics and in the civic life of their local communities,[13] and there is evidence that their offspring are becoming fluent English speakers at a pace identical to that of earlier, European migrant cohorts.[14]

In this regard, it appears that a large cross section of the immigrant population is trying to integrate into the American mainstream by following a path very similar to that taken by prior immigrant cohorts. Meanwhile, immigration has become the fastest-growing sector of federal law-enforcement spending over the past two decades—easily dwarfing public spending on services aimed at assisting immigrants with settling into their new lives in the United States.[15]

Some pundits and policy analysts have argued that this is justified by increases in immigrant crime, but most criminologists and sociologists have found little evidence that immigrant crime rates are greater than crime rates for the native born.[16] In fact, some social scientists have observed that first-generation immigrant populations—of the type that are growing in urban and semiurban areas throughout the United States—may actually help to curb crime rates.[17] What is clear, however, is that the federal population of incarcerated noncitizens has mushroomed over the past two decades. Noncitizens compose almost one-third of the federal prison population and, within the past decade, immigration violations have become the primary focus of a federal enforcement agenda that used to be dominated by the war on drugs.[18]

These trends shed an entirely new light on the phrase "Give me your tired, your poor, your huddled masses." It appears that the prison cell block has become a more fitting metaphor than the melting pot for the experience of today's low-income immigrant. This is, perhaps, a fair illustration of the dual status of the United States as the world's leading immigration nation and the leading exemplar of the global penitentiary.[19] But it also begs the question, Should the Statue of Liberty be holding the sword of freedom in one hand and a pair of handcuffs in the other?

This provocative question underscores some genuine ambiguities in the way immigrants are perceived in the United States today. Many supporters of get-tough immigration enforcement are concerned about security issues underscored by the attacks of September 11, 2001. But outside of this concern, there is still a desire to identify with America's immigrant heritage and to celebrate the "hardworking immigrants" who are willing to pick themselves up by their bootstraps. There are also anti-

immigrant pundits who blame immigrants for lowering wages and imposing an unfair fiscal burden on local governments. From this perspective,
the so-called immigration problem will be solved not by finding more effective ways of integrating newcomers into the mainstreams of U.S. society but by making it more difficult for them to become citizens or
permanent residents and developing more expedient ways of removing
them from the nation. There are other factions that support immigration
for purely economic reasons. In this case, the desire for noncitizen workers
is not necessarily correlated with support for immigrant rights, and quite
often it is accompanied by pragmatic support for immigration enforcement. In fact, this perspective does not even require new flows of immigrant labor; rather, it calls for nonimmigrants, or guest workers, who are
admitted on temporary visas that limit the terms and length of their employment in the United States.

These are just a few of the agendas contributing to the expansion of immigration enforcement in the United States. They can also filter down into
the standard operating practices of different branches of federal, state, and
local government. On the positive side, these different perspectives can
check and balance each other, limiting the spread of draconian interpretations of existing policy. For example, the federal court system—and even
the Supreme Court—has issued a number of decisions over the past twenty
years that have limited some of the more "creative" enforcement practices
of the Department of Homeland Security (DHS) and local police departments.[20] But on the other hand, these variations in the way that immigration enforcement is interpreted and implemented can also lead to extreme
abuses. For example, many local prisons that house immigrant detainees
have ignored even the meager standards that have been adopted by the
DHS.[21] The White House might criticize the vigilantism of the armed
Minutemen volunteers who patrol the U.S.–Mexico border, only for these
same people to be encouraged by state and local government officials and
individual border-control agents who praise them as "loyal Americans."[22]
The chances of an immigrant with a prior conviction being deported often
depends on the immigration judge's idiosyncratic evaluations of the person's moral character and the likelihood that he or she may participate in
future "terrorist" activity.[23] In a similar vein, the experience that noncitizens have with local law enforcement and DHS agents can vary widely, depending on how these agents interpret their responsibilities and their own
views about immigration. Some law enforcement departments (and individual officers) turn a blind eye to unauthorized migrants as long as these

individuals do not commit what are considered serious (criminal) violations, whereas other departments will use any opportunity (such as a faulty taillight or riding a bicycle on the wrong side of the street) to screen noncitizens for their legal status.[24] As a result, enforcement practices that are perceived to be necessary and practical from the vantage point of the mainstream can appear extremely arbitrary from the perspective of the noncitizens who are targeted by them.

The general American public may find it enough to know that these practices are being used to safeguard them from dangerous people. These practices also appeal to the commonsense rationale that immigrant convicts and unauthorized migrants are lawbreakers and that lawbreakers should be held accountable for their actions. This reasoning, however, distracts attention from the complicity of U.S. policy in growing the size of the immigrant detainee population. For example, a string of legislative developments—ranging from the Immigration Reform and Control Act to the 2005 REAL ID Act—has curtailed the ability of noncitizens to question the terms of their detention or to challenge unjust decisions (see the Appendix for a summary of the most significant provisions of these federal laws). As a result, it is not always possible to assess the reasoning behind the decisions that lead some immigrants to be deported while others, charged with similar convictions, are allowed to return to society. In some cases it is not even possible to determine the reason that a noncitizen has been detained. Many an immigrant family has had loved ones taken away by immigration enforcement agents in the early hours of the morning and placed in deportation proceedings before their families were able to determine where and why they have been taken.[25]

Meanwhile, media coverage of these issues rarely acknowledges that more immigrants are being deported because the criteria for deportation have been dramatically expanded and not because more immigrants are committing "dangerous crimes." There is also virtually no acknowledgment that many unauthorized migrants are persons who entered the United States legally, with temporary visas, or that nonimmigrants (persons admitted with temporary, nonrenewable legal status) have become the fastest-growing class of noncitizens admitted to the United States over the past fifteen years.[26] As a result, more people are "becoming illegal" because of a growing gap between the number of people who are being admitted to the United States as workers, and the number of persons who have been granted the right to apply for permanent residence.

Immigration raids may expedite the process of removing these deportable aliens, but they obscure a very important dynamic. These stepped-up enforcement practices are not just a response to an actual increase in unauthorized migration or to a burgeoning immigrant crime wave. They are also a product of changes in legal-administrative practice that have expanded the criteria determining how and why a noncitizen becomes "illegal" and a candidate for deportation.

Immigration Enforcement Today: Mapping the Terrain

The contributions to this anthology provide several different windows into this Kafkaesque world. Some of the chapters deliver an overview of media discourse and macro social trends, but most offer detailed accounts of the implementation of immigration enforcement in different parts of the United States on a day-to-day basis.

Most of our contributors have extensive experience working with immigrant communities that have been directly affected by immigration enforcement practices, and their writing reflects the concerns and frustrations of these populations. The contributors include lawyers who represent noncitizens facing deportation and whose work has established legal landmarks for immigrant rights at the national and international level, activists whose foray into antideportation work stems from seeing the effect of these enforcement practices on their own family and friends, former immigrant detainees who have struggled against abusive treatment in immigration prisons, and journalists and freelance writers whose investigative research has played a leading role in exposing abusive and authoritarian practices in the current immigration system.

We hope this anthology will expand the readers' understanding of the scope and range of immigration enforcement practices, the various ways they are implemented, and their impact on noncitizen populations. It bears emphasizing, however, that this information cannot be neatly separated from the critical perspective of the contributing writers. As other theorists and researchers have noted, some forms of knowledge—and modes of explanation—can only be produced by entering into a sympathetic engagement with a given experience.[27] Most of our contributors adopt this mode of explanation, which can also be described as a form of critical ethnography. They interpret interview data, case studies of deportation, and thick descriptions of how the immigration system "works" that they could not have accessed if they were not driven by their concern for immigrant rights and had been unable to gain the trust of noncitizens who have been directly targeted by these practices.

We do not present these critical perspectives with the expectation that the reader will agree with all of them. But we do believe that they all provide compelling insights into policy trends, ethical questions, and social justice issues that should be discussed and debated. It also bears noting that our contributors do not all share the same perspective on the underlying causes of immigrant marginalization or on priorities for reforming the immigration system. Some contributors, for example, couch their critiques of immigration enforcement in an appeal to constitutional law and the defense of civil liberties. Others emphasize forms of structural inequality and institutional discrimination that are only tangentially related to civil liberties arguments. Several contributors provide varying perspectives on the racialization of immigrant groups that, in turn, are informed by debates within immigrants' rights circles over the causes of immigrant exclusion. Underlying all of these perspectives, however, is a concern for safeguarding immigrants' rights.

Even so, we feel it would be disingenuous to either ignore or exaggerate these differences in perspective. Instead, we have allowed the loose ends of these views to dangle, so as to challenge the reader to elucidate some of the possible points of intersection between them and to encourage new ways of thinking about these issues.

National (In)Securities? Immigration Enforcement
Before and After 9/11

The tragic events of September 11, 2001, haunt most of the current policy discourse surrounding U.S. immigration enforcement. Even so, the shift toward more deportations and greater spending on immigration enforcement was already under way several years before 9/11. As most of our contributors note, the Illegal Immigration Reform and Immigrant Responsibility Act of 1996 (IIRAIRA) and the Antiterrorism and Effective Death Penalty Act of 1996 (AEDPA) set the tone for current enforcement practices.

This is why we begin the book by both acknowledging and decentering the significance of 9/11 as a turning point in U.S. immigration enforcement. In chapter 2, Mark Dow argues that a driving force behind current immigration enforcement practices is a desire for unchecked power that is only incidentally tied to issues of national security. Dow's discussion, which is derived from his investigative work, focuses on the government's treatment of Haitian asylum seekers, Cuban Mariel detainees, and noncitizens held at the U.S. detention facility for enemy combatants at Guantánamo Bay, Cuba. In each of these cases, Dow traces the arguments that have been used to curtail the legal remedies available to noncitizen detainees and others who have been labeled specially dangerous or security risks. Dow explains how these developments rely on a disturbing Orwellian reasoning in which the severity of the charges levied against a noncitizen also become the rationale for preventing them from questioning the validity of these charges (such queries, it is claimed, requiring federal agents to disclose top-secret information). He convincingly argues that these developments have set off a downward spiral resulting in the deterioration of immigrant rights, such that restrictions on the legal rights of terrorist suspects provide the legal precedent for restrictions on the rights of asylum seekers, which also provide the legal precedent for restricting the rights of all immigrant detainees.

Dan Malone explores similar issues in chapter 3. Whereas Mark Dow focuses on legal precedents in the federal court system, Malone documents changes in internal bureaucratic practice, with an emphasis on the developments that paved the way for secret prisons. Drawing on his research as an investigative journalist, Malone elucidates the obscure history of the secret prison system and explains how it was expanded after the attacks of September 11, 2001. He tells the stories of some of the noncitizens who are being held in secret prisons and recounts several of his failed efforts to persuade immigration authorities to release information about persons admitted to this system. Malone acknowledges that many of the persons held in these prisons are likely to be genuine security risks but also finds that a number of individuals are being held on baseless charges. However, because the government considers the names and ages of these persons—and even the reason for their detention—to be a matter of top security, it is nearly impossible to seek the release of individuals who have been falsely imprisoned.

In chapter 4, Ira Kurzban provides a more expansive overview of the policy and socioeconomic context that has set the stage for today's immigration enforcement practices. Kurzban argues that explaining get-tough enforcement is impossible without accounting for the popularity of anti-immigrant attitudes and that today's nativism is a reaction to the economic restructuring of the U.S. economy. Kurzban notes that these developments are responsible for many of the social tensions that are unfairly blamed on immigrants. Just as important, they set the stage for the centralization of decision-making authority that has allowed a small group of elites to monopolize the framing and discussion of important policy issues—immigration being chief among these.

In chapter 5, Irum Sheikh introduces the reader to the post–9/11 enforcement climate as it has been experienced by Arab-Muslim males (as well as "Muslim-looking" people). She explains how, right after 9/11, federal agents deported hundreds of Arab-Muslim males as possible terrorists, despite the fact that none of these men was ever charged for conspiring to participate in terrorist activity. She argues that federal enforcement agencies used a common formula involving highly publicized arrests of "terror suspects," distributing information that racialized and criminalized these suspects on the basis of their religion and ethnicity and then quietly deporting them for violations that had nothing to do with the stated reasons for the initial arrest. Sheikh notes that unfortunate circumstantial factors, and the fact that many of these young men were unauthorized migrants (in most cases, they had overstayed their visas), made them convenient scapegoats. She also notes that in several of these cases compelling evidence exists—supported by testimony from government officials—that the scapegoating process was deliberately orchestrated to convince the general public that progress was being made in the War on Terror.

Arsalan Iftikhar explores these issues further in chapter 6 with a detailed examination of four prominent cases of post–9/11 Arab-Muslim profiling. His discussion addresses the cases of former army captain James Yee, attorney Brandon Mayfield, religious scholar Tariq Ramadan, and entertainer Yusuf Islam (formerly Cat Stevens). Whereas Sheikh's chapter focuses on the categories of Arab-Muslim men who were most often targeted, Iftikhar focuses on "outlier examples" that illustrate the irrational extremes of these enforcement practices. It is in these extremes, however, that it is possible to identify some of the most typical features of the profiles that have guided the targeted enforcement of Arab-Muslim persons in the post–9/11 era. Iftikhar illustrates how Mayfield and Yee, who had no criminal record—and who were never convicted of a criminal or civil offense during the entirety of the terror investigations pursued against them—became suspicious to the FBI simply because they were recent converts to Islam. In the cases of Yusuf Islam and Tariq Ramadan, it appears that their progressive views on Islam were sufficient criteria to prevent their entry into the United States.

From today's perspective, it would appear to be a fairly safe assumption that the kinds of enforcement operations documented by Sheikh and Iftikhar are now things of the past. An important turning point was the federal government's 2003 decision to relax its criteria for the registration of Arab-Muslims in the National Security Entry-Exit Registration System (NSEERS).[28] However, the anti-Muslim climate that was exacerbated by these practices is still, unfortunately, part of U.S. popular culture. There is some evidence, for example, that anti-Muslim violence and hate speech have *increased* in recent years.[29] It is also likely that anti-Muslim stereotypes continue to inform a range of immigration enforcement practices that are no longer guided specifically by the objectives of counterterrorism (for example, operations that target unauthorized migrants and legal residents with felony convictions).

Even so, we should not lose sight of the fact that Arab-Muslim persons have always composed only a small minority of the noncitizens who are detained or deported by the U.S. government.[30] In light of this, post–9/11 dragnet operations should not be discussed only in terms of their direct impact on the Arab-Muslim community. It is also important to consider how the profiling of Arab-Muslim immigrants and U.S. citizens relates to the kinds of immigration enforcement experienced by the broader noncitizen population.

Chapter 7 concludes the section by providing some of this broader context. In this chapter, Michael Welch and Liza Schuster use moral panic theory to compare how the media in the United States and the United Kingdom have constructed asylum seekers as security threats and tax burdens, among other negative characterizations. Like the prior two chapters, this discussion focuses on the immigration enforcement climate following 9/11. Welch and Schuster also provide a theoretical framework for a question that resonates with many of the chapters in this volume: How is it that unprecedented increases in incarceration—which have little connection to actual crime rates—and curtailments in the civil liberties of citizens and noncitizens can be presented to the public as routine, even desirable, developments that are perfectly consistent with the ideals of a democratic society?

From Incarceration to Detention to Deportation

Some of our contributors point out that incarcerated immigrants are not generally viewed as people who deserve the same legal and human rights as citizens. The situation of the immigrant-convict contradicts the romanticized image of the hardworking, law-abiding immigrant that activists often appeal to in their efforts to lobby for more humane immigration laws.

It bears noting, however, that many of the noncitizens being held in immigration detention—or, more baldly, immigration prison—are *not* deemed to be "criminal aliens."[31] Some of these noncriminal detainees are unauthorized migrants who, in the eyes of many people today, are no less criminal. But others are adults and children who entered the United States seeking asylum and individuals whose legal status has been thrown into question because of the expiration of their temporary visa, or Temporary Protected Status (TPS).

Even so, just over 50 percent of noncitizen detainees are persons with criminal convictions.[32] Individuals with prior felony convictions also represent a growing share of the noncitizens who are being put through formal deportation proceedings. Like most of the native-born persons who are doing time in the criminal justice system, these immigrant detainees are not perfect people and the contributors to this volume do not attempt to sugarcoat their life stories. Instead, they depict the lives of immigrant detainees in all their complexity, acknowledging the civil or criminal violations they have committed and situating these violations in the context of their migration stories, their personal aspirations, and their ties to friends and family living in the United States.

It can be argued that people who make mistakes should still be entitled to basic legal rights. In fact, this presumption underlies most ideas about due process and civil liberties, which are inextricably tied to the way that *justice* is defined in liberal, democratic societies. But this, in turn, raises questions about what democracy and equality really mean. For example, what does it mean when a native-born person who is convicted of shoplifting, drug possession, or drunk driving is allowed to return to society after serving their time—but a noncitizen convicted of the same charge automatically faces the prospect of deportation and the likelihood of spending several more years in immigration prison after serving time for the original offense?

The mere act of posing such a question has been complicated by the discourse swirling around the immigration debate. For example, the discourse on immigrants-as-criminals obscures the fact that, under current law, different definitions of what counts as an aggravated felony are used to judge the actions of citizens and noncitizens. So when we read about the growing number of noncitizens being deported for aggravated felonies, it is important to note that many of these violations would not be defined as aggravated felonies if committed by a native-born citizen.[33]

It is also common to be told that immigrants do not deserve the same rights as citizens precisely because they are *not* citizens. However, this national sovereignty approach obscures the fact that current law does not simply distinguish between the rights of citizens and noncitizens—it also distinguishes between the rights of native-born citizens and foreign-born persons. Hence, a foreign-born person with a green card, or even a naturalized citizen, still runs the risk of deportation if they commit a criminal violation. It should be emphasized that these are among the rarest kind of deportations, but it is just as significant that the current policy climate has sent signals that make these sorts of deportations possible and less likely to be challenged.[34]

This is the most compelling example of how current immigration laws are creating a tiered system of rights applying to different classes of citizens—a native-born group whose rights are irrevocable and another group, of foreign-born persons, whose legal status can always be called into question. The implications of this tiered system of legal rights has not fostered much public debate because, at present, the people most affected are foreign-born persons with criminal convictions. However, as many of our contributors point out, this is precisely why it is important to understand the factors driving the transformation (and intersection) of the federal immigration system and the prison-industrial complex.

In chapter 8, David Brotherton provides a compelling introduction to this system as it is experienced daily by noncitizens. He provides an ethnographic account of Dominican migrants who are routinely processed through the immigration court system of New York City. Brotherton illustrates how the inflexible standards established by recent immigration laws fracture immigrant families, usually because of minor criminal violations that trigger compulsory deportation proceedings. In his concluding discussion he reflects on the impact that these sentencing practices are having at the macrosocial level. He makes connections between social control theory and theories of structural assimilation, pointing toward a form of unequal incorporation (or segmented assimilation) that is being shaped by immigration enforcement practices.

In chapter 9, Abira Ashfaq touches on similar themes. But whereas Brotherton focuses on the dangers of inflexible deportation guidelines (established under the Illegal Immigration Reform and Immigrant Responsibility Act of 1996), Ashfaq examines how these guidelines have been supplemented by new forms of judicial discretion (introduced by the 2005 REAL ID Act) that, ironically, have only made matters worse. Drawing on her experiences as an immigration attorney, Ashfaq explores how noncitizens are routinely processed through the courts and into the immigration prison system. She tells the stories of noncitizens who have been detained and deported as security risks, asylum-seekers and others with Temporary Protected Status who unsuccessfully seek to avoid deportation, and noncitizens facing deportation because of prior convictions. Despite their different legal options, Ashfaq finds, the experience of most of these noncitizens remains essentially the same: they are subjected to an array of formal and informal bureaucratic practices grounded in a presumption of guilt.

Officially speaking, detainees are not criminal convicts. As Ashfaq explains, many detainees are people whose legal status has become indeterminate, or has expired, for a variety of reasons. Even the ones in detention because of prior convictions are not being held as punishment for these offenses. Instead, they are being held while the immigration system makes its final determination on their legal status, which will determine whether or not they will be deported. Regardless of the reasons for their apprehension, most detainees are housed in prisons and jails that also house incarcerated persons, and most find that they are treated no differently from any other prisoner. Unlike prisoners who have been convicted of a criminal offense, however, immigrant detainees can be held indefinitely and are not eligible for many of the due process rights afforded to other prisoners because, ironically, they are not considered to be incarcerated persons. Although some court decisions (such as *Zadvydas v. Davis*[35] and the more recent *Clark et al. v. Martinez*[36]) have challenged the authority of the immigration system to hold detainees indefinitely—this has done little to alter the day-to-day workings of the immigration courts or the continuing growth of the U.S. detention system.

In chapter 10, Tamara K. Nopper provides a macrolevel description of this system. She draws on government data to review recent trends in deportation and detention, with a special emphasis on the experience of black immigrants. Like the other chapters in this section, Nopper points out that the expansion of immigration enforcement has to be situated in light of the continuing expansion of the prison-industrial complex. However, Nopper recenters the discourse of immigrant rights activists around a history of black incarceration that predates the recent rise of immigrant incarceration. Because of this, she engages immigration issues from a political perspective that is informed by post–civil rights era black radicalism and the U.S. prison reform movement. She challenges the way many immigrant rights advocates have chosen to frame antiblack racism and immigrant exclusion as mutually exclusive issues or as complementary issues that belong to different social justice constituencies. Nopper explains that this way of framing the issues ignores the integrative connection between antiblack racism and anti-immigrant policies and practices. Toward this end, Nopper argues that strategies for social control that have targeted black populations form the basis for the current forms of immigrant exclusion. She uses this argument to illustrate the ways in which black immigrants are disproportionately targeted by immigration enforcement and to explain how the black immigrant experience sheds light on issues that are relevant to the immigrant population as a whole.

Chapters 11 and 12 provide an activist perspective on the immigration prison system, written by people who have been intimately affected by current enforcement practices.

Chapter 11 looks in detail at the abuses that can occur in immigration prisons, as told from the perspective of a former detainee. Malik Ndaula and Debbie Satyal recount several examples of substandard conditions inside immigration prisons and the difficulties that immigrant detainees face when they try to become educated about their legal rights. Ndaula and Satyal explain how prison workers routinely subvert the minimum standards for humane treatment of detainees as stipulated by the regulations of the DHS. In then end, though, they conclude that it is still possible for detainees to struggle for change, with the help of family, friends, and immigrant rights activists on the outside. They also reveal encouraging glimpses into the unbroken idealism of some immigrant detainees who still consider the United States their only real home, despite the treatment received at the hands of immigration authorities.

In chapter 12, Subhash Kateel and Aarti Shahani provide another account of how the experience of being targeted for deportation can be transformed into a struggle for equal rights. Their trenchant critique of immigration enforcement practices reflects their experiences working with hundreds of immigrant families whose loved ones have been deported, often for very minor offenses.

Kateel and Shahani explain that the efforts of immigrant rights advocates to expand avenues for noncitizens to "become legal" do not address the factors driving immigrant incarceration, because this process revokes the legal status of noncitizens who were admitted to the United States through formal legal channels. They further point out that it is not possible to improve immigrant rights without addressing the factors behind the rise of immigrant incarceration.

The final section of the book explores similar issues—concerning targeted enforcement practices, immigrant incarceration, and racial profiling—but as they relate to the controversies surrounding unauthorized migration. In chapter 13, Kathleen Staudt describes grassroots struggles over immigration policy and border control in El Paso, Texas, which sits on the U.S.–Mexico border. Her discussion focuses on the efforts of state police to enforce federal immigration laws against unauthorized border crossers (also known as "local enforcement"). Staudt explains that these practices authorized new forms of anti-Latino racial profiling but that precisely because of this, they quickly became a volatile issue for a large cross section of the El Paso population.

Staudt also gives an account of the unique resistance culture of El Paso border communities, which has been shaped by social-economic networks that bind El Paso to its sister city, Ciudad Juárez, on the Mexican side of the border. She explains how local residents challenged the local enforcement practices of state police. However, she also notes that the debate over border control has created new divisions within the Mexican American and Mexican national population of El Paso.

In chapter 14, Jorge Capetillo-Ponce has a different take on the controversies surrounding unauthorized migration. He explores several aspects of the tax-burden argument as it has been applied to undocumented migrants and chronicles its use in justifying get-tough immigration enforcement measures. Capetillo-Ponce also looks at the discourse on balanced-budget conservatism and its role in framing arguments for immigration control in ways that appeal to both far-right immigration control advocates and moderate conservatives. He concludes his discussion by fleshing out some workable policy alternatives to the proenforcement solutions being proposed by immigration restrictionists. However, he also notes that these proenforcement arguments are being informed by a new climate of nativism more concerned with the cultural-demographic "threat" posed by Latino-Mexican immigrants than it is with finding a practical solution to the tax-burden debate.

Philip Kretsedemas's discussion of unauthorized migration and local enforcement in chapter 15 builds on Staudt's and Capetillo-Ponce's discussions. Kretsedemas notes that the costs and benefits of immigration *are* unequally distributed between the federal government and local governments and that these inequalities have been intensified by the last decade of social-spending cuts. However, this does not explain the rapid expansion of illegal-immigrant laws that have expanded the authority of local police and other government workers to screen noncitizens—and even people who look like they might be immigrants—for legal status.

Kretsedemas notes that these laws are being used to accomplish a diverse, and not entirely coherent, set of goals. In addition, the public discourse surrounding these local enforcement efforts obscures some rather counterintuitive trends. For example, although these laws are being enacted by local governments, they have been made possible by policy statements issued by federal agencies. It is also telling that a large number of the noncitizens who are being apprehended by local police are not unauthorized border crossers. Instead, they are noncitizens who have had their legal status revoked because of prior felony convictions. So, it appears that local enforcement measures are also being shaped by a broader set of institutional dynamics that are related to the ongoing reorganization and integration of the immigration and criminal justice systems.

The concluding chapter provides a summary discussion of the issues raised by all the contributors and ties them into some of the latest developments on the immigration policy front. We also make some observations about future trends for U.S. immigration enforcement. Unfortunately, the most apparent trend is that immigration enforcement will continue to expand and intensify for the foreseeable future, at both the state and federal levels. For example, at the time of this writing, Immigration and Customs

Enforcement (ICE), the enforcement arm of the DHS, has begun to expand its raids on factories and offices that employ unauthorized migrants. One of these raids in the New England area received a great deal of attention. It involved a leather factory in New Bedford, Massachusetts, that received government contracts to manufacture items for the U.S. military.[37] The raid resulted not only in the apprehension of dozens of undocumented workers but in the arrest of some of the factory's management team, who were charged with assisting their employees in the acquisition of false documents. These raids send a clear message to employers about the perils of employing immigrant labor, and they mark a decisive departure from the approach that the immigration system had previously taken, focusing more on incentives to comply rather than scare-tactic sanctions.[38] But the raids also reveal how thoroughly integrated unauthorized migrants have become within U.S. labor markets.

The New Bedford raid raised difficult questions about the fate of the U.S.-born children of the undocumented workers currently facing deportation. From a human rights standpoint—and even under certain interpretations of existing immigration law—it would appear unnecessarily cruel to separate these children from their parents and make them wards of the state. On the other hand, some immigration restrictionists are pushing for laws that would revoke the legal status of children born to undocumented migrants—a development that would effectively overturn the Fourteenth Amendment, which introduced jus soli citizenship to the U.S. Constitution.

This scenario provides a glimpse into how polarizing immigration policy has become. Anxieties about immigration are giving rise to plans for radically restructuring legal rights, the Constitution, the way the political system works, and even the economy.[39] Of course, it can just as easily be argued that these reactionary attempts to seal off U.S. society from "immigrant invaders" undermine the best, and most hopeful, ideals of the movement for democracy in the United States—ideals that are certainly worth preserving even if they have only been imperfectly realized. This is why the question of immigration enforcement can never be far removed from the question of democracy and civic participation. Only a few of the contributions to this volume directly explore this question—but in different ways, all the contributors raise political and ethical questions about the consequences of allowing get-tough enforcement to become the primary orientation of the U.S. immigration system.

As noted earlier, this enforcement focus has come to dominate in an era when the United States is becoming increasingly more reliant on immigrants for workforce replenishment and population growth in general. Given this context, it is telling that the predominant form of social spending on immigration focuses on routing out so-called undesirables and that most of the state and local legislation on immigration matters is geared toward capturing unauthorized migrants and other immigration violators. The dismantling of the Immigration and Naturalization Service (INS), and the incorporation of its duties within the Department of Homeland Security, provides as a good a metaphor as any of this shift in emphasis.[40] Although the shift toward an enforcement paradigm was already occurring within the former INS and arguably has always been a dominant feature of the immigration system, the organization of the DHS solidified the institutional and symbolic linkages between immigration, national security, and the federal prison system. In this light, it is not only important to question current policy trends but also to critically examine the emphasis on security that has threaded its way through the past fifteen years of immigration policymaking. It is possible, however, to reinterpret *security* as pertaining to improving the legal rights, social mobility, and well-being of all U.S. residents—immigrants and native born alike. We hope that this collection of essays contributes toward laying that groundwork.

Notes

1. For a history of these exclusionary measures, see Bill Ong Hing, *Defining America Through Immigration Policy* (Philadelphia: Temple University Press, 2004); Mae Ngai, *Impossible Subjects: Illegal Aliens and the Making of Modern America* (Princeton, N.J.: Princeton University Press, 2005); and Aristide Zolberg, *A Nation by Design: Immigration Policy in the Fashioning of America* (Cambridge, Mass.: Harvard University Press, 2006). For an overview of exclusions contained in the Illegal Immigration Reform and Immigrant Responsibility Act of 1996 and its impact on immigrant populations, see Philip Kretsedemas and Ana Aparicio, eds., *Immigrants, Welfare Reform, and the Poverty of Policy* (Westport, Conn.: Greenwood-Praeger, 2004).

2. As some researchers have suggested, immigration enforcement has also been used to regulate flows of migrant labor and to impose selective restrictions during peak periods of immigration. See Kitty Calavita, *Inside the State: The Bracero Program, Immigration, and the I.N.S.* (New York: Routledge, 1992); Grace

Chang, *Disposable Domestics: Immigrant Women Workers in the Global Economy* (Boston: Beacon Press, 2000).

3. In the year following the attacks, immigration levels remained relatively high (exceeding 1 million), then dipped to a four-year low of 700,000 in 2003. But immigration levels have since climbed back to pre-2001 levels, reaching 1.2 million as of 2006. See Department of Homeland Security, *Annual Flow Report: U.S. Legal Permanent Residents 2006* (2007), 1–2.

4. It has been noted that the United States has a special obligation to resettle Iraqi asylum seekers, given the leading role it has played in the invasion of Iraq. Even so, the United States has granted asylum to little more than 400 Iraqi refugees, while other nations in the immediate vicinity of Iraq have absorbed over 2 million Iraqi refugees. See Human Rights Watch, *Iraq: Neighbors Stem Flow of Iraqis Fleeing War; U.S. and U.K. Bear Special Duty to Aid Refugees* (New York: Human Rights, 2007). Meanwhile, the United States remains open to Arab-Muslim immigrants largely because of the growing preference for business-class immigrants and individuals who are not likely to become a financial burden on the state. On the other hand, criteria for admitting asylum seekers have become more stringent to discourage a mass influx of refugees from poorer and war-torn nations and hence to reduce the government's obligation to support these refugees. In recent years, some of the most austere measures to discourage refugee flow have been taken against Haitian asylum seekers. See "Handling Haitian Immigrants," *PBS NewsHour with Jim Lehrer*, October 30, 2002. UK and European Union immigration policies reflect similar priorities toward discouraging asylum seekers—who are increasingly being depicted as both a financial burden and a security risk— while increasing incentives for business-class immigrants. See Alan Travis, "Britain Competes to Attract Migrants," *Guardian*, June 19, 2007; Human Rights Watch, *An Unjust 'Vision' for Europe's Refugees* (New York: Human Rights Watch, 2003).

5. The number of formal removals remained level (at approximately 100,000 per annum) between 1998 and 2001 and did not begin to accelerate to the current figure of over 140,000 formal removals until after 2002. However, the biggest single-year jump in formal removals in recent history occurred shortly after the passage of the Illegal Immigration Reform and Immigrant Responsibility Act of 1996. Department of Homeland Security, *2005 Yearbook of Immigration Statistics*, http://www.dhs.gov/xlibrary/assets/statistics/yearbook/2005/OIS_2005_yearbook.pdf, 91–109.

6. See Wayne Cornelius, Takeyuki Tsuda, Phillip Martin, and James Hollifield, eds., *Controlling Immigration: A Global Perspective* (Stanford, Calif.: Stanford University Press, 2004).

7. Daniel Tichenor has characterized this combination of left-leaning labor and racial minority support for immigration control as "Nationalist Egalitarian," in that it ties immigration control to strategies for tighter regulation of the labor market and increased government investment in the low-income and middle-class working population. See Daniel Tichenor, *Dividing Lines: The Politics of Im-*

migration Control in America (Princeton, N.J.: Princeton University Press, 2002). In addition to this coherent political perspective, there are also rising tensions between native-born racial minorities and new immigrants that have been channeled in a variety of directions, including (though only rarely) support for far-right, anti-immigrant groups. See Brentin Mock, "Smokescreen: Activists Say a Black Anti-immigrant Movement Is Gathering Steam, but It Seems to Be Largely the Creation of White People," *Intelligence Report* 123 (2006): 18–23; Miriam Jordan, "Blacks vs. Latinos at Work: More African-Americans Claim They Are Passed Over for Hispanics in Hiring," *Wall Street Journal*, January 24, 2006.

8. Calavita, *Inside the State.*

9. Ngai, *Impossible Subjects*, 127–166 and 225–264.

10. This is the case throughout much of the New England area, especially in Massachusetts, where immigrants have been responsible for more than 100 percent of population growth for the past decade (counteracting the net loss of native-born persons emigrating from the state to other parts of the United States). See Andrew Sum, Johan Uvin, Ishwar Khatiwada, and Dana Ansel, *The Changing Face of Massachusetts* (Boston: Mass Inc. and Northeastern University Center for Labor Market Studies, 2005).

11. Randolph Capps, Michael Fix, Jeffrey Passel, Jason Ost, and Dan Perez-Lopez, *A Profile of the Low Low-Wage Immigrant Workforce* (Washington, D.C.: Urban Institute, 2003).

12. Jeff Chapman and Jared Bernstein, "Immigration and Poverty, How Are They Linked?" *Monthly Labor Review* (April 2003): 10–15.

13. This was illustrated most dramatically by the 2006 mass mobilizations of immigrants and undocumented workers against laws that would have made unauthorized migration a felony and criminalized individuals who assisted unauthorized migrants. In addition to this, however, there is ample evidence that many immigrants are deeply involved in local organizing efforts and state-policy advocacy and that, in addition, they stay active in the politics of their countries of origin. For a recent overview, see Taeku Lee, S. Karthick Ramakrishnan, Ricardo Ramirez, eds., *Transforming Politics, Transforming America: The Political and Civic Incorporation of Immigrants in the United States* (Charlottesville: University of Virginia Press, 2006); Janelle Wong, *Democracy's Promise: Immigrants and American Civic Institutions* (Ann Arbor: University of Michigan Press, 2006).

14. For a review of the recent literature on this matter, see Mary Waters and Tomas Jimenez, "Assessing Immigrant Assimilation: New Empirical and Theoretical Challenges," *Annual Review of Sociology* 31 (2005): 105–125.

15. In 2005, for example, approximately $430 million was appropriated for refugee-asylee assistance services, and approximately $1.7 billion for U.S. Citizenship and Information Services (the branch of the DHS that issues green cards and processes immigrant benefit applications, among other duties that do not involve direct service provision). In contrast, the budget for immigration

enforcement exceeded $5 billion (the enforcement budget had already approached $4.9 billion as of 2003). See House Committee on the Judiciary, *U.S. Citizenship and Immigration Services, Immigration Provisions in the FY05 Budget, Statement of Eduardo Aguirre Jr., Director, before the Subcommittee of Immigration, Border Security and Claims,* February 25, 2004, http://www.uscis.gov/files/testimony/AguirreBudget022504.pdf (accessed November 6, 2007); National Conference of State Legislatures, 2005 Federal Update, August 1, 2005, http://www.ncsl.org/programs/immig/Immig2005FedUpdate.htm (accessed November 6, 2007); and Migration Policy Institute, Immigration Enforcement Spending Since IRCA, November 2005, http://www.migrationpolicy.org/ITFIAF/FactSheet_Spending.pdf (accessed November 6, 2007).

16. The debate around immigration and crime hinges on distinctions between first-generation immigrants and the situation of their U.S.-born children and grandchildren. Most research has shown that first-generation immigrants are incarcerated at much lower levels than the native born. Ruben Rumbaut found, for example, that native-born males were incarcerated at a rate five times higher than immigrants, as of the 2000 census. See Ruben Rumbaut, Roberto Gonzalez, Golnaz Komaie, and Charles Morgan, *Debunking the Myth of Immigrant Criminality: Imprisonment Among First and Second Generation Young Men* (Washington, D.C.: Migration Policy Institute, June 2006). Also see Ramiro Martinez Jr. and Abel Valenzuela Jr., eds., *Immigration and Crime: Race, Ethnicity and Violence* (New York: New York University Press, 2006). But insofar as immigrants are tracked into poor neighborhoods and the lowest-paying segments of the economy, the life chances and incarceration rates of the second and third generation tend to approximate those of other working-poor, native-born groups. It bears emphasizing, however, that the label "second generation" or "third generation" is a misnomer here, since we are essentially addressing the situation of the native-born persons of immigrant parents whose incarceration patterns are a product of factors that are largely indigenous to the United States rather than being imported by immigrant groups.

17. Robert J. Sampson, Jeffrey D. Morenoff, and Stephen Raudenbush, "Social Anatomy of Racial and Ethnic Disparities in Violence," *American Journal of Public Health* 95 (2005): 224–232.

18. There also appears to be a reflexive, parallel relationship between immigration violations and drug convictions. On one hand, the number of individuals prosecuted for immigration violations has increased dramatically in recent years (now composing the single largest segment of federal prosecutions), but at the same time, immigrants are becoming a growing share of the individuals being prosecuted for drug offenses. For recent data, see Transactional Records Access Clearinghouse, "Prosecution of Immigration Cases Surge in U.S.," 2005, http://trac.syr.edu/tracins/latest/131/ (accessed November 6, 2007).

19. The most ominous landmark in recent history occurred in 2002, when the U.S. prison population topped 2 million (or, 1 incarcerated person for every 142

U.S. residents). This not only made the United States the world leader in the percentage of its national population that it is holding behind bars, it also gave the United States the dubious honor of holding 25 percent of the global prison population. Reuters, "U.S. Prison Population Surpasses 2 Million," April 6, 2003. Unfortunately, these incarceration rates have increased further since that time. As of June 2004, for example, 1 out of 138 U.S. residents were imprisoned. Associated Press, "U.S. Prison Population Soars in 2003, '04," March 24, 2005.

20. For example, the Supreme Court's *Zadvydas vs. Davis* decision declared that immigration authorities do not have the right to hold detainees indefinitely (but provided no guidelines as to what reasonable limits for detention should be. A number of recent federal circuit and district court decisions have challenged the legality of immigration-enforcement practices adopted by local governments and police departments. See Pam Belluck, "Towns Lose Tool Against Illegal Immigrants," *New York Times*, August 13, 2005; Michael Rubinkam, "Illegal Immigrant Laws Face Setbacks," Associated Press, January 20, 2007; "Hazleton Anti-immigrant Law Declared Unconstitutional," *El Diario/La Prensa*, July 26, 2007.

21. See chapter 11 in this volume.

22. Carla Marinucci and Mark Martin, "Governor Endorses Minutemen on Border: Schwarzenegger Parts with Bush on Group of Armed Volunteers That Stops Immigrants," *San Francisco Chronicle*, April 29, 2005; Associated Press, "Anti-immigration Conference in Las Vegas Spurs Plan for Protest," May 25, 2005.

23. See chapter 9 in this volume.

24. See chapter 15 in this volume.

25. The immigrant organizing coalition Families for Freedom has posted several of these stories—taken from first-person testimonials—in an online archive. See Families for Freedom, "Our Families," http://www.familiesforfreedom.org/?q=our-families (accessed November 6, 2007).

26. DHS, *2005 Yearbook of Immigration Statistics* (2006), 63–85.

27. This notion of producing knowledge through sympathetic engagement can be distinguished from the atheoretical inductive reasoning that has been criticized in some quarters, mostly that associated with the work of Barney Glaser and Anselm Strauss, *The Discovery of Grounded Theory* (New York: Transaction Books, 1967). Instead, this approach uses empirical data to explain processes that cannot be engaged through any other means and uses these insights, in turn, to generate new theory and reflect on prior theory. This approach has a precursor in the radical empiricism of William James (see *The Will to Believe and Other Essays in Popular Philosophy* [1896; New York: Cosimo Classics, 2006]) and more recently in the extended case study method of Michael Burawoy. See Michael Burawoy, Alice Burton, Ann Ferguson, and Kathryn Fox, *Ethnography Unbound: Power and Resistance in the Modern Metropolis* (Berkeley, Los Angeles: University of California Press, 1991).

28. See U.S. Immigration and Customs Enforcement, "Fact Sheet: Changes to National Security Entry-Exit Registration System (NSEERS)," December 1, 2003, http://www.ice.gov/pi/news/factsheets/nseersFS120103.htm (accessed November 6, 2007). See chapters 5 and 6 for a critical discussion of this development, including an overview of the US-VISIT program that was created as a supplement to NSEERS in January 2004.

29. Arsalan Iftikhar, *The Status of Muslim Civil Rights in the United States, 2005: Unequal Protection* (Washington, D.C.: Council on American Islamic Relations, 2005).

30. For example, Arab-Muslim nationals rank nowhere among the top ten groups for formal removals or criminal removals in recent years (1998–2005). DHS, *2005 Yearbook of Immigration Statistics* (2006), 91–109.

31. A 2004 report estimated this figure at 51 percent (based on 2002 data). Alison Siskin, "Immigration-Related Detention: Current Legislative Issues," Congressional Research Service Report for Congress, Library of Congress, April 28, 2004, http://www.fas.org/irp/crs/RL32369.pdf (accessed November 6, 2007). An earlier report, drawing on data from 1994–2001, indicates that the proportion of criminal alien detainees has fluctuated from 40–50 percent over the past decade or so. U.S. Department of Justice, Office of the Federal Detention Trustee, "Detention Needs Assessment and Baseline Report: A Compendium of Federal Detention Statistics" (2002): 14, http://www.usdoj.gov/ofdt/compendium_final.pdf (accessed November 6, 2007). However, if the continuing increase in immigrant incarceration is any indication, it is very likely that the proportion of criminal aliens held in immigration detention will continue to increase.

32. Siskin, *Immigration-Related Detention.*

33. Under current immigration law, convictions that may not count as an aggravated felony under the criminal justice system, or which were not deemed to be an aggravated felony when originally sentenced, can be treated as an aggravated felony for immigration purposes, justifying the mandatory deportation of the noncitizen. The expanded definition of *aggravated felony* as it applies to deportation proceedings is discussed by many of the contributors to this volume. In particular, see chapters 8, 9, 10, 11, and 12.

34. For a recent example, see Associated Press, "Haitian Immigrant Stripped of U.S. Citizenship Is Man Without a Country," December 9, 2006.

35. 533 U.S. 678 (2001). Argued February 21, 2001, decided June 28, 2001.

36. 125 U.S. 716 (2005). Argued October 13, 2004, decided January 12, 2005.

37. Ray Henry/Associated Press, "Federal Raid Leaves Town a Mess," March 8, 2007.

38. This accommodative approach toward employers was most characteristic of the immigration enforcement practices authorized by the Immigration Reform and Control Act of 1986 and the Immigration Act of 1990. For an overview of the recent policy history on this matter, see Marc Rosenblum, "Immigration Enforce-

ment at the Worksite: Making It Work," Migration Policy Institute Policy Brief, no. 6 (November 2005).

39. For an overview of the arguments that have been used to support this perspective—and corresponding policy priorities and proposals—see Patrick Buchanan, *State of Emergency: The Third World Invasion and Conquest of America* (New York: Thomas Dunne Books, 2006).

40. President Bush announced his intentions to create an Office of Homeland Security within ten days of the attacks of September 11, 2001. However, the dissolution of the INS and its incorporation within the new DHS did not occur until 2002. Unlike the former INS, the DHS is not limited exclusively to immigration matters. It places all the major immigration-regulation responsibilities of the federal government alongside federal drug and criminal enforcement operations and a wide range of security, antiterrorism, and intelligence operations.

PART I

The Expansion of Immigration Enforcement: Before 9/11

CHAPTER 2

Unchecked Power Against Undesirables
Haitians, Mariel Cubans, and Guantánamo

MARK DOW

IN THE EARLY POST–9/11 ARGUMENTS over Guantánamo prisoners, Vice President Dick Cheney said the military tribunal "guarantees that we'll have the kind of treatment of these individuals that we believe they deserve."[1] In other words, we have a sham process that cannot interfere with our doing what we want to do with these people. Cheney's statement provided a pithy summary of the administration's various policies aimed at loosening legal and moral restraints that might keep us from administering the deserved treatment, whether inside our borders, at our Cuban enclave, or in the estimated thirty-nine prisons around the world—in Iraq, Afghanistan, and other countries—where "we" are hiding detainees.[2]

What many of these policies have in common is their aim of justifying the mistreatment of disfavored groups by applying certain labels to them. The "deserved treatment" strategy came into view after September 11, 2001, and the media eventually started looking at who "these individuals" really were. But the strategy of categorizing certain people in ways intended to justify their mistreatment was not new, and it did not begin with the terrorist attacks here. I will discuss such strategies by successive administrations with regard to mistreatment of Haitian refugees and Mariel Cuban refugees, two of the main groups historically victimized by U.S. immigration policies. But first I'll turn to Guantánamo, where anti-Haitian policies were encapsulated long before the world knew about "Gitmo."

Our Lawless Enclave

For all the criticism the second Bush administration deserves, it is important to remember that federal law enforcement abuses did not appear out of thin air on September 12, 2001. Neither did Guantánamo. What we call "Guantánamo" is actually the U.S. naval base occupying some 45 square miles (118 square kilometers) of the Guantánamo province in eastern Cuba. Since 1961, the Cuban government has protested the legitimacy of the U.S. base. It can be argued that the Platt Amendment and the 1903 treaty leading to the U.S. presence in Guantánamo were the result of coercion and that the United States has been in breach of the treaty, which granted the U.S. a presence for the purposes of its own defense, Cuba's defense, and coaling and navy stations. Even Supreme Court justice Antonin Scalia acknowledged in *Rasul v. Bush*, the first post–9/11 Guantánamo case heard by the court, that the Cuban acreage was "merely leased for a particular use."[3]

All of this became part of the legal disputes in which the U.S. government made the argument that precisely because it did *not* exercise sovereignty over its own naval base in Guantánamo, it could do whatever it wanted there. In an impressive bit of logic, the dissent in *Gherebi v. Bush*—that is, the judge for the Ninth Circuit Court of Appeals who agreed with the government's position—said that the ability of the United States to violate the lease with impunity does not mean that the United States has sovereignty; it only means, wrote Judge Susan Graber, that the United States "simply is big enough and strong enough that Cuba has been unable to enforce its legal entitlements."[4] But let's go back.

In 1991 a group of uniformed U.S. military men filed into a Miami courtroom, filling the front rows so that federal district court judge Clyde Atkins would have a clear view of them. One of the attorneys later told me that it was the kind of military tactic for intimidating a judge that one expects in many Latin American countries. Here the message was national security, military necessity, and that the local judge should know his place. The case, *Haitian Refugee Center, Inc. v. Baker*, involved the forced repatriation of Haitians fleeing military violence and being picked up at sea by the U.S. Coast Guard.[5] A restraining order had already been issued "barring the government from continuing to repatriate Haitians on board Coast Guard cutters or at the U.S. naval base at Guantánamo Bay, Cuba."[6] At this hearing, Judge Atkins heard arguments about the temporary restraining order, about the court's jurisdiction, and about the enforceability of Article 33 of the United Nations Protocol Relating to the Status of Refugees discouraging the forced return of potential refugees. As I recall, the government's lawyer told the judge, in answer to a direct question, that yes, the interdicted Haitians now in U.S. custody had certain rights, but no, those rights were not enforceable. It seemed, and seems, an extraordinary thing for anyone, but especially a government lawyer, to say. The lawyer was pre–Monica Lewinsky Kenneth Starr, then solicitor general. When a president sends the solicitor general to argue a case in a district court, he is sending a message. When, against the executive branch's wishes, Judge Atkins extended the restraining order, Starr said, "At the highest level of the government there is profound concern about this litigation."[7]

Why make the government's attempt to win a case sound so sinister? There are several reasons, all related to double standards and executive lawlessness justified under the pretext of national security. First, the authority on which the U.S.'s interdiction of Haitians at sea was based was an executive agreement between the Reagan administration and a dictatorship, that of François ("Papa Doc") Duvalier. Second, the United States had supported the Duvalier dictatorship. Third, the United States supported and funded the paramilitary group Revolutionary Front for the Advancement and Progress of Haiti (FRAPH), responsible for the murder and repression that after the 1991 coup against President Jean Bertrand Aristide forced Haitians to flee their country[8]—Haitians whose forced repatriation led to the scene in the Miami courtroom. Fourth, the detention of Haitian asylum seekers as a means of deterring other potential refugees from fleeing persecution violates international standards of refugee protection, according to the late Arthur Helton, a refugee policy expert, and others. (Helton was killed in the August 2003 bombing of the United Nations headquarters in Baghdad.) Fifth, the U.S. government's long-standing claim in the absence of case-by-case determinations that "the majority of Haitian boat people, and the majority of asylum applicants . . . [are] intending economic migrants"[9] is considered a violation of international law. As early as 1980, the U.S. government was asserting that repatriated Haitians were not persecuted on their return, though a Carter administration official later admitted that "'no one inside or outside the government really believed it.'"[10]

After forced repatriations from Guantánamo, U.S. officials made false claims about U.S. monitoring of returned asylum-seekers.[11] *Haitian Refugee Center, Inc. v. Baker* and subsequent litigation concerned the fairness of asylum screening procedures at Guantánamo and on board U.S. Coast Guard cutters. The United Nations High Commissioner for Refugees (UNHCR) refused to participate in the "cursory screenings," saying that the procedures "deviate[d] significantly from international and U.S. law."[12] But there was little or no recourse against what attorney John Gibbons, in the oral arguments on *Rasul v. Bush,* would call a "lawless enclave."[13] And just in case the screenings did, as a result of pressure, become fair, the United States changed its policy in 1992 "from using Guantánamo as a site for conducting refugee screenings . . . to the policy of automatic interdiction and return of all Haitians interdicted on the high seas."[14] The UNHCR called the Supreme Court ruling in *Sale v. Haitian Centers Council,* upholding the legality of interdiction and repatriation, "a setback to modern international refugee law."[15] Most of the Haitians would indeed be repatriated, many of them handed over directly to the Haitian military on the Port-au-Prince docks, some forced off the U.S. cutters with high-powered water hoses. Chinese have also been interdicted at sea by the United States, held at Guantánamo, and "quietly and summarily returned."[16] So have would-be immigrants from several other countries. Cubans, too, have been detained in large numbers at Guantánamo, though most have been allowed into the United States.

The mistreatment of Haitians in the "lawless enclave" demands its own full-scale history. Here I will just mention that they were unnecessarily confined behind razor wire; their peaceful protests were met by assaults from military-police riot squads; they were subjected to the "psy-ops" (psychological operations) technique of blaring music—a technique also used against Manuel Noriega in the Vatican embassy; David Koresh and his followers in Waco, Texas; and, more recently, "enemy combatants" at Guantánamo. Unaccompanied Haitian refugee children reported being "cracked" at Guantánamo, "their hands cuffed behind their back, their feet cuffed and then stepped on. . . . The cuffings often occur[red] in conjunction with other punishments, such as . . . being forced to kneel for hours on hot cement or beds of ants."[17] More than two hundred Haitians, despite having passed the stringent screening procedures that should have allowed them into the United States to pursue asylum claims, were further detained because they tested positive for HIV. District court judge Sterling Johnson, who would rule in 1993 to allow the HIV-positive Haitians into the United States, wrote that the two hundred or so sick refugees were "subjected to pre-dawn military sweeps as they sleep by as many as 400 soldiers dressed in full riot gear."[18] In his dissent in *Rasul,* Scalia would write, as if the naval base itself were the victim, that the court's majority was "subjecting Guantánamo Bay to the oversight of the federal courts."[19] At least one HIV-positive refugee said she and other women at Guantánamo were forcibly injected with the contraceptive Depo-Provera.[20] All this must remain beyond the oversight of any court, the executive argues, because of issues of national security and because the judiciary has traditionally shown great deference in matters of immigration policy. This makes sense only if intimidation and violence against asylum seekers are legitimate means of securing our borders. The Haitians were getting "the kind of treatment . . . that we believe they deserve."

That the executive's arguments were pretexts becomes clearer when we note a few continuities from the 1990s into the so-called War on Terror. The Justice Department refused to release the names of some two hundred unaccompanied Haitian children on Guantánamo to the Haitian community in the United States because, it claimed, it was protecting their safety, even though around the same time it released the names of unaccompanied Cuban children on Guantánamo to Miami's Cuban community.[21] After the post–9/11 domestic roundups, the Justice Department refused to release the names of detainees because, it claimed, it was protecting the detainees' privacy and safety. When the American Civil Liberties Union of New Jersey attempted to force the release of the names, based on a New Jersey statute saying records of inmate names "shall be open to public inspection,"[22] the federal government argued that these were detainees and not inmates, so the statute did not apply. It further argued that because these were federal detainees held in state jails under contract with the federal government, a federal policy prohibiting the release of names superseded the local statute. But two months after making the argument in the Superior Court of New Jersey, the federal government argued in the press that a United Nations plan to monitor prisons worldwide "would be unconstitutional in the United States because it does not recognize states' rights."[23] According to news reports, the United States opposed the prison monitoring plan "because of potential demands for access" to the post–9/11 Guantánamo prisoners—for reasons that soon became clear.[24]

Asylum Seekers, Terrorists, et Cetera

In October 2002 a boat carrying 216 people from Haiti and the Dominican Republic sailed into Biscayne Bay off Miami. Most of the passengers were taken into custody. In November of that year an immigration judge found that one of these Haitians, eighteen-year-old David Joseph, or "D.J.," could be released on bond. The Board of Immigration Appeals upheld the release decision. Attorney General John Ashcroft intervened, however, so that neither D.J. nor the other Haitians could be freed, even on the basis of individualized case determinations. Ashcroft cited "national security interests" together with "sound immigration policy."[25] He ordered the young Haitian man and others "similarly situated" to remain in detention pending their asylum proceedings—even if an immigration judge or the Board of Immigration Appeals ordered them released. And once again the post–9/11 terror pretext was pressed into the service of anti-Haitian policies.

Ashcroft cited a statement from a Defense Department official invoking the "war on terrorism" and claiming that the release of the Haitian asylum applicant could "trigger a large-scale migration event" from Haiti, which "would also create an opportunity for terrorist infiltration into the United States Department of Defense installations in the region."[26] Ashcroft used the magic words "national security interest" and, even more immune to argument, "the terrorist attacks of September 11," then informed us that the State Department had "noticed an increase in third country nations (Pakistanis, Palestinians, etc.) using Haiti as a staging point for attempted migration to the United States."[27] That "etc." seems like a tip-off, but we even have an anonymous State Department official—like a twenty-five-year delayed echo of that Carter State Department official—saying, "we are all scratching our heads" about the source of the Attorney General's assertion.[28]

While aspects of the second Bush administration's anti-Haitian policies go back more than twenty-five years, a new shamelessness revealed itself when it came to U.S. participation in forcing President Aristide from office, supporting antidemocratic forces, and discriminating against Haitians trying to immigrate. In early 2004 groups that were apparently "armed by, trained by, and employed by the intelligence services of the United States" pulled off a second coup against Aristide.[29] One of Aristide's former bodyguards told of U.S. troops running the show in the unmarked plane that removed Aristide from Haiti: "They sat us down and didn't tell us where we were going."[30] Cheney said Aristide had "worn out his welcome," and that "we helped facilitate his departure when he indicated he was ready to go."[31] According to attorney Ira Kurzban—who argued the 1991 case in that Miami courtroom—the United States had made "contingency plans for Guantánamo" weeks before the operation.[32] On the same day that Kurzban described the links between U.S. and Haitian paramilitary forces, George W. Bush told the Haitian people, "We will turn back any refugee that attempts to reach our shore."[33] The U.S. Committee for Refugees and Immigrants noted that Bush "has finally spoken the truth about American practice toward Haitian refugees"—that he had "flagrantly rejected the legal and ethical obligations" of refugee protection which "no [other] state claims the right to violate."[34] Three out of two thousand interdicted Haitians were found to have a credible fear of persecution in the summer of 2004. Despite widespread political violence, hurricane damage, and a humanitarian crisis caused by flooding, the Department of Homeland Security (DHS) continued to deport Haitians, while Nicaraguans and Hondurans in the United States had been granted extensions of Temporary Protected Status here after recent hurricane damage in their home countries.[35]

Anti-Haitian policies and the War on Terror, different as they are, have at least three things in common: if you categorize a person in a certain way, that person's rights and protections are gone; if you categorize the place where you hold that person in a certain way, that person's rights and protections are gone; and by using the pretext of war or national security, you can do anything at all to a person—certainly to a noncitizen.

Mainland Guantánamo

Solicitor General Theodore Olsen opened his argument in *Rasul* by reminding the Supreme Court justices, "The United States is at war."[36] Justice John Paul Stevens soon interrupted with a question: What if the war were finished? Wouldn't the government still be making the same argument about sovereignty and jurisdiction at Guantánamo, and about the prisoner's access to U.S. courts (as indeed it had in the Haitian cases)? So isn't the war irrelevant? Olson essentially conceded the point but could not let it go: "It is not irrelevant because it is in this context that that question is raised. . . . It doesn't depend on that"—that is, his argument does not depend on the war—"but it's even more forceful [a]nd more compelling" because of it.[37] Since this war would never be clearly finished, the argument was for ongoing limitless power.

In the arguments in *Rumsfeld v. Padilla* about the executive's authority to detain a U.S. citizen indefinitely, Justice Ginsburg asked Deputy Solicitor General Paul Clement, "If the law is what the executive says it is, whatever is necessary and appropriate in the executive's judgment"—here she was alluding to the post–9/11 congressional authorization for the president to use "necessary and appropriate force"—"what is it that would be a check against torture?"[38] Justice Ginsburg tried two or three times to get an answer. Clement was evasive, but he did answer that there is no check on torture if the president or his people want to use it: "The fact that executive discretion in a war situation can be abused is not a good and sufficient reason for judicial micromanagement and overseeing of that authority."[39] Clement said that "the military ought to have the option of proceeding with" its captives in such a way that it can "get actionable intelligence to prevent future terrorist attacks."[40] In *Hamdi v. Rumsfeld,* Clement again referred to the necessity of "interrogation without counsel" when the citizen being interrogated might be of "paramount intelligence value."[41] This time Justice Stevens asked whether anything in the law limits interrogation methods. Clement reassuringly told the court that "the last thing you want to do is torture somebody or try to do something along those lines," since that would affect the "reliability" of information obtained.[42] Practical considerations aside, the argument was that in the ongoing war, the executive could do anything. (That evening, in order to beat out its competition, CBS News broadcast the Abu Ghraib photos. Up until then, it had been withholding them at the Pentagon's request.)[43]

In its next term, the Supreme Court again heard arguments related to torture and summary execution (*Clark v. Martinez,* October 2004). But this case was not about alleged terrorists or "enemy combatants"—which, paradoxically, is part of the reason it received so little attention, even among those with civil liberties high on their agendas. This time the victims were Mariel Cubans and other so-called inadmissible aliens.[44] Once again the premise is that if we categorize certain people in a certain way, they cease to be persons at all—at least as far as due process and their humanity are concerned. In defense of a sort of mainland Guantánamo, the government argued that it could do anything at all to certain people who are here because—in a bizarre legalistic sense—they are not people and they are not here.

Allowed by Fidel Castro to depart the island in 1980 from the port of Mariel, some 125,000 Cubans came to the United States over a six-month period. Many of them committed crimes in the United States, and detention typically began upon completion of a criminal sentence for crimes ranging from murder to shoplifting—though one Mariel Cuban was locked up because he could not afford necessary medical care on the outside.[45] Cuba refused to take them back, and the United States argued it could detain them for any length of time, which was exactly what the law had been allowing the government to do. In 2001 at least 160 Mariel Cubans had been detained by the Immigration and Naturalization Service (INS) for a decade or more *after* completing criminal sentences.[46] In 2004, 33 Cubans were reported to have been detained—again, after completing criminal sentences—for fifteen years or more, and counting.[47] Many would be released, but the immigration agency could detain them again, as one court put it, for "almost any reason."[48]

U.S. Immigration and Customs Enforcement (ICE), a successor to the INS and a component of the DHS, is authorized to detain noncitizens so that it can deport them. In 2001 the Supreme Court ruled in *Zadvydas v. Davis* that when a detainee's deportation cannot be carried out within a "reasonably foreseeable" period, defined by the court as six months in most cases, he or she must be released. Obviously, the *Zadvydas* ruling applied to immigrants present in the United States. But the government argued that the ruling did not apply to the Mariel Cubans, who have been here since President Jimmy Carter welcomed them almost thirty years ago. That's because the Mariel Cubans were paroled into the United States by the executive and are thus legally considered not to have entered. Exploiting this so-called entry fiction—never intended to apply to circumstances like those of the Mariel refugees—the U.S. government argued that the 917 Mariels in detention when the case reached the Supreme Court (as well as the thousands of others subject to arbitrary detention) had no right to be freed from detention here, ever.

Yet according to the government's duplicitous logic, because the prisoners received annual custody reviews by low-level bureaucrats, their detention was not "indefinite" at all: "the passage of time is irrelevant to [their] claim," according to the government. Never mind that those reviews were often *not* given annually, that the decisions were notoriously arbitrary, that there was no appeals process, that the prisoners were not entitled to lawyers, or that when they did receive representation, the legal representatives were regularly barred from the proceedings in violation of the government's own guidelines. In the words of a classic Supreme Court decision, "Whatever the process authorized by Congress is, it is due process as far as an alien denied entry is concerned."[49]

Here are just a few examples of the victims of this policy.

Soon after his arrival on the boatlift, one man was given probation for attempted robbery. Then he served two years for misdemeanor marijuana possession, a parole violation. And then the INS imprisoned him for twenty years.

Another Mariel Cuban was sentenced to ninety days for misdemeanor cocaine possession after a series of prior misdemeanors. Then the INS held him for fifteen years. Then one day, apparently, he was no longer dangerous, and he was released.

A Mariel Cuban man who served five years for attempted murder was, after the completion of his sentence, imprisoned for another fifteen years by the INS. After one custody review, immigration officials denied him release on the basis that he showed insufficient remorse. After a subsequent review, they denied him release on the basis that his expression of remorse was merely a "tactic" to gain release.

The logic is not only arbitrary, it mirrors that of the meaningless crime of *pelegrosidad,* or dangerousness, in Cuba, for which many of the Mariel Cubans were imprisoned by Castro—and for which many had fled to the United States in 1980. Others left Cuba after local police threatened them with prison for the crime of *pelegrosidad* if they did not leave.

I have been discussing Mariel Cubans who were taken into custody after committing crimes here. A study remains to be written on the truth about the number of Cubans among the Mariel exodus who had been released from Cuban jails. The INS commissioner told the press that 21,000 of the oft-cited 23,000 so-called criminals in the Mariel boatlift "were involved in very minor misdemeanors or, in many cases, political kinds of crimes that would not be crimes in the U.S."[50] But the meticulous writer Joan Didion, for instance, took the high numbers at face value, writing simply that 26,000 of the Mariel refugees had "prison records."[51] In U.S. law enforcement circles the term "Marielito" became synonymous with "criminal." Speaking about crimes allegedly committed here, the INS commissioner said that the numbers of Mariel criminals were greatly exaggerated: "There's an unfortunate tendency now in some quarters for every Hispanic arrested to be labeled a Marielito. For example, there were some 800 names that New York officials gave us of suspected Marielitos who were involved in criminal activity. It turned out that *only 80 of them were actually Cuban* and only 19 were Marielitos."[52] Conversely, some criminals were actually welcomed because of their crimes. In 1980 the Cuban government "noted that the United States had welcomed as heroes those Cubans who had forcibly hijacked boats."[53]

But the *Scarface*-assisted version of reality persists. That film's opening repeats that Castro sent "the dregs of his jails," repeating the figure of 25,000 prisoners that apparently includes Castro's political prisoners. In a twentieth-anniversary DVD release of the movie, screenplay writer Oliver

Stone also informs viewers that he performed actual law enforcement research in three Florida cities. When the movie was in danger of receiving an X rating—which would have meant less profit—producer Martin Bregman "appealed to the ratings board, bringing along some law enforcement officers . . . who said that the movie carried an anti-drug message."[54] In the 2004 Supreme Court arguments, Stone's explanation of the Mariel boatlift was echoed through the views of Antonin Scalia: "they just open their jails and say, hey, you know, go wherever you want."[55] The U.S.–Cuban collaboration would continue for decades as the Mariel prisoners were held as pawns in diplomatic maneuvering and "migration talks."

After doing time on drug charges, a Mariel Cuban woman was denied release by the INS because she had nowhere to live. Denied her antidepressant medication, she became suicidal, and after a subsequent custody review she was denied release because of a suicide attempt. Even the warden of the Louisiana jail holding her for the federal government had recommended her release. "The last thing they have to do is just kill us," she said, "but see, they can't do that."

Or could they? If Mariel Cuban prisoners were not entitled to any more due process than the administration claimed, wrote the Sixth Circuit Court of Appeals in 2003, "we do not see why the United States government could not torture or summarily execute them."[56] In the *Clark v. Suarez Martinez* arguments, Justice John Paul Stevens raised the same question, wondering whether the government could just "shoot" the Mariel Cubans. Government attorney Edwin S. Kneedler replied, "Absolutely not."[57] But he avoided saying clearly why the claimed authority for endless detention could not also be used for summary execution.

In the hallway of the Supreme Court, after the argument, I asked Kneedler for the reason. When I declined to go off the record, he declined to answer and said only that the government does not argue cases in the media. So it was not quite accurate to say the government asserts it can do anything at all to these people. In this case, lacking the terrorism cover, even the government mouthpiece was unwilling to articulate the deeper truth of what he was arguing for.

Afterword

In 2005, bound by its decision in *Zadvydas*, the Supreme Court ruled 7–2 against the government in *Martinez*, with Scalia writing for the majority.

Mariel Cubans and others like them, with certain exceptions, could no longer be indefinitely detained. So legislators went to work to legalize the indefinite detention outlawed by the Supreme Court. At this writing, these efforts remain in progress. For now, ICE uses the label "specially dangerous" to justify the continued, potentially indefinite detention of some immigrants who would otherwise be covered by *Zadvydas* and *Martinez*, and the agency keeps those prisoners' identities and locations from organizations who seek to help them.

ICE also simply breaks the law, violating regulations governing the release of long-term detainees.[58] While unknown numbers of administrative prisoners in immigration custody were released in compliance with the *Zadvydas* and *Martinez* rulings, the General Accounting Office (GAO) reported that three years after *Zadvydas*, ICE was detaining hundreds of persons who should have been released under that decision. Yet the GAO simply recommended that the agency violating the law remedy the problem.[59] In other words, someone who is being illegally incarcerated by ICE has no option other than trying—without the right to court-appointed counsel—to file suit in district court asking for justice from an agency already violating the Supreme Court ruling on the matter.

The Mariel Cuban case was never about the "hordes of aliens" conjured by government attorney Kneedler in his scare tactics before the Supreme Court. Nor was it about "the fundamental power of the United States to protect its borders." And it was certainly not about the al-Qaeda attacks on New York and Washington—the "events of recent years," as Kneedler delicately put it, joining them in a sentence with "migration crises involving Haitians and Cubans."[60] This case was about the limits of executive authority against those whose humanity would be, and has been, denied for the sake of nothing more than that very authority. It is the same circular, self-justifying logic of power that Cheney articulated so well.

Notes

1. Remarks by Vice President Dick Cheney to the U.S. Chamber of Commerce, November 14, 2001, http://www.whitehouse.gov/vicepresident/news-speeches/speeches/vp20011114-1.html (accessed November 6, 2007).

2. Human Rights Watch, "The United States' 'Disappeared': The CIA's Long-Term 'Ghost Detainees,'" October 2004, 4.

3. *Rasul v. Bush*, 542 U.S. 466 (2004), Scalia dissent, 17.

4. 352 F.3d 1278, 1310 (9th Cir. 2003).

5. 789 F.Supp. 1552 (S.D. Fla. 1991).

6. "Eleventh Circuit Twice Overturns Bar on Repatriation of Haitians," *Interpreter Releases* 68, no. 48 (1991): 1845.

7. Author's notes of hearing, December 2, 1991.

8. See Mark Dow, "Occupying and Obscuring Haiti," *New Politics* 5, no. 2 (1995), http://www.wpunj.edu/~newpol/issue18/dow18.htm#r18 (accessed November 6, 2007).

9. Cable from U.S. Embassy, Port-au-Prince, April 12, 1994. Reproduced in James Ridgeway, ed., *The Haiti Files: Decoding the Crisis* (Washington, D.C.: Essential Books/Azul Editions, 1994), 188.

10. Quoted in David W. Engstrom, *Presidential Decision Making Adrift: The Carter Administration and the Mariel Boatlift* (Lanham, Md.: Rowman and Littlefield, 1997), 145, 174, n. 47.

11. See Mark Dow, "A Refugee Policy to Support Haiti's Killers," *New Politics* 5, no. 1 (1994), http://www.wpunj.edu/~newpol/issue17/dow17.htm (accessed November 6, 2007).

12. Bill Frelick, "Safe Haven: Safe for Whom?" *World Refugee Survey*, U.S. Committee for Refugees and Immigrants (2002), 2.

13. *Rasul v. Bush*, transcript of oral argument, 3.

14. Frelick, "Safe Haven," 8.

15. Ibid., 8.

16. Ibid., 14.

17. "Haitian Children Imprisoned at Guantanamo: Cruel and Unusual Punishment," *Haïti Progrès* 13, no. 5 (1995), 9.

18. Paul Farmer, *The Uses of Haiti* (Monroe, Maine: Common Courage Press, 1994), 277.

19. *Rasul v. Bush*, Scalia dissent, 11.

20. Farmer, *Uses of Haiti*, 280.

21. Mark Dow, *Keeping the Haitians Out: A Conversation with Cheryl Little*, published in conjunction with the exhibition "Ghosts of Guantánamo," shown at Tap Tap Haitian Restaurant in Miami Beach, Fla., May 1995, 14.

22. Quoted in ACLU of New Jersey, "ACLU of New Jersey Files Lawsuit Seeking Information on Post-September 11 Detainees," press release, January 22, 2002.

23. Barbara Crossette, "U.S. Fails in Effort to Block Vote on U.N. Convention on Torture," *New York Times*, July 25, 2002.

24. Ibid.

25. In re D-J-, 23 I & N Dec. 572 (Attorney General, 2003), Interim Decision #3488.

26. Ibid.

27. Ibid.

28. "Ashcroft Leaking Logic," *Palm Beach Post,* April 29, 2003.

29. Ira Kurzban interview in Noam Chomsky, Paul Farmer, and Amy Goodman, *Getting Haiti Right This Time: The U.S. and the Coup* (Monroe, Maine: Common Courage Press, 2004), 47.

30. Franz Gabriel interview in Chomsky, Farmer, and Goodman, *Getting Haiti Right This Time,* 151.

31. Eric Green, "Cheney Says Aristide Made Own Choice to Resign as Haiti's President: Vice President Says Aristide Had 'Worn Out Welcome' in Haiti," U.S. Department of State, U.S. Info.State.Gov, March 3, 2004. http://usinfo.state.gov/xarchives/display.html?p=washfile-english&y=2004&m—arch&x=20040303173424AEneerG0.5541803&t=livefeeds/wf-latest.html (accessed November 6, 2007).

32. Kurzban in Chomsky, Farmer, and Goodman, *Getting Haiti Right This Time,* 47.

33. U.S. Committee for Refugees, "President Bush Finally Speaks the Truth About America's Unlawful Treatment of Haitian Refugees," press release, February 26, 2004.

34. Ibid.

35. "U.S. Policy Grants TPS to Many—Except Haitians," *Miami Herald,* October 20, 2004.

36. *Rasul v. Bush,* transcript of oral argument, 26.

37. Ibid., transcript of oral argument, 26–27.

38. *Rumsfeld v. Padilla,* 542 U.S. 426 (2004), transcript of oral argument, 22.

39. Ibid., transcript of oral argument, 23.

40. Ibid., transcript of oral argument, 24.

41. *Hamdi v. Rumsfeld,* 542 U.S. 507 (2004), transcript of oral argument, 30, 28.

42. Ibid., transcript of oral argument, 50.

43. Stephen J. Berry, "CBS Lets the Pentagon Taint Its News Process," *Nieman Report* 58, no. 3 (2004), 76–78.

44. See "Mariel Cubans: Abandoned, Again and Again," chap. 14 in Mark Dow, *American Gulag: Inside U.S. Immigration Prisons* (Berkeley and Los Angeles: University of California Press, 2004).

45. Daniel Golden, "U.S. No Haven for These Cuban Refugees," *Boston Globe,* March 29, 1987.

46. Dan Malone, "851 Detained for Years in INS Centers: Many Are Pursuing Asylum, Agency Challenges Own Records," *Dallas Morning News,* April 1, 2001.

47. Gaiutra Bahadur, "Court to Consider Detention of Mariel Boat Lift Refugees," *Philadelphia Inquirer,* October 12, 2004.

48. *Rosales-Garcia v. Holland* and *Carballo v. Luttrell,* 2003 FED App. 0070P (6th Cir.).

49. *Shaughnessy v. United States* ex. rel. Mezei, 345 U.S. 206 (1953).

50. "U.S. Won't 'Let Another Mariel Happen': Interview with Alan Nelson," *U.S. News & World Report*, January 16, 1984.

51. Joan Didion, *Miami* (New York: Simon and Schuster, 1987), 42.

52. Ibid. Emphasis added.

53. Engstrom, *Presidential Decision Making Adrift*, 122.

54. Bernard Weinraub, "A Foul Mouth with a Following," *New York Times*, September 23, 2003.

55. *Clark v. Suarez Martinez*, 543 U.S. 878 (2005), transcript of oral argument, 45.

56. *Rosales-Garcia v. Holland;* and *Carballo v. Lutrell.*

57. *Clark v. Suarez Martinez*, 24–25.

58. Kathleen Glynn and Sarah Bronstein, *Systemic Problems Persist in U.S. ICE Reviews for "Indefinite" Detainees* (Washington, D.C.: Catholic Legal Immigration Network, 2005).

59. General Accounting Office, *Immigration Enforcement: Better Data and Controls Are Needed to Assure Consistency with the Supreme Court Decision on Long-Term Alien Detention*, GAO-04-434, May 27, 2004.

60. *Clark v. Suarez Martinez*, 3–4, 55.

CHAPTER 3

Immigration, Terrorism, and Secret Prisons

DAN MALONE

LONG BEFORE THE TERRORIST ATTACKS of September 11, 2001, or the War on Terror or Camp X-ray or ghost detainees,[1] the United States began to create what amounted to a secret prison system within its own borders, a system that continues to exist and thrive today. If that assertion seems incongruous for a nation with traditions of transparency spanning more than two centuries, the assertion that follows is even more so. Some of those prisoners secretly detained for years have not been convicted of any crime. The words "secret prison" and "United States," at least in the era before September 11, 2001, describe an institution and a nation at odds with each other's essence. One might expect to find a secret prison in the Soviet Union, Iraq, North Korea, or any of the other countries U.S. leaders frequently criticize for human rights violations, but surely there are no gulags in America. And if there were, surely they would not be populated by men and women who have not been convicted of any crime.

But facts, as President Ronald Reagan once said, are stubborn things. And the stubborn fact about America's secret prisoners is that in the years immediately before September 11, 2001, some 850 persons were being detained in virtual secrecy by U.S. immigration officials in a web of municipal lockups, county jails, state and federal prisons, and privately run for-profit institutions across the country.[2]

Virtually nothing about these prisoners, beyond the fact that they were incarcerated and came from foreign lands, was a matter of public record. Further, the government considered the identities of these prisoners to be a secret worth fighting in court to protect.[3] This chapter explores the recent history of these secret prisons and explains the contradictory rationales that have been used to justify their existence. I also describe my own efforts, successes, and failures, and those of my students, in trying to get the government to reveal basic information about the people it is keeping in these prisons.

Following the attacks of September 11, 2001, a similar blanket of secrecy was thrown over persons detained in the war in Afghanistan. To accommodate the swelling population of prisoners, the United States began to use bases abroad, such as the naval station at Guantánamo Bay, Cuba, where it was even harder to determine who is locked up or why they were being detained. Common among all these cases is the government's claim that the prisoners pose a significant threat—either as common criminals, flight risks, suspected terrorists, or "enemy combatants"—to the lives and safety of ordinary Americans.[4] While that claim may well be true for many or even most of the prisoners, the threat posed by others is far from certain. In some cases, the threat itself seems to be a phantom. Among those who have been secretly imprisoned, some for years,[5] are asylum seekers,[6] men so old that they cannot "answer simple questions,"[7] disabled[8] and mentally ill persons,[9] and children as young as twelve.[10] As with the foreigners held in facilities on American soil before September 11, 2001, the government resisted requests that it identify people rounded up in domestic terror sweeps or the enemy combatants held in prisons on foreign soil. And when information about the identities of the prisoners themselves became public, the government moved to plug holes through which information about those in detention sometimes leaked out.[11] Local jailers who housed foreigners detained in post–9/11 roundups and who considered the prisoners' presence in their facilities to be public record, subsequently were barred by the Justice Department from ever again releasing such information.[12] Further, information released by local governments about persons detained by federal officials in post–9/11 sweeps was subsequently removed from public databases.[13] Records of a person's presence in a jail were here one day, gone the next. The U.S. military even thwarted attempts by student journalists to contact prisoners the students had identified from press clippings.[14]

Information on the vast majority of the nation's 2.3 million prisoners[15]—from garden-variety petty thieves to serial killers and convicted terrorists—is a matter of public record. Public information officers for jails and prisons around the country are accustomed to being asked and answering basic questions about people behind bars. Jailers routinely make available public information about their wards. Many jurisdictions now place information about their prisoners online. The names, ages, physical descriptions, and conviction histories of prisoners are routinely are available for the price of a phone call, a stamp, or a few clicks on a computer. "It's pretty fundamental. When the state takes custody of someone, they have to account for what they've done with that person," said James Castlebury, a spokesman for the Texas Department of Corrections Institutional Division, which manages the nation's second-largest state prison system.[16] But for many prisoners held by federal immigration authorities or by the U.S. military or intelligence agencies, no such accounting exists. They are counted but not named. Detailed records about their cases from the nation's immigration courts are not available without the prisoner's written permission—and that is not possible to request, much less obtain, unless the prisoner's identity is known.

So how many such prisoners are there? At the end of 2005, 19,562 prisoners, or less than 1 percent of the nation's total incarceration population, were being detained by U.S. Immigration and Customs Enforcement (ICE).[17] ICE's prisoner population historically includes large numbers of illegal immigrants waiting to be deported. In most cases, the agency is able to return the prisoners to their home countries or send them elsewhere within weeks or months of being picked up. Of those ICE prisoners, a full 40 percent, or 7,826, had neither been convicted of nor charged with a crime.[18] In addition to immigration prisoners, the U.S. military has held some 600 "enemy combatants" at military facilities in Guantánamo Bay and an unknown number at facilities in other countries.[19] Though the total population of these two groups constitutes only a tiny fraction of the nation's incarcerated population, it represents a dramatic and unprecedented departure in how the United States treats those it has deprived of freedom. And the secrecy surrounding those prisoners makes it difficult for the public to know what the government is doing and why.

This departure from transparency came to my attention in the late 1990s while I was working as a reporter for the *Dallas Morning News*. For several years, I had followed the story of a young Vietnamese immigrant named Luan Van Hoang, who had been questionably convicted of a high-profile home invasion robbery in North Texas's burgeoning Vietnamese community.[20] Luan was scheduled to be released a few days before Christmas in 1997 and had pledged to call me collect as soon as he was free. But when he called, it was not, as I had expected, from a phone booth outside a state prison. It was from inside yet another detention facility. The instant Luan was released from state prison, he was greeted by an Immigration and Naturalization Service agent who informed him that while he may have discharged his state prison sentence, a change in federal law and policy required that he now be detained indefinitely as a "criminal alien." The language of immigration law is, to a layman, maddeningly deceptive. A "criminal alien" sounds like a character in the *Men in Black* movies. Foreigners serving virtual life sentences in American prison are not "lifers" or even "prisoners," they are "indefinite detainees." People ejected from the country are no longer deported, but subject to "removal proceedings." Other noncitizens with feet firmly placed on U.S. soil are labeled "excludables"—meaning they are not legally considered to be present in the United States. Perhaps there is something inherently objectionable in the way a nation founded by immigrants treats the immigrants it encounters today that also prevents us from describing them as human beings and what happens to them in simple, straightforward terms.

While Luan did his time in a series of state prisons in the late 1980s and 1990s, Congress was reworking the nation's immigration laws. And laws enacted in 1996 required that immigrants convicted of certain crimes in the United States be deported after their release from prison.[21] The stated purpose of this change was to rid the streets of violent criminals who had no respect for U.S. laws. But the law was worded in such a way that even immigrants convicted of some relatively minors offenses were *required* to be deported. Further, the 1996 change in law was retroactive—meaning that, in some cases, a person who might have been convicted for a minor crime a decade earlier and who had no further problems with the law would now be required to surrender to immigration officials for deportation. Luan's case and those of hundreds of others were additionally complicated by nationality. Luan's family had legally immigrated to the United States after the fall of South Vietnam. But two decades later, relations between Vietnam and the United States remained so strained that Vietnam routinely refused to provide travel documents for any of its citizens that the United States ordered deported—making their repatriation an Immigration and Naturalization Service (INS) *Mission Impossible*. Such diplomatic impediments to carrying out the requirements of federal law meant that INS officials soon found themselves dealing with hundreds of foreigners they were required to deport but could not. Congress, in essence, gave INS orders it could not carry out. The agency's solution to this dilemma was to detain these undeportable aliens until some theoretical juncture in the future when their deportation might become possible. In cases where the immigrant came from Cuba, Vietnam, Laos, and a handful of other nations with severely strained diplomatic relations with the

United States, the chance of eventual deportation was usually nil. That impasse is reflected in the growing population of foreigners detained in immigration facilities. The imprisoned population of foreigners has more than doubled in the last decade—from 8,177 in 1995, the year before the immigration law changed, to 19,562 at the end of 2005.[22]

The change in the law the year before Luan was "released" had not registered at the time on either Luan or myself. We were both startled to learn that Luan, after having "paid his debt" to society, now faced a potential life sentence in federal custody because the United States did not have diplomatic relations with Vietnam. At the time, immigration officials in Washington told me that on any given day, their agency detains thousands of foreigners. The vast majority would be held only a few days or weeks until they were deported. But a growing number were being held indefinitely. The agency could not tell me how long the longest-held indefinite detainees had been in custody, but a spokesman said that there was a small group of a few dozen or so prisoners who had been in detention for three years or more. Thinking there might be an interesting story to tell about the lives of three dozen prisoners no nation wanted—an international roster of *personae non grata*—I asked for their names. The names of those our nation deprives of their liberty, for whatever reason, were surely public, or so I thought.

But the immigration agency said it could not reveal the identities of its longest-held prisoners because of another recent change, not in the law this time, but in policy at the U.S. Department of Justice. The new policy, officials said, forbid the release of "personal information" about immigration prisoners on the strange theory, or so it seemed to me, that identifying prisoners violated their rights to privacy. In June 1996, the same year that Congress changed the law to require the deportation of immigrations convicted of crimes, then–Attorney General Janet Reno approved a Justice Department policy change that "extended the right to privacy to everyone in the United States, regardless of their immigration status."[23] That policy stated that basic information about immigrants "ordinarily must be withheld [when requested by the news media or through the Freedom of Information Act] as a matter of law—except where disclosure would reflect agency [INS] performance."[24] The change in privacy policy, coupled with the change in immigration law, meant that the federal government was now holding hundreds of prisoners it could neither deport nor discuss without the prisoner's prior written permission—which, as a practical matter, was virtually impossible for an outsider to obtain.

This policy change had been politically driven by the 1994 Senate race in California, in which candidates Dianne Feinstein and Michael Huffington had both been accused of employing undocumented immigrants.[25] When journalists began to seek information about the workers in question, the Justice Department, which had routinely provided such information in the past, lowered its new curtain of secrecy.[26] "The object was to give aliens the same protections under the Privacy Act that was provided for U.S. citizens and permanent resident aliens," Carl Stern, who served as a spokesman for the Justice Department from 1993 to 1996, explained in a 1999 interview.[27] Information on immigrants in or out of prison that was available one day was, simply, not available the next. Before the policy change, Russ Bergeron, a spokesman for the immigration agency, said the agency "routinely released" information on immigrants. But the policy change, he said, took the matter "out of my hands."[28]

As a practical matter, the government seems to forget about prisoners' rights to privacy when it serves the government's political interest to do so. Both the federal government and the U.S. military, for example, consider the identities of condemned prisoners a matter of public record. And when high-profile suspected terrorists or military leaders are captured, government officials often trumpet the news. Following Saddam Hussein's extraction from a "spider hole," for example, the world was treated to photographs that would arguably violate even the privacy rights of a dictator—images of Hussein in his underwear and during a medical examination. In contrast, a list of asylum seekers in indefinite detention might be fodder for unfavorable news stories about the immigration agency or the courts if information about those prisoners became public. Intentionally or not, the privacy policy also had the effect of shielding the Justice Department and the INS from scrutiny from the media and immigrants' advocates about whom it was holding—and it did so in the name of protecting its prisoner' rights to privacy.

In May 1998 I filed a request under the Freedom of Information Act (FOIA) with the INS for the identities of its longest-held prisoners. When the agency responded to that request in August that same year, it made what seemed to be an incredible claim that it could not locate any records about its longest-held prisoners. The agency responded in a letter that stated it had "conducted a search of our Headquarters offices including our public affairs office, and did not locate any records" about the longest-held prisoners.[29] The agency seemed to be saying that not only were the identities of the prisoners not a matter of public record, they were not a matter of any record whatsoever. They had become apparitions.

The newspaper subsequently filed a lawsuit in the Northern District of Texas that sought to force the agency to release the names of its prisoners. As discovery in that lawsuit progressed, it became clear that not only did the agency maintain detailed records on its prisoners, but also that the number of prisoners being held for long periods of time was far greater than the government had previously acknowledged. At the time, immigration records placed prisoners into groups based on how long they had been detained. Those held for more than three years—whether it might be three years and a day or three decades—were lumped together in a final group. In interviews, immigration officials had given several accounts of how many prisoners fell into that category of longest held, but certainly no number that approached one hundred. In response to one round of interrogatories in a FOIA lawsuit, however, the INS released records showing that there were 294 prisoners who have been locked up for at least three years.[30] In a second round of interrogatories, the number grew to 851 persons from 69 nations.[31] The records came to us in the form of a spreadsheet with each prisoner's first name, date of birth, and country of origin. The records also had a code for the location of the facility in which the prisoner was being held and a code denoting the reason each prisoner was being held. What the records did not contain, and what the INS still refused to give up, was any prisoner's last name, the final bit of information that would make it possible to send a letter to an individual prisoner requesting information about his or her situation.

One of the disturbing issues raised by the records was whether the prisoners posed, as the immigration agency had contended, some threat to the public. The 1996 immigration reform law passed by Congress required the INS to deport any foreigner convicted of an aggravated felony. And the records show that of the 851 persons held for more than three years, 489, or about 60 percent, in fact had one such conviction.[32] That still left, however, 362 prisoners who had been detained for at least three years and had no such conviction. Whether they had been convicted of some lesser crime that did not require their deportation or had been convicted of no crime at all the records did not say.

In the end, the *News* settled its lawsuit against the INS when the agency, although still refusing to fully identify any of its secret prisoners, agreed to hand-deliver a letter from us to each of the 851 longest-held prisoners. Using the spreadsheet as a mailing list, and guessing at each prisoner's likely native tongue based on his or her home country, we drafted a "dear un-known prisoner" letter to each, had the letters translated when it seemed appropriate, and sent the 851 letters to the INS for delivery.[33]

Before long, the responses began to arrive—first a trickle, then a flood of correspondence from people from countries around the world who now called an INS detention facility their home. By the spring of 2001, we had boxes of letters from prisoners from countries around the world who were now being held in U.S. facilities. Many of the stories they told were quite compelling—and raised more disturbing questions about why they were in detention in the first place.

On July 22, 2001, the *News* published a package of articles written by me and by Frank Trejo, another reporter, who had spent years covering im-migration issues for the paper. Our stories documented the cases of a dozen asylum seekers who had been detained for up to six years and who the INS contended posed a threat to society or a flight risk.[34] As best we could determine, however, the only law any of these men and women had violated in the United States was entering the country illegally for the pur-pose of seeking asylum.

Jimmy Johnson, a thirty-seven-year-old Liberian, was detained for more than six years because he could not prove his identity. There did not seem to be any compelling evidence that he was not who he said he was, but Johnson, like many asylum seekers who leave their homeland under less-than-ideal circumstances, lacked the paperwork required to prove who he was.[35] Immigration officials detained him even after he was granted asy-lum and released him only after the Board of Immigration Appeals con-cluded that he likely faced torture if deported.

Johnson was the longest-held asylum seeker we found in the group—and he was one of only two to have been released by the time the stories were published. Ten others from Sri Lanka, Ivory Coast, Nigeria, Uganda, and Ghana, each citing fears of torture, imprisonment, or death if de-ported, had arrived in the United States only to be placed behind bars with dim hope for release.

In interviews with these prisoners, their attorneys, and their friends, there was nothing we found to indicate that they posed a threat to anyone. But immigration officials found some reason to doubt their often hard-to-document stories, and had, while their appeals of deportation orders lin-gered in the court, ordered their prolonged detention.

This bleak prospect for freedom facing any of these detainees was brightened somewhat in the summer of 2001 when the U.S. Supreme

Court ruled that the INS practice of indefinitely detaining prisoners that it could not deport was unconstitutional. That ruling stemmed from the case of a then–fifty-three-year-old stateless man named Kestutis Zadvydas. Zadvydas was born to a German couple living in Lithuania in the years immediately following World War II.[36] After he immigrated to the United States, where he was subsequently convicted of crimes that required his deportation, the INS tried to deport him only to find that neither Lithuania nor Germany considered him a citizen. So, for a time, Zadvydas joined the swelling population of imprisoned immigrants that the INS could not deport and would not release. The Supreme Court ruling said the practice of detaining people indefinitely when there is no hope of being able to deport them was unlawful—and the Zadvydas ruling offered the hope for freedom to hundreds of other immigrants who found themselves in similar situations. But even as the government was trying to determine which of its detainees must be released under the Zadvydas ruling, and what conditions might be imposed on their release, another group of immigrants committed a crime—the terror attacks of September 11, 2001—that would bring down a new, heavier curtain of secrecy on foreigners in or soon to be in U.S. custody.

In the five years between the government's imposition of a new privacy policy for foreigners and September 11, 2001, the federal government, while refusing to identify the prisoners in its custody, still remained willing to let its prisoners maintain contact with the outside world through the mail, personal interviews, or visitation.

In the years after September 11, 2001, however, the government took additional steps to keep the identities of people detained in post-terror roundups or captured on the battlefields of Afghanistan from becoming public knowledge.

In the panic that ensued after the attacks of September 11, 2001, federal agents across the country questioned and arrested hundreds of men, mostly of Middle Eastern extraction, for possible leads. Federal agents working in North Texas used a rural jail outside Dallas as a central repository for these prisoners. Federal agents considered the identities of those it picked up to be a secret—even though, as things turned out, none of the 1,200 persons rounded up after September 11, 2001, had anything to do with the attacks.[37] While the federal government considered their identities a secret, the Denton County Sheriff's Department's public access computer did not.[38]

In the fall of 2001, a group of graduate students at the Mayborn Graduate Institute of Journalism at the University of North Texas was assigned the task of scouring the online database maintained by the sheriff for leads to the identities of those who had been picked up. By querying the database for people who were jailed after September 11, 2001, and who were being detained on INS holds, the students identified about seventy prisoners, wrote each of them a letter inquiring about the circumstances of their detention, and waited for a response.[39] Those letters yielded a single response—a phone call from an attorney who represented a man named Anwar Al-Mirabi, a Saudi Arabian businessman who had been picked up two days after the attacks and who would spend the next ten months in detention for reasons that remain unclear almost six years later. In the first few days after September 11, Al-Mirabi certainly looked suspicious. The twenty-nine-year-old Saudi Arabian businessman had a long, unruly beard, ran an export business from Arlington, Texas, had recently traveled through both Boston (where two of the airplanes that were part of the attacks originated) and New York. Further, he was married to the widow of Bassam Kanj, a man identified in published reports as an associate of Osama bin Laden. He also knew, by virtue of having attended the same mosque, Wadih el Hage, who was convicted and sentenced to life in prison for perjury and conspiracy in connection with embassy bombings in Africa in 1998. When agents, acting on a tip about a suspicious Middle Eastern man who had just returned from Boston and New York, knocked on Al-Mirabi's door two days after September 11, 2001, Al-Mirabi and his wife consented to a search. The search netted no known evidence of involvement in a terror plot. But it did turn up Al-Mirabi's expired visa. And that was enough to land the young Saudi in the Denton County Jail. While he was in jail, a federal prosecutor named him as a material witness in an ongoing investigation, presumably into terrorism, being run out of Chicago. And Al-Mirabi eventually testified three times before a federal grand jury in Illinois before he was deported, after ten months in detention, to Saudi Arabia.[40]

Until the North Texas graduate students queried the sheriff's database, Al-Mirabi's detention was swathed in official secrecy and known only to his family and attorneys. Little is known today about why he was detained for ten months, why he was named as a material witness, or what he might have told grand jurors. Repeated attempts by a reporter to interview Al-Mirabi failed "as he was moved jail to jail, state to state, a human checker on a board." (Records on his case are sealed. Federal officials familiar with the government's interest in Al-Mirabi declined to discuss his case.)[41]

What is known comes from his wife, Marlene Kanj Al-Mirabi, and his attorneys. Yes, they say, he was in Boston and New York—but it was to accompany his pregnant wife on a cross-country driving trip for medical appointments for her pregnancy. And yes, he ran an export business—exporting automobiles. And yes, he had a beard and knew people who may have been associates of bin Laden. But those facts amounted to mere coincidences—not evidence to keep a man locked up, often in solitary confinement, for almost a year.

One of Al-Mirabi's attorneys, Gerhard Kleinschmidt of Fort Worth, said he understood how "the coincidences in Anwar's situation made (terror investigators) want to talk with him." But he also said how the government treated Al-Mirabi served no useful purpose:

> "He cooperated fully from the first interview. . . . If word gets out to these other [persons the government thinks might have information about September 11, 2001] . . . that all the time they are cooperating they're going to be locked up in maximum security cells and treated as if they are axe-murders, how is that going to encourage anyone to cooperate?

> From his initial cooperation, the questions ceased after two or three days. Then we have months and months where nobody bothers to see him, but he is locked in solitary confinement. He is sick and has a hard time getting treatment. He's constantly transferred. And then when the grand jury finishes with their investigation . . . they again ignore him."

Kleinschmidt also said, "Once they had him locked up, they didn't give a damn about him, his problems or his family."[42]

The government may not have cared about Al-Mirabi's problems, but it did care about what the public knew about his case. In April 2002 the Justice Department announced that local jailers would no longer be permitted to release information about federal prisoners being held in their facilities. "Information regarding certain federal detainees is extremely sensitive. . . . Officials at non-federal detention facilities will not release information relating to detainees, reserving the decision for release of such information, to the INS."[43] By the time of the information clampdown, the

INS had been operating for six years under the Justice Department policy that forbid the release of information about foreigners in detention on the grounds it might violate their privacy rights.

Denton County is one of the more transparent local governments in the United States. Its jail Web site, for example, makes detailed information, including photographs and criminal charges, available to the public for free. But if you check it today, as the graduate students did in 2001, you will find that it has been scrubbed clean of any mention that it once housed Anwar Al-Mirabi.[44]

While Al-Mirabi was in the Denton County Jail, the War on Terror shifted from American soil to Afghanistan, and U.S. troops were soon moving suspected terrorists to Camps X-ray and Delta on Guantánamo Bay in Cuba. Like asylum seekers and post–9/11 detainees, they, too, were cloaked in secrecy. In the fall of 2002, another group of graduate students from the Mayborn Graduate Institute of Journalism attempted to identify and contact as many of the Camp X-ray prisoners as possible. Initially, the only contact these prisoners had with the outside world was mail delivered by the International Committee of the Red Cross or the U.S. military. By September, letters from these prisoners began to trickle out to family members around the world, and news of the letters began to appear in the international press. Using news-clipping databases and scouring the world's media, the class was able to identify fifty-four of the six hundred or so prisoners by name and nationality. Prisoners in that group came from Afghanistan, Australia, Bahrain, Canada, Egypt, England, France, Germany, Jordan, Kuwait, Pakistan, Saudia Arabia, Sudan, Sweden, Tajikistan, and Turkey.[45]

Courts in the United States have long upheld the right of prisoners to correspond with the free world. And judging by their public pronouncements, both the Red Cross and the Pentagon were happy to deliver mail to these prisoners. The Pentagon, stung by early criticism of conditions at Guantánamo, seemed particularly interested in bragging about its own mail delivery system if only to counter the suggestion that the prisoners were being held in isolation.

In an article the students wrote about their attempt to interview the prisoners by mail, they reported:

> The Red Cross says it has delivered 3,300 personal letters to and from the prisoners and their relatives during the last year—"a precious link," the organization says, to the outside world. . . . The

Defense Department operates an independent mail delivery system for the prisoners. Military officials said in July [2002] that they had delivered an additional 1,900 pieces of mail. . . .

"We ensure the detainees are allowed to write and receive letters," Army Reserve Master Sgt. Debra A. Tart is quoted as saying in an Armed Forces Press Service article dated July 23, 2002.

"The detainees are not limited to our service. They can also send and receive mail through the International Committee of the Red Cross."[46]

The Geneva Convention further provided some guarantees that, at a minimum, prisoners of war "shall be allowed to send and receive letters and cards."[47] These prisoners, however, were considered neither traditional criminals nor prisoners of war. The students reported that "Bush administration officials have refused to categorize the detainees as 'prisoners of war,' instead labeling them 'enemy combatants,' a designation that the international accord does not address."[48]

Harold Heilsnis, the Defense Department director for public inquiry and analysis, reiterated the Defense Department's unwillingness to provide information about its prisoners. "It is our policy that, due to operational security considerations, we will not provide specific information on any individuals detained in our ongoing war on terrorism," Heilsnis wrote in an e-mail to Mitch Land, the director of the Mayborn Graduate Institute. Then he added, " "President Bush has established that all detainees in control of the United States will be treated humanely and consistent with the Geneva Convention." He further quoted Defense Secretary Donald Rumsfeld's assurance that "the treatment of the detainees in Guantánamo Bay is proper, it's humane, it's appropriate and it's fully consistent with international conventions."[49]

The students bundled their letters together in two packages—one to the International Committee of the Red Cross and another to the Pentagon—and put them in the mail.

The letters, which were written in English and translated into Arabic, requested basic information about the prisoners. The envelopes addressed to the detainees were left unsealed so their contents could be inspected.

"You are receiving this letter because we want to know the facts surrounding your capture, detention and life at Camp Delta at Guantánamo Bay, Cuba," the letters said. "We would be interested to know what you were doing when apprehended by U.S. forces, what your daily life is like in Camp Delta, and what your hopes for the future are. We would like to know your views about the United States and Al Qaeda."[50]

With their letters in the mail, the students began interviewing family, friends and attorneys of the prisoners they identified. The stories that emerged from those interviews hinted at the abuses that are now well established. Their story reported that:

The family of Murat Kurnaz, for example, said in a telephone interview from Germany that the 20-year-old detainee is a devout Muslim with no military training who traveled to Pakistan solely to study the Quran. Rabiye Kurnaz said through a translator that her son had been in Pakistan for two months and was trying to return when U.S. forces detained him.

"He was asked for more money when he wanted to buy his ticket. Since he had no money, he was sold to Americans," she said. The students were unable to corroborate her assertion. Rabiye Kurnaz said her family had received three letters and two postcards but had heard nothing from her son since June. She said she had seen photographs of him, however, "with his hands tied, tape on mouth, kneeling and eyes isolated." She said she had been told that the interrogation of her son could be lengthy and that "the procedures could last a couple of years."

Bernhard Docke, Murat Kurnaz's attorney in Germany, said his client had wanted to join the Taliban but, for reasons that are unclear, could not. "German investigators found no links between Murat and the Taliban," Docke said. "Murat hoped to get involved with the Taliban but he didn't manage to. He was a wannabe."

A relative of a Kuwaiti prisoner also raised questions about why his brother has been detained. In a telephone interview from Kuwait, Mansour Kamel said his brother Abdullah Kamel is disabled and lacks the ability to be a soldier. He said he last heard from his brother, one of a dozen Kuwaitis being detained, in August.

"He can't be a terrorist," Mansour Kamel said. "He can't even use his hands. He has no fingers on his hands. He was injured by a booby trap during the Persian Gulf War. I have the papers to prove that the Kuwait government excused him from military service because of his handicap. I have pictures of his hands."

Mansour Kamel says he's confident that his brother will be absolved of any connection with terrorism—if only the United States will allow an outside review of his case. "I'm not asking for my brother's release, just for his case to be heard in court," he said. "They will see what he has told them is the truth."

Kurnaz has written several cards to his family through the Red Cross. In one dated March 2, 2002, he expressed his uncertainty about the future. "I am fine with God's protection, but I don't know when I am going to return," he said in a note written in Turkish and translated for the students into English. "God knows best, and whatever he says, will happen to us."[51]

In the end, of course, neither the Red Cross nor the U.S. military was willing to do for student journalists what they said they have done for thousands of others who have corresponded with these prisoners—deliver the mail.

The assistant to the International Committee of the Red Cross's chief of delegation in Washington, D.C., a man named Frank Sieverts, responded to the request to deliver fifty-four letters from student journalists. Returning the undelivered letters to the students, Sieverts said the Red Cross delivered mail only to and from families of prisoners, not mail from journalists and other media workers. He suggested the students might have better luck with the Department of Defense.

The letters to the Defense Department were mailed in November 2002 to Victoria Clarke, the assistant secretary of defense for public affairs in Washington. Clarke's office said she forwarded the package to . . . Heilsnis. In an e-mail to Mitch Land, Heilsnis said he would, "contact my colleagues at the U.S. Southern Command to discuss the potential delivery that you seek. I will then be back in touch with you as soon as possible after that."[52]

Heilsnis' e-mail was dated November 25, 2002. Land made repeated unsuccessful attempts to contact Heilsnis during December and January. In February, Land again contacted Clarke and inquired about the letters. "We have heard nothing. It has now been two months and we would like to know where things stand," Land wrote in a letter. "All we are asking the Department of Defense to do is deliver the mail—just as the Department has done hundreds if not thousands of times for others."

On February 4, 2003, Heilsnis again said he would check with "my colleagues at U.S. Southern Command regarding your specific request. I should have an answer by tomorrow and will convey that to you."[53] That was the last the students heard about their attempt to interview the prisoners.

Eventually the government was forced by the Associated Press to give up the identities of its prisoners. The AP had filed a FOIA lawsuit against the Pentagon over its refusal to identify its secret prisoners. Even as the Pentagon turned over the documents, a Defense Department spokesman stuck to the company line, first uttered a decade earlier, about immigration prisoners. "Personal information on the detainees was withheld solely to protect detainees' privacy and for their own security," Lieutenant Commander Chito Peppler told the Associated Press. Disclosing such information, he said, "could result in retribution or harm to the detainees or their families."[54]

The United States was founded on the premise that governments derive "their just powers from the consent of the governed." For the governed to give their consent, however, they must know what it is their government is doing—and whom it is doing it to. When it comes to foreigners being held by the United States—whether they are asylum seekers, immigrants who have been accused of crimes, accused terrorists, or enemy combatants—the federal government under both Democratic and Republican administrations has made it difficult if not impossible to tell whom it has deprived of their liberty and the reasons for so doing. Without that knowledge, consent is meaningless.

Acknowledgments

Much of this chapter is based on the reporting of graduate students I taught and worked with at the Mayborn Graduate Institute of Journalism at the University of North Texas in 2001 and 2002. Kay Colley, Ahren

Hemberger, Karen Lim, Marty Newman, Laura Short, and Charles Siderius contacted detainees being held in the Denton County Jail following September 11, 2001. Joshua Baugh, Kathryn R. Clark, Sonya Cole, Seth Gonzales, Kwami Koto, Christina Koutalis, Molly McCullough, Jon O'Guinn, Carey Ostergard, Nikela Pradier, and Mark Saffold identified fifty-four of the early detainees in the so-called War on Terror held at Guantánamo, and interviewed some of their attorneys and family members. Gulden Wyatt and Maike Rode helped with translations. Special thanks go to Gene Zipperlen, who also taught the class that identified the Guantánamo detainees, and Mitch Land, the director of the Mayborn Graduate Institute, who gave our class the chance to explore an unpopular subject during a time of war. Gayle Reaves, editor of *Fort Worth Weekly*, published stories other editors would not have touched. I also am indebted to former *Fort Worth Weekly* interns Naureen Shah, Julian Aguilar, and Shomial Ahmed. Finally, I would like to acknowledge Howard Swindle (1945–2004), the editor at the *Dallas Morning News* who told me about Luan Van Hoang and who, ten years ago, launched me down this exploration of America's secret prisons.

Notes

1. Julian Borger, Jailed Iraqis Hidden from Red Cross, Says U.S. Army, *Guardian*, May 5, 2004.

2. Dan Malone, "851 Detained for Years in INS Centers, Many Are Pursuing Asylum, Agency Challenges Own Records," *Dallas Morning News*, April 1, 2001.

3. Complaint 4:00-cv-00060, *Malone et al. v. U.S. Department of Justice et al.* (N.D. Tex. 2000).

4. Mayborn Graduate Institute of Journalism, "Report on Terrorism Prisoners Stonewalled," March 6, 2003, http://www.alternet.org/story/15317/ (accessed November 6, 2007).

5. Based on data obtained in discovery through Complaint 4:00-cv-00060, *Malone et al. v. U.S. Department of Justice et al.* (N.D. Tex. 2000).

6. Malone, "851 Detained for Years in INS Centers."

7. Mayborn Graduate Institute, "Report on Terrorism Prisoners Stonewalled."

8. Ibid.

9. Frank Trejo, "Suffering from Mental and Health Problems, Sri Lankan Is Detained for Years in at Least 6 Facilities," *Dallas Morning News*, July 22, 2001.

10. James Astill, "Cuba? It Was Great, Says Boys Freed from Guantánamo Bay Who Recall the Place Fondly," *Guardian*, March 6, 2004.

11. Dan Malone and Naureen Shah, "Prisoners? What Prisoners? INS Detainees in Denton Have Disappeared from Files," *Fort Worth Weekly*, July 11, 2002.

12. Ibid.

13. Ibid.

14. Mayborn Graduate Institute, "Report on Terrorism Prisoners Stonewalled."

15. Bureau of Justice Statistics, "Prisoners in 2005," *Bureau of Justice Statistics Bulletin* (November 2006).

16. Dan Malone, "INS Faulted for Secret Detentions," *Dallas Morning News*, December 12, 1999.

17. Bureau of Justice Statistics, "Prisoners in 2005."

18. Ibid.

19. Ibid.

20. The information in this passage is derived from Dan Malone, "Lies, Justice and American Ways," *Dallas Morning News*, June 25, 2000.

21. The two most significant legal developments were the 1996 Illegal Immigration Reform and Immigrant Responsibility Act (Public Law 104-208, div. C., 110 *Stat.* 3009-546, Sept. 30, 1996) and the 1996 Anti-Terrorism and Effective Death Penalty Act (Public Law 104-132, 110 *Stat.* 1214, Apr. 24, 1996).

22. Bureau of Justice Statistics, "Prisoners in 2005."

23. Malone, "INS Faulted for Secret Detentions."

24. Richard L. Huff and Daniel J. Metcalfe, codirectors, Office of Information Privacy, U.S. Department of Justice, memorandum on third-party requests for INS file information for the attorney general, May 10, 1996.

25. Ibid.

26. Ibid.

27. Ibid.

28. Malone, "INS Faulted for Secret Detentions."

29. *Malone et al. v. U.S. Department of Justice et al.*

30. Malone, "INS Faulted for Secret Detentions."

31. Ibid.

32. Malone, "851 Detained for Years in INS Centers."

33. Ibid.

34. Dan Malone and Frank Trejo, "Trapped in America," *Dallas Morning News*, July 22, 2001.

35. Ibid.

36. *Zadvydas v. Davis*, 533 U.S. 678 (2001).

37. See chapter 6 in this volume for a more detailed discussion. Also see Arsalan Iftikhar, *The Status of Muslim Civil Rights in the United States, 2005: Unequal Protection* (Washington, D.C.: Council on American Islamic Relations, 2005).

38. Malone and Shah, "Prisoners? What Prisoners?"

39. Dan Malone, "Cell Without Number, Prisoners with Arab Names," *Fort Worth Weekly*, May 9, 2002.

40. All of the information in this passage is derived from Malone, "Cell Without number."

41. Ibid.

42. Ibid.

43. Ibid.

44. Malone and Shah, "Prisoners? What Prisoners?"

45. Mayborn Graduate Institute, "Report on Terrorism Prisoners Stonewalled."

46. Ibid.

47. As cited in ibid.

48. Ibid.

49. Ibid.

50. Ibid.

51. Ibid.

52. Ibid.

53. Ibid.

54. Associated Press, "U.S. Reveals Details on Guantánamo Detainees After AP Lawsuit," March 7, 2006, http://www.associatedpress.com/FOI/foi_030706a .html (accessed November 6, 2007).

CHAPTER 4

Democracy and Immigration

IRA J. KURZBAN

TODAY, ANTI-IMMIGRANT SENTIMENT in this country is on the ascent. Self-described vigilante "minutemen" are stationed at the border. Congress has appropriated funds to begin building a wall along the Southern border. Cities are passing ordinances to prevent citizens from renting to or selling goods to undocumented persons.[1]

Anti-immigrant sentiment is not something new. Our history is replete with examples of bigotry and hatred directed toward those we call "aliens," as if they were from another planet, or "illegals" as if a human being can be illegal. Whether it was legislation in the form of the national origin quota system barring Asian immigrants because of the color of their skin or Southern and Eastern European immigrants because of their Catholic or Jewish faith, the fears and prejudices of our people have been clear, if only in hindsight. We have been a country of Know-Nothings whose anti-immigrant agitation had significant effects on the new Republican Party of the last century, just as today's vigilante minutemen push both political parties toward an enforcement agenda. Although our history is replete with these reflexive anti-immigrant responses, today's response is entirely different. As I will argue in this chapter, it is not possible to understand anti-immigrant views in the United States today without also understanding the forces that have destabilized both the middle class and the institutions that traditionally formed the bulwark of democracy in this country.

The current wave of anti-immigrant sentiment has its roots in the anti-drug and anticrime rhetoric that was used in the 1980s and 1990s to support overtly repressive legislation against noncitizens. From 1986 to 1996, under the guise of attacking "illegal" immigration and particularly "criminal aliens," anti-immigrant and antidemocratic organizations and their supporters in Congress were successful in laying a foundation for the elimination of the basic features of a procedurally fair immigration system that is consistent with the fundamental rules of a democratic society, by permitting mandatory detention, abolishing independent administrative review of many procedures, and restricting judicial review of errant administrative conduct. How did this begin?

Within a period of approximately thirty years, we went from the 1965 civil rights act for the foreign born, which eliminated the National Origins Quota System,[2] to the Illegal Immigration Reform and Immigrant Responsibility Act of 1996,[3] which literally rewrote the immigration laws to severely restrict due process and most forms of immigration relief.

This dramatic change began when anti-immigrant legislators incorporated immigration issues into antidrug legislation. Since the foreign born have little political clout in the United States and the foreign born who commit crimes have even less, there was no political constituency, with the exception of civil rights and immigration lawyer groups, to stop what became a legislative steamroller.

The Anti-Drug Abuse Act of 1986[4] was the first legislation that tied any drug offense to the federal schedule of drug classifications as a basis for inadmissibility into the United States. These measures were also made retroactive. Thus, a person who—before the passage of the act—had been fined in the United States or in his or her own country for the possession of, for instance, a small quantity of marijuana now faced deportation or was barred permanently from entering the United States. The law did not distinguish between a simple user of drugs or a major drug trafficker and made no allowance for persons married to U.S. citizens or who had U.S.-citizen children. These kinds of distortions of common sense were often overshadowed by press reports and congressional statements promoting tough measures against drug trafficking.

Through the 1980s and until the mid-1990s, Congress continued to pass antidrug legislation and continued to incorporate immigration provisions. The Omnibus Anti-Drug Abuse Act of 1988[5] began the slow descent into the establishment of "aggravated felony" legislation that has been used to strip away virtually all the rights of anyone who has committed a crime—including those of long-term lawful permanent residents of the United States. This act narrowly defined aggravated felons as drug and weapons traffickers and murderers, and made aggravated felonies a new ground for deportation. It also stated that aggravated felons were not eligible for certain kinds of immigration relief, were barred for a longer period of reentry into the United States, and were required to undergo special, restrictive appeals processes.

The Violent Crime Control and Law Enforcement Act of 1994[6] expanded restrictions on aggravated felons and permitted, for the first time, a summary form of removal for certain nonresident aggravated felons. This small change had major repercussions. For the first time, we had legislation that took away due process in the guise of fighting "criminal aliens," whose deportation could now be ordered by an immigration officer in a summary proceeding. Because they were "criminal aliens" they were no longer entitled to a due process hearing before an immigration judge where the government had to prove deportability by clear and convincing evidence. In the same year, restrictionist legislators used a technical amendment bill to vastly expand the definition of aggravated felonies to now include ordinary felonies.[7] In today's Orwellian world, felonies and aggravated felonies have become virtually one and the same.

This antidrug, anticrime legislation reached its zenith in the Illegal Immigration Reform and Immigrant Responsibility Act of 1996, which changed our legal system in profound and unprecedented ways. It restricted the right of immigration judges and immigration officers to grant relief, and then it insulated them from judicial review for their mistakes or, worse, their prejudices.[8] Scores of statutes preclude judicial review of most major issues in immigration proceedings. Persons wronged by immigration authorities, even long-term lawful permanent residents of the United States, can no longer go to federal court to challenge any discretionary decision made in their case, any discretionary decision to incarcerate them, or any decision regarding their physical removal from the country. Congress instituted the anti-American idea of allowing, for the first time in our history, mandatory detention of people who pose no threat to society and are not likely to abscond. Thus, immigration authorities can now incarcerate a noncitizen without any bond until the completion of his or her immigration proceedings, which in many cases takes months or years. Although a sitting president of the United States can be sued for sex discrimination while in office,[9] an immigration officer can no longer be sued for any discretionary decision he makes, no matter how wrong or mean-spirited the decision.

The 1996 Act also allowed, for the first time, summary removal at our borders. The immigration officer became the judge, jury, and executioner. He or she now makes the final decision as to whether someone can enter the United States or whether the person can be deported and barred from returning to the country for five years. This process is also insulated from judicial review. At the same time, immigration judges and immigration officers were stripped of the right to grant most forms of relief to long-term lawful permanent residents and other deserving noncitizens, who are now simply being separated from their U.S. citizen families and deported. The act also insulated these actions from judicial review.

The antidrug and anticrime rhetoric made major inroads into the elimination of fundamental due process rights. This rhetoric could be dragged out and used or reused to keep people in a state of fear and anxiety by recalling specific cases of noncitizens who may have been dangerous and/or engaged in criminal conduct. Often one story, repeated endlessly in the corporate media, was sufficient to demonstrate how necessary undemocratic measures were to protect we the people.

This fear and terror reached its zenith after September 11, 2001. Now the anti-immigrant and antidemocratic forces had a far more powerful analogy to drag through the streets of public discourse. They could now raise the specter of illegal aliens who are terrorists coming across the border like Huns at the gates of Europe.

With the use of terrorism rhetoric, it was easy to mount a full-scale assault on fundamental democratic principles as they applied to both citizens and noncitizens. The USA PATRIOT Act opened the floodgates to spying on United States citizens and noncitizens alike. While we were repeatedly reminded of the terror that lurks all around us, Congress passed the REAL ID Act of 2005[10] with little more than a whimper from the public. REAL ID not only established a program to initiate a national identification card, it abolished, in most respects, the writ of habeas corpus, the All Writs Act, and the Declaratory Judgment Act with respect to immigration matters.[11] These developments have severely limited the ability of any person charged with an immigration violation to contest the charge or even to determine the basis for the charge. An alien or even a citizen mistakenly put in removal proceedings can no longer go to federal court on a writ of habeas corpus to review his or her final order of removal. In addition, measures that protect the discretionary decisions made by immigration authorities from public review have been expanded in an unprecedented manner to include all discretionary decisions of immigration officers whether or not they are related to removal proceedings. And the improper or even illegal revocation of a visa is no longer reviewable in federal court. None of these issues was discussed in the national media, which focused exclusively on whether it was proper for the REAL ID Act to require people to have a standardized national driver's license.[12]

The manipulation of the fear of alien terrorists attacking the United States made citizens too preoccupied with the next terrorist attack to worry about the continued erosion of political and civil rights. Perhaps we failed to recognize that when Congress abolishes the writ of habeas corpus for one purpose, it becomes easier to abolish it for another, as we recently learned with the passage of the Military Commissions Act of 2006.[13] This act now gives the president the authority to detain indefinitely and in secret locations noncitizens (or persons who are mistaken as noncitizens), subject them to torture, and preclude them from bringing a writ of habeas corpus—all because the president has designated them "alien enemy combatants."

Although the anticrime, antidrug, and now antiterrorist rhetoric have been powerful tools in the hands of those who wish to radically depart from fundamental constitutional protections in our society, they cannot, alone, explain the current anti-immigrant fever sweeping the United States. Something far more dramatic is at work today.

Today's anti-immigrant sentiment has developed alongside the economic struggle of a rapidly deteriorating middle class. Most Americans do not need a statistician to tell them their real wages are decreasing while corporations and those at the very top are reaping windfall profits. While their schools, their health care, their neighborhoods, and their quality of life deteriorates, middle- and low-income Americans are painfully aware that they, and not those at the very top, are suffering in the current economic situation. It is apparent that class divisions in the United States have deepened and that those with means control the economy and are protected, while the middle class slides slowly into poverty.

The resultant anger and frustration at the deterioration of everyday life, however, has been channeled into anti-immigrant sentiments by politicians and the media. Because of the alliance between corporate and political systems and the concentration of ownership in the media by large corporate interests, the root causes of economic deterioration are never addressed. It is better to go after aliens with a different culture than to go after the real culprits. We are told that it is the undocumented workers who are stealing our jobs and abusing our schools and health-care systems, as if this were the reason for our dilemma.[14] It is not that citizens' grievances are not real. Indeed, our schools, our health care, our wages, and our quality of life are all deteriorating as Americans work longer and harder to earn less and less. But it is contrary to reality to believe that this is attributable, other than in the most insignificant way, to undocumented workers.[15] While the attack on undocumented workers and immigration reaches a fever pitch, the government does little to enforce employer sanctions or occupational safety, thereby perpetuating the cycle of depressed wages in unsafe working conditions.

The decline of the middle class is quite evident statistically. In 1970, those at the very top of the income ladder earned one hundred times more than the rest of Americans. Today they earn 560 times more.[16] For every additional dollar the bottom 99 percent of wage earners made in America between 1970 and 2000, the top 13,500 families earned a shocking $7,500.[17] Four out of five Americans in 2000 were making less or were no better off than they were in 1970.[18] In 1970, 70 percent of Americans fell into the top tax bracket. Today it is 35 percent.[19] By the year 2002, the portion of federal revenues that came from corporations was below 10 percent, down from over 30 percent during the Eisenhower years.[20] The median hourly wage for American workers has declined 2 percent since 2003, while the amount an average worker produces has risen steadily. We spend more time at work than people do in any major industrial nation in Europe.[21] Wages and salaries now make up the lowest share of the nation's gross domestic product (GDP) since the government first recorded these statistics in 1947. At the same time, corporate profits have soared to their highest share of the GDP since the 1960s.[22]

The disparity between the rich and the poor grows each year within the United States. In recent years it has been proudly touted that this country has 313 billionaires—a record for the United States, and more than any other country in the world. Today, the Forbes 400 are worth $1.13 trillion, up from $221 billion in 1985.[23] While the inflation-adjusted average annual pay for CEOs in roughly the same period went up by $1.8 million, the inflation-adjusted median annual household pay went down by $1,699.[24] We also have 46.6 million people who do not have health insurance, representing 16 percent of the population[25]—an increase of 1.3 million in one year.[26] In addition, an estimated 40 to 44 million Americans are functionally illiterate,[27] and between 17.6 percent and 22.4 percent of our children live in poverty, making the United States the second-worst country in its treatment of children in the industrialized world, besting only Mexico.[28] These gloomy statistics are understandable in a nation that has lost 2.8 million manufacturing jobs in the four-year span from 2001 through 2004.[29]

The economic disparity is not only internal. As a world superpower, we have ignored the growing disparity between rich nations and poor nations. The actual number of people living in poverty in the last decade of the twentieth century, despite so-called poverty-reduction programs, has actually increased by almost 100 million.[30] This occurred at the same time that the total world income actually increased by an average of 2.5 percent annually.[31] Globalization has clearly favored the rich nations over the poor ones. The consequences of this are manifested in many ways, including mass migration to the United States and other industrialized countries; internal displacement; destabilization of democracies in developing countries, which also leads to emigration to the United States and elsewhere; and anger, frustration, and contempt against the United States as a world power.

The widening gap between the rich and super-rich and the rest of America has also had profound effects on our democratic institutions. Today, more than 80 percent of identifiable political contributions come from 1 in 833 Americans, which reflects the fact that most political contributions now come from the very wealthy at the very top.[32] Companies now spend millions of dollars in lobbying to obtain returns of tens or hundreds of millions in government contracts. Everything in the government is for sale, whether it is the Lincoln Bedroom or war contracts in Iraq that are decided by noncompetitive bids (the top-ten defense contractors in 2005 received almost $350 billion in noncompetitive and cost-plus contracts). Corruption is rampant and grossly underreported. The Special Inspector General for Iraqi Reconstruction reported on October 24, 2005, that more than 50 percent of funds going to reconstruction actually went to overhead, thus leaving far less money than expected to provide the oil, water, and electricity needed to improve Iraqi lives.[33] Halliburton, the company that Vice President Dick Cheney continues to receive dividends from, went from being thirty-seventh to seventh on the list of defense contractors and received more than $4.3 billion in defense contracts in 2003.[34]

And how do we measure our democracy and determine whether it is working? The disintegration of the middle class has been accompanied by the diminution of political participation in elections. Democracy is a far more subtle, far more fragile project than the election of officials every few years. The immigration Minutemen and other "self-help" groups have been a reaction to how little is altered through traditional democratic elections given corporate dominance of political parties and redistricting that prevents competitive races. We know that today, because so few positions are contested in political life. In the 2006 congressional elections, only approximately thirty seats changed hands in the "people's" House of Representatives, representing less than 7 percent of the membership of that government body.[35] Major, substantial change in political alignment is unlikely because redistricting, sanctioned by the courts, has made so few seats truly competitive. In 2002, 98.2 percent of incumbents won reelection.[36] Turnout in the 2000 presidential election fell to 54.5 percent of eligible voters from 63.1 percent in 1960, thereby ranking the U.S. electorate in terms of participation as 139th out of 172 countries that hold democratic elections.[37] Even with both major political parties engaged in an all-out effort to bring people to the polls, the U.S. electorate turned out in lower percentages in 2004 than in 1960.[38]

If democracy is not just about going to the polls every few years, what is it? Perhaps it can be found in the words of de Tocqueville, who said that democracy flourished in the United States not because of the free-market entrepreneurial spirit but because of what he called "the general equality of conditions."[39] But in a democracy in which economic equality is rapidly deteriorating and political participation in elections has lessened, meaningful change can only occur when the population is educated and empowered. Political education assumes public education, and it can only be a meaningful part of a democratic progress when the media serves in an independent capacity. Without clear voices to expose governmental wrongdoing, to discuss facts rather than opinions, and to investigate matters to determine truth, the public is subject to gross manipulation.

Theoretically, the role of the media should be to expose government malfeasance and corruption, investigate and examine issues of great national importance, be as impartial a forum as possible for discussion of these issues, and empower those who are traditionally voiceless to participate in the democratic process, because unlike the powerful and rich, they do not have access to the media. Today, the media does virtually none of this. Investigative reporting is rarely done; the issues addressed are usually those raised by the government or the political parties; and the reporting on a wide breadth of issues is skewed far to the right side of the political spectrum. Media empires like Fox, owned by foreign interests, are used almost exclusively to spew right-wing propaganda in the United States.[40]

The concentration of the media in the hands of the few is also an extremely dangerous precedent. Today, fewer than ten companies own most of the media.[41] Five conglomerates dominate television news.[42] Together they control two-thirds or more of the programming that appears on prime-time television, including news and program channels.[43] In 1984 some fifty corporations controlled most of the media outlets in the United States, but by 1993 the number of corporations controlling those outlets had dropped to fewer than twenty.[44] At the end of World War II, 80 percent of daily newspapers in the United States were independently owned, but by 1989 that number was reversed, with 80 percent owned by corporate chains.[45] The merger of AOL and Time Warner, for example, now means that one company owns CNN, TNT, HBO, Cinemax, Warner Brothers Television, Court TV, New Line Cinema, Little, Brown and Co., Time-Life Books, Atlantic Records, Elektra, Warner Brothers Records, *Time* magazine, *Fortune* magazine, *Life* magazine, and *Sports Illustrated,* as well as owning shares in Comedy Central, E!, and Black Entertainment Television. And the list continues.

In *What Liberal Media?* Eric Alterman noted that the two heads of AOL-Time Warner earned a combined income of $210 million in 2001, and Michael Eisner, the former CEO at Disney, earned $73 million, not counting stock options and other income. This might lead you to ask, as it did Eric Alterman, whether "the men and women who earn numbers like these are really sending forth aggressive investigators of financial and political malfeasance" who are charged with the responsibility, as journalists have historically been, to "afflict the comfortable and comfort the afflicted."[46]

The inability to engage in critical journalism, the pressures to cut costs and produce entertaining pieces, and the decided turn to the right through the punditocracy on TV, radio, and the press have reduced the media, as we learned in the war in Iraq, to little more than cheerleaders for the government.

A shocking example of the deteriorating standards of the media occurred on November 3, 2006, when a fifty-two-year-old man named Malachi Ritscher committed suicide by dousing himself with gasoline and setting himself on fire in a very prominent and public area in Chicago. He videotaped the suicide to be broadcast on TV and left a detailed, meticulous note explaining his opposition to the killing of people during the Iraq war. Although the protest-suicide occurred four days before the midterm elections, there was a complete blackout of the story until several weeks after the election.[47] Was it incompetence? Or was it purposeful action by those few corporate giants not to release the story because it would give heightened visibility to an issue that the Republican Party was not anxious to defend? When media is so concentrated in the hands of a few, one can only speculate.

And what of the other pillar of democracy—the judicial system? The fundamental principle of the rule of law—a rule that fosters consistency, legitimacy, fairness, and equality—has been severely tarnished. The Supreme Court's election decision in 2000 politicized and polarized the judicial system in a way rarely acknowledged in our legal history. A decision by Justice Antonin Scalia to insist on deciding a case involving Vice President Cheney, despite his close personal relationship with him, further tarnished the highest court's credibility.[48] A recent study demonstrated that we currently have the most conservative judges, in terms of the protection of civil liberties, of any known Republican or Democratic administration. Today's judicial appointees are 25 percent more conservative and less interested in protecting civil liberties than judges appointed under Ronald Reagan and Richard Nixon.[49] If we can politicize the Supreme Court over the election of a president, isn't it easy to politicize every other legal decision?

In addition, the diminution of judicial review demonstrates how far we have strayed from the fundamental principles of democracy that are considered core values of our system. There is no more fundamental principle in our constitutional system than the right to challenge government authority in court. The Supreme Court wrote in *United States v. Lee:*

> No man in this country is so high that he is above the law. No officer of the law may set the law at defiance with impunity. All the officers of the government from the highest to the lowest are creations of the law and are bound to it. It is the only supreme power in our system of government and every man who by accepting office participates in its functions is only the more strongly bound to submit to that supremacy and to observe the limitations which it imposes upon the exercise of authority which it gives.[50]

Unfortunately, the political consensus of both parties appears to be that the diminution of these rights is of little concern to the public. Because the media has failed to fulfill its functions in a democratic society and because the judiciary no longer can function as a break on executive power on immigration policy, or other matters the fabric of our constitutional system is in crisis. We all understand on some level that the constitutional system we were taught in school is malfunctioning. The widening gap between rich and poor and between truth and public pronouncements and the closing gap between fact and opinion and government and religion represent an assault on our system that affects not only immigrants but all of us.

Since 2005, new "enforcement" legislation has emerged in the wake of the anti-immigrant hysteria.[51] These bills would abolish what little remains of judicial review, including denying even courts of appeal the right to review motions to reopen and district courts the right to review the denial of citizenship applications. This full-scale assault on the judiciary remains largely unreported in the media, which again has focused on border enforcement, in line with the most extreme elements of the anti-immigrant movement.

The effort to ramp up anti-immigrant sentiment ensures that due process and basic procedural fairness to immigrants and citizens alike will continue to be eroded through legislation. The building frustration of the declining middle class, the breakdown of democratic institutions, and the lack of media investigators of gross misconduct and corporate greed, all contribute to a sense of powerlessness for the vast majority of citizens. Their anger and frustration has been channeled into attacking immigrants because undocumented persons lack the political influence to withstand such attacks and are a convenient diversion from the growing disparity of wealth in the United States. For the last two decades, Congress and its anti-immigrant adherents have skillfully used fear of drugs and terrorism to manipulate citizens and diminish the rights traditionally accorded all persons in the United States.

The anti-immigrant sentiment also has direct effects on our economy. For one, the antiforeigner sentiment has so diminished the numbers of people entering the United States that trade has been substantially affected. Yet we rarely see news articles that discuss the effect of visa restrictions on the developing world and on our own economy. We have not heard from any political leader that in a world economy the United States can no longer simply close its doors and expect its own people to maintain their own lifestyle.

When the process becomes so difficult to enter the United States, people simply take their business and their tourism elsewhere. Today, the nations of Southeast Asia are turning more and more toward business and travel to China than to the United States. How has that affected the economies of their countries? How has it affected the economy of our country? We do not know, because the media and our political leaders would rather discuss one person in 10 million who obtained a visa by fraud. This leads to disruptive and dysfunctional policies.

The elimination of the current anti-immigrant sentiment will only occur when citizens are not being pitted against immigrants to divert public attention from the current economic transformation concerning the depletion of the middle class. Polls repeatedly indicate that most Americans are aware of the facts of their own circumstances and that they are far more progressive than the leadership in Congress. In 2005, public opinion polls demonstrated that the people of the United States, despite the lack of progressive leadership, are far ahead of the politicians who purport to lead us. In May 2005, a Pew Research Center survey demonstrated that 65 percent of respondents favor providing health insurance to all Americans, even if it means raising taxes; that 86 percent said they favor raising the minimum wage; and that 77 percent said they believe the country "should do whatever it takes to protect the environment."[52] Numerous polls now say that a solid majority of Americans consider the war in Iraq a mistake and that U.S. forces should be partially or completely withdrawn.[53] These sentiments need to be directed toward those responsible, not toward hapless immigrants who share the same values as citizens. Political participation needs to be directed toward the root causes of the conflict between middle-class citizens and undocumented immigrants—the inequality of wealth, the lack of meaningful political choices as a result of redistricting, and the busting of media monopolies in the United States.

If we wish to address the "problem" of immigration, we, as a nation, should consider the following: (1) establish and fund a national program (a) to pay for the education and retraining of U.S. workers on a scale similar to the G.I. bill after the Second World War for occupations needed in the twenty-first century; (b) to reinvest in our public school system; and (c) to provide educational grant programs for all Americans desiring to attend college; (2) establish a living (not a minimum) wage in the Untied States; (3) enforce the Occupational Safety and Health Act, Title VII, and the Unfair Immigration-Related Employment Practices Act as well as employer sanctions; (4) renegotiate NAFTA in the interest of workers, not agribusiness or large U.S. corporations, to preserve and create agricultural and other employment in Mexico, and to preserve and create employment in the United States; (5) establish a national health-care program; (6) identify demographic employment needs, in both the short and long term, that will not be filled by U.S. workers, and provide programs that allow temporary workers into the United States with full employment protections and at wages that will not adversely affect U.S. workers; (7) end the era of impunity of immigration and all other U.S. officials by restoring full judicial review and meaningful waivers and forms of relief; (8) legalize the existing population of undocumented persons in the

United States by moving up the registry date to the present; (9) reinstate the fairness doctrine, the fundamental principle that radio and television is owned by we, the American people, and demand the deconcentration of the media; (10) stop privatizing public services, from prisons to child welfare to the military; (11) reinstitute term limits and establish national legislation that ends current redistricting designed to prevent meaningful competitive elections; and (12) eliminate restrictions that prohibit votes from being counted, by insisting on a paper, verifiable process, and eliminate restrictions that prohibit votes from being cast by ending onerous identification requirements and other barriers to voting. For those who would say the cost is too great, one can only say, "Imagine if the over $1 trillion we spent in Iraq was available to fund these programs, what a strong democracy we would have at home."

Notes

1. See chapters 13 and 15 in this volume for a more detailed discussion of this trend.

2. The act also removed race, gender, and national origin discrimination in the grant of residency. It is more commonly known as the Immigration and Naturalization Act of 1965 (Public Law 89-236, 1, 79 *Stat.* 911 [October 3, 1965]) or the Hart-Cellar Act, which amended the 1952 (McCarran-Walter) Immigration and Nationality Act.

3. Public Law 104-208, div. C., 110 *Stat.* 3009-546 (Sept. 30, 1996).

4. Public Law 99-570, 100 *Stat.* 3207 (Oct. 27, 1986).

5. Public Law 100-690, 102 *Stat.* 4181 (Nov. 18, 1988).

6. Public Law 103-322, 108 *Stat.* 1796 (Sept. 13, 1994).

7. This amendment was the Immigration and Nationality Technical Corrections Act of 1994, Public Law 103-416, 108 *Stat.* 4305 (Oct. 25, 1994).

8. For a detailed summary of the provisions of the Illegal Immigration and Immigration Reform Act (IIRAIRA), see Ira J. Kurzban, *Immigration Law Sourcebook,* 10th ed. (Washington, D.C.: American Immigration Lawyers Association, 2007); and for a more specific discussion of IIRAIRA as it pertains to drug offenses, see National Immigration Project of the National Lawyers Guild, Dan Kesselbrenner, and Lory D. Rosenberg, *Immigration Law and Crimes* (Eagan, MN: Thomson West, 1984).

9. *Clinton v. Jones*, 520 U.S. 681 (1997).

10. Public Law 109-13, div. B., 119 *Stat.* 231.

11. Habeas corpus is the name of a legal action that can be addressed to a prison official, demanding that a prisoner be brought before a court of law to determine if he or she is serving a lawful sentence or should instead be removed from custody.

The writ of habeas corpus is frequently used by detainees who are seeking relief from unlawful imprisonment and is generally regarded as an important instrument for the safeguarding of individual freedom against arbitrary state action. It was traditionally used in immigration matters to challenge unlawful decisions resulting in deportation. The All Writs Act and the Declaratory Judgement Act are informed by similar principles, which stem from the precedent of habeas corpus. Both acts grant federal courts the power to check the decisions (and deportation orders) of the immigration court system. The All Writs Act (28 *U.S. Code* § 1651[a]), allows any federal court to issue a writ to protect its own jurisdiction. Thus, a court could issue a writ to stop someone's deportation from the United States to protect the court's right to issue a final decision in a deportee's case. The Declaratory Judgment Act (28 *U.S. Code* § 2201) permits federal courts to issue orders declaring acts by immigration authorities illegal or unconstitutional.

12. For an example, see Donna Leinwand, "Real ID Act Edges Closer to Passage," *USA Today,* May 5, 2005, http://www.usatoday.com/news/nation/2005-05-05-dmv-changes_x.htm (accessed November 6, 2007).

13. Public Law 109-366, 120 *Stat.* 2600 (Oct. 17, 2006).

14. For some recent examples of how these anti-immigrant arguments have been covered in the mainstream media, see Shane Anthony, "Feel Strongly About Immigration? Joe Buehrle Does," *St. Louis Post-Dispatch,* October 15, 2006; Kimberly Hefling, "Santorum Steps Up Tough Talk Against Illegal Immigration," Associated Press, October 15, 2006; Sarah Lynch, "Pearce Calls on 'Operation Wetback' for Illegals," *East Valley Tribune* (A2), September 29, 2006.

15. See Roger Lowenstein, "The Immigration Equation," *New York Times Magazine,* July 9, 2006. There has also been a fairly extensive academic debate over how and to what degree the "benefits" of immigration outweigh the "costs" for lower- and middle-income workers. Although some researchers have shown that low-income males with lower levels of education, and racial minorities in particular, are most vulnerable to displacement by low-skilled immigrant labor, most research has shown no transparent connection between immigration and job displacement for the native-born working class. This is evident in the fact that national levels of unemployment have decreased over the past fifteen years as immigration flows have increased. The problem of substandard wages and workplace conditions for native-born persons is better explained in light of domestic strategies for economic structuring as well as the sociopolitical aspects of labor-market formation and organization, which cannot be reduced simply to the ebb and flow of immigration. For a fairly recent and detailed application of these arguments, see Rodger Waldinger, *Still the Promised City? African-Americans and New Immigrants in Postindustrial New York* (Cambridge, Mass.: Harvard University Press, 1999).

16. David Cay Johnston, *Perfectly Legal* (Penguin, 2003), 36.

17. Ibid., 39.

18. Ibid.

19. Ibid., 40.

20. Ibid., 41.

21. Nancy Gibbs, "An In-Depth View of American by the Numbers," *Time*, October 30, 2006, 48.

22. Steven Greenhouse and David Leonhardt, "Real Wages Fail to Match a Rise in Productivity," *New York Times*, August 28, 2006.

23. Clara Jeffery, "A Look at the Numbers: How the Rich Get Richer," *Mother Jones*, May/June 2006.

24. Ibid.

25. John Graves and Sharon K. Long, "Why Do People Lack Health Insurance?" Urban Institute, http://www.urban.org/publications/411317.html (accessed November 6, 2007).

26. Ibid.

27. National Institute for Literacy, "Factsheet Overview," http://www.nifl.gov/nifl/facts/facts_overview.html (accessed November 6, 2007).

28. UNICEF, "A League Table of Child Poverty in Rich Nations," Innocenti Report Card No. 1, www.unicef-icdc.org/publications/pdf/repcard1e.pdf (accessed November 6, 2007).

29. Thom Hartmann and Mark Crispin Miller, *Screwed: The Undeclared War on the Middle Class* (New York: Berrett-Koehler Publishers, 2006), 4.

30. Joseph E. Stiglitz, *Globalization and Its Discontents* (New York: Norton, 2002), 5.

31. Ibid., 5.

32. Ibid., 43.

33. James Glanz, "The Struggle for Iraq: The Budget, and an Ally; Idle Contractors Add Millions to Iraq Rebuilding," *New York Times*, October 25, 2006, 1.

34. Seth Borenstein, "No-Bid Pentagon Contracts Frequently Go to Biggest Firms," *Miami Herald*, September 30, 2004.

35. For a quantitative summary of election results see CNN Com, "Democrats Retake Congress," November 9, 2006, www.cnn.com/ELECTION/2006/(accessed November 6, 2007).

36. Jennifer E. Duffy and Amy Walter, "How the Hill Was Lost: Two Analysts for the Cook Political Report Examine the 2002 Election and Come to a Startling Conclusion," *Blueprint*, February 11, 2003.

37. *Business Week*, "Special Report—Democracy in America: The Few Decide for the Many," June 14, 2004, http://www.businessweek.com/magazine/content/04_24/b3887070.htm (accessed November 6, 2007).

38. Ibid.

39. Alexis de Tocqueville, *Democracy in America*, ed. Richard Heffner (New York: Signet Classics, 2001).

40. Eric Alterman, *What Liberal Media?* (New York: Basic Books, 2003).

41. Irwin P. Stotzky, "The Indispensable State," *University of Miami Law Review* 58, no. 201 (2003): 227–228.

42. Consumer Reports, "Fighting Media Monopolies," April 2006, www .consumerreports.org/cro/aboutus/mission/viewpoint/fightingmediamonopolies703/index.htm?resultPageIndex=1&resultIndex=1&searchTerm=Fighting %20Media%20Monopolies (accessed November 6, 2007).

43. Ibid.

44. Stotzky, "Indispensable State."

45. Ibid.

46. Alterman, *What Liberal Media?* 27.

47. For detailed commentary from an independent media perspective, see Nitsuh Abebe, "Malachi Ritscher, 1954–2006," *Pitchfork,* November 14, 2006, http:// www.pitchforkmedia.com/article/feature/39663-malachi-ritscher-1954-2006 (accessed November 6, 2007).

48. For a summary of this issue, see "Public Citizen Litigation Group and Sierra Club, Motion to Recuse," Supreme Court Hearing No: 03-475. *Richard B. Cheney et al. v. U.S. District Court for District of Columbia,* http://fl1.findlaw.com/ news.findlaw.com/hdocs/docs/scotus/chny22304scrbrf.pdf (accessed November 6, 2007).

49. Reuters, "Study: Bush Judges Most Conservative on Rights," September 9, 2004.

50. *United States v. Lee,* 106 U. S. 196 (1882).

51. The House bill was originally titled the Border Protection, Antiterrorism, and Illegal Immigration Control Act of 2005, HR 4437. The Senate bill was originally titled the Comprehensive Immigration Reform Act of 2006 (CIRA), S 2611. However, since Republican politicians initially drafted these bills and their party is no longer the majority faction in the Congress (as of the fall 2006 midterm elections), these bills have undergone significant revision.

52. Susannah Fox, "Health Information Online," Pew Internet and American Life Project, Pew Research Center, May 17, 2005, http://www.pewinternet.org/ pdfs/PIP_Healthtopics_May05.pdf (accessed November 6, 2007).

53. Dana Milbank and Claudia Deane, "Poll Finds Dimmer View of Iraq War: 52% Say U.S. Has Not Become Safer," *Washington Post,* June 8, 2005; CBS News Polls, "Poll: Fading Support for Iraq War: 55% Say War Was a Mistake; 59% Want U.S. Troops Home ASAP," October 10, 2005, http://www.cbsnews.com/stories/ 2005/10/10/opinion/polls/main930772.shtml (accessed November 6, 2007).

PART II

Noncitizens as Security Threats: After 9/11

CHAPTER 5

Racializing, Criminalizing, and Silencing 9/11 Deportees

IRUM SHEIKH

SINCE SEPTEMBER 11, 2001, the U.S. government has continued to arrest and deport immigrants predominantly from Muslim countries on the suspicion of terrorism.[1] The stories all follow a familiar pattern: the arrest of a Muslim or Muslim-looking individual,[2] sizzling news stories about the individual's connection to al-Qaeda, and, months later, deportation on minor charges unrelated to terrorism. Deportation occurs quietly, in vivid contrast to the arrest. But even when the media does follow through on the stories, the deportees are described as lawbreakers, illegals, and suspected terrorists—not distinguishing among these terms. Weeks or months later, more headlines appear about the arrest of yet another alleged terrorist. These sensational arrests keep the general public preoccupied with the fear of new attacks by Muslim terrorists who are intent on killing Americans.

Over the last five years, I have interviewed more than forty individuals and researched fifty other cases connected with terrorism. In reviewing these, I found a pattern very similar to what I have just described. Based on my research, I argue that the state is using enforcement practices as part of a two-tiered strategy that first racializes and then criminalizes Muslims. The racialization process draws on widespread stereotypes that equate terrorism with Muslim-looking individuals, allowing the state to dehumanize Muslims who have been targeted for deportation. This creates a climate of fear in which the general public assumes that the state is protecting them from dangerous individuals. The general public therefore consents to provide the state with unprecedented and unchecked powers in the name of national security.

The criminalization process deprives these individuals of their legal, human, and civil rights. It also safeguards the state against public or legal scrutiny by invoking a plethora of immigration laws to frame individuals—who are often arrested on no other basis than racial profiling—as immigration violators and criminals. In the process, the state justifies its actions in the court system and silences opposition from legal, human rights, and other activist groups. Last but not least, this experience silences deportees and traps them in a state of shame and fear.

In the first part of the chapter, I provide several examples illustrating how the government has racialized and criminalized post–9/11 deportees. In the second half of the article, I explore the social and psychological trauma that unfolds in the lives of deportees because of this experience. I also explain how this process forces deportees into silence.

Racializing Muslims and Muslim-Looking Individuals

Michael Omi and Howard Winant argue that racial categories are socially constructed and are constantly being contested and transformed.[3] Racialization can be defined as a political process through which frameworks for defining racial difference are manipulated by institutional actors and used to subjugate specific groups. This usually results in the creation of a field of discourse that imputes negative stereotypes to racialized minorities. Latinos, African Americans, Native Americans, and Asian Americans are the primary groups that Omi and Winant refer to in their discussion of racialization in the United States. Nadine Naber, however, has extended Omi and Winant's theory of racial formation to argue that Muslims are now being racialized in ways that they had not been before. Just as blacks have been racialized and, historically, been associated with crime, Muslim males are now being racialized and associated with terrorism.

In the case of Arab Americans and Muslim noncitizens, the racialization process draws on interpretations which associate phenotype with religion, resulting in profiles that are based on what a Muslim "looks like."[4] In addition, the post–9/11 racialization process equates Islam with terrorism. Within this framework, it is relatively uncontroversial for an enforcement officer to frame a Muslim-looking individual as a terrorist and later deport him on minor immigration and/or criminal charges. In the vast majority of cases, Muslims and Muslim-looking individuals who are detained on and deported under immigration charges have no connection to terrorism.[5] However, the state's discourse on national security rationalizes these procedures by implying that these individuals have the potential to become terrorists in the future. Therefore, it is safer to either deport or imprison them. The following example illustrates how this process works.

On September 12, 2001, Mohammad Azmath was traveling with his friend Ayub Khan from New Jersey to Texas on an Amtrak train. The train stopped close to Fort Worth, Texas. Some officials from the federal Drug Enforcement Agency came to Azmath and Ayub's cabin and started to investigate them based on a "suspicious tip." Both Azmath and Ayub had lost their jobs at a newspaper stand in New Jersey the day before. At a friend's invitation they decided to move to San Antonio, Texas. On September 11, 2001, the attacks on the Twin Towers forced their plane to stop in St. Louis, Missouri. Instead of waiting for the flights to resume, they took an Amtrak train to continue their journey. They were both carrying cash for their journey and had some leftover box cutters in their luggage from their work at the newsstand.

Both Azmath and Ayub were immigrants from India who had come to the United States in pursuit of better opportunities. They were living in the United States on expired visas and worked at various low-wage jobs to support their families back home.[6]

They were arrested, and within hours, every national and international newspaper published stories about new terrorists with box cutters. Their faces were on television news and in major newspapers. Everything about them was rendered suspicious. These Muslims with box cutters were prime suspects.

Instead of placing them in immigration prison, the police transferred Azmath and Ayub to the Special Housing Unit of the Metropolitan Detention Center (MDC) in Brooklyn, New York, a place designated for individuals connected with the attacks on the World Trade Center. Here they lived in solitary confinement for almost a year. They did not receive access to legal counsel for ninety days, during which they were interrogated about their role in the September 11, 2001, attacks. Ayub wrote about his experience in a letter:

I was locked up 11 months in solitary confinement. The cell was 6 by 10 foot with nothing to read but the Koran. Cells were lit twenty-four hours a day with a bright light. The windows were painted white. Recreation consisted of standing alone in a small cell for 1 hour a day. When it was cold weather there was a punishment recreation for

5 hours in rain. I was allowed to get a social phone call a month, and legal call twice a week. . . . I was cursed and threatened, thrown into walls and told by guards [that] I would be killed. Even the agents and prosecutor threatened me during interrogation. . . . I was told I would not be released and I would not be able to see my family. I would get life imprisonment. [They asked,] "How would you like to die?"[7]

During Azmath and Ayub's eighteen-month detention, FBI officers, in collaboration with Indian intelligence, visited their homes in Hyderabad to investigate their families, neighbors, and friends. Local police took Azmath's wife, Tasleem, a Pakistani national, to the local police station with her infant child, and placed her in jail for an immigration violation that was connected to Azmath's detention in the United States. Azmath and Ayub were ultimately charged with credit card fraud and eighteen months after their arrest were deported to India. The stigma of terrorism and the surrounding publicity has lingered for both of them. Ayub Khan writes:

Where ever I go people know me that this is the guy who was arrested in connection with 9/11. This makes me embarrassed and makes me upset. I am not getting any job. The American government did bad publicity of my name with no reason. I have to carry the stigma and scar of 9/11 my entire life.[8]

Right after the arrests of Azmath and Ayub, I remember seeing their photographs all over the *New York Times* and CNN, with repeated references to box cutters, cash, and another wave of attacks. I remained fearful of additional terrorist attacks until I started to research the matter and discovered that these "terrorists" were individuals, no different from my brothers and friends who had been racially profiled just because they were in the wrong place at the wrong time. A systematic pattern of nationwide arrests of Muslims, the release of suggestive information to the media, and speeches by high-level officials all contributed to a political climate under which all Muslims became suspect as possible terrorists.

The interrogation of Azmath and Ayub could have been carried out without controversy. After enforcement officials established that both men had expired visas, they could have been placed in immigration proceedings and their backgrounds quietly researched. There is an established legal process to prosecute and deport immigration detainees who have overstayed their visas, and it could have been followed. However, the manner in which they were arrested and displayed in the media created a sensationalized image that deliberately blurred the distinction between immigrants with civil violations and persons who could be the next terrorist hijackers.

This process of framing immigration detainees as terrorists was not limited to the actions of lower-level enforcement officers. Top administration officials, including President George W. Bush and Attorney General John Ashcroft were very keen to inform the public about the success of the government's intelligence operation. For example, speaking in October 2001, the attorney general stated:

> Our anti-terrorism offensive has arrested or detained nearly 1,000 individuals as part of the September 11 terrorism investigation. Those who violated the law remain in custody. Taking suspected terrorists in violation of the law off the streets and keeping them locked up is our clear strategy to prevent terrorism within our own borders.[9]

In June 2002, when most of the detainees had been deported or released, President Bush praised the Department of Homeland Security by declaring that the homeland defense coalition, "has hauled in about 2,400 of these terrorists, these killers—there's still a lot of them out there."[10]

In public, government officials boasted about the success of the intelligence operation. Behind closed doors, however, some were skeptical about these arrests. Colleen Rowley, an FBI whistleblower and *Time* magazine's Person of the Year for 2002, characterized these arrests as a public relations strategy. In her letter dated March 6, 2003, addressed to the FBI director, Rowley pointed out:

> After 9-11, Headquarters encouraged more and more detentions for what seem to be essentially PR purposes. Field offices were required to report daily the number of detentions in order to supply grist for statements on our progress in fighting terrorism. . . . Particular vigilance may be required to head off undue pressure (including subtle encouragement) to detain or "round up" suspects—particularly those of Arabic origin.[11]

This PR strategy becomes more apparent when we look at the patterns of arrests and the way they were carried out after September 11, 2001. For example, on September 13, 2001, dozens of FBI agents raided the one-bedroom apartment of a naturalized Pakistani citizen who worked as a pilot for United Airlines. All of the streets adjoining the apartment were sealed off with yellow "Do not enter" tape. Floodlights lit up the night, creating a circuslike atmosphere, inviting curiosity and an audience. Local television and newspaper reports sensationalized the investigation. As a consequence, this retired U.S. Air Force major was recast as a "mysterious . . . pilot" over night. According to a news article, FBI agents found "terrorist paraphernalia" in the pilot's house; in fact, they had found spy novels written in Urdu.[12] Neighbors and other residents living in the area watched the FBI investigation and became concerned.[13]

Ahmed Khalifa, an Egyptian, was a medical student with a valid tourist visa who was kept in a high-security jail in New York for months. He was brought to jail in a motorcade of police cars with blaring sirens. He felt that through the spectacle of the motorcade, FBI agents wanted to show the public that they were doing their job. In my interview with him, he explained that everyone on the street was staring at the motorcade with frightened expressions.[14]

On November 28, 2001, two police officers paraded a Pakistani American businessman in handcuffs through downtown Manhattan from the East side police precinct to the West side precinct. Apparently, the fingerprinting machine at the former was too busy, and the officers decided to walk instead of driving the five or six blocks. Syed Ali has described his walk in handcuffs through downtown Manhattan as a setup that was designed to show off the success of federal agents in capturing another supposed "terrorist suspect."[15]

Through these theatrics, federal agents effectively framed Muslims as terrorists in the national imagination. These actions were also used to appease the fears and concerns of the general public, and to attract the attention of the media and politicians. In many ways, these dramatizations resembled the staged FBI raids of Japanese American communities during World War II.[16] And just as members of the media were present for many of the government raids on Japanese American communities, so were they for the FBI's post–9/11 raids on Muslims.[17] Hungry for quick answers and eager to satisfy the curiosity of the general public, the media ran stories of these investigations and arrests without confirming or checking sources. The mainstream media televised and published images of

Muslim-looking men in chains, implying their connection to terrorism on the basis of little more than their religion, ethnicity, and racial appearance.

As the government paraded shackled, Muslim-looking bodies, it also reinforced popular stereotypes about Muslim males. Immediately after the attacks of September 11, 2001, the state launched the Terrorism Information and Prevention System (also known as Operation TIPS). Through Operation TIPS, the state encouraged the public to call FBI hotlines with leads on suspicious persons. By September 18, one week after the attacks, "the FBI had received more than 96,000 tips or potential leads from the public, including more than 54,000 through an internet site."[18] Most of the callers attributed suspicious activities to "Arab men." In one of her speeches, Colleen Rowley describes the kinds of tips that were often received through the FBI hotlines right after September 11:

> The most common "citizen tip" we receive is something to the effect of, "I don't want you to think I'm prejudiced because I'm not, but I just have to report this because one never knows and I'm worried and I thought the FBI should check it out." This precedes a piece of general information about an "Arab" or "Middle-Eastern" man who the tipster lives by or works with that contains little or nothing specific to potential terrorism activities.[19]

This was not simply a matter of thousands of U.S. citizens "turning racist" over night. These attitudes developed in response to a climate of fear that had been created by the state and reinforced through repeated references to the "arrest of 1,000 terrorists" and slogans like "United We Stand." President Bush defined *patriotism* with binary statements, like "Either you are with us, or you are with the terrorists." Even when it became clear that Operation TIPS was not providing any substantial information about terrorists, the state continued to encourage the public to report "suspicious people."

Displays of American flags on houses, cars, and office buildings were a common spectacle after September 11, 2001. Within this context it became very easy for state officials and right-wing groups to label people as unpatriotic if they questioned brutal interrogations, detentions, and deportations. This climate led many people to see the racial profiling of Muslim-looking individuals as a civic duty. It also emboldened some U.S. citizens to engage in hate crimes and racially motivated killings. On

September 15, 2001, Balbir Singh Sodhi, a Sikh immigrant from India, was shot to death in Mesa, Arizona, while he was planting flowers outside his Chevron station. After killing him, Frank Roque drove to an Afghani family's house and opened fire but missed the people inside. Later, he shot at a man of Lebanese heritage at a nearby convenience store, but missed him also. Mesa police arrested him a few hours later as he yelled that he was a patriot and an American.[20]

On November 26, 2001, two Somali men praying in a parking lot in Texas City, Texas, were reported as taking part in "suspicious activity." Arrested on minor technical violations, they were released after a day.[21] Ahmad Abdou El-Khier, an Egyptian, was picked up after a hotel clerk in Maryland told police that he appeared suspicious. He was initially charged with trespassing at the hotel where he was staying. He was deported on November 30, 2001, on a separate immigration violation.[22] Ali Yaghi, a Palestinian with a Jordanian passport, was deported after five months of solitary confinement. He was arrested in October 2001 in Albany, New York, because a neighbor called to say that he was expressing anti-American sentiment and dancing in the streets. He, too, was deported on an immigration violation.[23] Ali Raza, a Pakistani American, was picked up from his home in New York City in October 2001 after the police received a tip from a concerned neighbor who insisted that "people make bombs there." He spent about six months in jail for an immigration violation.[24]

These attitudes toward Muslims and Muslim-looking individuals have not subsided. As recently as December 2006, talk radio host Jerry Klein suggested that all Muslims in the United States should be identified with a crescent-shaped tattoo or a distinctive armband.[25] One of the callers responded, "Not only do you tattoo them in the middle of their forehead but you ship them out of this country. . . . They are here to kill us." Another called and suggested that tattoos and other identifying markers don't go far enough. "What good is identifying them? . . . You have to set up encampments like during World War Two with the Japanese and Germans."

Unfortunately, these opinions are shared by a cross section of the American public. A Gallup Poll in the summer of 2006 showed that 39 percent were in favor of requiring Muslims in the United States, including American citizens, to carry special identification. A third of those polled thought that Muslims in the United States sympathized with al-Qaeda.[26]

The discourse on national security has been a truly hegemonic force negating the human rights and civil liberties of Arabs and Muslims and, specifically, young males. Through the eyes of the state, these infringements on the rights of Muslims and their families were small sacrifices when compared against the greater goal of national security. Even when the details of many of these cases were brought to light, the circumstances of the post–9/11 climate were still seen to justify the interrogations, detentions, and deportations. As I have explained, this process of racialization continues today. Racist stereotypes of Muslims still operate under the guise of national security. They render Muslim bodies disposable, in much the same way that black bodies are rendered disposable within the growing prison-industrial complex. Another incarcerated black male or another Muslim-looking terrorist body behind bars hardly raises any eyebrows, since the War on Crime and War on Terror have both normalized the incarceration and racialization of these groups.

Criminalizing Deportees

The discussion so far has illustrated how the state deployed theatrical strategies that racialized Muslims and equated them with terrorism. Enforcement officers used racial profiling to stop Muslim-looking individuals. If the interrogation uncovered an immigration violation, the suspect was detained and framed as a terrorist. Later, the person was either quietly released or deported on minor immigration or criminal charges. Since many of these individuals were undocumented, they made very convenient targets. They were arrested not because they had terrorist connections but because they could be held under immigration laws as illegal aliens and criminals. This formed the core of the state's criminalization process, which is explained in greater detail in this section.

Despite being widely disseminated among the American public, overt racial stereotypes could not be used in the court of law as a rationale for keeping thousands of individuals behind bars for months or years. Immigration laws became convenient tools in this charged environment, and the state scapegoated undocumented immigrants from Muslim countries as it has done to other immigrant communities in the past. At congressional hearings, public forums, and press conferences, Department of Justice officials insisted that this was a cut-and-dried legal matter and that they had acted within the bounds of the law by arresting and detaining individuals without legal status.

Even though civil and human rights groups questioned the government's discriminatory practices, the discourse of illegality and criminal aliens prevailed. Most newspapers and television stations uncritically accepted the government's rationale, and in situations when the media publicized these arrests, the undocumented or criminal status of the detainee was highlighted without any additional context.

These immigration violators included people with expired visas, people without employment authorization (who had only been granted a visiting visa), people with incomplete paperwork, and others who failed to inform the immigration office of a change in address. The heavy concentration of undocumented immigrants in high-security jails also suggests that the government targeted vulnerable individuals. Because many of them were new to the country, undocumented Muslims were unfamiliar with the U.S. immigration and legal system and lacked resources and connections to the right people. Sandra Nicholas, an attorney who worked with several of these detainees, describes a typical immigration courtroom in the days after September 11, 2001, as follows:

> I was going in for their first hearings. And it was a mob scene when I got there. There were forty or fifty prisoners shackled to each other, packed into courtrooms. Relatives, lawyers, court personnel, guards, were all just wandering around the halls and trying to get things organized. . . . It was so chaotic. I said, oh, my God what a mess. . . . It was like a zoo, a three-ring circus. I have never seen such chaos in the immigration court. Everybody was still very anxious and nervous because of 9/11. The judges did not want to erroneously free someone who might be a terrorist. . . . All of [the detainees] were in on [immigration charges]—anyone who would interview them . . . anybody in their right mind talking to these guys would know in a minute that they were not terrorists. . . . They would not know how to light the match . . . how to get the fuse into the bomb. . . . They were the guys who overstayed the visas. . . . They just wanted to send money back home.[27]

Nonetheless, the attorney general was pleased to claim that "our antiterrorism offensive has arrested or detained nearly 1,000 individuals as part of the September 11 terrorism investigation."[28]

This concentration on undocumented immigrants was deliberate and systematic. Individuals who had legal status were generally let go. For example, in October 2001 enforcement officials entered the Brooklyn apartment of five Arab men. One out of the five had a green card and thus was not arrested. The remaining four were classified as "high interest" cases, which translated into having a strong connection with terrorism. These four spent months in a high-security jail in New York. Months later, they were deported for expired visas and working on a visiting visa.[29]

The Office of the Inspector General's (OIG) 2003 report[30] criticized the Department of Justice for violating the legal, human, and civil rights of individuals arrested during their post–9/11 investigations. The report noted that men without any connection to terrorism were placed in solitary confinement and held under restrictive conditions for weeks and even months. Held incommunicado, these pretrial detainees "were locked down 23 hours a day, were placed in four-man holds during movement, had restricted phone call and visitation privileges, and had less ability to obtain and communicate with legal counsel [than ordinary prisoners]."[31] The OIG workers who wrote the report watched hundreds of videotapes that recorded the movements of detainees and "administratively compelled" interviews with MDC staff. They concluded that there was

> evidence that some officers slammed detainees against the wall, twisted their arms and hands in painful ways, stepped on their leg restraint chains, and punished them by keeping them restrained for long periods of time. . . . We determined that the way these MDC officers handled some of the detainees was in many respects unprofessional, inappropriate, and a violation of . . . policy.[32]

The OIG report also points out that after September 11, 2001, certain government polices, such as "Communication Blackout," "Hold Until Cleared," and "No Bond Policy," as well as delays in removal proceedings were developed and handed down from the very top level. Implementation of these policies resulted in the loss of freedom and civil liberties for hundreds of individuals. With the exception of one person, all the detainees kept at MDC have been deported to their homelands.

These reports were alarming, since they pointed fingers at high-ranking officials in the Department of Justice and could be used as evidence in a lawsuit. Thus, the state needed a legal framework to justify its position. Barbara Comstock, a spokeswoman for the Justice Department, emphasized the criminal and the illegal status of the detainees in her response to the OIG report:

Those detained were illegal aliens. They were all charged with criminal violations or civil violations of federal immigration law. . . . Detention of illegal aliens is lawful. We detained illegal aliens encountered during the 9-11 terrorist investigation until it was determined they were not involved in terrorist activity, did not have relevant knowledge of terrorist activity, or it was determined that their removal was appropriate. . . . Our policy was to use all legal tools available to protect the American people from additional terrorist attacks. . . . We make no apologies for finding every legal way possible to protect the American public from further terrorist attacks.[33]

This statement implies that, because the detainees were "illegal aliens," the state had the right to place them in solitary confinement without any evidence to connect them to terrorism, abuse them physically and emotionally, and ignore their civil and legal rights. A month later, at the request of human and legal rights groups and a few politicians, a Senate Judiciary Committee hearing was held to examine the findings of the OIG report. The hearing amounted to little more than a slap on the wrist for the Department of Justice officials. At the opening, Senator Orrin Hatch's remarks set the tone for the rest of the proceedings:

It is also important to acknowledge that the 762 detainees who are the subject of the OIG's report were illegal aliens who had no right to be in this country. They were individuals who had violated our nation's immigration laws, and they were individuals who well-intentioned law enforcement agents believed at the time may have had ties to, or knowledge of, terrorism or terrorists.[34]

During the hearings, Michael Rolince, assistant director of the FBI's Washington, D.C. field office cited the case of Azmath and Ayub as an example of the criminals who were successfully apprehended during the post–9/11 investigations although well before the June 2003 hearings both Azmath and Ayub had been deported to India on only credit card fraud charges:

Two people down in Texas that were taken off a train, for instance, comes to mind, that had box cutters and shoe polish and an inordinate amount of money, and it just looked suspicious on the front end. We didn't get a lot of cooperation. But ultimately they would plead guilty to charges relative to that money, and I believe there were some sort of bank fraud charges.[35]

Citing a single, specific case with erroneous information was not enough, however. Later in the same hearing, Rolince again connected deportees to terrorism without any evidence, and he suggested that by deporting illegal aliens, the state had been successful in averting future terrorist attacks:

> It is also important to clarify another point which I believe has been significantly confused in the media. That is the issue of some individuals being, quote, "cleared," unquote, of terrorism ties. The fact that an illegal alien was prosecuted for nonterrorism crimes or deported rather than prosecuted does not mean that the alien had no knowledge of or connection to terrorism. . . . In many cases the Department of Justice, in conjunction with the FBI, determined that the best course of action to protect national security was to remove potentially dangerous individuals from the country and ensure that they could not return.[36]

After listening to this and other, similar official testimonies, most of the congressmen present at the Senate hearing felt that the detentions were justified.[37] Many also claimed that the detentions were a necessary sacrifice for national security.[38]

This public hearing is just a glimpse into the political system's complicity in the enforcement strategies used to scapegoat immigrants. This public hearing was not an exception. The discourse around the illegality of the detainees dominated every venue.

However, this treatment was not limited to undocumented immigrants. In the following section, I provide an example of a legal immigrant who was arrested, deported, and criminalized like the rest of the undocumented immigrants. Ansar Mahmood, a Pakistani American in his early twenties who held a valid green card, was arrested in October 2001 in the Hudson Valley region of New York state. Ansar had asked one of the two security guards watching the reservoir to take his photograph next to the scenic view. While one took the photo, the other called the local police to report a suspicious person. Enforcement officers suspected that Ansar intended to throw anthrax in the reservoir; Ansar insisted that he only wanted the photo because he was struck by the serenity of the scenery. Since Ansar possessed a valid green card and the FBI had no evidence connecting Ansar to terrorism, it was difficult to detain him. However, during the interrogation, the FBI agents found that Ansar had helped an undocumented couple from his hometown in Pakistan to get an apartment and jobs. The FBI officers coerced him into admitting that he was aware of the undocumented status of the young couple before he helped them, which constitutes a crime that made him subject to deportation. Approximately three years later, Ansar was deported, despite widespread protests from local community members, politicians, and the media. In his final letter on the matter dated June 29, 2004, William Cleary of Immigration and Customs Enforcement emphasized Ansar's crime of "harboring and smuggling of illegal aliens" and evoked the concept of "national security" to deny Ansar's appeal to stay in the United States.

Crime is a dynamic concept that takes on different meanings in different places and time periods. Helping a childhood friend—a moral responsibility in Pakistani culture—was manufactured into a crime after the U.S. Congress adopted the Antiterrorism and Effective Death Penalty Act of 1996, and enforcement officers decided to strictly enforce it after the attacks of September 11, 2001. It is also important to note that Ansar was barred from ever returning to the United States, as compared with the more typical five to ten years. It is not that Ansar's crime was more serious than that of other deportees. It is that he has a stronger case for suing the American government for violating his rights because he was a legal resident.

Silencing Deportees

Today, in Pakistan, Ansar is very well aware that he was made into a scapegoat.[39] Like Ansar, other deportees understand very well the political reasons for their detention. On an intellectual level, they know they were innocent and that what happened to them was unjust, as described by Walid:

> We are innocent. We did not do anything. This was injustice. We had punishment for something that we did not do. Somebody did worse things than that. Drug dealers got released after 24 hours. We did not do anything. . . . FBI arrested and punished us for their illusions. We are the victims of their illusions.[40]

However, almost all the post–9/11 detainees were individually prosecuted for immigration or criminal violations. Consequently, at a very personal level—beneath their intellectual criticism of the post–9/11 climate—they also perceive themselves to be violators. Some of them have internalized the stigma of having been in the United States illegally and feel embarrassed. The shame of being criminalized makes it very difficult for them to talk about their experience. Most of them want to leave this episode in their lives behind them, yet they carry a deep sense of shame and guilt.

The deportees have also been deeply affected by the physical and emotional abuse they experienced in prison and the lengthy deportation proceedings. For the most part, they want to forget the unpleasant experience and are afraid that by merely talking about it they may be linked with terrorism and end up being jailed again. Because some of them were imprisoned immediately after arriving in their home countries, they live in perpetual fear of further imprisonment. This fear silences the deportees, which helps the United States continue illegal arrests and deportations without repercussions.

Most of the Japanese Americans who were interned during World War II were able to stay in the United States after they were released because they were already citizens or permanent residents. In contrast, most of the post–9/11 detainees were deported and dispersed to more than thirty countries.

When I visited Pakistan, I asked many deportees about their contacts with others who were in similar situations. I learned that most of them had not talked with any other deportees since their return. In some cases they had lost or misplaced contact information. One deportee gave me contact information for other deportees in other Pakistani towns. I asked him if he had spoken to them since he had returned. He explained that he had not, but asked me to convey his regards. Even so, I did not sense a strong desire on his part to connect with others.

Most of these deportees feel ashamed to admit that they were detained by the U.S. government for charges related to terrorism and have told a limited number of people about their detention experiences. Some had told their close family members but not the entire community. One told his extended family that he was on vacation and would be returning to the United States soon. Another deportee, Ahmad Aly, in Alexandria, Egypt, had called his friends from the jail during his ten months of detention and told them that he was calling from his Brooklyn apartment.[41] Some specified the reasons for not being able to talk about what had happened to them:

> I talked to only those people who already know that I have been deported. . . . I did not feel comfortable in telling people that I was deported or in jail. I don't think that it feels good. People over here don't understand. They would be surprised of my detention story. . . .

> I did not tell my brother that I was in jail. . . . I was afraid that he would feel bad about it. . . . [He] asked, "Was everything ok? How come we could not locate you?" I told him, "People were getting arrested so I went to another place." . . . I don't want to tell people that I was in jail. It is an insult for me. I don't like it. . . . I don't want to tell even my brothers and sisters because they would make different kind of stories. . . . When people started to get arrested, everybody in the world knew about it. They already guessed that I was arrested. . . . They already know about it, but they don't confront me.[42]

Deportees' inclination to remain silent about their detentions is not surprising. Donna Nagata documented the lack of an intergenerational dialogue between *nisei* (first generation) and *sansei* (second generation) around the World War II internment of Japanese Americans.[43] Jere Takahashi used Erving Goffman's framework analysis to explore feelings of shame and guilt that developed from the institutional culture of internment camps in which close surveillance prevented internees from talking freely with each other.[44] Although Japanese Americans on the West Coast were notified as a group and placed collectively in internment camps, most of them felt the impact of internment on an individual level. The tall guard towers, barbed-wire fences, and lack of privacy created a sense of constant surveillance. Unable to talk freely among themselves while they were interned, most internees internalized their shame and continued this culture of silence even after they were released from the camps.

This internalized sense of *haji* (shame) and fear contributed to the disarticulation of their collective sense of injustice for a long time. To compensate, most of the Japanese American internees became 200 percent American. Some took up arms to protect U.S. soil. "Don't rock the boat" and "Obey the orders" were among the many messages sent by the Japanese

American Citizen League (JACL) right after Pearl Harbor and during internment. It was the *sansei* who took the lead in challenging the government's internment policy in the 1980s by demanding an apology and reparations for each surviving Japanese American internee.

The sense of shame and guilt that Japanese Americans felt in the aftermath of the internment was, arguably, even more intense for post–9/11 detainees. They were much more alienated from each other than the Japanese American internees and were returned to home communities that did not necessarily understand or sympathize with their situation. As explained earlier, the U.S. government capitalized on the notion that all post–9/11 detainees were guilty of immigration or criminal violations. To further complicate matters, no meaningful assistance from human rights or legal organizations materialized after they arrived in their homelands. In addition, deportees were often reluctant to take legal action because they are afraid of the retaliation that could follow if they talked about their experience. One of the deportees expressed these fears in my interview with him:

When I came back, I was thinking that I should publish the entire story in detail, in twenty to thirty episodes, in a local newspaper. . . . But later, I thought that this writing could harm me. I met a person. His son was detained in the U.S. . . . I told him that I want to write about this incident in detail in the newspapers. He said, "You should try to forget all the things that happened to you. If you write something against the FBI, it could be constructed against you. It could create some problems for you in the future." I became quiet and decided not to write. Otherwise, I had a lot of things to write about.[45]

Another expressed similar concerns:

There should be a lawsuit because what happened to us was injustice. . . . An American attorney should file it. . . . Whether there is a benefit of filing a lawsuit or not, at least [the U.S. government] would get a whip[ping]. People over here are afraid. The FBI is coming to homes in Pakistan, like guests come over. . . . We have to be careful here. Let's say that we file a lawsuit and FBI starts knocking at our doors and asking why did you file the lawsuit? Where we are going to go?[46]

These concerns were shared by most of the Pakistani deportees with whom I spoke. Most of them were hesitant to talk to journalists or researchers. To gain access, I worked closely with the Islamic Circle of North America (ICNA), an organization that was tremendously helpful to these detainees after September 11, 2001. Adem Caroll of the ICNA gave me the names and addresses of a few deportees who felt comfortable talking in each country that I visited. I also mailed approximately thirty letters explaining the scope of my research along with a letter of support from the ICNA. I received two responses. Many people who scheduled interviews did not show up, and some rescheduled several times. Of those I did meet with, some refused to talk after I arrived, and others questioned me about my research and my identity. Interviews were arranged through word of mouth, and it was only after a trusting relationship was established that the deportees would in turn give me contact information for other people.

A family friend deported to Pakistan was living in a remote village. He knew about my research because I had talked to his wife in the United States. After speaking to him on the phone in Pakistan, he invited me to his home. I hired a taxi to go to his village. He asked his family to prepare an elaborate lunch for me, including chicken, lamb, biryani, and everything else under the sun. When it came time to talk about his detention experience, he hesitated. His wife was a U.S. citizen, and she had filed papers for his return. I assume Mohammad was worried that by talking with me, he might jeopardize his chances of returning to the United States. He did not allow me to even write down our conversation. After lunch, he gave me a tour of the village in his car and took me to the bus station. By the time I returned to the hotel, it was late and I had no interview. On at least three other occasions I again traveled long distances to find that people were uncomfortable talking with me for various reasons.

A team of American Civil Liberties Union (ACLU) members, including some journalists, had completed several interviews with deportees before my arrival in Pakistan. I talked with one of the people who conducted these interviews. He shared many of my impressions and wrote the following e-mail about his experiences interviewing deportees:

> They thought that I might be an intelligence man. If they talk to me they might get in another trouble. They had an impression that the Pakistani government was cooperating with USA. If they tell me anything against USA authorities, they will be in jail again.[47]

A deportee in Egypt noted the sense of fear and mistrust that has emerged since his arrest and deportation:

> As soon as I came over there, I started to be afraid to be with people. . . . I was not like that before. . . . Now I don't want to know any new person or any new community. . . . Something physiologically . . . I don't know. Fear, to some extent . . . afraid . . . scared to try anything new. When you came by, I thought to myself that you were from FBI. I didn't want to talk to you. . . . I don't want to talk about something that can hurt me.[48]

For some, the ordeal was far from over even when they returned to their homelands. Some of the deportees were sent back with travel documents informing local authorities about their political asylum applications filed in the United States. These papers made the deportees appear suspicious to their home governments, and many underwent additional investigation, imprisonment, and even torture.

The Egyptian deportee (quoted above) recorded his U.S. detention experience in detail on an audio recorder. When I asked him about the Egyptian government, he said, "no comment." He agreed to talk about it after I stopped the audio recorder. I inquired about this hesitation. He said, "I don't have any other place to go. I have already been thrown out of the U.S."[49]

Mohamed Elzeher is another Egyptian deportee. He talked to a *New York Times* reporter in early 2003 about being tortured by the Egyptian government after his return.[50] After he spoke with the *Times,* the local authorities arrested him again and warned him that he could not talk about his torture. When he met me at a large sporting complex in Cairo in April 2003, we spent over twenty minutes entering and exiting the facility at various points to ensure that no one was watching us. He told me that he was arrested in October 2001 on an alleged immigration violation even though he is married to a U.S. citizen. After he had spent fourteen months in a Passaic County, New Jersey, jail, two deportation officers escorted him to Cairo with travel documents, including a report entitled "Significant Incident Report." The travel document erroneously established Mohamed's connection to Al-Jihad, an Egyptian organization responsible for the assassination of Egyptian president Anwar el-Sādāt in 1981. Mohamed had applied for political asylum to obtain a visa in the United States and withdrew the application after his marriage to a U.S. citizen.

Mohamed believed that enforcement officials were aware of the history of his immigration case but deliberately highlighted his connection to Al-Jihad. The travel document read as follows:

Subject Mohamed ElZaher . . . an Egyptian National is a crewman that jumped ship. On 1/18/02 he withdrew his asylum & withholding claim before (Judge) I.J. Cabrera. A review of the file indicated that on his asylum application he admitted to being a member of the terrorist organization Al-Jihad (courier & recruiter) between 1996 and 1998.[51]

After arriving at the airport in Cairo, Mohamed was taken to a jail, where he was interrogated, and tortured with electric shocks. His brother's military connections in Egypt and a strong plea from international human rights organizations won his release from jail after three months. He currently lives in Switzerland as a political asylee.[52]

Azmath Mohammad, who was deported to India, also described the negative publicity associated with being connected to terrorism:

It is very difficult for me to move around due to the difficulties I am facing from government officials and strangers. I don't know them, but they know me very well. Forget about the friends and associates. They have become strangers to me. . . . Maybe they are afraid to see me because they don't want to get into any trouble. . . .

My family applied for a passport for my son eighteen months ago. Until now, they have not issued the passport. . . . [The authorities said] they need a police investigation report. I told them the kid is an infant. He can't even speak. Why would you need a police report for a minor? . . . Two weeks after that a few police officers came to my home regarding my kid's passport. They asked me so many stupid questions [that I felt like I was being] interrogated. After a few weeks they called me to the police office and asked me the same questions again about my kid's passport. I am still waiting.[53]

Furthermore, many of the deportees feel that their local communities do not understand them. Family members and people in the community at large have limited knowledge of FBI harassment and the post–9/11 detentions. In the media, the American government has manufactured an image of the United States that is synonymous with the ideals of democracy, due process, equality, and freedom for all. It is hard for the general public to believe that people are placed in solitary confinement for months simply because they've overstayed their visas. The deportees understand these limitations:

> I don't know what people think of me. I don't know what people believe. If I would tell someone the (same) story, I don't know if he would believe me or not. For some people, it is a very strange thing to happen, especially in the United States. It is hard for them to believe. Even if I was lucky and did not go through this experience and I was here in Egypt and somebody came from the States and started telling me a story like this I won't believe him. From my past experience with the United States, I won't believe him. I would say that he was lying.[54]

Being surrounded by people who they feel cannot understand their stories hinders the deportees from talking openly about their experience of discrimination. An ACLU journalist in Pakistan summarized the community's response as follows:

> As far as the larger community response towards them is concerned, that was bad. I mean the community did not feel sympathetic towards them but [instead there was] a little bit of harassment. The community thought that they might have a relation with Taliban. Most of them felt satisfied when they came to know that they came back and lost everything . . . they had earned and now they are no more rich.[55]

Alia, a Pakistani woman who was arrested in upstate New York for an immigration violation and spent approximately three months in various detention centers in New York State, recollected:

> My parents live in a village. It is a small place and everybody knows everything. . . . This girl from a family . . . who works as servant in my parents' house . . . and we know since our childhood asked my younger sister about me. I was in Pakistan at that time. . . . She asked her if I had any children. My sister replied no. The girl said, "How

could she have a child? She must be rotting in the jails over there." I felt so bad after hearing that.[56]

Besides having a limited understanding, the larger community also harbors mixed feelings toward these individuals. Due to the economic opportunities that the United States provides, many people in developing countries perceive the country as a dreamland, a place where you can find work easily and live in freedom. Many believe that the social and economic barriers that impoverish the majority of people in developing countries are nonexistent for people living in the United States. The distance of the United States and its increasingly restrictive immigration policies make this "utopia" seem unattainable—adding another layer of desire. This glamorized and distorted picture of America is reinforced by American television and movies.

Hate crimes and detentions, on the other hand, create anger. This love/hate relationship toward the United States produces an ambivalent attitude toward Muslim deportees. Although critical of U.S. foreign policy, many citizens of Arab/Muslim nations believe that Muslims living in the United States should be responsible for their own actions. One of the standard reactions is to admonish and blame the victim by saying "I told you so."

For example, one of my family friends in Sialkot, Pakistan, knew a man deported on an immigration violation after living for ten years in the United States. He told me that it was the deportee's fault for not having the proper paperwork. It is a common belief that people should be able to come to the United States and obtain all the necessary legal papers within one year. He questioned the deportee's long stay in the United States: "What was he doing there? He came back after ten years with nothing. Now what is he going to do here? He should have thought about it." There were a variety of responses from community members. Most of them were sympathetic yet critical. Some were relieved that it did not happen to them. Only a handful fully understood the complexity of the circumstances. Despite the recent surge in deportations, many have friends and relatives living in the United States with insufficient papers who have not been arrested or deported. It is hard for them to understand why some individuals become targets while others in similar situations are not targeted.

All of this serves to illustrate that, for deportees, the candle of stigma and blame burns at both ends. Deportees are misunderstood not only by

Americans but also by people in their home nations. The following is a comment from a deportee about this situation:

Our culture is not easy. It is very difficult here for people to understand. They make talks and insult you. They talk like, "Oh, look at that person. He came back. He spent so much money to go there. Now do you know what happened to him when he was there?"[57]

Unable to be fully understood, most of the deportees feel alone and alienated. Alienation prevents deportees from assessing their collective experience of discrimination and fighting for their civil rights and thus minimizes lawsuits. These barriers are compounded by the deportees' lack of adequate access to the U.S. legal system, their dispersal to more than thirty countries, and the differences among facts in their cases.

Despite these barriers, some nonprofit organizations have been addressing the legality of post–9/11 detentions and deportation in the U.S. courts. The Center for Constitutional Rights filed a class-action lawsuit, *Turkmen v. DOJ*.[58] This lawsuit challenges the Department of Justice for arresting Arabs and South Asian individuals "on the pretext of minor immigration violations, and secretly detaining them for the weeks and months that the FBI took to clear them of terrorism charges. It claims that the U.S. government violated the U.S. Constitution and international human rights law."[59] The Urban Justice Center's lawsuit addresses the issue of physical abuse of detainees kept at the MDC.[60] Other lawsuits, filed by individuals, are also pending. None of these, however, demands reparations for all post–9/11 detainees. Because of this, the U.S. government has not been held fully accountable for violating the legal and human rights of the deportees. But just as the U.S. government apologized for its internment of Japanese Americans, my hope is that it will also eventually apologize to the immigrants who were unfairly targeted by its "security" operations and will look back to the post–9/11 era as a dark period in American history. I only hope I won't have to wait very long for that to happen.

Notes

1. Some U.S. citizens and residents have been arrested in connection with terrorism. Examples include Captain Yee and Brandon Mayfield. However, these

cases are rare and require a different analysis; therefore, they are not included in this chapter for discussion.

2. I use the term "Muslim-looking" to indicate that many non-Muslims, especially Sikhs, have become victims of racial profiling, hate crimes, and detentions.

3. Michael Omi and Howard Winant, *Racial Formations in the United States: From the 1960s to the 1980s,* 2nd ed. (New York: Routledge and Kegan Paul, 1994).

4. Nadine Naber, "Arab San Francisco: On Gender, Cultural Citizenship, and Belonging (California)" (Ph.D. diss., University of California, Davis, 2002), 4.

5. For a detailed discussion of the spurious definitions that have been used to categorize segments of the U.S. population as security risks, see David Cole, *Enemy Aliens: Double Standards and Constitutional Freedoms in the War on Terrorism* (New York: New Press, 2005).

6. Azmath Mohamad, interview by author, tape recording, Hyderabad, India, March 2003.

7. Ayub Khan, personal letter to author, York County Jail, Pennsylvania, December 25, 2003.

8. Ayub Khan, e-mail to author from India, October 6, 2003.

9. Attorney General John Ashcroft, Department of Justice, prepared remarks for the U.S. Mayors Conference of October 25 (2001 [cited March 15, 2002]).

10. "President Convenes Homeland Security Advisory Council: Remarks by the President at Meeting of Homeland Security Advisory Council, the Indian Treaty Room," Office of the Press Secretary, June 12, 2002.

11. Colleen Rowley, "Letter to FBI Director, Mr. Robert Muller," *New York Times,* March 6, 2003.

12. FBI Investigates Mysterious United Airlines Pilot: Anjum Pervaiz Shiekh Vanished Two Days Before Attack (Click 10.com, September 17, 2001 [cited October 21, 2001]).

13. Author's conversations held with the residents of the apartment building, South Beach, Florida, July 2002.

14. Ahmed Khalifa, interview by author, tape recording, Alexandria, Egypt, April 2003.

15. Syed Ali, interview by author, tape recording, Upstate New York, January 2003.

16. Emily Colborn, "Staging the Home Front: Spectacle, Spectatorship, and Post-Pearl Harbor Raids" (paper presented at the Dokkyo International Forum on Performance Studies, Japan, December 2002). Many scholars, including Emily Colborn, discussed the theatrical performance of FBI raids on Japanese Americans during World War II and the performance they created for anxious neighbors, outraged politicians, and sensation-hungry journalists.

17. See note 15. Videos stored in the National Archives also document that the media and the FBI collaborated on these raids. These propagandistic videos were used to demonstrate the government's success in the espionage operation.

18. Department of Homeland Security, Office of the Inspector General, "The September 11 Detainees: A Review of Aliens Held on Immigration Charges in Connection with the Investigation of the September 11 Attacks," April 2003, p. 12.

19. Colleen Rowley, "Balancing Civil Liberties with the Need for Effective Investigation," *Patriotism, Democracy and Common Sense: Restoring America's Promise at Home and Abroad* (Lanham, Md.: Rowman & Littlefield, 2004).

20. Sikhnet.Com, "Two Sodhi Brothers Shot in the Backlash of 9/11 Death Penalty Overturned," August 21, 2006, http://www.sikhnet.com/Sikhnet/news.nsf/NewsArchive/346896D867EB03EB872571D100683355!OpenDocument (accessed November 6, 2007).

21. Kevin Moran, "Praying Muslims Find Selves in Jail: 2 Face Charges Over License Knife," *Houston Chronicle*, November 29, 2001.

22. Human Rights Watch, "Presumption of Guilt: Human Rights Abuses of Post September 11 Detainees," 14, no. 4 (2002).

23. Shokeria Yaghi, interview by author, tape recording, Albany, New York, December 2002.

24. Ali Raza, interview with author, tape recording, New York, New York, December 2002.

25. Bernd Debusmann, "In U.S., Fear and Distrust of Muslims Runs Deep," Reuters, December 1, 2006.

26. Ibid.

27. Sandra Nichols, interview with author, tape recording, New York, January 2003.

28. Attorney General John Ashcroft, Prepared remarks for the U.S. Mayors Conference of October 25.

29. Khalifa, interview by author.

30. The Office of the Inspector General is an oversight agency located within the Department of Homeland Security.

31. Office of the Inspector General, "September 11 Detainees," 17.

32. Office of the Inspector General, "Supplemental Report on September 11 Detainees' Allegations of Abuse at the Metropolitan Detention Center in Brooklyn, New York," 46.

33. Department of Justice, "Statement of Barbara Comstock, Director of Public Affairs, Regarding the OIG's Report on 9/11 Detainees," June 2, 2003, http://www.immigration.com/frame/statementreseptiireportfr.html (accessed November 6, 2007).

34. Federal Document Clearing House, *Senate Judiciary Committee Hearing on the Inspector General Report on the 9/11 Detainees,* Washington, D.C., June 25, 2003.

35. Ibid.

36. Ibid.

37. The Office of the Inspector General report is incorrect in stating that all post–9/11 detainees except one were undocumented. The Human Rights Watch report includes references to several post–9/11 detainees who had valid green cards. I personally met two individuals with valid green cards. One of them, Ansar Mahmood, was criminalized and deported to Pakistan despite his valid green card.

38. Federal Document Clearing House, *Senate Judiciary Committee, Hearing on the Inspector General Report on the 9/11 Detainees.*

39. Ansar Mahmoud, interview by author, Islamabad, Pakistan, December 2005.

40. Walid [last name withheld], interview by author, tape recording, Alexandria, Egypt, April 2003.

41. Ahmad Aly, interview by author, tape recording, Alexandria, Egypt, April 2003.

42. Sultan Mahmood, interview by author, tape recording, Siālkot, Pakistan, February 2003.

43. Donna Nagata, "The Japanese-American Internment: Exploring the Transgenerational Consequences of Traumatic Stress," *Journal of Traumatic Stress* 3 (1990): 47–69.

44. Jere Takahashi, *Nisei/Sansei: Shifting Japanese American Identities and Politics* (Philadelphia: Temple University Press, 1997).

45. Azhar Bahri, Interview by author, tape recording, Islamabad, Pakistan, March 2003.

46. Tanveer [pseud.], interview by author, tape recording, Gujrat, Pakistan, March 2003.

47. Ali Gohar Butt, e-mail to author, Lahore, Pakistan, October 24, 2003.

48. Sharif [pseud.], interview by author, tape recording, Cairo, Egypt, April 2003.

49. Ibid.

50. Mohammad Elzeher, interview by author, tape recording, Cairo, Egypt, April 2003.

51. Do James Carroll, "Significant Incident Report" (Newark: U.S. Department of Justice, 2002).

52. Mohamed Elzeher, interview by author.

53. Mohammed Azmath, interview by author, tape recording, Hyderabad, India, March 2003.

54. Raheem [pseud.], interview by author, tape recording, Alexandria, Egypt, April 2003.

55. Butt, e-mail to author.

56. Alia [pseud.], interview by author, tape recording, Gujrat, Pakistan, February 2003.

57. Mohmad, interview by author, tape recording, translated from Punjabi, Siālkot, Pakistan, February, 2003.

58. *Turkmen v. Ashcroft*, Class Action Complaint and Demand for Jury Trial 02-cv-2307 (USDC E.D. NY 2002).

59. Center for Constitutional Rights, *Turkmen v. Ashcroft*, cited on May 28, 2005, http://www.ccr-ny.org/ourcases/current-cases/turkmen-v.-ashcroft (accessed November 6, 2007).

60. Nina Bernstein, "2 Men Charge Abuse in Arrests After 9/11 Terror Attack," *New York Times*, May 3, 2004.

CHAPTER 6

Presumption of Guilt

September 11 and the American Muslim Community

ARSALAN IFTIKHAR

IN THE MONTHS FOLLOWING SEPTEMBER 11, 2001, Attorney General John Ashcroft used his powers under section 412 of the USA PATRIOT Act[1] to round up and imprison over 1,200 Muslim and Arab men. At the time, the most disconcerting fact about these mass roundups was that the Justice Department refused to disclose the detainees' identities, give them access to lawyers, or allow them to have contact with their families. In addition to this indiscriminate immigration dragnet, several high profile "terrorism" related cases further stigmatized the American Muslim community. All these cases were tried in the court of public opinion before ever being convicted in a court of law.[2]

This chapter takes a detailed look at four of these cases. The first case is that of Captain James Yee, who spent over seventy-six days in solitary confinement, being labeled a "spy" in most media circles—despite the fact that he was never convicted of any offense. The second case involves Brandon Mayfield, who was falsely linked by the FBI to the Madrid train bombings of March 11, 2004. The third and fourth cases involve Professor Tariq Ramadan and Yusuf Islam (formerly Cat Stevens) who were placed on the Transportation Security Administration's terrorist suspect "no fly" list. Each of these cases provides a different insight into the ethnoreligious profiling and egregious violations of civil liberties and legal rights that have been experienced by thousands of American Muslims since the attacks of September 11, 2001.

Under United States immigration law, an absconder is defined as an "alien who, though subject to . . . [deportation], has failed to surrender for removal or to otherwise comply with the order."[3] According to a January 2002 memorandum sent to federal immigration and law enforcement officials, the deputy attorney general of the United States estimated that there are approximately 314,000 absconders, or deportable illegal aliens, living in the United States today.[4] Of these 314,000, only about 6,000, fewer than 2 percent, originate from Muslim or Arab nations.[5]

Although over 90 percent of absconders come from Latin American countries, after September 11, 2001, the Justice Department began selectively targeting absconders primarily from predominantly Muslim and Arab countries. However, their selective targeting of Muslims and Arabs yielded almost no criminal convictions. By the end of May 2002, the Justice Department admitted that out of 314,000 absconders, only 585 had been located. More embarrassingly, not a single terrorist had been apprehended in that mass roundup.[6]

Although there is no doubt that all Americans have been affected by the attacks of September 11, 2001, and their aftermath, young males from Arab and Muslim countries have been most directly affected by the dragnet conducted by the Justice Department in our ongoing "war on terror." In addition to the law enforcement dragnets conducted by the Justice Department, newly passed congressional legislation has stirred debates as to how best to balance national security interests while safeguarding the civil liberties guaranteed to every American by our Constitution.

THE SECRET ROUNDUP
Glenn A. Fine, Inspector General for the Department of Justice, reported that at least 1,200 men from predominantly Muslim and Arab countries were detained by law enforcement officials nationwide within two months of September 11, 2001.[7] The Inspector General conceded in his official report that a senior officer in the Office of Public Affairs stopped reporting the cumulative count of detainees after 1,200 because the "statistics became too confusing."[8]

In August 2002 Human Rights Watch (HRW) released a ninety-five-page report, entitled *Presumption of Guilt*, that documented cases of prolonged detention without any charge, denial of access to bond release, interference with detainees' rights to legal counsel, and unduly harsh conditions of confinement for the more than 1,200 detainees.[9]

HRW's findings were later confirmed by Inspector General Fine's report, which also identified a pattern of "physical and verbal abuse" by correctional staff at the Metropolitan Detention Center (MDC) in Brooklyn, New York.[10]

In terms of demographics, the group of post–9/11 detainees comprised citizens from more than twenty countries. The largest number, 254 (33 percent), were from Pakistan, more than double the number of any other country.[11] The second largest number (111) were from Egypt, and there were also substantial numbers of detainees from Jordan, Turkey, Yemen, and India.[12] The ages of the detainees varied, but by far the greatest number, 479 (63 percent), were between the ages of twenty-six and forty.[13]

The fruits of these legally suspect and egregiously overarching dragnets were summed up by Georgetown University law professor David Cole, who said that, "Thousands were detained in this blind search for terrorists without any real evidence of terrorism, and ultimately without netting virtually any terrorists of any kind."[14]

THE "LIST OF FIVE THOUSAND," THE NATIONAL SECURITY ENTRY-EXIT REGISTRATION SYSTEM (NSEERS), AND US-VISIT PROGRAMS

On November 9, 2001, Attorney General John Ashcroft directed the FBI and other federal law enforcement officials to seek out and interview at least five thousand men between the ages of eighteen and thirty-three who had legally entered the United States on nonimmigrant visas in the two years preceding 2001 and who came from specific countries linked by the government to terrorism.[15] The list of individuals was compiled solely on the basis of national origin. Even the Justice Department acknowledged that it had no basis for believing that any of these men had any knowledge relevant to an ongoing terrorism investigation.[16]

Subsequently, the FBI and other law enforcement officials began arbitrarily visiting mosques, schools, and homes to conduct interviews with these five thousand Muslim and Arab men, all of whom were lawfully residing in the United States. According to the American Civil Liberties Union (ACLU), although these were allegedly voluntary interviews, "the interviews were highly coercive and few felt free to refuse."[17]

In March 2002 the Justice Department announced another round of interviews. This time, they were targeting three thousand Arab, Muslim, and South Asian men who again were legally residing in the United States as students or visitors.[18] This time, however, many law enforcement officials expressed concern over the mistrust that these legal witch hunts would cause in certain immigrant communities.

A hallmark of American law enforcement is community policing, which is characterized by local community members reporting crimes in their area to law enforcement officials. Many law enforcement officials anticipated the problems that the implementation of this new federal policy targeting immigrant populations would create for their local communities.

For example, in relation to post–9/11 federal law enforcement initiatives, Denver chief of police Gerry Whitman once said, "Communication is big . . . and an underpinning of that is trust. . . . If a victim thinks that they're going to be a suspect in an immigration violation, they're not going to call us, and that's just going to separate us even further."[19]

In June 2002, Attorney General John Ashcroft instituted the National Security Entry-Exit Registration System, more commonly referred to as NSEERS.[20] One of the most ambiguous and publicly debated aspects of NSEERS was known as Special Registration. Special Registration required all male nationals over the age of fourteen from twenty-five countries to report to the federal government to be registered and fingerprinted. With the sole exception of North Korea, every single one of these countries[21] on the Special Registration bulletin was either a Muslim or Arab nation.[22] The ACLU denounced the plan as "a thinly veiled effort to trigger massive and discriminatory deportations of certain immigrants."[23]

In December 2002 up to seven hundred men and boys from Iran, Iraq, Libya, Sudan, and Syria were arrested in Southern California by federal immigration authorities after they had voluntarily complied with the NSEERS call-in program. Some of these people were college students who were guilty only of not attending enough classes for a given semester. Others were just awaiting the outcome of their green card applications.

In response, the Center for Constitutional Rights, the Council on American-Islamic Relations, the American-Arab Anti-Discrimination Committee, and other plaintiffs filed a class-action lawsuit against Attorney General John Ashcroft on behalf of these hundreds of men and boys who had been unfairly arrested in Southern California in violation of their Fourth and Fifth Amendments rights.[24]

In one year alone, the Special Registration program registered 83,310 foreign nationals. Out of these 83,310 people, the NSEERS program placed 13,740 into deportation proceedings. Of these 13,740 deportations, not a single one involved a person convicted of a terrorism-related crime.[25]

In January 2004 the Department of Homeland Security (DHS) suspended Special Registration, which had been operating under the National Security Entry-Exit System (NSEERS) program, and officially launched the U.S. Visitor and Immigrant Status Indicator Technology, or US-VISIT, program.[26] Many American advocacy groups, communities, and individuals who had roundly criticized Special Registration for its blatantly prejudicial design and shoddy implementation foresaw similar potential problems with the implementation of the US-VISIT program.

"Contrary to assertions by the Homeland Security Department, the US-VISIT program is an addition to—not a substitute for—the notorious Special Registration program that singled out Arab and Muslim men because of their national origin and that continues to subject them to special and confusing requirements," said Timothy Edgar, former legislative counsel for the ACLU.[27] "Only one part of the special registration program—the part that requires reregistration at local immigration offices—was suspended last year. But Arab and Muslim men are still subject to different requirements than other visitors."[28]

THE USA PATRIOT ACT (HR 3162)

The editors of *Esquire* magazine once wrote that "if there is one thing that always comes out of a terrible tragedy, it is really dumb legislation."[29] On October 25, 2001, a mere forty-five days after the attacks of September 11, 2001, Congress passed with virtually no debate House Resolution 3162, entitled "Uniting and Strengthening America by Providing Appropriate Tools Required to Intercept and Obstruct Terrorism" Act,[30] which has come to be ominously known worldwide as the USA PATRIOT Act.

USA PATRIOT, at over 340 pages in length, amends over fifty current federal statutes and was passed in the Senate by a vote of 98–1, with the lone dissenting vote being Democratic senator Russell Feingold of Wisconsin.[31] Many provisions of USA PATRIOT opened a new chapter in the debate on the application of constitutionally suspect laws in a time of war. Although not all 340 pages of USA PATRIOT Act were considered legally controversial, major sections of the law concern tremendously those who cherish due process, free speech, and other fundamental protections guaranteed by the United States Constitution.

For example, Sections 411 and 802 of the USA PATRIOT Act broadly expanded the official definition of "domestic terrorism" so that college student groups who engage in certain types of protests could very well find themselves labeled as terrorists. Initially, under Sections 215 and 505 of the

USA PATRIOT Act, law enforcement officials are given broad access to any type of record—sales, library, financial, medical, etc.—without having to show probable cause of any crime. The USA PATRIOT Act also forbids the holders of this information, such as university librarians and college registrars, from disclosing that they have ever provided such records to federal officials.

A University of Illinois survey of American public libraries once found that at least 545 libraries had been asked for records by law enforcement in the year following 9/11 alone. According to the American Association of Collegiate Registrars and Admissions Officers, approximately 200 colleges and universities have turned over student information to the FBI, INS, and other law enforcement agencies.[32]

The "sneak-and-peak" provision of the USA PATRIOT Act (Section 213) allows law enforcement agencies to conduct secret searches of anyone's home or apartment without a warrant or even notification to the owner. This meant that investigators could potentially enter anyone's place of residence, take pictures, download computer files and seize items without informing them of the search until days, weeks, or even months later.[33]

Since its inception in October 2001, the debate over privacy and constitutional issues raised by the USA PATRIOT Act has motivated 357 local legislatures, representing over 55 million people in 44 states, to pass resolutions officially condemning portions of the USA PATRIOT Act.[34] In addition to resolutions passed in more than 200 smaller cities, the list of successful resolutions includes those passed in the large metropolises of New York,[35] Los Angeles, Chicago, Detroit, St. Louis, and Philadelphia.[36] In addition, the states of Hawaii, Alaska, Maine, and Vermont have passed statewide resolutions condemning portions of the USA PATRIOT Act as being unconstitutional and infringing on individual rights.

Privacy and civil rights advocates, both Democratic and Republican, have called for greater congressional oversight on any extensions of or additions to the USA PATRIOT Act. In addition to state and local governments, several bipartisan national organizations have adopted similar pro–civil liberties resolutions condemning the USA PATRIOT Act. Among them are the National League of Cities, the American Conservative Union, the American Library Association, the Japanese American Citizens League, the National Association for the Advancement of Colored People, the Organization of Chinese Americans, and Veterans for Peace.[37] Even traditionally conservative voices like former speaker of the House Newt Gingrich, Republican Senators Larry Craig of Idaho, Arlen Specter of Pennsylvania, and Lisa Murkowski of Alaska, have all publicly voiced criticism of the USA PATRIOT Act.[38]

Douglas Dow, professor of government at the University of Texas, perfectly summarized the national grassroots movement in opposition to the USA PATRIOT Act: "It is necessary for us to secure our values in those institutions closest to home and to rely on ourselves and our local officers, rather than waiting for the courts or Congress to defend minorities from racial targeting, or protect the privacy of our personal records."[39]

The Case of U.S. Army Chaplain James "Yusuf" Yee

James Yee was born in Springfield, New Jersey, to Chinese American parents, and he graduated from West Point in 1990. In 1991 he converted to Islam and adopted the Islamic name Yusuf, which is the Arabic version of the name Joseph.

Captain Yee left active military duty in 1993, joining the United States Army Reserves so that he could go to Syria to learn Islam and Arabic to prepare to become one of the U.S. Army's first Muslim chaplains.[40] It was during this visit to Damascus that he met and married his wife, Huda.[41] When he returned from Syria, Captain Yusuf Yee became a chaplain with the 29th Signal Battalion at Fort Lewis, Washington, and was stationed there during the attacks of September 11, 2001.

In November 2002 Yee was transferred as an army chaplain to Guantánamo Bay, Cuba, where he ministered to Muslim prisoners and advised his superiors on Islam-related issues pertinent to the 660 detainees being held at Camp X-Ray.[42] During this time, Captain Yee and other Muslim workers used a vacant office in the prison compound for prayers and meals.[43]

ACTS OF ESPIONAGE?
On September 10, 2003, Captain Yee arrived at the Jacksonville, Florida, Naval Air Station on leave for a one-week vacation. Investigators at Guantánamo Bay had alerted customs agents at the airport that Yee was possibly carrying classified materials. A customs agent testified at an Article 32 military investigation[44] that he had been "tipped" to stop Captain Yee and that he confiscated "suspicious" documents from him.[45] Federal agents say the captain was found in possession of sketches of the military prison at Guantánamo Bay and lists naming U.S. interrogators and imprisoned Taliban and al-Qaeda fighters.[46] After being searched and

found in possession of these classified documents, Captain Yee was arrested.

Thus began Captain Yee's seventy-six-day confinement;[47] he spent the vast majority of this ordeal in solitary confinement without being convicted of any crime.

At his confinement hearing on September 12, 2003, a Navy prosecutor argued that Yee should be held under maximum-security conditions since he was a flight risk. This determination was made despite the fact that Captain Yee was a commissioned army officer with no history of fleeing a subpoena.

According to records, on September 16, 2003, Yee was subjected to sensory-deprivation treatment and driven to Charleston, South Carolina. Shackled, blindfolded, and deafened by ear covers, he was then transported to the navy brig and given the same treatment used on Camp X-Ray prisoners being flown to Cuba. Court papers from the initial confinement hearing reported that Captain Yee was being charged with espionage, spying, aiding the enemy, mutiny or sedition, and disobeying an order. At the time, some media reports were already speculating that Captain Yee could face the death penalty if convicted.[48] Surprisingly, details of Yee's arrest appeared in the media before he was ever charged with a crime in a court of law.

A September 20, 2003, *Washington Times* headline proudly proclaimed "Islamic Chaplain Is Charged as Spy," and the article proceeded to lay out details about the charges against him.[49] Such media reports before any charges were levied against Captain Yee led many to believe that there had been leaks by government officials to the media.[50] Captain Yee was finally brought to trial on October 10, 2003. Despite the severity of the accusations originally levied against Captain Yee, he was indicted on two lesser charges, counts of failing to obey orders.[51]

The Department of Defense's Southern Command, which oversees Guantánamo Bay, reported that Yee was charged with "taking classified material to his home and wrongfully transporting classified material without the proper security containers or covers."[52] Air Force Master Sergeant Jose Ruiz, a spokesman for the Southern Command, reported that the Army "had sufficient evidence that [Yee] violated the procedures in place for classified material given what he had in his possession."[53] After his trial, Yee's security clearance was lowered.[54]

INHUMANE TREATMENT

Without being convicted of a crime, Captain Yee was imprisoned under maximum security conditions in twenty-three-hour solitary confinement for an astonishing grand total of seventy-six days.[55] According to his army-appointed civilian lawyer, Eugene Fidell, Yee was let out of confinement for only one hour a day, for exercise that he had to perform while wearing leg irons and handcuffs.[56] Personnel at the Navy brig in Charleston refused to recognize his status as a commissioned officer and required him to identify himself as an E-1, the lowest enlisted rank.[57]

Fidell also reported that brig personnel were "needlessly interfering with his daily prayers and religious practices" by refusing to provide him a prayer rug, a liturgical calendar or telling him the time of day or direction of Mecca.[58] "They let him languish in solitary confinement for 76 days. That's outrageous. When he saw his legal counsel, he was in leg irons," said John Fugh, a retired army judge advocate general. "We don't treat commissioned officers that way. I don't care what they did."[59]

FROM TREASON TO PORNOGRAPHY?

Captain Yusuf Yee was finally released from prison on November 25, 2003, after two and a half months of confinement. Instead of issuing an official apology for unjustly imprisoning a commissioned officer, the army instead found it prudent to charge Captain Yee with adultery and storing pornography on a government-issued computer.[60] The alleged adultery was said to have occurred with U.S. Navy lieutenant Karyn Wallace between July and September 2003.[61] The pornography was said to have been stored on his computer at Guantánamo Bay.

Yee was now scheduled to face an Article 32 hearing.[62] Meanwhile, a U.S. Southern Command spokesman said the military would graciously "allow" Captain Yee to return as a chaplain to the base at Fort Benning, Georgia, noting that he would not be allowed to have contact with any prisoners at Guantánamo.[63]

The Article 32 hearing on the new charges against Captain Yee was postponed six times before being cancelled altogether.[64] The first postponement occurred on December 2, 2003, after military officials realized they had "mishandled classified information," which was one of the initial charges in Captain Yee's litany of treason charges. Apparently, officials accidentally released pages from Yee's diary to his defense attorneys. At this time, the prosecution even admitted that it was uncertain if Yee even possessed classified materials when he left Guantánamo Bay in September 2002.[65]

Finally, on March 19, 2004, all criminal charges against Captain James Yee, including the charges of failure to obey orders and mishandling of classified information, were dropped. However, the army would not admit

Captain Yee's innocence. General Geoffrey Miller's dismissal of the charges was instead due to "national security concerns that would arise from the release of the evidence."[66]

Although Yee had by that time been transferred to a post at Fort Meade, Maryland,[67] his ordeal was, unfortunately, far from over. Although not a criminal offense, adultery is punishable under the Uniform Military Code of Justice, the legal standard for soldiers in the armed forces. At a noncriminal administrative hearing on March 22, 2004, Yee was reprimanded for the adultery and pornography charges.[68] Although he was never convicted of a crime and would now be a free man, Yee and his civilian defense attorney, Eugene Fidell, reiterated his innocence and appealed the reprimand.

COMPLETE EXONERATION AND FREEDOM

On April 14, 2004, General James T. Hill, head of the Southern Command, granted Captain Yee's appeal, dropping all remaining reprimands from Captain Yee's record.[69] General Hill stated that he granted Yee's appeal because of the "extensive media attention given . . . [to] Chaplain Yee's personal misconduct. . . . While I believe that Chaplain Yee's misconduct was wrong," General Hill said, "I do not believe, given the extreme notoriety of his case in the news media, that further stigmatizing chaplain Yee would serve a just and fair purpose."[70]

Cleared of all charges against him, Captain James Yee finally returned as an army chaplain to his home post of Fort Lewis, Washington, in early May 2004. He was, however, placed under a strict gag order not to wear his uniform in public when making comments about his case and was told he should be careful when speaking publicly so as not to undermine military "loyalty, discipline or unit morale."[71]

DENUNCIATIONS OF ARMY ABOUND

Throughout Captain Yee's case, numerous critics, including former military prosecutors, judges, and congressmen, had demanded further examination. Pointing to media leaks, lack of evidence, unjust confinement, and unusual courtroom procedures, critics of the army often felt that Yee was treated unfairly and was being targeted because of his faith. Most observers found it odd that despite the severity of the espionage charges for which Captain Yee was initially arrested—charges for which he could have been given the death penalty—Captain Yee received only a simple reprimand for adultery. Eventually, even that reprimand was rescinded.

Retired Coast Guard judge Kevin Barry would be one of the first to speak out against the injustice against Captain Yee. He said, "This is a case that's so obviously wrong that [even] people who don't know military law are, if not outraged, then very concerned about what happened." Speaking about the dismissal of charges, Judge Barry said, "There apparently was no evidence. If they had the goods, they would have prosecuted."[72]

Bob Barr, a former Republican congressman from Georgia, noted that certain patterns emerge when Captain Yee's case is compared with other terrorism-related cases. Congressman Barr explained that "what we're seeing in Guantanamo, and perhaps in this case, is what happens when you've removed any judicial oversight over what the government is doing."[73]

Captain Yee's lawyer, Eugene Fidell, has consistently spoken out against major discrepancies in the case and has often called on the army to apologize for their vilification of Captain Yee. Fidell spoke about the lack of evidence against his client: "When you see a gulf between the shrill charges and this anthill of evidence . . . you have to wonder." He also noted that the prosecutors never showed the defense any evidence of the classified materials Yee was suspected of carrying. "The government has never produced the evidence that it believes was classified, so I am somewhat at a loss. . . . We were playing Hamlet without Hamlet here."[74]

In finally realizing the blatant injustice committed against Captain Yee, four United States congressmen called for a formal investigation into the army's unjust actions against Captain Yee. The four representatives were Michael Honda (Democrat, California), House Armed Services Committee ranking member Ike Skelton (Democrat, Missouri), House Armed Services Total Force Subcommittee ranking member Vic Snyder (Democrat, Arkansas) and Armed Services Committee member Adam Smith (Democrat, Washington state), who also happens to be Captain Yee's congressman. All four congressmen wrote a letter to Joseph Schmitz, inspector general of the Department of Defense, demanding an investigation into the criminal probe and court martial hearings against Captain Yee. The following are excerpts from the congressional letter:

We write to formally request that your office investigate the U.S. Army's criminal probe and court martial of Army Chaplain Captain

James Yee. The Army's decision to drop all charges against Captain Yee raises important questions about the strength and legitimacy of initial assertions by Army officials that Captain Yee had engaged in espionage and treasonous conduct at Guantanamo Bay, Cuba.

Press reports alleged that while confined, Captain Yee, a commissioned officer of the United States Army, was not afforded the military courtesies commensurate with his rank and that he was unduly targeted because of his religious affiliation with Islam. Given the unusual facts of this case, it is critical to determine whether Captain Yee was appropriately investigated, arrested and charged for criminal conduct by the U.S. Army.[75]

In addition, Senators Carl Levin (Democrat, Michigan) and Edward M. Kennedy (Democrat, Massachusetts) separately demanded that Secretary of Defense Donald Rumsfeld start an investigation into the Captain Yee fiasco.[76]

In response to this request by the congressmen and senators, the inspector general of the Defense Department agreed in August 2004 to investigate the case. Assistant Inspector General John Crane said the investigation would be launched in the fall of 2004 and could not be started sooner because of "other ongoing and urgent matters."[77] Though the Inspector General's Office did not comment on what the probe would include, at the time, Congressman Mike Honda expected that it would explore whether the army ever had sufficient probable cause and evidence to suspect Captain Yee at all.

Eugene Fidell commented that the inspector general's investigation was long overdue. He hoped that the probe would eventually lead to an official apology, something that Captain Yee had been demanding for months. Fidell rightly noted that congressional intercession should not be required for the army to finally apologize to Captain Yee for its blatant mistakes and the undue hardships imposed on him and his family. "The more tooth-pulling involved, it seems to me," said Fidell, "the less the apology."[78] Understandably, these trials and tribulations had a profound effect on Captain Yee and his family. In August 2004 Captain Yee tendered his resignation to his superiors, asking to be discharged effective January 7, 2005. A portion of Yee's letter cited several reasons for his resignation. Some relevant excerpts of his letter are as follows:

In 2003, I was unfairly accused of grave offenses under the Uniform Code of Military Justice and unjustifiably placed in solitary confinement for 76 days. Those unfounded allegations—which were leaked to the media—irreparably injured my personal and professional reputation and destroyed my prospects for a career in the United States Army. The only formal punishment I received (on matters having nothing to do with national security) was overturned, but at the same time official statements again unfairly tarnished my reputation.[79]

Yee went on to write that "because of the gag order, my ability to defend myself against this pattern of unfairness has been impeded by official correspondence, the clear purpose of which is to chill the exercise of my right to free speech." Yee wrote that he waited for months for a government apology, "but none has been forthcoming. I have been unable even to obtain my personal effects from Guantanamo Bay, despite repeated requests. In the circumstances, I have no alternative but to tender my resignation."[80]

After his ordeal and honorably completing his tenure with the U.S. Army, Captain Yee plans to complete his master's degree in international relations and return to his home in Washington, D.C.

The Case of Brandon Mayfield and the Madrid Train Bombings

On March 11, 2004, ten bombs exploded on four commuter trains in Madrid, Spain. The death toll exceeded 190 people, and at least 1,800 people were injured.[81] A partial fingerprint found on a bag containing detonators was matched by FBI analysts, and the Justice Department proclaimed the match to be a "100% identification" of American lawyer Brandon Mayfield, who was subsequently arrested and jailed as a "material witness" in the bombings.[82]

Two weeks later, as Mr. Mayfield languished in prison, Spanish federal authorities confirmed their previous suspicions that the fingerprint did not belong to Mr. Mayfield. After two weeks in jail and hundreds of media stories labeling him a "terrorist," he was finally released with a rare official apology from the FBI, which claimed that errors in fingerprint analysis were the sole cause for the catastrophic mistake.[83]

Said Mayfield about his arrest: "I am a Muslim, an American, and an ex-officer of the U.S. military. I believe I was singled out and discriminated against . . . [for being] a Muslim."[84]

Brandon Mayfield was a forty-year-old licensed attorney who lived with his wife, Mona, and three children in a suburb of Portland, Oregon. After graduating from high school, he joined the army and also spent time serving in the U.S. Army Reserves.[85] After an honorable discharge, he served in the ROTC program and was commissioned as a second lieutenant. Mayfield returned to active duty as an air defense artillery officer and was later honorably discharged following a shoulder injury.[86]

After completing law school and passing the Oregon State Bar Examination, Mayfield began to work as a family law attorney in Oregon.[87] Mayfield embraced Islam in the late 1980s after he had married his wife, an Egyptian American. He became a regular attendee of Friday prayers at a mosque in the Portland suburb of Beaverton.[88]

THE FINGERPRINT

According to the affidavit issued by FBI Special Agent Richard K. Werder requesting Mayfield's arrest, the Spanish National Police (SNP) sent the FBI digital photographic images of fingerprints found during the investigation of the Madrid bombings. Latent Finger Print (LFP) #17, found on a plastic bag containing detonators believed to be used in the Madrid bombings, was run through the Automated Fingerprint Identification System.[89]

Brandon Mayfield was one of more than twelve people who emerged as a "potential match" for the fingerprint.[90] After the print was identified at fifteen points and after a confirming second opinion, fingerprint analysis experts determined that LFP #17 was "a 100% identification" of Brandon Mayfield.[91] Two senior law enforcement officials told the Associated Press that Mayfield and his home had been under FBI surveillance for several weeks before his arrest, mainly because of the fingerprint analysis.[92]

Agent Werder's affidavit also states that surveillance agents observed Mayfield drive to his regular mosque on several occasions beginning on March 21, 2004. The surveillance did not go unnoticed by the Mayfield family, who believed their house had been searched. Upon seeing the agents, neighbors of the Mayfield's also questioned the officers about why they were in the neighborhood.[93]

One would hope that before arresting an American citizen for links to a major international terrorist attack, the FBI would have investigated all leads and fully verified the fingerprint before rushing to judgment and informing the media of a "terrorist" arrest. However, despite that Spanish law enforcement and investigative officials remained doubtful about the print's match with Mayfield, the Muslim lawyer from Oregon was arrested anyway.

On March 20, 2004, the FBI analyzed the partial fingerprint sent from Spain and concluded that it did indeed belong to Brandon Mayfield, notwithstanding the fact that a Scotland Yard fingerprint expert found any claim of a fingerprint match "horrendous."[94] Also, "miscellaneous Spanish documents" that the FBI found in Mayfield's home were part of the evidence used to detain him.

The absurdity of the Justice Department's case was revealed when the *New York Times* reported that these miscellaneous "documents" were later identified as nothing more than his children's Spanish homework.[95] Unfortunately, since the story had already leaked to the media and many major news outlets were now carrying the breaking story of the "American connection"[96] to the Madrid bombings, the damage to Mayfield and the American Muslim community had already been done.

Less than a month later, however, Spanish forensic experts officially informed the FBI of their doubts, and the two groups met in Madrid on April 21, 2004. Werder's affidavit cites the same meeting as such: "Before the meeting SNP personnel indicated that their examination of LFP #17 was preliminary and that a final determination had not been rendered. The SNP also indicated that they had not gone into the level three characteristics . . . utilized by the FBI when making their initial comparison. At the conclusion of the meeting it was believed that the SNP felt satisfied with the FBI Laboratory's identification of LFP #17. . . ."[97]

Spanish forensic experts and officials on the case had quite a different take on that meeting. It seems that the Spanish officials had little success in convincing the FBI of its mistake and commented on the FBI's unwillingness to accept its error. Said one Spanish police official: "The Spanish officers told [FBI representatives] with all the affection in the world that it wasn't [Brandon Mayfield]. . . . We never wanted to simply come out and say the FBI made a mistake. We tried to be diplomatic, not to make them look bad."[98]

The head of the SNP fingerprint unit, Pedro Lledo, noted that in the Mayfield case, the FBI "had a justification for everything. . . . But I just couldn't see it."[99] A commissioner of the SNP's science division, Carlos Corrales said, "It seemed as though they had something against him and they wanted to involve us."[100] The Werder affidavit went on to highlight that Mr. Mayfield had no record of international travel or border crossing.[101] In fact, Mr. Mayfield's passport had been expired for almost a year before the Madrid attacks, and he had never filed for its renewal. Although some federal officials claimed that Brandon Mayfield may have traveled under a false or fictitious name, Agent Werder concedes in his affidavit that no known aliases for Brandon Mayfield were ever found by the FBI, nor had he ever left the United States.[102]

Nonetheless, in his affidavit, Agent Werder requested Brandon Mayfield's arrest because "based upon the likelihood of false travel documents in existence, and the serious nature of the potential charges, Mayfield may attempt to flee the country if served with a subpoena to appear before the federal grand jury."[103] Agent Werder went even further by requesting that the court issue a seal on the affidavit, thereby making unavailable to the public any of the "evidence" linking Mayfield to the Madrid terrorist attacks.

FBI "APOLOGIZES" TO MAYFIELD

On May 24, 2004, after Mayfield's complete exoneration, noisy public outrage, and scathing criticism from dozens of newspaper editorial boards, the FBI finally issued an official apology to Mayfield after his harrowing ordeal. In its one-page press release, the FBI blamed their monumental error simply on the "substandard image quality"[104] of the fingerprints involved. The vast majority of the FBI's press release dealt with the technical and scientific fingerprint analyses. Only in the last line does it state, "The FBI apologizes to Mr. Mayfield and his family for the hardships that this matter has caused."[105]

The *New York Times*, like most Americans, believed that this apology was insufficient. The editorial board proclaimed that "the Justice Department and the Federal Bureau of Investigation ought to hang their heads in shame."[106] Mayfield summed up his ordeal in a written statement saying that "the government's handling of this case has been prejudicial and discriminatory in the extreme. Upon initially being arrested, I was informed by the arresting officers that the media was close behind. Within minutes of my arrest the allegations of my involvement in the Madrid bombing were being disseminated through the media. Notwithstanding the judge's gag order, the government put out its theory and its facts while we were prevented from saying anything."

"The whole thing was unbelievable," said William Mayfield, Brandon's father. "It was a witch hunt."[107] The *Washington Post* reiterated this sentiment, stating that "an apology is not enough" and roundly criticized the Justice Department for their treatment of Mayfield and their abusive use of the material witness statute.[108]

JUSTICE DEPARTMENT MISUSE OF THE MATERIAL WITNESS STATUTE

Many critics of the Justice Department's tactics and procedures in the Mayfield case repeatedly pointed to the FBI's continuing abuse of the material witness statute, which allows the government to arrest and hold witnesses who have information essential to a case but are considered a flight risk.[109] These material witnesses, many of whom are never charged with or convicted of any crime, can be held secretly and indefinitely, without any access to counsel. This is the unfortunate method that has been used since September 11, 2001, to detain many terrorism suspects for long periods of time without informing them of the charges against them or allowing them access to their lawyers. As occurred in the case of Mayfield, the media often portrays people detained pursuant to the material witness statute based solely on selective government leaks and not on the evidence.

The government conveniently sealed all the evidence related to Mayfield's case and selectively leaked information to the media that helped form negative public opinion. Usually, in order to obtain a material witness warrant, a prosecutor is required to prove that a witness is likely to flee when summoned to court.[110] No evidence was ever presented that an officer of the court like Mayfield—especially given that his passport had expired and he had no history of foreign travel—would not respond to a subpoena or flee upon being served with a subpoena.

Many legal experts and critics have spoken out against the Justice Department's use of the material witness statute to round up Muslims who have not been charged with any criminal act. The former second-in-command in the Clinton administration's Justice Department said that former attorney general John Ashcroft was converting the statute into a preventive detention policy without congressional approval. "After all, if they can pick people up like this, anyone can be picked up like this," said Michael Greenberger, who now teaches at the University of Maryland School of Law. "I am fearful that this is a long line of dramatic detentions, and we will find as time goes on that the evidence just peels away," Greenberger said.[111]

The material witness statute was issued a severe legal blow on May 1, 2004, when a federal judge called the imprisonment of material witnesses in the government's terrorism probe "unconstitutional."[112] U.S. district judge Shira Scheindlin wrote that "imprisoning a material witness for a grand jury investigation raises a serious constitutional question under the Fourth Amendment," which prohibits unreasonable searches and seizures.[113] She added that "since 1789, no Congress has granted the government the authority to imprison an innocent person in order to guarantee that he will testify before a grand jury conducting a criminal investigation."[114]

BRANDON MAYFIELD FIGHTS BACK

On August 26, 2004, Brandon Mayfield hired one of the nation's most successful plaintiffs' attorneys to represent him in a civil lawsuit against the Department of Justice.[115] Celebrity lawyer Gerry Spence says he decided to help Brandon Mayfield sue the government because "it's an important case to Mr. Mayfield, and it's an important case to all Americans."[116]

In his suit, Mayfield claimed the federal government targeted him solely because of his Muslim faith and violated his Fourth Amendment rights by searching his home and office, seizing his family's belongings, and incarcerating him for two weeks. "It's called the Muslim factor," Spence said. "It's profiling. It even affects what you see on a fingerprint, which is supposed to be science."[117]

After such a catastrophic blunder by the Justice Department and the FBI, the case of Brandon Mayfield serves to remind all Americans about our nation's legal hallmarks of due process, evidential analysis, and every person's right to be presumed innocent until proven guilty in a court of law. Kent Mayfield, Brandon's brother, accurately summed up the frustrations of many Americans when he said that Mayfield's only crimes were that "he is of the Muslim faith and that he is not super happy with the Bush administration. So if that's a crime, well, you can burn half of us."[118] In late 2006 the United States government agreed to settle the civil lawsuit by Brandon Mayfield for $2 million.[119]

The "No-Fly" List, Tariq Ramadan, and Cat Stevens

The Transportation Security Administration (TSA) was created by the Aviation and Transportation Security Act of 2001[120] and is charged with overseeing the security of all modes of interstate transportation. The TSA's current system for preventing terrorist access to airplanes relies on airline watch lists compiled from a variety of government sources. At least two types of watch lists are maintained: a no-fly list of terrorist suspects, and a selectee list targeting people who must be subjected to rigorous screening before they are allowed to fly.[121]

Since the inception of these lists, the TSA has refused to supply details on whom or why someone is on the no-fly or selectee lists. However, according to TSA documents obtained through a Freedom of Information Act (FOIA) suit filed by the ACLU on behalf of six racially diverse plaintiffs,[122] the list of targeted people has been growing daily in response to requests from the intelligence community, DHS, and other agencies.

The ACLU asked the court to declare that the no-fly list violates airline passengers' constitutional rights of freedom from unreasonable search and seizure and also violates due process under the Fourth and Fifth Amendments.[123] The ACLU also asked the TSA to develop satisfactory procedures that will allow innocent people to fly without being treated as potential terrorists and without being subjected to humiliation and unnecessary delays.

Reverend John Shaw was one of the six plaintiffs in the ACLU lawsuit and one of the many names on the no-fly list. "I am joining the ACLU lawsuit because I have been repeatedly interrogated, delayed, and have experienced enhanced screening procedures and detention since 2002. I have also tried without success to have my name removed from the list," said the seventy-four-year-old Presbyterian minister from Sammamish, Washington.[124]

THE CASE OF TARIQ RAMADAN

Tariq Ramadan is a world-renowned Swiss Muslim scholar who was recently named one of *Time* magazine's "100 Innovators of the 21st Century."[125] Because of his prolific academic record, Ramadan was appointed to the Henry R. Luce Professorship of Religion, Conflict, and Peace Building[126] for the fall 2004 semester at the Joan B. Kroc Institute for International Peace Studies at the University of Notre Dame in South Bend, Indiana.[127]

Ramadan's visa application for admittance to the United States was initially accepted, and he subsequently received a visa from the U.S. State Department. After receiving his visa, Ramadan was preparing to move his family and young children to Indiana and was scheduled to begin teaching his classes at Notre Dame in late August 2004. But just days before Ramadan was set to travel, his visa was summarily revoked without any explanation at the behest of the Department of Homeland Security.[128]

It turns out that Ramadan's visa was revoked pursuant to section 411 of the USA PATRIOT Act, which bars entry to foreigners who have used a "position of prominence . . . to endorse or espouse terrorist activity."[129] Although government officials had provided no explanation concerning Ramadan's visa revocation, some noted scholars said they suspected the government's decision to bar Ramadan could have been influenced by certain right-wing pro-Israeli groups that have "waged a campaign" against moderate Muslim scholars and intellectuals whose views on Islam and the Middle East conflict with their own.[130]

Middle East expert Graham Fuller, a senior Rand analyst and former vice chair of the National Intelligence Counsel, once told the *Chicago Tribune* that "pro-Likud organizations want to block people who can speak articulately and present the Muslim dilemma in a way that might be understandable and sympathetic to Americans." In talking about the Arab-Israeli crisis, he said, "They succeed by presenting this as a security matter. There is no way homeland security would initiate this on its own."[131]

For example, Web sites that seek to chill the First Amendment and academic freedom, such as Campus Watch, initiated by neoconservative Daniel Pipes, seek to "expose" professors who allegedly hold views critical of the right-wing Likud government of Ariel Sharon in Israel.[132] "They want to say all Muslims are a monolithic threat," said John Esposito, a professor at Georgetown University, who describes Ramadan as "an established academic . . . with a strong record."[133]

Scott Appleby, director of the Kroc Institute, challenged Ramadan's critics to provide any credible evidence of nefarious links. "If Mr. Pipes or anyone else has solid evidence that Tariq Ramadan has connections with [terrorists]—whatever that might mean—I would like to see it," Appleby said. "Otherwise, unsubstantiated charges intended to defame a Muslim intellectual is troublingly reminiscent of some of the darkest moments in U.S. history."[134]

Commenting on the arbitrary denial of a visa to Ramadan and his appointment to Notre Dame, Professor Appleby further states that despite the numerous requests to DHS and federal government officials, the University of Notre Dame has been given "no substantial evidence of any of the various things that have been said about him."[135] Professor Appleby goes on to further state categorically that "we stand behind Tariq fully, and are proud of the appointment, and believe and continue to believe it's the proper appointment."[136]

THE CASE OF YUSUF ISLAM (FORMERLY CAT STEVENS)

"It started with a simple spelling error."
—*Time*, September 25, 2004[137]

On September 21, 2004, United Airlines Flight 919[138] was en route from London to Dulles International Airport in suburban Washington, D.C., when American officials realized that the pop star Cat Stevens, now known as Yusuf Islam, was aboard that flight. After learning of Mr. Islam's presence on the flight, the plane was diverted six hundred miles to Bangor International Airport in Maine, where federal authorities began questioning Mr. Islam at 3:00 P.M. Eastern Standard Time.[139]

After a lengthy interview, U.S. officials ordered Mr. Islam's deportation, saying that he was on a "security watch list because of suspicions that he was associated with potential terrorists."[140] After being held in Bangor, Mr. Islam, a British citizen, was then transferred to Logan International Airport in Boston, where the Massachusetts Port Authority said he would be put on a flight to Washington. From Washington he was subsequently sent back to London.[141]

Yusuf Islam was born Stephen Demetre Georgiou in London to a Greek Cypriot father and Swedish mother.[142] In the 1970s he took the stage name Cat Stevens and had a string of musical hits, including "Wild World" and "Morning Has Broken."[143] Last year he released two songs, including a re-recording of his 1971 international hit "Peace Train," to express his opposition to the war in Iraq. He left his music career in the late 1970s after his conversion to Islam and later became a teacher and an advocate for his religion, founding the Islamia Primary school in London in 1983. In 1998 it became the first Muslim school in Britain to receive government support on the same basis as Christian and other religious schools.[144]

Yusuf Islam is also the founder of Small Kindness, a charity whose purpose it is to raise money for children and families suffering from poverty and war in the Balkans and Middle East. He has also donated, both personally and through his charities, to victims of the September 11, 2001, tragedies and to victims of the AIDS pandemic in Africa.[145]

Upon his return to London after his ordeal, Mr. Islam told a crowded press conference that he was "shocked and slightly amused" that U.S. offi-

cials had determined that he was on a terrorist watch list and was not allowed to enter the United States. Islam said that he was a victim of an
"unjust and arbitrary system," and that he has consistently denounced terrorism in his speeches and even on his official Web site.[146]

With regard to the no-fly list, the former pop singer was allegedly in
the same league as Senator Edward Kennedy, who apparently shares a
name with someone on the no-fly list and had also been told several
times that he could not fly.[147] Senator Kennedy told the Senate Judiciary
Committee that he was stopped and questioned at airports on the East
Coast five times in March 2004 because his name appeared on the
government's secret no-fly list.[148] Senator Kennedy said that he had to
personally enlist the help of DHS secretary Tom Ridge to get his name
removed from the list.[149] Federal air security officials said the initial error that led to the scrutiny of the senator should not have happened, and
they have acknowledged in the past that the no-fly list is imperfect. Privately, however, many officials were embarrassed that it took a United
States senator and his staff "more than three weeks to get his name
removed."[150]

As is the case with Yusuf Islam and Senator Kennedy, most of the other
people ensnared in the no-fly list debate have absolutely no links to terrorism. At least one person says he was told that he would need to "have his
name legally changed to avoid the problem in the future."[151]

Subsequently, the case of Yusuf Islam would become humorous fodder
for newspaper editorial pages and for late-night talk show monologues.
The Washington Post commented that in the case of Islam and the no-fly
list, what the government was "missing was common sense."[152] The Pittsburgh Post-Gazette called the fiasco a "ridiculous overreaction."[153] "What
did federal authorities think he was going to do? Threaten to sing Peace
Train over and over until certain demands were met?" said the Post-Gazette
editorial. "Here was someone who was traveling with his daughter and
had been to the United States several times, most recently in May, when he
met with officials of the White House Office of Faith-Based and Community Initiatives to discuss philanthropic work."

Other notable figures have spoken up against the arbitrary and secre-
tive denial of Yusuf Islam's entry into the United States. Islam's detention
and return to Britain sparked a protest to the Bush administration by then
British foreign secretary Jack Straw. On September 22, 2004, Secretary
Straw personally told U.S. secretary of state Colin Powell that the action
against Mr. Islam "should not have been taken."[154]

A final validation to the injustice committed against Mr. Islam occurred on November 10, 2004, when Yusuf Islam was presented with the Man for Peace award by former Russian president Mikhail Gorbachev at the opening of a meeting of Nobel Peace Prize laureates in Rome, Italy.[155] The Gorbachev Foundation said the peace award was for Yusuf Islam's dedication to "promoting peace and condemning terrorism."[156] The award is given annually "to a distinguished personage of culture and entertainment for peace messages, fraternity and integration between nations."[157]

At the presentation of the peace prize, President Gorbachev kissed Islam on the cheeks and praised him for standing by his convictions despite personal hardships. "Cat Stevens' life has not been simple," Gorbachev said. "Every person who takes a critical stance to make the world a better place . . . has a difficult life."[158] In summing up the receipt of this prestigious international award and his recent ordeal in the United States, Yusuf Islam told reporters that "perhaps it's part of the irony that sometimes you have to go through a test in order to achieve a prize. So maybe that's a symbol. Today I'm receiving a prize for peace, which is actually, I would say, a bit more descriptive of my ideas and my aims in life."[159] The *Miami Herald* called Islam's receipt of the Gorbachev Foundation award "sweet vindication."[160]

Conclusion

The American Muslim community has always categorically condemned acts of terrorism and believed that those who break the law should be prosecuted to the fullest extent of the law. In order to remain consistent with the constitutional hallmarks of due process and "equal protection" under the law, however, it is essential that our law enforcement agencies enforce and apply the law in a consistent manner to all people rather than selectively target people based on their race, religion, or ethnic affiliation.

Although the post–9/11, mass dragnets against American Muslim, Arab, and South Asian communities may have tapered off, we as a nation are still at a legal crossroads. As we did with Japanese Americans after World War II, as well as other minority groups before and after WWII, demonizing and targeting a minority community is antithetical to every democratic and constitutional foundation upon which our country was founded.

Even as we continue to relegate American Muslims to second-class citizenry in the United States American Muslims will, as in all other prior civil rights movements, struggle to overcome the "guilty until proven innocent" paradigm and will one day rightfully take their place as the next chapter in the civil rights history of America.

Notes

1. Public Law 107-56, 115 *Stat.* 272 (Oct. 26, 2001).

2. See also Arsalan Iftikhar, *The Status of Muslim Civil Rights in the United States, 2005: Unequal Protection* (Washington, D.C.: Council on American Islamic Relations, 2005).

3. Memorandum, Office of the Deputy Attorney General, "Guidance for Absconder Apprehension Initiative," January 25, 2002.

4. Ibid.

5. Ibid.

6. See Dan Eggen and Cheryl W. Thompson, "United States Seeks Thousands of Fugitive Deportees; Middle Eastern Men are Focus of Search," *Washington Post,* January 8, 2002.

7. U.S. Department of Justice, Office of the Inspector General, "The September 11 Detainees: A Review of Aliens Held on Immigration Charges in Connection with the Investigation of the September 11 Attacks," April, 2003.

8. Ibid.

9. Human Rights Watch, "U.S. Supreme Court Should Review and Reject Secret Detentions," press release, September 30, 2003, http://www.hrw.org/press/2003/09/us093003.htm (accessed November 10, 2007).

10. Kelli Arena and Terry Frieden, "U.S. Report Critical of 9/11 Detainee Treatment," CNN, June 3, 2003 http://edition.cnn.com/2003/LAW/06/02/detainees/ (accessed November 10, 2007).

11. Ibid., 21.

12. Ibid.

13. Ibid.

14. American Civil Liberties Union (ACLU), "Sanctioned Bias: Racial Profiling Since 9/11," February 2004, http://www.aclu.org/SafeandFree/SafeandFree.cfm?ID=15102&c=207 (accessed November 10, 2007).

15. Memorandum, Office of the Deputy Attorney General, "Guidance for Absconder Apprehension Initiative."

16. ACLU, "Sanctioned Bias."

17. Ibid.

18. All changes that were made to the Special Registration program, from its inception to cessation, are summarized by Department of Homeland Security, U.S. Immigration and Customs Enforcement, "Fact Sheet: Changes to National Security Entry/Exit Registration System (NSEERS)," December 1, 2003.

19. Arena and Frieden, "U.S. Report Critical of 9/11 Detainee Treatment," 6.

20. U.S. Department of State, "Fact Sheet: National Security Entry-Exit Registration System," June 5, 2002.

21. In addition to Iran, Iraq, Libya, Sudan, and Syria, the twenty-five "Special Registration" countries include Afghanistan, Algeria, Bahrain, Eritrea, Lebanon, Morocco, North Korea, Oman, Qatar, Somalia, Tunisia, United Arab Emirates, Yemen, Pakistan, Saudi Arabia, Bangladesh, Egypt, Indonesia, Jordan, and Kuwait.

22. U.S. Department of State, "Fact Sheet: National Security Entry Exit Registration System."

23. Arena and Frieden, "Report Critical of 9/11 Detainee Treatment," 6.

24. American Arab Anti-Discrimination Committee et al. v. Attorney General John Ashcroft et al., No. 02-70605 (USDC C.D. Ca. 2002).

25. Cam Simpson, Flynn McRoberts, and Liz Sly, "Immigration Crackdown Shatters Muslim Lives," *Chicago Tribune,* November 16, 2003.

26. American Civil Liberties Union (ACLU), "ACLU Says New Border Fingerprinting System Likely to Sow Confusion, Tracking of Arab and Muslims Based on National Origin Will Continue," press release, January 5, 2004.

27. Ibid.

28. Ibid.

29. Editors of Esquire Magazine, *Esquire: The Rules: A Man's Guide to Life* (New York: Hearst Books, 2003).

30. Public Law 107-56, 115 *Stat.* 272 (Oct. 26, 2001).

31. U.S. Congress Senate, U.S. Senate Roll Call Votes, 107th Cong., 1st sess., http://www.senate.gov/legislative/LIS/roll_call_lists/roll_call_vote_cfm.cfm?congress=107&session=1&vote=00313 (accessed November 10, 2007).

32. Sara Gamay and Diane Lee, "Patriot Act Encourages National Insecurity," *(Georgetown) Hoya,* November 7, 2003.

33. See Mike Barber, "Yee Reunited with Family," *Seattle Post-Intelligencer,* April 6, 2004.

34. American Civil Liberties Union (ACLU), "Largest City to Date Passes Pro-Civil Liberties Resolution; Los Angeles Rejects Bush's Call to Continue Civil Liberties Curtailment," press release, January 21, 2004.

35. Michelle Garcia, "N.Y. City Council Passes Anti-Patriot Act Measure," *Washington Post,* February 5, 2004.

36. American Arab Anti-Discrimination Committee et al. v. Attorney General John Ashcroft et al., No. 02-70605 (USDC C.D. Ca. 2002).

37. Ibid.

38. Ibid.

39. Douglas Dow, "Liberty Starts at Home," Fort Worth (TX) Star-Telegram, March 8, 2004.

40. Ray Rivera, "Pentagon to Investigate Case of Fort Lewis Chaplain," Seattle Times, August 5, 2004.

41. Laura Parker, "The Ordeal of Chaplain Yee." USA Today, May 16, 2004.

42. Topics ranged "from the history of Islam to insights on the rise in suicide attempts" among the detainees. See FOX News, "Yousef Yee Charged with Adultery, Storing Porn on Gov't Computer," November 26, 2003.

43. U.S. Department of Justice, Office of the Inspector General, "The September 11 Detainees."

44. An Article 32 hearing is the military equivalent of a grand jury proceeding or hearing.

45. Rowan Scarborough, "Yee Case on Hold as Military Falters," Washington Times, December 12, 2003.

46. Eggen and Thompson, "United States Seeks Thousands of Fugitive Deportees."

47. U.S. Department of Justice, Office of the Inspector General, "The September 11 Detainees."

48. Arena and Frieden, "U.S. Report Critical of 9/11 Detainee Treatment."

49. Rowan Scarborough, "Islamic Chaplain Is Charged as Spy," Washington Times, September 20, 2003.

50. U.S. Department of Justice, Office of the Inspector General, "The September 11 Detainees."

51. CBS News, "Gitmo Chaplain Charged," October 10, 2003.

52. Guy Taylor, "Muslim Chaplain Charged by Army." Washington Times, October 10, 2003.

53. Al-Jazeera, "Guantanamo Muslim Chaplain Charged," October 11, 2003.

54. Barber, "Yee Reunited with Family."

55. CNN.com, "Chaplain's Prosecutors Focus on Porn, Sex Charges," December 8, 2003 http://www.cnn.com/2003/LAW/12/08/yee.hearing.ap/ (accessed November 10, 2007).

56. Eggen and Thompson, "United States Seeks Thousands of Fugitive Deportees."

57. Arena and Frieden, "U.S. Report Critical of 9/11 Detainee Treatment."

58. Eggen and Thompson, "United States Seeks Thousands of Fugitive Deportees."

59. Ibid.

60. Fox News, "Yousef Yee Charged with Adultery."

61. U.S. Department of Justice, Office of the Inspector General, "The September 11 Detainees."

62. Ibid.

63. Ibid.

64. See JusticeForYee.Com, http://www.justiceforyee.com/Media.htm (accessed November 10, 2007).

65. Barber, "Yee Reunited with Family."

66. Parker, "Ordeal of Chaplain Yee."

67. Rowan Scarborough, "Army, Captain Near Deal in Espionage Case," *Washington Times*, March 16, 2004.

68. Parker, "Ordeal of Chaplain Yee."

69. CNN.com, "Muslim Army Chaplain Wins Adultery Appeal," April 14, 2004, http://www.cnn.com/2004/LAW/04/14/yee.appeal/index.html (accessed November 10, 2007).

70. Ibid.

71. Ibid.

72. Ibid.

73. Ibid.

74. Ibid.

75. Mike Honda, Fifteenth District of California, "Letter Requesting Investigation of Captain Yee," May 20, 2004.

76. Eggen and Thompson, "United States Seeks Thousands of Fugitive Deportees."

77. Ibid.

78. Ibid.

79. Mike Barber, "Army Chaplain Yee to Resign," *Seattle Post-Intelligencer*, August 3, 2004.

80. Barber, "Army Chaplain Yee to Resign."

81. British Broadcasting Corporation (BBC), "Timeline: Madrid Investigation," August 11, 2004.

82. U.S. Department of Justice, "Statement on Brandon Mayfield Case," May 24, 2004; Affidavit of Richard K. Werder, Federal Grand Jury 03-01, No. 04-MC-9071 (USDC W.D. Or. 2004), 3. *USA Today*, "Family: Oregon Lawyer Has No Connection to Madrid Attacks," May 8, 2004.

83. Kevin Johnson, "Bomb Case Against U.S. Lawyer Dropped," *USA Today*, May 24, 2004.

84. Johnson, "Bomb Case Against U.S. Lawyer Dropped."

85. Ibid.

86. Ibid.

87. Ben Jacklet and Todd Murphey, "Now Free, Attorney Brandon Mayfield Turns Furious," *Washington Report on Middle East Affairs* (July/August 2004).

88. Daniel Wools, "Fingerprint Evidence Cited," *Topeka Capital-Journal*, May 8, 2004.

89. Johnson, "Bomb Case Against U.S. Lawyer Dropped."

90. According to the affidavit by Special Agent Werder, the prints were on file from his service as an army officer and because of an arrest for burglary in 1984. Robyn Blumner, "All the Fear That's Fit to Print." *St. Petersburg Times,* June 6, 2004.

91. Daniel Wools, "Fingerprint Evidence Cited."

92. Ibid.

93. Ibid.

94. David Sarasohn, "In Mayfield case, Fingers Are Pointing," *Oregonian,* June 9, 2004.

95. Ibid.

96. Michael Isikoff, "An American Connection?" *Newsweek,* May 7, 2004.

97. Christopher Brauchli, "Third Time Is Not the Charm for FBI," *Boulder Daily Camera,* June 12, 2004.

98. Ibid.

99. Ibid.

100. Ibid.

101. U.S. Department of State, "Fact Sheet: National Security Entry Exit Registration System."

102. Ibid.

103. U.S. Department of Justice, Office of the Inspector General, "The September 11 Detainees."

104. FBI National Press Office, "Statement on Brandon Mayfield Case," May 24, 2004, http://www.fbi.gov/pressrel/pressrel04/mayfield052404.htm (accessed November 10, 2007).

105. FBI National Press Office, "Statement on Brandon Mayfield Case."

106. Editorial, "The FBI messes up," *New York Times,* May 26, 2004.

107. Johnson, "Bomb Case Against U.S. Lawyer Dropped."

108. *Washington Post,* "Apology Is Not Enough," May 27, 2004.

109. The text of the material witness statute says that a person may be arrested and detained as a "material witness" only "if it is shown that it may become impracticable to secure the presence of the person by subpoena" (18 *U.S. Code §* 3144).

110. See Brett Zongker, "Secret Legal Process Misused, American-Islamic Group Says," Associated Press, August 30, 2004.

111. Honda, "Letter Requesting Investigation of Captain Yee."

112. Larry Neumeister, "Judge Declares Imprisonment of Material Witnesses Unconstitutional," Associated Press, May 1, 2004.

113. Ibid.

114. Ibid.

115. Rukmini Callimachi, "'Smoking Gun' Author to Represent Brandon Mayfield," Associated Press, August 26, 2004.

116. Ben Jacklet, "Mayfield Calls in Heavy Hitter," *Portland Tribune*, September 28, 2004.

117. Associated Press, "Judge Quits Wrongly Accused Lawyer's Suit," November 9, 2004.

118. See Arsalan Iftikhar, "Worst Since J. Edgar Hoover Era," *South Florida Sun-Sentinel*, November 16, 2004.

119. Dan Eggen, "U.S. Settles Suit Filed by Oregon Lawyer: $2 Million Will Be Paid for Wrongful Arrest After Attack," *Washington Post*, November 30, 2006.

120. Public Law 107-71, 115 Stat. 597 (Nov. 19, 2001).

121. Human Rights First, "Airline Watchlists: Overview," http://www.human rightsfirst.org/us_law/privacy/airwatch_overview.htm (accessed November 10, 2007).

122. *Green et al. v. Transportation Security Administration et al.*, No. C04-763Z (USDC W.D. Wa. 2004).

123. Stella Richardson, "ACLU Challenges 'No-Fly' Lists: Citizens Targeted as Terrorists," ACLU News of ACLU of Northern California, Spring 2004.

124. Ibid.

125. See Nicholas Le Quesne, "Trying to Bridge a Great Divide," Time.Com: Innovators, http://www.time.com/time/innovators/spirituality/profile_ramadan .html (accessed November 10, 2007).

126. Jay Tolson, "Should This Man Come to the U.S.?" *U.S. News & World Report*, December 6, 2004.

127. Democracy Now! "Interview with Tariq Ramadan and Scott Appleby: Leading Muslim Scholar Tariq Ramadan Denied U.S. Visa to Teach at Notre Dame," September 13, 2004, http://www.democracynow.org/article.pl?sid=04/09/13/ 1428249 (accessed November 10, 2007).

128. Ibid.

129. U.S. Department of Justice, Office of the Inspector General, "The September 11 Detainees."

130. Genieve Abdo, "Muslim Scholar Has Visa Revoked," *Chicago Tribune*, August 24, 2004.

131. Ibid.

132. Ibid.

133. Ibid.

134. Ibid.

135. Ibid.

136. Ibid.

137. Sally Donnelly, "You say Yusuf, I say Youssof," *Time*, September 25, 2004.

138. Associated Press, "Britain Complains to U.S. About Cat Stevens' Detention," September 23, 2004.

139. Kevin Anderson, "Cat Stevens to Be Deported After Jet Diversion," Associated Press, September 21, 2004.

140. Ibid.

141. Jeanne Meserve, "Detained Cat Stevens Heading Home," CNN.com, September 22, 2004, http://www.cnn.com/2004/US/09/22/plane.diverted.stevens/ (accessed November 10, 2007).

142. British Broadcasting Corporation (BBC), "Cat Stevens Denied Entry into U.S.," September 22, 2004.

143. Associated Press, "Britain Complains to U.S. About Cat Stevens' Detention."

144. Ibid.

145. Associated Press, "Cat Stevens Wins Peace Prize," November 11, 2004.

146. Ibid.

147. Editorial, "Moonshadow Boxing," *Washington Post,* September 25, 2004.

148. Sara Kehaulani Goo, "Sen. Kennedy Flagged by No-Fly List," *Washington Post,* August 20, 2004.

149. Associated Press, "Ted Kennedy's Airport Adventure," August 19, 2004.

150. Editorial, "Moonshadow Boxing."

151. Ibid.

152. Ibid.

153. Editorial, "National Insecurity: Keeping America Safe from Cat Stevens," *Pittsburgh Post-Gazette,* September 26, 2004.

154. British Broadcasting Corporation (BBC), "Cat Stevens 'Shock' at US Refusal," September 23, 2004.

155. Associated Press, "Cat Stevens Wins Peace Prize."

156. British Broadcasting Corporation (BBC), "Cat Stevens Honoured by Gorbachev," November 9, 2004.

157. Ibid.

158. Associated Press, "Cat Stevens Wins Peace Prize."

159. Ibid.; Associated Press, "Cat Stevens Named 'Man of Peace,'" November 10, 2004.

160. *Miami Herald,* "Sweet Vindication," November 10, 2004.

CHAPTER 7

American and British Constructions of Asylum Seekers
Moral Panic, Detention, and Human Rights

MICHAEL WELCH AND LIZA SCHUSTER

DETENTION, ESPECIALLY FOR LONG PERIODS, is among the gravest acts the state can take against individuals. The current practice of the governments of both the United States and the United Kingdom of detaining asylum seekers is a particularly serious matter and has drawn the attention of human rights organizations, since this clashes with the United Nations Convention Relating to the Status of Refugees. The controversy has, however, taken different forms in these otherwise similar nations, most notably along lines of social constructionism and moral panic. While there is considerable public and political attention directed at asylum seeking in Britain, the putative problem in the United States remains muted; nevertheless, the consequence is the same: the subjection of asylum seekers to unnecessary confinement in harsh conditions.[1]

This chapter compares the ways asylum seekers are depicted in the United States and the UK while also shedding light on matters pertaining to human rights and the regulation of human mobility within a global context.

Moral Panic: Noisy and Quiet Constructions

For decades, moral panic theory has been used to decipher key social problems ranging from drug use to pornography, thereby capturing interlocking aspects of negative societal reaction. This work draws on Stanley Cohen's writings on moral panic in an effort to identify the distinctive ways in which asylum seekers are portrayed, particularly since they are commonly viewed as a problem and a threat to the social order. In illumi-

138

nating that phenomenon, Cohen defines a moral panic as "a condition, episode, person or group of persons [that] emerges to become defined as a threat to societal values and interest; its nature is presented in a stylized and stereotypical fashion by the mass media and politicians."[2]

In the third edition of *Folk Devils and Moral Panics*,[3] Cohen explores three extensions of moral panic theory. These include social constructionism, media and cultural studies, and risk. In approaching these domains, Cohen confronts a significant problem facing moral panic analysis; namely, its subjective nature. "Why is reaction to Phenomenon A dismissed or downgraded by being described as 'another moral panic' while the putatively more significant Phenomenon B is ignored, and not even made a candidate for moral signification?"[4] As a partial remedy to this predicament, Cohen calls for a comparative sociology of moral panic that provides researchers an opportunity to discern why a certain condition manifests as a pseudodisaster in one nation but not in another. Moreover, comparative research invites critical analysis in determining the many forms and nuances of moral panic.

Further refining the sociology of moral panic, Cohen distinguishes between noisy and quiet constructions. As the name suggests, noisy constructions manifest in moral panic accompanied by high levels of public, political, and media attention. By contrast, quiet constructions emerge as a more contained entity in which the "claims makers are professionals, experts, or bureaucrats working in an organization with little or no public or media exposure."[5]

At first glance, the idea of a quiet panic appears oxymoronic: How can a moral panic be quiet? Unfortunately, Cohen offers little guidance on how to resolve this dilemma other than the aforementioned quote. Still, we eagerly pursue this facet of moral panic theory in an attempt to break new ground. In particular, this work attempts to decipher why reaction to asylum seekers has taken the form of noisy panic in Britain while remaining muted in the United States even though the state interventions—detention—are identical. Taking a comparative approach between two similar societies contributes tremendously to our efforts to reveal the nuances of moral panic. Moreover, our reality check of the unnecessary detention of those fleeing persecution shows that these constructions in the UK and the United States are not merely benign pseudodisasters but instead constitute serious human rights abuses.

Previous research displays the utility of this paradigm in understanding the processes and consequences of moral panic with regard to immigrants in the United States during the 1990s.[6] That work demonstrates how exaggerated claims were used to justify an official crackdown on so-called illegal aliens, creating a greater reliance on detention. In the UK, moral panic has generated similar campaigns against asylum seekers. According to Cohen, "in media, public, and political discourse in Britain the distinctions between immigrants, refugees, and asylum seekers have become hopelessly blurred."[7] Furthermore, asylum issues in the UK "are subsumed under the immigration debate, which in turn is framed by the general categories of race, race relations and ethnicity."[8] Beginning in the 1990s, growing numbers of asylum seekers were met with hostility in the UK.[9] Consider the following headlines in the British press: "Warning Over New Influx of Gypsies,"[10] "Handouts Galore! Welcome to Soft Touch Britain's Welfare Paradise: Why Life for Them Here Is Just Like a Lottery Win,"[11] "Script for a Scam: In Letters Back Home Asylum Gypsies Tell Their Friends How to Get into Britain."[12] Compounding rejection, many of those persons faced accusations of being bogus asylum seekers and therefore not entitled to compassion or safe refuge.[13] Cohen explains:

> Governments and media start with a broad public consensus that first, we must keep out as many refugee-type foreigners as possible; second, these people lie to get themselves accepted; third, that strict criteria of eligibility and therefore tests of credibility must be used. For two decades, the media and the political elites of all parties have focused attention on the notion of "genuineness." This culture of disbelief penetrates the whole system. So "bogus" refugees and asylum seekers have not really been driven from their home countries because of persecution, but are merely "economic" migrants, attracted to the "Honey Pot" or "Soft Touch Britain."[14]

Researchers have tracked the formation of moral panic, particularly in the British media, where so-called bogus asylum seekers are publicly vilified.[15] In 1995 the Runnymede Trust surveyed asylum coverage in the print media, finding a pattern of racist rhetoric that likened migration and asylum seeking to natural disasters. Those metaphors, such as "tides," "waves," "floods," and "swamps," serve to dehumanize migrants and refugees while exaggerating the size, scale, and threat of the phenomenon. In doing so, so-called bogus asylum seekers are blamed for placing an undue burden on the social welfare system and taking jobs from British citizens.[16] In a similar examination of the British press, Ron Kaye found that 58 percent of all relevant articles in his sample contained labels characterizing asylum seekers as bogus rather than genuine.[17]

Furthering a critical understanding of the media and its facility at shaping representations of refugees, Zrinka Bralo[18] analyzed the discourse of news coverage in the UK. Borrowing from Stuart Hall,[19] Bralo recognizes that representation through language is pivotal to the process by which meanings are reproduced and that language does not merely reflect reality in a transparent manner but constructs a certain version of social reality. Bralo discovered that asylum seeking is portrayed as a social problem for Britain rather than as an opportunity to provide safe haven for people fleeing persecution. In this way, refugees are labeled as Others who should be met with suspicion.[20] Like other researchers, Bralo found evidence of natural disaster metaphors used to describe strains on the welfare state. Consider the headline "The Flood of Bogus Asylum Seekers into Dover Has Left the Local Council Facing a Potential 10 million [Pounds] Crisis That Could See Basic Social Services Slashed, It Emerged Yesterday."[21]

Likewise, other labels are frequently attached to asylum seekers, depicting them as "benefit scroungers," "cheats," and "fraudulent." In some instances, asylum seekers are criminalized as "hoodlums," "gangsters," or, in another sweeping demonization, "Evil Foreigners."[22] Additionally, examples of modern racism are common, particularly in reference to Islamic fundamentalism.[23] Consider the inflammatory title "Lying Guerrilla Wins Thousands for a Few Weeks Behind Bars."[24] In that article, a detainee is described as "an Islamic guerrilla fighter [who] is to be paid 'substantial' damages by the Home Secretary despite lying about his asylum case. . . . A judge has ruled that he was 'illegally detained' for nearly five weeks by suspicious immigration authorities."[25] Bralo concludes her discourse analysis by noting, "The exclusion and discrimination are produced by the media through the use of language, contextualization, prominence of voices and agenda setting and reproduced from the primary definers, in our case official/government sources. Immigration discourse cuts deep into the issues of power and is therefore of great importance for dominant ideologues."[26]

Containing Asylum Seekers on Both Sides of the Atlantic

The tragic events of September 11, 2001, have had a tremendous impact around the world and particularly on American society.[27] Regrettably, the government's initial response to the threat of terrorism has been fraught with civil and human rights infractions, particularly in the form of profiling and detentions concealed behind a thick wall of secrecy.[28] The crackdown on undocumented immigrants and foreigners also extends to another vulnerable subset of the immigrant population—namely, asylum seekers. Along with an undifferentiated fear of terrorism, crime, and nonwhite immigrants, there is growing suspicion that under existing asylum proceedings, "People would show up, ask for asylum and then disappear, and of course stay in this country indefinitely."[29] However, experts insist that using asylum seeking as a means of gaining entry to the United States is tremendously risky for terrorists because all asylum applicants are fingerprinted and thoroughly interrogated and face the prospects of months or years in detention.[30]

From the port of entry, asylum seekers are transported to jail, often in handcuffs and usually without any clear understanding of why they were being detained. In detention, once they pass a screening interview, asylum seekers are legally eligible to be paroled if they satisfy the Department of Homeland Security (DHS) parole criteria (i.e., community ties, no risk to the community, and their identity can be established). However, in practice, even asylum seekers who meet those criteria remain in detention.[31] Immigration officials too often ignore or selectively apply the parole criteria, which exist only in guideline form rather than as formal regulations. Compounding matters, when an asylum seeker's parole request is denied by DHS officials, they have no meaningful recourse; they cannot appeal the decision to an independent authority, or even an immigration judge.[32] Since the attacks of September 11, 2001, other strict measures have been established that adversely affect asylum seekers in the United States, including Operation Liberty Shield and the Blanket Detention Order of 2003.

Human rights advocates are appalled by Operation Liberty Shield, a recent program initiated by the DHS on the eve of the war with Iraq. That program requires the detention of asylum seekers from thirty-three countries where al Qaeda has been known to operate. Under Operation Liberty Shield, even asylum seekers who did not raise any suspicions of security or flight risks were slated for detention for the duration of their asylum proceedings (estimated by the DHS to be six months, or significantly longer if the case was appealed). Consequently, many of these detainees would be deprived of a meaningful opportunity to request release through parole.[33] While Operation Liberty Shield was launched as a comprehensive national plan designed to protect citizens, secure infrastructure and, most important, deter terrorist attacks, the initiative was terminated after only one month of operation. It is believed that the government quietly abandoned the program in the face of intense pressure from human rights organizations. Still, arriving asylum seekers from the designated countries and territories continue to be subject to mandatory detention upon their arrival in the United States under the Illegal Immigration Reform and Immigrant Responsibility Act of 1996.[34] Although asylum seekers from those nations are now technically eligible to apply for parole, it is unclear how many will actually be released.[35]

Adding to the government's escalating war on terror, Attorney General John Ashcroft issued a profoundly significant measure on April 17, 2003. Under that directive, illegal immigrants, including asylum seekers, can be held indefinitely without bond if their cases present national security concerns. Ashcroft firmly stated: "Such national security considerations clearly constitute a reasonable foundation for the exercise of my discretion to deny release on bond."[36] Whereas the blanket detention order is framed as being necessary for maintaining national security, the actual case involves a Haitian asylum seeker, David Joseph.[37] The DHS, which now has authority over most immigration matters, sought the opinion from the attorney general after the Board of Immigration Appeals upheld a judge's decision to release Joseph on a $2,500 bond. Ashcroft argued that "national security would be threatened if the release triggered a huge wave of immigrants to attempt to reach U.S. shores. That would overtax the already-strained Coast Guard, Border Patrol, and other agencies that are busy trying to thwart terror attacks."[38] The State Department weighed in on the controversy, claiming that Haiti has become a staging point for non-Haitians who are considered security threats (e.g., Pakistanis and Palestinians) to enter the United States.

Whereas most of the immigration issues have been transferred to the DHS, the measure promises to centralize further the power of the attorney general in the area of asylum seeking. Human rights groups and immigration attorneys swiftly opposed the blanket detention order. Amnesty International denounced Ashcroft's ruling to hold groups of asylum seekers and other noncitizens in detention indefinitely, noting that the provision extends to those who pose no danger to the United States. "To suggest that all Haitian asylum-seekers pose a threat to U.S. national security, as Attorney General Ashcroft has done, strains credulity and makes a mockery of our immigration system," said Amnesty International USA's executive director, William Schulz. "Ordering asylum-seekers to remain locked up simply because of their nationality is tantamount to discrimination and a violation of international standards."[39] Human rights organizations acknowledge the U.S. government's obligation to protect the country against terrorism, and the organization supports legitimate means of doing so. Still, the blanket detention policy violates international standards, which specify that the detention of asylum seekers be limited to exceptional cases under law. Furthermore, governments have the burden of demonstrating the need for detaining of asylum seekers in prompt and fair individualized hearings before a judicial or similar authority.[40]

It is important to note that, on the other side of the Atlantic, most European Union states are now bound by the European Convention on Human Rights. Article 5 of the convention guarantees the right of liberty and the security of the person. However, the convention does permit the detention of individuals to facilitate removal.[41] Until the 1990s, there were no permanent detention centers in Britain, because detention was an exceptional measure. When large groups of people were detained, barracks or similar buildings or camps would usually be commandeered, as happened, for example, during the two world wars. Otherwise, individuals would be held in prisons or, in the case of a group of asylum seekers mostly from Sri Lanka in 1987, on the ferry the *Earl William*.[42]

The detention of persons subject to migration control in the UK was first codified under the 1920 Aliens Act, and then elaborated further under the 1972 Immigration Act. This act empowered immigration officers to detain, among others, persons arriving in the UK while a decision was being made on whether to grant leave to enter; those refused leave to enter or suspected of having been refused leave to enter, pending directions for their removal; illegal entrants and those reasonably suspected of being illegal entrants, pending directions for their removal and actual removal; and those found to be in breach of conditions attached to their leave to enter, including overstaying. Powers to detain are very broad, and there is no automatic or independent scrutiny of the lawfulness, appropriateness, or length of detention.

New detention center rules were introduced in 2001 to covering matters including conditions in the centers and the provision of reasons for detention.[43] Their introduction is significant in that they make statutory provision for rules by which detention centers must be run. However, the operating standards that flesh out the rules have yet to be completed and there are significant differences between centers. People detained under the 1972 act were usually overstayers (people who had entered on a tourist, visitor's, or other visa and remained after the visa had expired), frequently brought to the attention of the immigration authorities through denunciations, traffic accidents, or crimes (whether as victims or perpetrators). Before 1988, asylum seekers averaged approximately five thousand a year and were rarely deported or detained. Those granted the status of refugee tended to come as part of a resettlement program or came from the Soviet Bloc and were readily granted asylum. Occasionally, people would be stopped on entry and detained awaiting removal, but at any one time there would usually be 200–300 people in detention. This situation changed significantly in the 1990s. From 250 people in early 1993, the numbers of people detained increased to just over 2,260 ten years later.[44] More facilities were soon built to house a growing detainee population. In spite of government promises to end the practice, asylum seekers continue to be held in prisons; moreover, nongovernmental organizations (NGOs) report that transfer from a detention center to a prison is sometimes used to punish detainees. All the detention centers (except Haslar and Lindholme) are run by private security firms, such as Group 4 and Wackenhut.

In the UK—unlike in most other European countries, and contrary to the recommendations of the UN Working Group on Arbitrary Detention, which visited the UK in 1998—there is no legal limit to the time a person may be held.[45] The longest known detention was of an Indian national, Karamjit Singh Chahal (six years, two months). He was finally released on November 15, 1997, after the European Court of Human Rights in Strasbourg ruled it would be illegal to deport him. That decision forced the Home Office to introduce the Terrorism Act of 2000.[46] Given the long periods for which people may be detained, among the most pressing concerns of NGOs working with detainees is the issue of bail. In the Immigration and Asylum Act of 1999,[47] the British government promised to introduce the right to automatic bail hearings, vital given the length of time individuals may be detained. The provision was, however, never implemented and was withdrawn in the Nationality, Immigration and Asylum Act of 2002.[48] Detainees now have to request a bail hearing, and many are unaware of this possibility. Furthermore, because people are now often detained upon or shortly after arrival, it is difficult for them to find sureties.

The Home Office argues that only those believed to be likely to abscond are detained, and usually at the end of the process. To underline that claim, detention centers have been renamed removal centers. However, the majority of those held in these removal centers are eventually released, because of conditions in the country of origin prevent their removal, because travel documents for the persons to be removed cannot be issued, because they are allowed to appeal, because they are released on bail (only in the UK), because they are granted leave to remain on compassionate grounds, or because their claim for asylum is eventually allowed. Increasingly, organizations such as Bail for Immigration Detainees, National Coalition for Anti-Deportation Campaigns, and Barbed Wire Britain are reporting an increase in people detained upon arrival, and it seems likely that the goals of this policy, for New Labour as much as for the Conservatives before them, are deterring people from seeking asylum and facilitating removals.

Interpreting Anglo and American Constructionism

The invention and dramatization of so-called bogus asylum seekers as a popular stereotype is much more of a British phenomenon than an American one. As discussed throughout, the perceived threat of asylum seekers in the United States is quietly contained within government agencies and not a publicly shared construction. That divergence is recognized by Cohen, who points to a discursive formula of moral panic; specifically, some panics are transparent and others opaque. Societal reaction to asylum seeking in the UK manifests as a transparent moral panic, since "anyone can see what's happening."[49] Whereas there have been spikes of panic over foreigners (most recently, those perceived as being Arab and Muslim) and undocumented workers (mostly Latino) in the United States since September 11, 2001, the putative problem of asylum seeking does not resonate in the public mind. Privately, however, American government officials have quietly embarked on a detention campaign similar to those in Britain. Although such detention practices existed before September 11, 2001, the war on terror provides American authorities an urgent rationale for greater reliance on that form of control. Specifically, U.S. government officials insist that policies calling for the detention of asylum seekers serve national security interests.[50]

Beyond those developments, it is important to survey other key distinctions between British and American societies that help explain their different constructions of asylum seekers. While the prevailing literature on social control, notably the writings of David Garland,[51] demonstrates that criminal justice systems in the United States and UK are similar in their heavy-handed responses to crime, there remain important cultural distinctions that shape popular and political perceptions of asylum seekers. Among the most obvious cultural features of the United States is its history—and identity—as an immigrant nation, which is the foundation of contemporary liberal movements toward multiculturalism. Although the United States has experienced periods of anti-immigrant sentiment, even as recently as the 1990s, there has yet to be any large-scale public panic directed specifically at asylum seekers.[52] Although the U.S. government continues to draw differences among various immigrant populations (e.g., asylum seekers, refugees, and undocumented workers), in the eyes of Americans they are all lumped together as immigrants, regardless of the circumstances that brought them ashore.

In England, however, historical forces underpinning asylum reveal a unique set of priorities, deeply intertwined in colonial politics. In his work *Frontiers of Identity*, Robin Cohen traces asylum provisions to the period of William the Conqueror, when there was a formal strategy to exert control over newly colonized territories. By extension, immigration and asylum—as well as expulsions and deportations—symbolized and reproduced the power of the monarch. Eventually, the "right to exclude" was legislated in Parliament in reaction to the wave of forced migration amid the French Revolution; in particular, the Aliens Act of 1793 granted the government authority to remove aliens. Conversely, awarding sanctuary served another key political function insofar as it demonstrated the seemingly benevolent side of the British government, displaying a sense of moral superiority over other nations that were reluctant to provide safe haven for those who had fled persecution.[53]

With those historical distinctions in full view, it is also important to address some contemporary features of British culture that remain relatively insignificant in the United States, most notably the role of the tabloid media. Certainly, in the United States, media sensationalism continues to influence popular and political views of crime and other social problems. Though by comparison, the degree to which British tabloid journalism penetrates politics, thereby shaping discourse over the putative threat of asylum seekers, is virtually unmatched by any American news outlet. Some headlines in Britain newspapers read, "Thousands Have Already [Come to the UK] Bringing Terror and Violence to the Streets of Many English Towns,"[54] "Fury as 20,000 Asylum Cheats Beat the System to Stay in Britain; Get Them Out,"[55] and "Kick Out All This Trash."[56] Negative reactions to migrants and asylum seekers have a long history in British political culture. Moreover, "successive British governments have not only led and legitimated public hostility, but spoken with a voice indistinguishable from the tabloid press."[57] In 2002 the Labour government instituted a campaign under the banner of "zero acceptance," including shutting down the Sangatte refugee camp on the French side of the English Channel, intercepting boats transporting illegal migrants, and expediting deportation.[58]

Due to the intersection of tabloid media, politics, and public opinion, the detention of asylum seekers in the UK conforms to a European-wide phenomenon of incarcerating foreigners, or "suitable enemies" who symbolically represent an array of social anxieties.[59] Loic Wacquant aptly summarizes those developments embodied in "Fortress Europe":

> This process is powerfully reinforced and amplified by the media and by politicians of all stripes, eager to surf the xenophobic wave that has been sweeping across Europe since the neoliberal turn of the 1980s. Sincerely or cynically, directly or indirectly, but with ever more banality, they have succeeded in forging an amalgam of immigration, illegality, and criminality.[60]

In Britain, the detention of asylum seekers as a noisy construction—and state ritual—reaffirms legality to the witnessing public, which is hungry for expressive punishments. That penal ceremony has reached a media theater onto whose stage politicians pronounce their claim to clamp down on so-called bogus asylum seekers fraudulently in search of welfare benefits, education, health care, housing, and jobs. In 2003 former cabinet member Stephen Byers set out to reassure working-class voters that Labour understood their concerns over immigration, proposing that all asylum seekers who fail to register with the government be deprived of access to British schools and hospitals. Byers defended his proposal, saying, "It is not racist to address the legitimate worries and concerns that people have about asylum and immigration, but that it would be irresponsible not to do so."[61]

By contrast, the quiet nature characterizing detention of asylum seekers in the United States is contoured along a different set of law enforcement priorities, namely the War on Terror, compounded by the Bush administration's commitment to government secrecy.[62] Months following the investigation of the attacks on the World Trade Center and the Pentagon, Attorney General Ashcroft repeatedly denied access to basic information about many of the people being held in detention, including their names and current location. Such secrecy was denounced by human rights and civil liberties advocates, as well as by news organizations and even some political leaders who have complained that the attorney general failed to explain adequately the need for those drastic measures. Kate Martin, director of the Center for National Security Studies, said: "The rounding up of hundreds of people secretly, secretly arresting them and putting them in jail where their families don't know where they are and not telling the public is unprecedented and extraordinary in this country."[63] Martin added, "This is frighteningly close to the practice of 'disappearing' people in Latin America," where secret detentions were carried out by totalitarian regimes.[64] Similar degrees of secrecy surrounding detention are evident in other spheres of the U.S. War on Terror, including Abu Ghraib (Baghdad), Baghram (Afghanistan), and Guantánamo Bay (Cuba).[65]

Regulating Human Mobility in a Global Context

Whereas this chapter set out to decipher the convergence and divergence of detention practices adversely affecting asylum seekers, there remain a few items worthy of further consideration. First, some contextual discussion is in order that may improve our understanding of asylum seekers as a constructed political problem. Second, it is important to realize that the societal and political reactions to asylum seekers are far from monolithic, since there exist key differences in how government entities shape their responses to perceived threats, and heated exchanges often occur on this issue between (and within) political parties, the courts, and human rights activists. Finally, in light of the numerous tactics deployed by governments, attention must also be turned to the multitude of carceral establishments aimed at controlling people fleeing persecution. At the heart of these developments, to be sure, is the politics of movement, or what Zygmunt Bauman refers to as the "global hierarchy of mobility," in which freedom of movement is a trait of the "dominant," and the "strictest possible constraints" are forced on the "dominated."[66] Indeed, Alessandro De Giorgi[67] makes a similar point that even in the wake of globalization, borders maintain their symbolic and material impact against the circulation of some classifications of people, most notably asylum seekers and underprivileged non-Western workers. "Therefore, what we witness is not so much the disappearance of borders, as their fragmentation and flexibilisation: these no longer operate as unitary and fixed entities; instead, borders are becoming flexible instruments for the reproduction of a hierarchical division between deserving and undeserving populations, wanted and unwanted others."[68]

In the realm of asylum seekers, it is important to realize that the recognition of the status of "refugee" is often based on arbitrary evaluations made by the nations of destination. Official decisions commonly are determined by political and economic contingencies to which humanitarian principles are easily subordinated.[69] Alessandro De Giorgi also reminds us that those frequently are the same governments whose "humanitarian wars" (e.g., Iraq, the Serb-Croat conflict in the former Yugoslavia, the conflicts in Kosovo and Somalia) are at least partly responsible for the humanitarian emergencies from which asylum seekers and refugees try to escape:

> A clear example is offered by the policies adopted by the Italian government with Kosovo refugees. During the Kosovo war, Italy recognised the status of "refugees" to all people coming from that region, offering them "temporary protection." However, as soon as military operations ceased, and the humanitarian emergency exploded, the Italian government changed suddenly its former provisions, turning thousands of refugees into illegal immigrants.[70]

Correspondingly, European countries have been known to impose political and economic pressures on undemocratic governments so as to prevent their victimized populations from fleeing to the West for sanctuary, or to readmit and refoule asylum seekers in transit. A clear example would be the return of thousands of migrants, including potential asylum seekers, by Italy to Libya in and since the summer of 2004; Libya is not a signatory of the 1951 Refugee Convention.[71]

Although there are both clear and nuanced distinctions in how a culture of control manifests in the United States and Europe, particularly in the realm of social constructionism, shared consequences persist, most notably the reliance on detention as a coercive measure of social control. In those nations, there are significant developments worth noting: growing detention populations and longer periods of confinement. Moreover, governments are increasing their efforts to expand detention capacity. Still, even more differences arise in the nature of the carceral systems implemented by governments. In the United States, immigration authorities rely on their own detention facilities, along with a network of private and state jails where asylum seekers commingle with prisoners charged (and convicted) of criminal offenses. Generally, conditions of confinement are punitive, and private facilities in particular lack adequate monitoring that would otherwise hold companies accountable for the abuse and mistreatment of detainees.

Similar detention patterns and complaints occur in Europe (and Australia). Britain has adopted, with its multitiered detention and removal system, a dispersal program comparable to those in Germany and the Netherlands. This program places asylum seekers in local communities scattered throughout the UK. That policy was met initially with considerable controversy insofar as the neighborhoods selected for dispersal were inner-city sections marked by social and economic deprivation. Some communities offer genuine support; however, there also are incidents of racist attacks on asylum seekers. "While tensions in these cities have denoted a considerable amount of racial intolerance, they have centered on perceived threats to material resources in the areas of social deprivation."[72] Still, even among the well-intentioned and seemingly benevolent programs intended to assist asylum seekers, the prevailing governmental response to those fleeing persecution is a combination of containment, punishment, and deterrence—all of which are chief elements of a culture of control driven by perceptions of difference and putative threat.

Conclusion

Despite their divergence on popular perceptions of asylum seekers, American and British governments have adopted similar strategies, namely detention. In the third edition of *Folk Devils and Moral Panics* Cohen predicts that more anonymous, or "nameless," folk devils will emerge. That forecast is especially pertinent to those fleeing persecution whose actual identity and biography are frequently obscured from public consciousness; instead they are commonly labeled as bogus and undeserving. As a result, "social policies once regarded as abnormal—incarcerating hundreds of asylum seekers in detention centers—run as punitive transit camps by private companies for profit—are seen as being normal, rational and conventional."[73]

These developments in the detention of asylum seekers, in both the UK and the United States, have strong implications for an emergent sociology of denial. In *States of Denial: Knowing About Atrocities and Suffering*[74]

Cohen critically examines the role of denial in perpetuating long-term social problems, including human rights violations. More to the point of this analysis, Cohen's framework concentrates on the content of denial manifesting in three forms: literal, interpretive, and implicatory. Literal denial is as blunt as it is blatant (e.g., officials insist that "atrocity did not occur"), serving as a blanket defense against acknowledging undisputed facts. Under interpretive denial, however, facts are not refuted but are given a different spin, thus altering the meaning (e.g., officials argue, "What happened is not what you think it is"). In the third form, implicatory denial, neither the facts nor their conventional meaning are refuted; rather, the psychological, political, or moral consequences are denied, minimized, or muted. By reducing the significance of the harm of human rights violations and other atrocities, officials evade their responsibility to intervene.[75]

At a higher level of abstraction, denial can permeate entire governments, societies, and cultures. Indeed, denial becomes official when it is public, collective, and highly organized. Unlike totalitarian regimes that go to great lengths to rewrite history and block out the present, denial in democratic societies is subtle, often taking the form of spin-doctoring and public agenda setting. But similarly to totalitarian states, democratic nations also build denial into the ideological facade of the state. Denial becomes even more ubiquitous when whole societies slip into collective modes of denial. For citizens, cultural denial becomes a potent defense mechanism against acknowledging human rights abuses within their own nation.[76]

In reading Cohen's *Folk Devils and Moral Panics*, together with *States of Denial*, we are reminded that sociologists investigating social problems ought to confront both polarities of societal reaction. Moral panic, exaggeration, and prejudice represent one extreme, namely overreaction. Still, we must not neglect underreaction at the other end of the spectrum, including apathy, indifference, and denial.[77] The unnecessary detention of asylum seekers in the UK is facilitated by over-reaction in the form of moral panic driven by politicians and tabloid journalists who characterize those fleeing persecution as bogus and threats to the welfare state. That overreaction simultaneously produces underreaction whereby human rights violations against those seeking refuge fail to reach a critical mass. Similarly, in the United States, quiet constructions of asylum seekers as threats to national security also serve to keep their unjust confinement from entering the collective conscience.

Notes

The discussion in this chapter is a revised version of Michael Welch and Liza Schuster, "Detention of Asylum Seekers in the UK and US: Deciphering Noisy and Quiet Constructions," *Punishment and Society: An International Journal of Penology* 7, no. 4 (2005): 397–417.

The authors acknowledge Malcolm Feeley and Jonathan Simon (University of California, Berkeley) and Tim Newburn (London School of Economics) for offering useful comments on a previous draft of this work. Additionally, thanks to Philip Kretsedemas and David Brotherton for their invitation to contribute this chapter.

1. See Welch and Schuster, "Detention of Asylum Seekers in the UK and US"; and Michael Welch and Liza Schuster, "Detention of Asylum Seekers in the US, UK, France, Germany, and Italy: A Critical View of the Globalizing Culture of Control," *Criminal Justice: The International Journal of Policy and Practice* 5, no. 4 (2005): 331–355.

2. Stanley Cohen, *Folk Devils and Moral Panics: The Creation of Mods and Rockers* (London: Routledge, 1972), 9. In this book, Cohen explored the roles of the public, the media, and politicians in producing heightened concern over British youths in the 1960s when the Mods and Rockers were depicted as threats to public peace as well as to the social order. Together, the media and members of the political establishment publicized putative dangers posed by the Mods and Rockers; in turn, such claims were used to justify enhanced police powers and greater investment in the traditional criminal justice apparatus. However, the term "moral panic" was used initially by Jock Young in "The Role of the Police as Amplifiers of Deviancy, Negotiators of Reality and Translators of Fantasy," in Stanley Cohen, ed., *Images of Deviancy* (Harmondsworth: Penguin, 1971). However, Cohen elaborated more fully on the concept in *Folk Devils and Moral Panics*. In its infancy, moral panic theory incorporated an emerging sociology of deviance and an embryonic cultural studies, reflecting the changing social mood of the late 1960s. Young and Cohen both concede, however, that they probably picked up the idea of moral panic from Marshall McLuhan's *Understanding Media: The Extension of Man* (New York: McGraw-Hill, 1964).

3. When *Folk Devils and Moral Panics* was released in its second edition in 1980, Cohen contemplated developments in subcultural theories of delinquency associated with the Birmingham Centre for Contemporary Cultural Studies. In 2002 the book's third edition was published, allowing Cohen to look back on how moral panic as a concept has been used—and misused—by academics and journalists. Chronicling its applications, Cohen reviews key advances in several areas of inquiry, including juvenile delinquency, school violence, bad drugs, pornography,

welfare issues, and asylum seekers. Nevertheless, a greater understanding of moral panic goes beyond recognizing its many territories of expansion; it is also crucial to reveal the depth and complexity of the concept.

4. Stanley Cohen, *Folk Devils and Moral Panics,* xxi.

5. Ibid., xxiii.

6. See Michael Welch, *Detained: Immigration Laws and the Expanding I.N.S. Jail Complex* (Philadelphia: Temple University Press, 2002): and Michael Welch, "Ironies of Social Control and the Criminalization of Immigrants," *Crime, Law and Social Change: An International Journal* 39 (2003): 319–337.

7. Stanley Cohen, *Folk Devils and Moral Panics,* xviii.

8. Ibid., xviii.

9. Asylum seekers have also been met with hostility throughout Europe. See D. Joly, *Refugees in Europe: The Hostile New Agenda* (London: Minorities Rights Group, 1997); and Saskia Sassen, *Guests and Aliens* (New York: New Press, 1999).

10. *Daily Mail,* "Warning Over New Influx of Gypsies," October 23, 1997.

11. *Daily Mail,* "Handouts Galore! Welcome to Soft Touch Britain's Welfare Paradise: Why Life for Them Here Is Just Like a Lottery Win," October 10, 1997.

12. *Daily Mail,* "Script for a Scam: In Letters Back Home Asylum Gypsies Tell Their Friends How to Get into Britain," October 24, 1997.

13. See Vaughan Robinson, *Spreading the "Burden"?* (Cambridge: Polity, 2003); Liza Schuster, *The Use and Abuse of Political Asylum in Britain and Germany* (London: Frank Cass, 2003); Liza Schuster, "Asylum Seekers: Sangatte and the Channel Tunnel," special issue on crisis management, *Parliamentary Affairs* 56, no. 3 (2003).

14. Cohen, *Folk Devils and Moral Panics,* xix.

15. See Oxfam, *Asylum: The Truth Behind the Headlines* (London: Oxfam, 2001); El E. Refaie, "Metaphors We Discriminate By: Naturalized Themes in Austrian Newspaper Articles About Asylum Seekers," *Journal of Sociolinguistics* 5, no. 3 (2001): 352–371.

16. Also see Teun Van Dijk, *Communicating Racism: Ethnic Prejudice in Thought and Talk* (London: Sage, 1987); M. Wetherell and J. Potter, *Mapping the Language of Racism* (London: Harvester Wheatsheaf, 1992).

17. Ron Kaye, "Redefining Refugee: The UK Media Portrayal of Asylum Seekers," in *The New Migration,* ed. Khalid Koser and Helma Lutz, Europe: Social Constructions and Social Realities (London: Macmillan Press, 1998).

18. Zrinka Bralo, "(Un)cool Britannia: Discourse Analysis of Construction of Refugees in the UK Press" (master's thesis, London School of Economics and Political Science, 1998).

19. Stuart Hall, "The Work of Representation," in *Representation: Cultural Representation and Signifying Practices,* ed. Stuart Hall (London: Sage, 1997).

20. See Angel-Ajani, "A Question of Races?" *Punishment and Society: An International Journal of Penology* 5, no. 4 (2003): 433–448; Jock Young, "To These Wet

and Windy Shores: Recent Immigration Policy in the UK," *Punishment and Society* 5, no. 4 (2003): 449–462.

21. *Daily Mail*, "The Flood of Bogus Asylum Seekers into Dover Has Left the Local Council Facing a Potential 10 million [pound] Crisis That Could See Basic Social Services Slashed, It Emerged Yesterday," October 21, 1997, 1.

22. Simon Heffer, "Why Are We a Haven for Evil Foreigners?" *Daily Mail*, December 20, 1997, 1.

23. See also Christopher P. Campbell, *Race, Myth and the News* (London: Sage, 1995): Paul Gilroy, *There Ain't No Black in the Union Jack: The Cultural Politics of the Race and the Nation* (London: Hutchinson, 1987); Paul Gilroy, *Problems in Anti-Racist Strategy* (London: Runnymede Trust, 1997).

24. Jason Burt, "Lying Guerrilla Wins Thousands for a Few Weeks Behind Bars," *Daily Mail*, December 18, 1997, 1, 13.

25. Ibid., 13.

26. Bralo, "(Un)cool Britannia," 24; Hugh Mehan, "The Discourse of the Illegal Immigration Debate: A Case Study in the Politics of Representation," *Discourse and Society* 8 (1997).

27. David Cole and James X. Dempsey, *Terrorism and the Constitution: Sacrificing Civil Liberties in the Name of National Security* (New York: Free Press, 2002); Michael Ratner, "Making Us Less Free: War on Terrorism or War on Liberty?" in *Implicating Empire: Globalization and Resistance in the 21st Century World Order*, ed. S. Aronowitz and H. Gautney (New York: Basic Books, 2003), 31–46.

28. General Accounting Office, *Better Management Oversight and Internal Controls Needed to Ensure Accuracy of Terrorism-Related Statistics* (Washington, D.C.: General Accounting Office, 2003); Human Rights Watch, "Presumption of Guilt: Human Rights Abuses of Post-September 11 Detainees," 14, no. 4 (2002).

29. F. Tulsky, "Asylum Seekers Face Tougher U.S. Laws, Attitudes," *San Jose Mercury News*, December 10, 2000: 1–9.

30. Amnesty International, "Amnesty International Condemns Ashcroft's Ruling to Indefinitely Detain Non-U.S. Citizens, Including Asylum-Seekers," press release, April 28, 2003.

31. *Asylum Protection News*, "Tibetan Nun Detained in Virginia Jail Denied Parole Again," 22 (2004): 1–4.

32. *Asylum Protection News*, "Court TV Film, Inspired by Lawyers Committee Case, Shines a Light on U.S. Detention of Asylum Seekers," 21 (2003): 1–6; Bart Jones, "Asylum Seeker Feels Sting of Post–9/11 Immigration Laws: A 'Culture of No' Casualty," *New York Newsday*, November 3, 2003: 1–4; Lawyers Committee for Human Rights, *In Liberty's Shadow: U.S. Detention of Asylum Seekers in the Era of Homeland Security* (New York: Lawyers Committee for Human Rights, 2004).

33. Lawyers Committee for Human Rights, "Operation Liberty Shield Quietly Terminated: Future of Detained Asylum Seekers Still Unclear," *Asylum Protection News* 15 (May 15, 2003).

34. This expedited removal authority was created by the 104th Congress in amendments to the 1996 Illegal Immigration Reform and Immigrant Responsibility Act (IIRAIRA); Public Law 104-208, div. C., 110 *Stat.* 3009-546, Sept. 30, 1996.

35. Lawyers Committee for Human Rights, "Operation Liberty Shield Quietly Terminated."

36. Curt Anderson, "Ashcroft Rules on Immigrants' Detention," Associated Press, April 4, 2003, 1.

37. *Haitian Refugee Ctr., Inc. v. Baker,* 949 F.2d 1109, 1110 (11th Cir. 1991).

38. Anderson, "Ashcroft Rules on Immigrants Detention."

39. Amnesty International, "Amnesty International Condemns Ashcroft's Ruling."

40. Ibid.; Allen S. Keller, *From Persecution to Prison: The Health Consequences of Detention for Asylum Seekers* (New York: Physicians for Human Rights, 2003).

41. Liza Schuster, "A Comparison of Asylum Policy in Seven European States," special issue, *Journal of Refugee Studies* 13, no. 1 (2000): 118–132.

42. See Robin Cohen, *Frontiers of Identity: The British and the Others* (London: Longman, 1994); United Nations, "Bail for Immigration Detainees," submission to the United Nations, Working Group on Arbitrary Immigration Detention in the United Kingdom, September 2000.

43. In conjunction with the UK *Anti-Terrorism, Crime and Security Act 2001* (c. 24).

44. See Schuster, *Use and Abuse of Political Asylum in Britain and Germany;* and Schuster, "Asylum Seekers: Sangatte and the Channel Tunnel."

45. United Nations, "Bail for Immigration Detainees."

46. UK *Terrorism Act 2000* (c. 11).

47. UK *Immigration and Asylum Act 1999* (c.33).

48. UK *Nationality, Immigration and Asylum Act 2002* (c. 41).

49. Cohen, *Folk Devils and Moral Panics,* viii.

50. See David Cole, *Enemy Aliens: Double Standards and Constitutional Freedoms in the War on Terror* (New York: New Press, 2003); Ratner, "Making Us Less Free."

51. David Garland, *The Culture of Control: Crime and Social Order in Contemporary Society* (Chicago: University of Chicago Press, 2001); David Garland, *Mass Imprisonment: Social Causes and Consequences* (London: Sage, 2002).

52. See Michael Welch, *Detained: Immigration Laws and the Expanding I.N.S. Jail Complex* (Philadelphia: Temple University Press, 2002); and Michael Welch, "Quiet Constructions in the War on Terror: Subjecting Asylum Seekers to Unnecessary Detention," *Social Justice: A Journal of Crime, Conflict and World Order* 31, no. 1–2 (2004) : 113–129.

53. Robin Cohen, *Frontiers of Identity*.

54. *Sunday People*, "Thousands Have Already [Come to the UK] Bringing Terror and Violence to the Streets of Many English Towns," March 4, 2001, 2.

55. *Daily Express*, "Fury as 20,000 Asylum Cheats Beat the System to Stay in Britain; Get Them Out," July 30, 2001, 4.

56. David Mellor, "Kick Out All This Trash," *People*, March 5, 2000, 10.

57. Cohen, *Folk Devils and Moral Panics*, xix.

58. Stephen Castles, "Confronting the Realities of Forced Migration," Refugee Studies Centre, University of Oxford Migration Information Source, May 1, 2004, http://www.migrationinformation.org/USfocus/display.cfm?id=222 (accessed November 6, 2007).

59. Nils Christie, "Suitable Enemy," in *Abolitionism: Toward a Non-Repressive Approach to Crime*, ed. H. Bianchi and R. van Swaaningen (Amsterdam: Free University Press, 1986).

60. Loic Wacquant, "Suitable Enemies, Foreigners and Immigrants in the Prisons of Europe," *Punishment and Society* 1, no. 2 (1999): 219; Loic Wacquant, *Deadly Symbiosis: Race and the Rise of Neoliberal Penality* (Cambridge: Polity, 2004).

61. Patrick Wintour, "Cut Health Care for Illegal Migrants Says Byers," *Guardian*, July 31, 2003, 6; Sarah Lyall, "Where Officer Died, Britons Blame Policy on Asylum Seekers," *New York Times*, January 17, 2003, A12.

62. John W. Dean, *Worse Than Watergate: The Secret Presidency of George W. Bush* (New York: Little, Brown, 2004); Mark Dow, "We Know What INS Is Hiding," *Miami Herald*, November 11, 2003, 1–3.

63. B. Donohue, "Rights Groups Prodding Feds for Information on Detainees," (New Jersey) *Star-Ledger*, October 30, 2001, 1–2.

64. P. J. Williams, "By Any Means Necessary," *The Nation*, November 26, 2001, 11; *Chicago Tribune*, "Concerns Rise of Civil Rights Being Ignored," October 2001, 1–3.

65. Michael Welch, *Scapegoats of September 11th: Hate Crimes and State Crimes in the War on Terror* (New Brunswick, N.J.: Rutgers University Press, 2006).

66. Zygmunt Bauman, *Globalization: The Human Consequences* (Cambridge: Polity Press, 1998), 9; J. Pratt, "Dangerousness and Modern Society," in *Dangerous Offenders: Punishment and Social Order*, ed. M. Brown and J. Pratt (New York: Routledge, 2000), 35–48.

67. Alessandro De Giorgi, *Re-thinking the Political Economy of Punishment: Perspectives on Post-Fordism and Penal Politics* (Aldershot, UK: Ashgate, 2006), 10; Alessandro De Giorgi, "Europe: New Penal State or New Citizenship? (paper presented at the European Society of Criminology Annual Congress, Kraków, Poland, August 31–September 3, 2005).

68. Nicholas P. De Genova, "Migrant 'Illegality' and Deportability in Everyday Life," *Annual Review of Anthropology* 31 (2002): 419–447; De Giorgi, "Europe: New

Penal State or New Citizenship?"; Nathalie Peutz, "Embarking on an Anthropology of Removal," *Current Anthropology* 47, no. 2 (2006): 217–241.

69. Jock Young, "To These Wet and Windy Shores."

70. De Giorgi, *Re-Thinking the Political Economy of Punishment.*

71. See J. Horowitz, "Italy Bangs the Door Shut on Castaways from Africa," *New York Times,* July 22, 2004, A4; *New York Times,* "Hiding the Refugee Problem Offshore," October 20, 2004, A26.

72. M. S. Malloch and E. Stanley, "The Detention of Asylum Seekers in the UK: Representing Risk, Managing the Dangerous," *Punishment and Society* 7 (2005): 61.

73. Stanley Cohen, *Folk Devils and Moral Panics,* xxxiv; Bente Molenaar and Rodney Neufeld, "The Use of Privatized Detention Centers for Asylum Seekers in Australia and the UK," in *Capitalist Punishment: Prison Privatization and Human Rights,* ed. A. Coyle, A. Campbell, and R. Neufeld (London: Zed Books, 2003), 127–139.

74. Stanley Cohen, *States of Denial: Knowing About Atrocities and Suffering* (Cambridge: Polity, 2001).

75. See Conor Gearty, *Principles of Human Rights Adjudication* (Oxford: Oxford University Press, 2004).

76. See Cohen, *States of Denial;* Michael Welch, "Trampling of Human Rights in the War on Terror: Implications to the Sociology of Denial," *Critical Criminology: An International Journal* 12, no. 1 (2003): 1–20; and Michael Welch, *Ironies of Imprisonment* (Thousand Oaks, Calif.: Sage, 2005).

77. Michael Welch, "Moral Panic, Denial, and Human Rights: Scanning the Spectrum from Over-Reaction to Under-Reaction," in *Sociology and Politics of Denial: Crime, Social Control and Human Rights—Essays in Honour of Stanley Cohen,* ed. David Downes, Paul Rock, Christine Chinkin, and Conor Gearty (Cullumpton, Devon, UK: Willan Publishing, 2007).

PART III

From Incarceration to Deportation

CHAPTER 8

Exiling New Yorkers

DAVID C. BROTHERTON

THIS CHAPTER IS DRAWN FROM FIELD NOTES and interview data that I have collected since 2001 regarding the social process by which Dominicans are expelled from the United States and the hidden stories behind their removal, eventual resettlement, and sometimes illegal reentry into the United States. I am currently writing a book with my colleague, Luis Barrios, on the life histories of Dominican deportees in Santo Domingo and New York City, highlighting the narratives of settlement, incorporation, expulsion, and resistance. The names of the subjects have been changed, due to a pledge of confidentiality.

During the recent past, the rate of expulsion of both legal and undocumented Dominicans has reached more than three thousand a year, the majority of whom resided in New York City and its environs. In this chapter I ask the reader to feel the lived experience of being deported, the anguish of the deportee, the absurdity and inhumanity of the courtroom drama, and the vindictiveness of the state and to consider the sociological background of the subject and the logic of immigration-related social control policies.

As has been analyzed in other chapters in this volume, the phenomenon of forced repatriation for noncitizens has grown exponentially since the passing of the Illegal Immigration Reform and Immigrant Responsibility Act of 1996 and the USA PATRIOT Act of 2001. It is the logical result of the three wars on the globalized "other": the war on drugs, the war on terror, and the war on the immigrant. What we need to remember, however, is what Jock Young calls the "bulimic" character of this process.[1] Here is the nation in all its mythical splendor, culturally sucking in the immigrant, socializing him in the factory system of schooling, feeding him the promise of social mobility through the avenue of sport, and then showing him the exit through a celebrated yet cruel performance of so-called due process. The actors and actresses play out similar roles on different stages of the criminal justice system across the United States every single day of the week. Sometimes the immigrant subject is not even given a court to perform in and has to make do with a cost-saving videoconference during which he or she is told of the inevitable by a judge who is hundreds of miles away. This chapter is based on notes taken during a recent deportation hearing for a Dominican-born man who had been living and working legally in Manhattan for twenty-seven years. He and his family lived "just off Bleecker," that fabled thoroughfare of the West Village where tens of thousands of immigrants have staked their claim as "Americans," where the Beats made poetry history, Dizzy Gillespie created a new musical genre, and Bob Dylan changed our notion of folk music forever. I mention this context because the immigrant, despite our attempts to humanize him or her, is often imagined to be in a different place, both spatially and culturally. We often forget how intrinsic the immigrant is to our sense of the everyday and how fragile the notion and experience of "place" is in the contemporary world, when the grid of the city is being mapped by the security state and lived by a vast mosaic of citizens, noncitizens, quasi-citizens, and categories yet to be named.

Because of my knowledge of Dominican deportees, I was called on to be an expert witness at the hearing. I was accompanied by a colleague who intended to interview family members on film for a future documentary. The day's events turned out to be harrowing, however, and in the end we decided against the intrusive use of the camera.

We arrive at Eastern New York Correctional Facility in Ulster County in upstate New York. The fortresslike maximum-security prison built for human disposables around the 1920s is impressive in its colossal, symbolic might, peering over the Catskills like some hungry ogre. Nearby is the facility that houses the immigration court. I enter its doors through a reception area and undergo the usual inspections by its security personnel. As we walk back and forth through the security scanner while our bags, coats, and shoes pass slowly through an X-ray machine, the guard in charge emphatically announces, "No keys, pens, cell phones, or pills. Just papers needed for the court for those who are testifying."

Meanwhile, seven guards lounge on two rows of padded black plastic chairs, hanging around in a relaxed, friendly way, and chatting while observing the events. Perhaps this is the end of their shift or they are await-ing the beginning of it. The guard in charge returns to the business at hand, directing a question at me.

"You're here for the Delgado trial?"

"Yes, and this is my assistant," I respond, motioning to my colleague.

"They only said one of you was coming. We only have a permission slip for one person. We've already had twenty-one of them come in. That's the most we've ever had here for a court appearance. Usually it's three or four, but twenty-one! That's almost more than our entire staff here sometimes," he adds with a wry smile. "Isn't that true, guys?" he says, addressing his fellow workers. "Sometimes we only have seven people here on duty, and there's this family with twenty-one of them!"

"Well, I guess they're all here to support him," I retorted.

The guard glances up, raising his eyebrows, "I suppose so. I suppose that's one way of looking at it. So you're the expert witness, are you? You do a lot of this? I mean, you know a lot about this deportation thing?"

"Yes, I do a lot of it," I reply. "I spent a year in the Dominican Republic seeing how deportees are living. It's very difficult for them, very difficult. There are no jobs, the cops blame them for everything. They don't have a chance."

The guard looks at me straight on, shakes his head, and says, "Crazy, isn't it? I mean, they've already done their bids [this refers to prison sen-tences–author] and then they get this at the end of it. I guess they'll have to come right back over here again, won't they? You know, they'll have to get in any way they can and just hope they don't get caught, 'cuz you know it's another three years in the federal pen if they do."

"Yes," I said, somewhat taken aback at the guard's sympathy and can-dor, "that's what some of them do, but then there's a lot that stay over there and try to make it."

Finally, he finds the permission letters, hands us each a visitor's badge, and escorts us to an office positioned next to two security gates. There, our hands get stamped with a special ink that can be read only by a special machine.

"There'll be another guard here in a minute to escort you," says our man-in-charge. "Here she comes now."

Standing on the far side of two gates is a tall Hispanic female who nods at us then signals to someone in the security office. Suddenly, the first gate on her side is opened electronically, and she enters into a sort of no-man's-land between the two gates. The gate behind her closes abruptly, followed immediately by the gate in front of her opening. After this security ritual is complete, she is standing next to us.

"You got everything?" she inquires.

I nod my head affirmatively, a little bemused at the question.

"Let's go, then." She gestures to a guard to open the gate again. Our escort is affable, and we quickly strike up a conversation as we traverse the grounds.

"How long have you worked here?" I ask.

"Ten years," she answers. "Came from Bedford Hills."

"Yes, I know it. It's the prison for female inmates," I reply. "Did you like it?"

Her pace slows slightly as she turns her head toward me, as if for emphasis.

"The women? Oooh! They're crazy," she answers, elongating the last word.

"Compared to the men—pure crazy."

"And here? How are the inmates here?" I respond.

"Here, they're fine, no problem."

We reach the immigration court via a path between several inmate dormitories. For a prison (or, more specifically, a distribution center for recently adjudicated inmates mainly coming up from Rikers Island), the accommodations look relatively cheery and clean. The surroundings are bucolic, with snow-capped hills providing a beautiful backdrop and the sound of a rushing stream breaking the silence. I am struck by how ironic it all is: the inmates so unfree amid this wintry natural openness.

At the entrance to the immigration court building another guard greets us, inspects our visitors' badges, and checks our names against a list. He then escorts us to a room where those asked to testify must congregate and wait to be called. While waiting, I talk with Mr. Delgado's father, mother, niece, and fourteen-year-old son. The father and mother are clearly agitated, talking almost manically about the need for their son to come home. They talk as if they are trying to wake up from a nightmare.

"He should never have pleaded guilty," he says in a heavily accented Dominican Spanish. "The lawyers said if he pleaded guilty he would only do three years. He never said anything about being deported. He said he might have to do fifteen years if he didn't plead guilty. My son didn't do anything. He's a good boy. He's always lived with his mother and father. How can they do this to us? All he wanted to do was play baseball. When he couldn't play anymore, he started to drink. He started to get depressed. But why does it end up with this? Oh God, oh Maria, we are good religious people, we go to church. He was raised a good boy. Why this?"

The father continues in the same desperate vein, speaking rapidly. He is not willing to accept what is happening or what might be about to take place. The mother starts to pray and calls upon God to help reunite her with her son.

"I am an old woman. I have terrible blood pressure, I cannot take the stress. My heart, my heart can't take it. I love my son. I don't want to see him taken away. He's my baby, my son. I can't stand it, I can't."

The niece then explains the background of the case to me. She recounts how her uncle got into a physical altercation with someone in a bakery when he was drunk, and how the owner of the bakery called the police two days later when her uncle returned to buy something.

"There was no evidence, nothing," the niece intones. "They couldn't produce anything that he stole, nothing. There was no weapon. It was just this guy's word, and my uncle was drunk. My uncle is a good man. He wouldn't hurt anyone. They forced him to do this, to say that he was guilty. You know how they do. We are a vulnerable people. We are Latino immigrants. When the lawyers tell these things to us we believe them. When they say that you'll do fifteen years you believe them. To us, they are the law. We are always afraid, always. That's why he's in this mess. It's crazy. What kind of justice is this?"

Suddenly a guard appears, "A Dr. Brotherton? Is there a Dr. Brotherton here?"

"Yes, that's me," I say, and bid my farewell to the family.

Inside the courtroom, seated along the back and the front side walls, are the rest of Mr. Delgado's family members, including his five sisters, seven-year-old son, nieces, nephews, and brothers-in-law. It is an example of the central importance of family in Dominican life, especially when this microcommunity is under pressure.

The judge beckons. "Dr. Brotherton, please stand here and raise your right hand." "Do you swear to tell the truth and nothing but the truth so help you God?"

"I do, sir."

"Please take a seat," says the judge.

The lawyer for Mr. Delgado looks at me, smiles, and begins his cross-examination. He first asks me to describe who I am and what I do. He then asks a series of questions that revolve around whether or not deportees are likely to be tortured by the Dominican government or whether the police will torture them with the complicity of the government. I do my best to paint a picture that fits this scenario, but I cannot honestly say that torture is something deportees should expect. Rather, I say that in the present climate, in which deportees are being scapegoated, it follows that the police, who are often authoritarian and out of control, will abuse them. It also follows that many deportees will land back in prison after being put in preventive custody. Given the nature of the Dominican prison system—its appalling lack of resources and the normalization of brutality that goes on inside—it is likely that deportees will suffer physical and psychological harm. The judge then counters that this is not the same as torture. Physical abuse and beatings by the police do not meet the criteria, he says. What is torture? It is the government-sanctioned use of extreme pain to extract information from a subject. It is the pulling out of people's fingernails, the attachment of electrodes to men's testicles, and the extraction of teeth without anesthetic. That is torture.

"As I have said time and time again, Mr. Crichter [Mr. Delgado's lawyer], you fail to make the case that deportees will be tortured at the behest of the Dominican government. Rather, you assert repeatedly that, in general, harm will come to these deportees. I have no doubt that the country we are sending them to is a bad place. I have no doubt that the deportees do not wish to go there and that life will be difficult for them. I have no doubt that for some of them it will lead to serious harm. But that, according to the law of the United States, is not the same as torture. If I were to allow such evidence, if I were to agree with you that that is torture, this appeal will simply be turned down at the next level, which is the Board of Appeals in Washington. They have done this to me already. I had a gentleman here who was going to be sent back to Barbados with full-blown AIDS. The man desperately needed his daily cocktails. His lawyer argued that if he were sent back there would be no chance that he would continue to be treated and therefore be kept alive. I agreed with him and I ruled that in such a case we would be sending this man to his death. The Board of Appeals disagreed with me and sent him to what I am almost certain was his death. That, Mr. Crichter, is the law of this land."

The judge's words unintentionally expose and explain the depth of cruelty and injustice that characterize these policies. Here was a judge condemning the U.S. legal system's lack of morality and rationality simply by recounting the evolution of a case he had just tried. I'm not sure how this is received by all who sit there, but for me it is absolutely clear that poor Mr.

Delgado will assuredly be spending much of the next twenty years in a country he hardly knows.

"If you wish to stay here and watch the rest of the proceedings, Dr. Brotherton, then please do so," the judge says.

"Thank you, your honor. I would very much like to observe the rest of the hearing," I answer and take my seat in the middle of the courtroom.

"Who is your next witness, Mr. Crichter?" booms the judge.

"I want to call Hector Delgado, the father of my client, judge," said the lawyer.

The next hour and a half proved to be the most dramatic demonstration I have ever witnessed of the barbarity of laws conceived by humans to control, condemn, and abuse other humans in a so-called democratic society. The seventy-five-year-old father enters the room escorted by a guard. He stands in the witness box next to the judge, who asks him if he speaks English.

"No, señor," he answers, whereupon the translator, a dark-skinned, middle-aged Latina seated in front of me to my right, begins to translate word for word, exclamation by exclamation, the statements of the next two experts in this hearing.

The lawyer for the defense asks Mr. Delgado how many times he has returned to the Dominican Republic during the last ten years. Mr. Delgado answers that he used to go regularly while his parents were alive. His father lived to be 95 and his mother 104, he proudly states. But when they died in the late 1990s, he would go less, and then when his son got locked up in 2003 he hardly went at all. The lawyer then asks him what he thought his son would be facing in the Dominican Republic. Mr. Delgado answers, "Nothing but crime and delinquency . . . nothing but hardship, problems, injustice."

"Do you think your son will be tortured when he goes back?" asks the lawyer. The father stands there and wonders for a while, grappling with the knowledge that only by saying yes could he get his son to stay in this country. Finally, he says, "Yes. He will face torture."

"How do you know, Mr. Delgado?" asks the lawyer.

"Because that is the kind of place my country is. It is a place where the police kill people for nothing, absolutely nothing. They don't care about anybody, especially the deportees."

"Have you seen the police kill anybody?" asks the lawyer.

"Yes, I have," answers the father.

"Can you tell us about it?"

"In the neighborhood where I used to live in Santiago, I saw a jeep full of police come up and pull out their rifles and go boom, boom to some guy. He fell dead. I couldn't believe it. I said to a neighbor, 'What are they doing?' 'The police have just shot a guy,' the neighbor said. I didn't want to stay there. I moved away immediately."

The father then makes a gesture with his hands as if he is pushing away the words he has just uttered, as if brushing away a memory.

"So you actually saw the police kill someone?" says the judge.

"Yes, I did. I saw them kill this man and then bundle him into the back of a jeep and drive off. That's what the police do in my country. That's why I am so afraid to let my son, my only son, go back there. I want him to stay here, judge. Oh God, oh Maria, I want him to stay here with his family. Please, please, give him clemency. We are all known in our neighborhood. We have been here for thirty years. America has been good to us. We love America. We had nothing when we came here. My son drinks and gets depressed. The police, the police, they find him and bring him home. They say, "Mr. Delgado, look after your son. We found him drunk again. He's got to take care of himself."

At this point Mr. Delgado starts to shake visibly. The people around the room are now wailing. The sisters, the brothers-in-law, the seven-year-old son, and the defendant: nobody is immune to the rising tension that has been created by the questions and by the desperation in the father's creaking voice. The guard picks up a box of tissues and hands them out. The judge then turns to the defense lawyer.

"Mr. Crichter, was all this necessary? Did you have to put this father through this? I am a man probably the same age or even older than Mr. Delgado, and I have a son like Roberto. I feel for this man, but he is unable to answer your questions in the way you would like. He has not been able to state factually that his son will face torture by the government when he returns, and that is the crux of this case. So why do you put your witness through this? Why are you putting this family through this? Your job is to present a case to me, Mr. Crichter. You cannot help it if you don't have a case, and I am afraid you don't have a case. We have been here now for four hours. Normally, this hearing would last one hour. But with all the family members here who have traveled so far from New York to see their brother, their uncle, their son, and to support him, I have decided that this trial has to play itself out. There is no other way. But, I must tell you that I find it disagreeable and unnecessary to put people through such emotional turmoil and pain like this."

"I'm sorry, judge," says the lawyer. "I am just trying to show the court the probability of what faces my client. I have to work with what I have. I am just doing my job to the best of my ability."

"Do you have any questions, counsel?" the judge asks the lawyer representing the government.

"No, judge," comes the reply.

"Mr. Delgado, please take a seat," instructs the judge in a pleasant but firm manner.

The father walks somewhat bewilderedly back to the center of the room and sits down a couple of seats to my left. I look at him and smile, but he fails to respond. His face expresses a mixture of disbelief, frustration, and anxiety. How can this be happening to him at this stage in his life? He has gone through countless hardships to raise his six children. He left the country of his birth in 1972, seven years after the Revolution and in the middle of the bloody Balaguer dictatorship, with his entire family. All of his children were born in the Dominican Republic. He has managed so far to keep his family together. Everyone was doing so well with the exception recently of his son. He still lives in the same house that he moved into when he first came to the United States. How could he prepare himself for this moment when the very country that he has believed in all these years, that gave him an opportunity to be somebody, to live decently, to experience joy and happiness—how can this country do this to him, to his son? It just does not make sense.

"Who do you want to call now?" the judge asks of Mr. Delgado's lawyer.

"I want to call the mother of Roberto Delgado," the lawyer replies.

"Are we going to see the same thing, Mr. Crichter? Are you going to put her through this, too? Does she know what torture is? Have you schooled her? Have you?" asks the judge.

"Yes, I think so," says the lawyer diffidently.

The mother is brought into the courtroom by the guard. She looks very tense. On entering the witness box, she goes through the ritual with the Bible and sits down. The defense lawyer begins questioning her.

"Do you follow what is going on in the Dominican Republic, Mrs. Delgado?"

"Yes, I try to," she says.

"How do you do this?" asks the lawyer.

"Through listening to the news, through friends," Mrs. Delgado replies.

"What do you think faces your son if he is deported to the Dominican Republic?" asks the lawyer.

"Delinquency, nothing but delinquency. Nothing good can come of this. I know he will face terrible things, I know this. My country will harm him, I know this."

"Do you think your son will be tortured if he is returned?" asks the lawyer.

The mother just sits after the question is translated. She looks apoplectically at the audience. God knows what is going through her mind. The question is too pointed, too agonizing, to be answered.

"Do you understand the questions?" asks the judge.

Again, the mother just looks at the audience and pats her chest. She then begins to talk, as if channeling something from another universe.

"Yes, I believe something terrible will happen to him. I believe the police will hurt him. I can't bear to think about it. I don't want to talk about it. I don't want to think about this evil. Can I say something? May I say something?" the mother asks the judge.

"Yes, you may," replies the judge, looking down at his feet as if to communicate, "Here we go again."

The mother then gets to her feet and raises her hands in the air as if praying in a Pentecostal church.

"Oh God, oh Jesus, oh Maria, I pray to you, release my son from this trial. Oh Judge, please forgive my son. Please have the power, the pity, to allow my son to go free. Allow him to come back to his mother and father, that's all we ask. He's a good boy. He doesn't mean ill to anyone. What use is this to take him away from us and his children? Please, please I beg you. . . ."

The mother continues for several more minutes beseeching the judge to release her son. The family members are again sobbing uncontrollably. Even one of the guards, a bulky African American man, is beginning to break down; tears start to run slowly down his cheeks. The mother suddenly stops, turns away from the judge, looking glassy-eyed, collapses into the chair, and closes her eyes. There is now pandemonium in the courtroom, the mother has fainted, and the judge orders one of the guards to call a nurse. After about three minutes, the mother comes around and is holding her chest and breathing heavily. One of her daughters runs over and holds her head, stroking her hair gently and whispering softly that "everything's all right," which is about the farthest thing from the truth right now.

At this point, a nurse comes into the room with a guard, and between them they get the mother to her feet and take her outside and place her in a chair. They are joined outside by someone who has a stethoscope around his neck, presumably a doctor. The mother does not return to the room, and we find out later that she has been taken to the hospital, where she is diagnosed with having suffered a mild heart attack. The judge, looking exhausted and exasperated, turns to the defense lawyer.

"Now what, Mr. Crichter? Now who are we going to have? Please don't let's go through this again. It is not helping your case. It is not helping Mr. Delgado." But his words are misdirected. It is not the lawyer who does not have a case, or the family. In a humane society, it is the U.S. government that is on the wrong side of the ethical, rational divide, and everyone in the courtroom knows it. I would wager that even the guards would agree that this inflexible policy leading to mass social exclusion and family fragmentation, targeting mainly black and Latino communities, is senseless. There are no winners, only losers, and it is costing the U.S. taxpayer hundreds of millions of dollars in wasted resources.

"I would like to call Jessina X . . . , the niece of Robert Delgado," answers the lawyer, somewhat chastened by the flood of undermining comments from the judge and, of course, by the inability of most of his witnesses to speak to the subject of torture, which has been so ill-defined and difficult to conceptualize.

The niece enters, led by a guard, and confidently strides to the witness box. I had spoken with her earlier, and she had told me that she had recently graduated from John Jay College of Criminal Justice. Though she was better informed than I was about the history of the case for which her uncle was sentenced, she had very little knowledge of the Dominican Republic except from time spent there on the occasional holiday. Neither did she know the finer details of the Illegal Immigration Reform and Immigrant Responsibility Act of 1996 or the 2001 USA PATRIOT Act, all of which were playing a role in her uncle's expulsion. After she takes the oath and sits down, the questions begin once more.

"Do you understand what is facing your uncle, Roberto Delgado?" asks the defense lawyer.

"Yes, I do. I have read about cases like his on the Internet, and I have tried to do some research around the subject."

"So you know that the only way we can halt your uncle's deportation is through proving the probability of torture when he arrives there?"

"Yes," says the niece, "I understand that this is his only chance."

"So, what do you understand by *torture?*"

"Well, for me, it is the application of extreme forms of pain and punishment to someone in an attempt to get information and just to terrorize someone. This punishment can be physical—it can come from beatings, but also from the denial of food to someone. It can also be psychological and emotional." The niece makes an impressive statement and surprises me at how cool, calm, and collected she can be under the circumstances.

"Thank you," says the lawyer. "So, do you think that this form of torture will be facing your uncle when he goes back to his homeland? If so, why do you think this will happen?" asks the lawyer, who is now regaining some of his composure.

"Well, let me see," says the niece. "I can't say for certain that this will happen to him, but I do know how Dominican society feels towards deportees, and I do know how violent and brutal the police are. I can tell you that Dominicans think of deportees as less than human. They are nothing to them and are blamed for everything that goes wrong in the country. And if they are thinking this, then you can imagine what the police are thinking. The police simply treat them like dirt. They beat them, kill them, torture them. They do whatever they like to them."

"How do you know this?" asks the defense lawyer.

"Because when I've been back there for holidays, when I've been staying in the capital, I hear what people say about them, and I have had dealings with the police just driving around," answers the niece.

"Now hold on here," says the judge. "None of this means anything. This has nothing at all to do with the conditions of torture that need to apply in this case. For a start, your definition of torture is all wrong. As I've said before, it is about pulling fingernails, taking out teeth, attaching electrodes to testicles. . . . That's torture. Not all this talk about being denied food and psychological punishment, that's not what we're talking about under this law. And as for giving testimony on the probability of torture, you've proceeded to talk about how bad the police are and how nasty the people can be toward deportees, but that's irrelevant, absolutely irrelevant. You have to be specific, factual. Mr. Crichter, once again I must ask you, have you prepared your witness?"

"Yes, judge, as much as I could. I am just trying to show that . . ."

"I know what you are trying to show, Mr. Crichter, and I am trying to keep this trial focused and it is proving impossible." The judge then turns back to Ms. X.

"Ms. X, do you understand what I am saying?"

"Yes, judge. I understand what you are saying, but do you understand what I am saying? I think I understand what torture is, and maybe it doesn't satisfy the needs of this court, and maybe I have it all wrong, but I don't think so. It is this court that has it all wrong. If you want to know what torture is, this is torture. What you are doing to my uncle is torture. Look at it here! Look at what the laws are doing! It is tearing up our family. It is tearing my uncle away from his children, his mother, his father, and his loved ones. What justice is there in this? I have done my research. I have studied criminal justice, and I don't see any here today. There is torture, yes, and it is here. This is torture, but there is no justice."

"Thank you, Ms. X," says the judge. "I understand your feelings. You may step down. Who do we have next, Mr. Crichter?"

"I would like to call the son of Roberto Delgado, Roberto Junior."

Led by a guard, the new witness enters somewhat hesitantly with his head bowed. He is a handsome boy with long, thick black hair. He stares at his father, who looks back at him with great intensity and tears in his eyes. The judge is kindly toward him and gently asks him to take a seat after he is sworn in. The judge turns to the lawyers.

"Mr. Crichter, I am allowing this witness, but only for very few, specific, and direct questions. Do you understand? I want no repeats of what has gone on before."

"Yes, judge," says the lawyer, "I understand."

"Mr. Delgado, do you understand what might happen to your father?"

"Yes," says the boy, "he's going to be deported."

"And do you understand what is meant by torture?"

The boy looks at the lawyer and slowly looks down at his feet. After a while, he shakes his head. The judge says, "You have to say something, Roberto. You cannot just nod for the court." The boy returns the judge's gaze.

"No," says the boy, "I don't understand."

The lawyer now looks down at his own feet and shakes his head.

"Okay," says the lawyer. "Okay, that's enough. You may step down, Roberto. Please step down."

The boy looks up and turns to the judge. The judge says gently, "It's okay, just take a seat."

The boy goes to the middle of the room and sits behind his father. He cups his head in his hands and begins to sob, silently, his shoulders and upper body moving up and down rhythmically, but there is no sound. As I look around, I see his little brother staring at him with tears running down his cheeks and his eyes swollen and red. It is heartbreaking for me, as I think of my own children and how they would be reacting if I were to be taken from them. The process is simply insane, insane.

"Now, we have had all the witnesses. Is that right, Mr. Crichter?" says the judge.

"Yes, that's correct, judge," the lawyer answers.

"I have allowed this court all the time it takes to come to some kind of judgment. Up till now I see nothing that alters the opinion of the court that Mr. Delgado will be deported. He will be returned to his homeland after completing his sentence, which I believe has five months more to run. Now, Mr. Delgado, before I fill out the forms confirming your deportation, do you have anything more to say?"

"Yes, judge, I do."

Mr. Delgado stands up and looks around the room. He has tears in his eyes, and his face is swollen from the strain and the crying.

"I want to tell you and my family that I am no thief. I've never taken anything from anyone in my life, not even a pair of nail clippers. What happened to me was wrong. It was a miscarriage of justice. I agreed to a plea for something I didn't do. I thought I was gonna get a short sentence and then be released. I thought if I didn't do that I was gonna get fifteen years. That's what they threatened me with. No one told me I was gonna get this. Okay, I have a temper and I can get violent. It happens when I drink, and I'd been drinking when all this happened. I don't remember much about it, except the guy gets the better of me and I go home. That's about it. But I didn't steal nothing from nobody. All I wanted to be was a baseball player, that's all. I got a scholarship to some university, but it didn't work out. I didn't get picked up, and so I got depressed. I get very depressed and I start to drink. I know I need treatment for this, but I don't need jail and I don't need to be torn away from everything I love. This is my life here. I've been here since I was a kid. This is all I know. Here's my family right here. I don't have no family where you wanna send me. What am I gonna do there? Where am I gonna live? How am I gonna see my children again? Where's the justice in all of this?"

"Why, Mr. Delgado, didn't you become a citizen like your sisters? Why?" asks the judge.

"Because I can't read or write, judge. I knew if I took the test I wouldn't be able to write down all those names of the states. I wouldn't be able to write down the answers to all those questions that they were gonna ask me, that's why. I got a scholarship to a college when I was a kid—somewhere in Oklahoma—to play baseball, but they never taught me to read or write. It's as simple as that."

The words that come out of Mr. Delgado's mouth are astounding in this theater of humiliation. I was thinking how much courage it took for him to make this statement. The bitter truth of his situation reveals itself in the suffering he experienced long ago, not just in the last few years. The marginality of his race and class, the cynical mass packaging of the American Dream, the shattered hopes of his parents' generation, the children left fatherless, resentful, and traumatized; these are all the truths embedded in his final plea. Only this time, there was no bargaining. The decision was nonnegotiable. Mr. Delgado did not even bother to ask for an appeal. At this moment he was a broken man. The unassailable logic of the immigration laws won the day. They had gotten their man. He was ejected, seemingly with due process in the American way, through the court system. Of course, objectively, the odds were massively against him from the beginning, but the appearance was maintained, and as the judge had remarked, this trial played itself out.

As we exit the prison, I turn to the translator who had performed so magnificently throughout, never wavering in her concentration.

"Do you do a lot of these hearings?" I ask her.

"Yes, all the time. I've been doing them for years," she answers.

"It was quite a day, wasn't it?" I follow up, rather inanely. "I bet these kinds of scenes are quite unusual aren't they? I mean, the intensity of it."

She looks at me, a bit puzzled, and then, in a quiet, matter-of-fact manner, she replies:

"No, they are quite common. I work under these conditions very frequently. It is a very emotional job. I try to keep calm and professional, to be of maximum service."

On the drive back to New York City, my colleague excitedly and vividly recounts the day's extraordinary events. After a while, he focuses on a single, seemingly undeniable conclusion: "What kills me about this country is its self-representation, how it continually tells the world that it's the freest, the most democratic place on earth and yet its practice is totally the reverse. What's the difference between what this country is doing and what the Soviet Union was doing? Tell me, what's the difference?"

Conclusion: A Comment on Theory

These field notes reveal much about the invasive properties of the security state in the current epoch, as well as the lived culture and practices of repressive immigration policies. While these "data" shed a much-needed humanistic light on processes of immigrant incorporation and removal, which are often obscured by legal discourse, they also raise some important issues regarding the state of contemporary immigration theory and its departure from one of sociology's founding concepts: social control.

In the early days when the discourse of immigration was dominated by the discipline of sociology, social control was a favored paradigm for analyzing processes of settlement for immigrants and what was believed to be their eventual assimilation into American society. Robert Park's four stages of ordered segmentation regarding the immigrant incorporation process are well known.[2] This process, according to the Chicago school pioneers, was supposed to be universal and voluntaristic and spoke to the degree to which society could "regulate itself according to desired principles and values."[3] Of course, there were many other approaches to social control,[4] and one could argue that the process of regulation was not at all so benign and that the state and its agents worked from a premise of coercion rather than consensus. Thus, in subsequent years Park's paradigm was subject to withering critiques as sociologists responded to the civil rights and national self-determination movements of the 1960s, and the ideological/epistemological blinders worn by so many white, middle-class social scientists were finally discarded.

In this fast-moving discursive terrain, however, instead of the various interpretations of social control being used to explore the rapidly growing studies on immigration, they have largely been ignored with the exception of the notion of assimilation, which is now conceived as three ideal-typical models. Portes and Zhou describe it as follows:

> [The first] replicates the time honored portrayal of growing acculturation and parallel integration into the white middle-class; a second leads straight in the opposite direction to permanent poverty and assimilation into the underclass; still a third associates rapid economic advancement with deliberate preservation of the immigrant community's values and tight solidarity.[5]

The problem with removing theories of social control and only rehabilitating part of the original paradigm is that processes of social exclusion, pathways into deviance, the varying roles of the state, the vicissitudes of socialization and social stratification under the impact of globalization, and the cultural meaning of citizenship become analytically separated, often appearing as foci in increasingly specialized peer-reviewed journals. Even in recent discussions around transnationalism,[6] the role of the state is insufficiently considered, there is little serious engagement with the relevant social control literature in criminology, no real analysis occurs of the disciplinary effects on immigrants courtesy of the Department of Homeland Security, and there has yet to be a fuller and more critical exploration of what Michael Smith calls "place-making" in this highly contradictory and culturally complex field.[7] In fact, it is rare to see deportation mentioned in any reputable immigration anthology, despite the extraordinary increase in human "removals."[8]

Consequently, there is a great deal to learn from Roberto's journey as he haplessly tries to understand the irrationality of society's rules. As the Chicago-schoolists saw it, the more society turns to coercive mechanisms for social control, the greater the failure of the project. This sociological insight needs to be borne in mind not only by the policymakers but by the students of our current immigration "crisis." Old theories need to be extended, not simply discarded, and social science needs more than ever to respond to a question often uttered—perhaps naively—in the heyday of 1960s sociology: Which side are you on?

Notes

1. Jock Young, *The Exclusive Society: Social Exclusion, Crime and Difference in Late Modernity* (London: Sage, 1999).

2. In his model, Park assumes that immigrant integration is a unidirectional process that is generally the same for all groups, leading from competition to conflict to accommodation and, finally, assimilation within the mainstream. Robert Park, s.v. "Assimilation, Social," in *Encyclopedia of the Social Sciences,* ed. Edwin Seligman and Alvin Johnson (New York: Macmillan, 1930), 281.

3. Morris Janowitz, "Sociological Theory and Social Control," *American Journal of Sociology* 81 (1975): 82–108.

4. Dario Melossi, "Theories of Social Control and the State between American and European Shores," in *Blackwell Companion to Criminology,* ed. Colin Sumner, 32–48 (London: Blackwell, 2004).

5. Alejandro Portes and Min Zhou, "The New Second Generation: Segmented Assimilation and Its Variants," *Annals of the American Academy of Political and Social Science* 530 (1993): 82.

6. Linda Basch, Nina Glick-Schiller, and Cristina Blanc-Szanton, *Nations Unbound: Postcolonial Predicaments and the Deterritorialized Nation State* (New York: Gordon and Breach, 1994); Michael Smith, *Transnational Urbanism: Locating Globalization* (Oxford: Blackwell, 2001); Robert Smith, *Mexican New York: Transnational Worlds of New Immigrants* (Berkeley: University of California Press, 2005).

7. Michael Smith, *Transnational Urbanism.*

8. There are a few exceptions, such as the following edited volumes: Michael P. Smith and Luis Guarnizo, eds., *Transnationalism from Below* (New Brunswick, N.J.: Transaction, 1998); Mary C. Waters, Ueda Reed, Helen B. Marrow, Richard Alba, and Roger Waldinger, *The New Americans: A Guide to Immigration Since 1965* (Cambridge, Mass.: Harvard University Press, 2007).

CHAPTER 9

Invisible Removal, Endless Detention, Limited Relief
A Taste of Immigration Court Representation for Detained Noncitizens

ABIRA ASHFAQ

WITH LIMITED OPPORTUNITIES to remain in the United States or be released on bond, noncitizens in removal or deportation proceedings in U.S. immigration courts are compelled to take removal orders. Within a structure of restricted legal relief, judges too are willing to stamp these orders. Not all noncitizens being deported are "illegal"—many are green card holders or lawful permanent residents (LPRs). Many have entered on valid visas, but those who have entered illegally may have lived in the United States for years and put down roots here. Many of the non-LPRs are arrested and detained for removal proceedings for violating their visa conditions or for being out of status. LPRs are usually arrested and placed in removal proceedings because of criminal convictions. If their crime is not defined as an aggravated felony, they may be able to apply for a form of relief called cancellation of removal, but with the Antiterrorism and Effective Death Penalty Act of 1996 (AEDPA) broadening the boundaries of what constitutes an aggravated felony, this relief is not available to most.

LPRs with aggravated felonies, as well as others, end up requesting relief under the U.N. Convention Against Torture, arguing that they would be tortured in their home country. Often this is a futile endeavor, since the grant rate in immigration court is low. Noncitizens not qualifying for relief in immigration court may still be eligible for release on bond and voluntary departure from the United States. In many cases, however, judges are not willing to exercise discretion and release them, considering them flight risks. Judges ruling within the xenophobic post–9/11 culture are particularly disinclined to release Muslim detainees so they may leave on their own within a prescribed period. Profiling based on religion and national origin, the FBI arrests and interrogates them.

Limited relief coupled with detention makes removal proceedings all the more insufferable. Being disallowed release and voluntary departure means a person is not allowed the courtesy of being able to take care of his or her belongings and any unsettled business. And winning a case in detention can be tricky. Simple acts such as accessing your lawyer, gathering evidence on equities in the United States (e.g., family ties, employment history, and other criteria that are used to establish the moral character of the noncitizen) or on country conditions, convincing and preparing your family and friends to testify in court, and contacting your country's consulate to secure travel documents all become very difficult. The following accounts, taken from my experiences as an immigration court attorney, illustrate how all these dynamics play out in the immigration court system.

A Glimpse of the San Francisco Immigration Court

Before the judge enters the courtroom, I have had a chance to look through four Notices to Appear and talk to an equal number of respondents. A man from Belize and two Mexicans tell me they want to take an order of removal, which would result in their deportation. It is the first hearing for each of them. They know they have the right to find a lawyer and contest the charges against them, but they think it is futile. One Mexican is charged as an illegal reentrant, which is an aggravated felony, and the other is an EWI, or someone who entered the United States without inspection. He has lived in the United States since 2002. Although I have explained to them their right to bond, as well as other forms of relief, I nod in assent after hearing their decisions. Frankly, their choices are wise. They will be put on a bus and be in Mexico within twenty-four hours. There is virtually no way they can stay in the United States lawfully. The judge conducts their removal hearings concurrently—advising them in unison about what they may give up by being deported. They listen attentively and respectfully, their hands touching as their handcuffs and chains clink softly.

The boy from Belize bothers me. His face is young, his features chiseled. He looks a young twenty. He has been awake and in transit since 3 a.m. to make it to court for his 9 a.m. hearing. He has fathered two children with a woman who is a U.S. citizen. I explain to him that he could adjust status if he were to marry her, but not without overcoming the legal obstacle of proving that he has a bona fide marriage. However, he, unlike the Mexicans, has relief available to him, because he is not an EWI. He came on a tourist visa in 2001 and overstayed, but is adamant about taking the order. His calm exterior belies the anger I sense in him. He wants the whole process abbreviated, to achieve closure quickly. He shakes his head when I mention the mother of his children. It is apparent they have a terrible relationship.

Three others take continuances. One is a Punjabi man from India who announces he does not speak English. I offer Urdu and he manages. I suspect he manages English as well. The "snakehead" (the person who secured him a fake visa) had died, and he needs more time to plan a strategy to continue to stay in the United States. We ask for a continuance, and the judge gives him a week. He is disheveled, his hair a premature gray. Leaning his head back, he sleeps through the rest of the hearing. A man from El Salvador has been an EWI since 2000. He entered as a child. He never applied for Temporary Protected Status (TPS) during the registration period and is now applying for asylum before the immigration judge.

TPS is granted to nationals of designated countries who cannot return home because of a political or environmental crisis in their home countries. Certain eligibility criteria apply, including registering during a certain period and a physical presence in the United States during the designated period. Most crimes render one ineligible. Burundi, Honduras, Liberia, and Sierra Leone are some of the designated countries.[1]

The Salvadoran requests a bond redetermination hearing. Immigration and Customs Enforcement (ICE), an arm of the Department of Homeland Security (DHS) has set bond at a high $20,000. The judge eventually settles for $7,500 after questioning my client about where he will live and work, and whether he has any arrests or convictions. The judge states that it is his policy to set bond at least in that amount for EWIs without convictions who have some, but not significant, relief available to them. The government's attorney, neutral and amused by the respondent's creatively fake ID, is willing to go as low as $1,500.

The judge asks the DHS guard how soon a certain very anxious young man will be deported. When the guard says "twenty-four hours," the judge looks over at the man, who nods eagerly. "I come back day-after," the youth whispers to me later in an unsolicited confession, flashing a gold tooth. I advise him that that would be a punishable felony. He retreats unsmilingly.

In a remarkable and distinct difference from my immigration courtroom experiences in Boston, San Francisco judges and DHS attorneys are uniformly courteous. The judge today, an avowed conservative, is respectful to respondents and diligently emphasizes rights instead of demeaning them with slurs about accent, race, or criminality. It is not that the two judges who handle detained cases are both people of color that makes them sensitive to the plight of noncitizens of color. San Francisco immigration courts maintain a culture of cordiality, taking a kinder, gentler approach to removal proceedings than I had been accustomed to. The court works with the American Bar Association to arrange a pro bono lawyer for every master calendar hearing. I hear a judge compliment a Bosnian respondent on his English. Another explains to a respondent maternally that he must not be fooled by the three-month-long continuance until his next hearing and should start looking for a lawyer instantly. Attorneys are not regularly chided, even if they fumble with the law or seem unknowledgeable about new Board of Immigration Appeals case law. Occasionally, one might get an impatient grunt.

Assembly-Line Removals

But it is this humaneness of the San Francisco Immigration Court that makes the inhumane nature of the deportation process all the more vivid. In assembly-line fashion, Mexicans are removed in daily master calendar hearings. Many of them have lived and worked as cooks, cleaners, guards, and construction workers in the United States for over five years. Many are leaving behind children in the care of their mothers and female relatives. They are ineligible for legal entry for years, and entering illegally following an order of removal is a punishable offense.[2]

In essence, the laws have created a class of children who must grow up without a father, of fathers who have lost all rights to live with their U.S.-born children on U.S. soil, and of women raising and rearing the young without the financial and emotional support of fathers; and if the fathers do show up, life has the stress and fear of their impending capture by the immigration authorities. A gritty, uncertain future awaits many of these young ones. Certainly, any child who has a parent who has been forever criminalized and deemed ineligible to live with them lawfully in the United States would be affected. But their future is not within the jurisdiction of this court that is entrusted to enforce the immigration laws enacted by Congress.

I see the children sometimes with the nondetained respondents. They remind me of when I was young and dragged by my own parents to a government office for official business. I do not recall whether the exchanges I have witnessed were pleasant or grim, or how precarious their future, or how close they were to losing a house. But I do recall that the children seemed happily oblivious, and I am glad for the general wholesomeness I detect in all the nondetained families that show up at court.

A high percentage of nondetained respondents seek and find attorneys, and their removal hearings carry an air of promise. Even with the limited relief available to most in removal proceedings, the lawyers make earnest, nonfrivolous cases for their clients.

One of the judges who presides over detained-persons calendars becomes impatient with my zealous advisement of detainees, which ends up delaying the removal proceedings (hearings for up to fifteen respondents that are usually crammed into a three-hour morning session). He asks me if I have many nondetained clients. "These guys want to get out of here as soon as possible," he says, swishing his arm over his head. "Over at Kearny Street it's a very different mentality. They'll make cases go on and on and on."[3]

Laws enacted since 1990 have gradually chipped away at the rights and relief available to people in removal proceedings. In 1996 Congress toughened laws covering deportation of legal immigrants with criminal convictions. The Antiterrorism and Effective Death Penalty Act of 1996 (AEDPA)[4] broadened the definition of aggravated felony to include many additional crimes and eliminated 212(c) waivers, which had allowed some respondents charged with an aggravated felony to stay in the United States based on their residence and equities in the United States. The Illegal Immigration Reform and Immigrant Responsibility Act of 1996 (IIRAIRA)[5] further created new grounds of inadmissibility. It did create a new waiver similar to 212(c), known as the seven-year cancellation of removal, for those who had held green cards for five years and had lawfully resided in the United States for at least seven; this waiver was not available to those charged as aggravated felons.[6]

IIRAIRA also mandated detention for most people convicted of crimes, thus limiting the discretion individual judges can exercise in considering humane and mitigating factors in a case that would justify the release of even the most sympathetic individuals. The situation has also become fairly desperate for detainees as many minor crimes became redefined as aggravated felonies. In addition, aggravated felons became ineligible for release on bond and for most forms of relief like cancellation of removal, voluntary departure, asylum, adjustment of status through a U.S. spouse (for a green card holder), and withholding of removal following conviction of a particularly serious crime. As previously mentioned, respondents are often forced to appeal to the United Nations Convention Against Torture in making their case, because this is the only form of relief from deportation available in immigration court.

The USA PATRIOT Act further enhanced the detention powers of the attorney general's office by allowing the detention of persons for seven days before they are charged, if there are reasonable grounds to believe that a person has engaged in terrorist activities or sought to overthrow the U.S. government. Under the REAL ID Act of 2005, an applicant must also prove that he or she meets the criteria of eligibility for relief from deportation and merits a favorable exercise of discretion. REAL ID also toughened evidentiary standards in asylum and withholding of removal cases, and it limited habeas corpus review for orders of removal in federal district courts.

Voluntary Departure as Relief

Requesting that one be allowed to leave voluntarily is often the only reprieve in immigration court, and today's aggressive enforcement practices mean that many people will find themselves unwittingly in removal proceedings, or in detention, without even that option.

I represented a family of five in such a fix. The unlucky father/husband of the family was apprehended when he applied for a second extension of his tourist visa. (A single six-month extension of stay is allowed under certain circumstances.) Instead of receiving a denial in the mail, he had DHS agents knocking on his door, and in an experience that the whole family found to be traumatic he was whisked away and put in the local jail in San Jose. His family was asked to show up in court. A respected businessman in his native Rawalpindi, Pakistan, his entire world went topsy-turvy.

He glanced at me with deep shame in his eyes. The jail uniform had stripped him of his identity, his honor. He thought he was doing the right thing by asking for an official extension. He said they needed it because the earthquake that ravaged Northern Pakistan in October of 2005 had hit their house. It was not a convincing story, but he needed all the sympathy he could muster. A motion to reopen was ruled out because there were no new facts since his first hearing. He and his family had no immediate relatives to sponsor them to stay, and they were not eligible for cancellation waivers, which would prevent their deportation, or for asylum. He was, however, eligible for release on bond and voluntary departure, since he had no arrests. But intimidated at his first hearing and wanting to please the judge, he acquiesced to an instant order of removal rather than asserting the rights read to him. And instead of availing himself of his right to have a bond hearing, be released, and depart the United States as a free man, he was incarcerated for an extra two months, until ICE finally removed him from the United States by putting him on an airplane. His wife and children left in the second week of their 120-day voluntary departure grant.

A respondent's request for voluntary departure is meaningless unless he or she can also secure release on bond and use the order to depart, without the assistance of DHS, within the time allotted to him or her, which is usually between 60 and 120 days.[7] Ironically, some judges consider eligibility for voluntary departure such a weak form of relief that they will not grant release on bond, considering all respondents a flight risk, even those who have never been convicted of a crime.[8] (Indeed, the Executive Office for Immigration Review does not consider voluntary departure a form of relief when compiling their statistics.)

An issue as well is the arbitrary nature of immigration proceedings. Mehmood and Shahid, two Pakistanis, were both arrested for immigration violations in early 2003 in a DHS raid on an apartment in North Dartmouth, Massachusetts. In February they both had their hearings, before different judges and with significantly different results.

Mehmood, a thin, bearded man in his fifties, appeared before a judge via videoconference. He was seated in a nondescript room in the Bristol County Jail—about fifty miles away from the judge. His voice and movements were transmitted with a delay. I sat in the courtroom with my back facing the video screen, aware that all he could see of me was the back of my head, and that I could not consult with him in private if the need arose.

Mehmood had no criminal convictions. He had overstayed his visa and was eligible for voluntary departure and release on bond. The judge was willing to grant both, but she asked the government attorney his position. The attorney said he opposed release and voluntary departure. She asked him for a reason. He had none. On examination, he asked Mehmood if he was a terrorist. "No, sir." Mehmood responded with a lilt that was a bit too servile. "Have you ever supported a terrorist group?" Mehmood said no, this time his tone even more grating to my ears. The judge was getting impatient by this time with this baseless line of questioning. The DHS attorney relented. The judge then issued an order for his release on his own recognizance and gave him about two months to leave the country, setting a voluntary departure bond at $2,000. Mehmood was released the next day, and with a slice of reclaimed dignity he prepared for departure.

Shahid had no such luck. He appeared before a different judge, again in front of a video screen at the same jail. Like Mehmood, Shahid had no criminal convictions and was simply present in the country without authorization. Unlike Mehmood, he was clean shaven, heavyset, and youthful, perhaps in his thirties. He requested the same relief—voluntary departure and release on bond.

A relatively new trial attorney sat back fumbling through the overload of detention files he had carted into the courtroom. "Where did you work?" the judge asked Shahid, taking over the cross-examination.

"Gas station," replied Shahid.

"What did you do at the gas station?"

"I pumped gas. Sometimes I checked oil if customers asked me to." Shahid responded with a tremor of earnestness.

"Checked oil, eh?" Shahid nodded a sincere yes, thinking in that moment that he had a chance, hoping that his courteousness to his gas station customers meant something in the bizarre scheme of immigration enforcement. The judge deliberated for a second, rocking in his seat. He then reached over his desk with catlike stealth, glared into the video monitor, and said, "Bond denied. You are a flight risk." He swiftly averted his eyes from the screen—unwilling, perhaps unable, to see the man's despair—stamped and signed his order, and read it out in his auctioneering style. Shahid spent the next two months sitting in jail, waiting to be deported. The judge granted voluntary departure, but because Shahid was detained and could not arrange for his departure, it converted to an order of deportation. An order of deportation in one's immigration record has much worse consequences than an order of voluntary departure (for example, it generally prohibits one from legally reentering the United States for ten years).

Feeling the pressures of a post–9/11 courtroom, some judges are more than willing to take the harshness of the laws one step further and not give someone like Shahid the benefit of the doubt, thus radically altering his immediate future. Technically, the rules of evidence do not apply in immigration court; but it is shocking how little the DHS trial attorneys adhere to these guidelines. Without any evidence whatsoever except for Mehmood's religion (Islam) and country of origin (Pakistan), the DHS attorney at his hearing asked if he had supported terrorism. Beneath that one question is a culture of racism, where being a Muslim is synonymous with something sinister and a person's country is a clue about his criminality. Incidentally, this DHS attorney, a seasoned and soft-spoken man in his fifties, eloquently made a case for racial profiling at a talk he gave at Boston College in 2003. I do not think it figured remotely in his consciousness and perception of the world what that meant within a human rights framework. I observed another DHS attorney carelessly suggest to an immigration judge that there was an FBI probe of an Algerian man and that he could not disclose its nature, hoping any allusion he made about an FBI investigation on a Muslim respondent would be enough for the judge to refuse release on bond. Moreover, when such assumptions and attitudes toward Muslims and other noncitizens are codified into law, the bureaucrats, judges, jail guards, and trial attorneys feel even more emboldened in their profiling.

He's Not a Terrorist, but Detain Him Anyway

The FBI's scrambling for terrorists often yields visa violators. I met Alim, a Muslim from Tanzania, on a stormy January day at the Bristol County Jail. He had had a bond hearing before I met him and had been denied release by the judge. I later examined his immigration court file, and scrawled across a page were the words "flight risk." Alim was a journalist in his native country and was on a brief stint with a convenience store. He had no criminal arrests or convictions and had entered the United States on a valid visa. His only violation was briefly overstaying this visa. His other mistake was breaking up with a woman who had attacked him several times, once in front of a Boston police officer outside a Cambridge courthouse, and a second time with a cup of scalding coffee at his workplace. She then called the Immigration and Naturalization Service (INS; now DHS), saying that he was wanted by the FBI.

The FBI took the call seriously. They showed up at his workplace, and having nothing on him, they used his visa overstay to arrest him. They sent him to the Bristol County Jail, where FBI agents interviewed him three times. Finding nothing on him, they walked away like bored lions leaving immigration hyenas to deal with him. Alim told me that the FBI agents had flipped through his passport and found a stamp for a transitory stop in Oman. This merited the FBI's three visits to the Bristol County Jail. When I conducted an informal survey among Muslim clients, mostly visa violators, I was alarmed by how many were visited by the FBI in jail. One client pointedly touched his long beard as we discussed his experience.

I filed a motion for a new bond hearing for Alim, based on "changed circumstances." Once a respondent has had a decision made on a bond hearing, he is only eligible for a new bond hearing if circumstances have evolved since that time, like a conviction being cancelled on appeal or the birth of a new baby. Although I knew there was not much of a chance with this judge, and Alim's circumstances had not changed substantially, there was not much hope for Alim anyway. I collected police reports and charging documents for the cases involving his ex-girlfriend, prepared his roommates for testimony, and put these before the judge the moment I arrived at the respondents' table. The courtroom was brimming with lawyers and respondents. It was a particularly busy master calendar with hearings for detained and nondetained respondents. An urgent whisper of consultation permeated the air, despite the clerk's plea for silence. The judge glanced at my motion as if I had placed a vegetarian treat before a hungry carnivore. Refusing to look at it, he yelled that hearings for release (bond) and hearings on the main case (merits) are different. Merits and bond hearing *are* different, but not in any material way. Bond hearings are off the record, whereas merits hearings are on the record. But the same judge conducts them, and in the same time slot, and there is no particular order or form besides the clicking shut of a tape recorder and the flipping open of a different manila folder.

Alim peered at us from the video screen, only half following the exchange. We had discussed that ultimately we would ask for voluntary departure, and we did. When I raised the bond question again, the judge fired back that he had no jurisdiction, since he had rendered a final order on the merits case by granting voluntary departure. I was appalled. Either he was being tricky procedurally or was anxious about making it through the rest of the cases. Without a bond grant, the voluntary departure order was practically meaningless. He could have easily gone off the record, ruled on the request for a new bond hearing, and returned to the issue of voluntary departure. Even if his ruling was a rejection of the motion, perhaps I would have been satisfied if our motion had been reviewed.

We continued the fight. Jurisdiction for release and bond shifts to the immigration district director after a final decision by the Executive Office of Immigration Review. I returned to my office and photocopied and re-packaged the motion and submitted it to the district director of the INS. They receive a million letters a day. I did not think it would be read. Two weeks later at a local meeting between immigration attorneys and immigration officials, I spoke to the assistant district director about Alim. With a professional politeness, nodding as he offered his listening face, he said I could call him about Alim's case.

I rushed out of my swearing-in ceremony at the U.S. District court the next day, where—in an ironic parallel to my universe—the pro bono coordinator made a pitch to ninety-four starry-eyed attorneys who were also being sworn in, that they must assist prisoners and noncitizen detainees who are filing their own requests for release through habeas corpus petitions. I called the assistant district director from the basement of this grandiose courthouse and asked him about Alim's case. He said he could not release Alim. He did not want to be the one taking the risk. Our conversation was over well before the thirty-five cents ran out on me.

Convention Against Torture Relief: Impossible to Prove

Often for someone charged with an aggravated felony, there is no relief except applying for deferral of removal under Article 3 of the United Nations Convention against Torture (CAT). Under the Convention (signed by the United States in 1998) a person may not be returned to a country where he or she may be tortured. In immigration court, this entails proving that government officials would intentionally inflict physical or mental pain on a person to obtain information or a confession from him, or to punish him.[9] CAT grant rates have remained low; 2 percent in 2005. Out of 33,640 requests, only 458 were granted by immigration judges in 2005.[10] Overall, 82,993 applications for relief were made in 2005, reflecting the high number of CAT applications in court.

After having two CAT cases denied—for one respondent from Liberia and the other from Vietnam—I finally had a CAT victory in the San Francisco Immigration Court. Rustom was in the mental health unit of a California jail when I first met him. He was a resourceful person and had contacted several agencies for assistance, including immigration nonprofits, Friends Outside (a group that assists detainees with personal business), and members of the local Muslim community. The Muslim community, frustrated by Rustom's incessant substance abuse, incurable homelessness, and inability to turn his life around, suggested forcefully that he return to Pakistan, where he would be united with his extended family. Rustom, charged with an aggravated felony (he sold a small amount of crack cocaine), was subject to mandatory detention and ineligible for most forms of relief. However, he was adamant. He needed to stay in the United States, his home for over twenty-five years, where several miles away (in Seattle), his two sons resided with their mother. He had not seen them or even a picture of them in years, but the distance seemed finite; moreover, he was on disability and took antipsychotic drugs that he believed were unavailable in his home country. A removal order as an aggravated felon would render him ineligible to return for twenty years.[11]

Rustom spent eight months in jail before his final individual hearing. Over this period, I became well acquainted with Rustom's colorful personality. After several sessions, he seemed to understand that he was ineligible for release on bond, the meaning of the term *aggravated felony* within the immigration context, and the difference between immigration and criminal proceedings. But he would still protest that he was eligible for release, since he had met his drug rehabilitation program requirements. He would repeatedly mention his excellent relationship with the California Drug court judge who had placed him in a diversion program for addicts where he received counseling, education, and testing. He had forced a business card in my hand of, in his words, a "beautiful" drug rehabilitation officer and insisted I call her. The conviction, however, was irreversible. In his lucid moments, when he grasped that immigration courts are a distinct entity from the criminal justice system, he would plead that the immigration judge would be sympathetic to his plight and release him.

Rustom was a deeply spiritual man. In his convoluted, nonlinear ramblings, he would express his deep fondness for religion. Although a Muslim by birth, he was a Sufi who had embraced Christianity, frequented Hindu temples, eaten at *langars* (free meals) in Sikh Gurudwaras, and gleefully become a Jehovah's Witness. He pontificated on Islamic mysticism endlessly. With the help of a psychological expert and a country conditions expert, we won CAT relief for him. Rustom appeared tense through the hearing. His psychologist had told me he has an overwhelming need to please authority figures. We rehearsed his testimony for the court several times, although I knew we would be playing much of it by ear. Not wanting to hear from the respondent, the judge called the trial attorney and me to his office for a conference. The trial attorney had only glanced through the four-inch-thick pile of reports on country conditions and mental illness evidence we had submitted in support of the case. The judge shrugged, addressing the trial attorney: "Do you really want him to go back to *Pakistan?*" he said, emphasizing the media manufacturing of the state as a hotbed for fundamentalism. Pakistan, a multifaceted country with traditions of religious tolerance and Sufi Islam, has many contradictions and also prosecutes apostasy and blasphemy. Human rights reports contain numerous stories of people imprisoned for defaming the prophet Muhammad, of violent mobs turning against lower-class Christian sweepers who have allegedly shown disrespect to a religious symbol. Prison conditions are deplorable, and many people have been tortured in custody. Thus, government acquiescence, instigation, and consent were present as per CAT regulations.[12]

Rustom was released a couple of months later as DHS fulfilled formalities, supposedly seeking a third country to which he could be removed or for conditions in Pakistan to change magically. He was released on an order of supervision, however, and required to report to DHS officials every month.

My Liberian and Vietnamese cases were strong, too—the Vietnamese had spent nine years in a reeducation camp, witnessing executions of fellow inmates, being subjected to grueling physical labor (breaking rocks) and beatings, and living on a diet of starchy roots. But past torture is merely a factor in the judge's decision when assessing whether a person is more likely than not to be tortured in the future.[13] Notwithstanding this fact, I had reason to believe that the judge had made up his mind before he examined our CAT evidence. He found my client's domestic violence conviction particularly distasteful, and my detained client, who shifted uneasily and modified his answers based on the judge's body language, particularly despicable. The judge had gone out of his way in a case earlier that day to hurry and grant asylum based on the applicant's suffering of domestic violence. The grantee's son was turning twenty-one and would lose his eligibility for a green card based on her grant of asylum in the United States. However, his paternalistic benevolence to one victim came out as excessive prosecutorial harshness to another kind of victim.

Under the REAL ID Act of 2005, a judge can deny an asylum request, withholding of removal (which prevents deportation), or a CAT case based simply on a respondent's demeanor, candor, responsiveness, consistencies, and accuracies. It thus legitimates a judge's bias or cultural misinterpretation of a respondent's testimony—a respondent who may also sink his case because of language barriers and courtroom pressures.

Similarly, the Liberian's case was viable. He was a young man in his twenties charged with an aggravated felony for a drug crime committed when he was seventeen. His father had naturalized before his eighteenth birthday, and he had lived in the United States as a permanent resident since he was ten. Had the Child Citizenship Act of 2000 come a few years earlier, he would have qualified as a United States citizen by derivation.[14] (The previous law required both parents to have been naturalized.) Given Liberia's volatile and violent political climate, we made the case that American deportees were treated with suspicion. We presented volumes of country conditions reports and an expert witness who had been a missionary in Liberia in the 1980s. Retired, he visited Liberia periodically and testified to the dangers my client would face even at the airport, where someone without any family and resources could be apprehended and taken to one of President Charles Taylor's dungeons.

Luckily, both the Liberian and the Vietnamese respondent were released several months after losing their cases, as DHS/ICE was unable to procure travel documents for them to be sent back.

While CAT remains an untenable form of relief, it is often a respondent's last or only resort. An unrepresented Thai woman who came to the United States as a refugee clutched her CAT application, ready to present it to the judge. When I advised her to at least attach the latest U.S. State Department Report to her application, she appeared to lack any knowledge of the rigorous evidentiary standard and the burden of proof she would be facing. The situation of Haitian asylum seekers provides another example of the increasingly rigorous standards applied to noncitizens seeking CAT relief. Before 2002, almost every Haitian charged with an aggravated felony would apply for or consider CAT relief, based on the fact that most Haitian deportees were sent to prison in Port-au-Prince, where they languished in overcrowded and disease-ridden jail cells, being fed only at the whim of prison guards. Then, in 2002, the Board of Immigration Appeals issued a decision, *Matter of J-E-*, in which it noted that indefinite detention of criminal deportees by Haitian authorities in substandard prisons was not torture, since there was no government intention to inflict pain or suffering.[15] With the REAL ID act of 2005, Congress eliminated habeas corpus jurisdiction for review of CAT claims in U.S. district courts, thereby further limiting CAT relief.

A pretty Vietnamese woman I met briefly was issued an order of removal (i.e., deportation) at her first hearing before the immigration judge. She was convicted of a drug-trafficking offense for which she served three years in prison. Having lived almost all her life in the United States with her family, she did not want to be exiled to Vietnam. However, because of her conviction, she was ineligible for all forms of relief from deportation. I told her CAT was her only option if she really wanted to try to fight her case, but it is very hard to prove. She shook her head with the wisdom of a prison survivor. The judge promptly granted her wish. She asked how soon she could expect to be back in Vietnam, and he responded, "You know what? I don't think you will be sent back, as Vietnam is still not issuing travel documents." This is bittersweet news. She may not be deported to Vietnam, a country she is unfamiliar with, but she could stay in jail for six months or much more, until DHS/ICE was convinced they would not be able to procure travel documents for her return.

Cancellation of Removal: The Lucky Few

Since September 11, 2001, many more Muslims have joined the ranks of ICE's detained populations. Still, a majority of the detainees are black and Latino. Most of them are detained for illegal reentry, criminal convictions for which they have completed their sentences, and immigration violations. Indeed, Mexico, El Salvador, Honduras, Brazil, and Guatemala accounted for about 66 percent of the court cases completed in 2005.[16] Haitians accounted for about 2.29 percent. These statistics have remained more or less the same over the last five years. Pakistan, India, and Iran have regularly been among the top twenty-five countries.[17]

Because most crimes meet the definition of an aggravated felony, it is the rare case that one finds a detainee eligible for this relief. A ten-year cancellation of removal is available to noncitizens without their green cards, but it is very hard to make a case for it. One must show good moral character, residence in the United States for ten years, and that the respondent's removal will result in exceptional and extremely unusual hardship to an LPR or U.S.-citizen child, parent, or spouse.[18] Most crimes render one ineligible. In a 2002 case, the Board of Immigration Appeals found that even though the removal of a noncitizen was going to result in the respondent's separation from his two young U.S.-citizen children, the "exceptional and extremely unusual hardship" standard still did not apply.[19]

Generally, though, in my experience, judges are fair and grant seven-year cancellations to the few who are eligible. Winning your case with a cancellation of removal is very different from winning on CAT. Equities are easy to stack up. Even homeless clients who have no work histories and who have lost all contact with families have won their cases. I had one client whose entire showing of equities was based on the testimony of his sole witness—his social worker—who attested to his good moral character and his struggle to turn his life around.

Being in jail, though, can be fiercely debilitating for an applicant seeking cancellation of his or her removal proceedings. A Haitian client who spent seven years, on and off, in immigration custody, beginning in 1992, had very little to show as equity, his life having been so ravaged by the incarceration. When his lawyer vacated his conviction in 1993, he was released and proceedings against him were terminated. Then came the 1996 laws and a previous offense (indecent assault/sexual abuse of a minor) was redefined as an aggravated felony although he had received only probation for the crime. He was back in immigration custody, and this time ineligible for cancellation of removal. It was not until the Supreme Court's decision in *INS v. St. Cyr* hat he was able to retroactively apply for 212(c) relief.[20] He placed in evidence all the rehabilitation programs he took and retook in jail—even though the violence of his experience in jail had permeated his existence—and he finally won a hard victory.

In March 2003 I represented another Haitian man, Michel, who lived in Cambridge, Massachusetts. He was eligible for cancellation of removal because his conviction for assault (which held a sentence of less than one year) was not categorized as an aggravated felony. If released on bond, he would be able to prepare for his cancellation trial in a more dignified manner, returning to court in suit and tie instead of appearing on a video screen in an orange jumpsuit or escorted in by guards, his hands and feet in chains. It is easier for a judge to deny relief to a person who is in jail and on the verge of being deported than to a person who is not being detained. Moreover, since cancellation decisions are based on a person proving that the good in his or her life outweighs the bad, looking like a prisoner is hardly a great starting point to having things tip in your favor.

Michel had been in federal immigration custody since January 2002, and in state custody for about a year and a half before that. During this time, he was shuttled between jails in Massachusetts, Georgia, and South

Carolina. Despite being bond eligible, he never once was granted a bond redetermination hearing. This right was lost somehow, overlooked in the web of bureaucracy and the perpetual shuttling up and down the coast. Although under the law a respondent must *ask* for a bond hearing, the court could prompt the respondent to request it and not compromise court rules. In vivid contrast, in another courtroom across the hallway, a homeless, mentally ill Jamaican man who was without family and also unrepresented was being informed by a judge about his right to a bond hearing, and asked if he wanted one. He said yes and she conducted it and issued an order for his release on his own recognizance. At his next hearing two weeks later, the judge was incensed to find that the government had taken no steps to release him.

I spoke to Michel through a soundproof tinted-glass screen and by telephone at Bristol. He had allegedly misbehaved and was in the "hole" for it. He had lost his privileges. Despite his imminent court date, I was not allowed to meet with him in an attorney-client meeting room, face-to-face, paper-to-paper, and with pens readily exchangeable for signatures. I could barely see him or even hear him over the clamor of a court-administered program that was being conducted in the background. County inmates were lecturing boys ages seven to fifteen on the ills of drug use. A guard hovered several inches too close for my comfort as he passed documents between Michel and me. But we managed, after four hours of trying to hear one another and decipher each other's expressions.

At his bond hearing, the judge insisted we skip the direct examination. The DHS attorney then grilled Michel for forty-five minutes about his arrests and convictions. When I asked for a redirect after his cross-examination (by the prosecuting attorney), the judge said I had only five minutes. Making the best of my five minutes, I asked Michel to talk about the circumstances of his arrests by the Boston police. The judge interrupted me saying he did not want to hear it. I gave up and moved on to rehabilitation, a perfectly legitimate area for direct examination given that the matter was whether Michel was fit for release, a flight risk, and/or a danger to the community. I asked him to talk about the programs he had attended while in jail. Even more irate this time, the judge pulled forward in utter disgust saying he did not want to hear it. "How is this relevant? This is a bond hearing not a cancellation hearing. We are concerned with his dangerousness only." He alternated his voice, loud and soft, to create an effect and instill just the right amount of terror. He went on to deny release on bond.

Michel was dragged away by the guards to the back elevator. Ten minutes later, I returned to the courtroom to collect a forgotten file and I found the judge and the government attorney who looked like a human version of Bluto from the Popeye cartoons engaged in an intimate discussion, probably about how they would tackle the next set of cases. They were unfazed by my appearance, unconcerned with any notion of bookish ethics.

I had told Michel during my clumsy meeting with him that he did not sound remorseful enough. He said he knew that. He said he knew the judge wanted him to accept responsibility, express remorse, say he was guilty, sorry and ashamed, look straight and sit upright, and grovel for release. This is the story they want to hear and nothing else. As soon as a respondent starts to explain how he was framed, what the extenuating circumstances were, or about the guy who got away, judges interrupt them and say they do not want to relitigate a conviction. Criminal convictions trigger deportation proceedings for noncitizens, and immigration judges cannot readjudicate the conviction. Most immigration and defense lawyers are fully aware that defendants often take guilty pleas for myriad reasons other than guilt. Still, they shudder at the thought of a respondent appearing before an immigration judge and claiming innocence on a certain conviction. Judges hold close to their hearts that conviction is fact and that guilt or innocence must not be redetermined. Regardless, judges delve into the nature and circumstances of the crime in their decision to grant cancellation of removal, and in a very important way, they do end up relitigating the alleged crime. But allowing the respondent to narrate the nature and circumstances of his arrest and conviction in a way other than embracing guilt and accepting responsibility is anathema to them.

The unfair workings of the criminal justice system and its routinization of defendants taking guilty pleas has perverse consequences in the immigration detention system—and no one seems to be challenging any of this. Law review articles abound on the prevalence of wrongful guilty pleas in the U.S. criminal justice system, but it is not a point one can raise in immigration court or even at professional conferences. The fact of the injustice of racial profiling and the criminalization of youth of color has gained acceptance in public consciousness, but it would not be accepted in a cancellation of removal hearing, since the law is perceived to be applied fairly and equally.

Bassam, a Palestinian refugee from Syria, showed up at my office at Boston College. It took me a few seconds to recognize him. For two years I had seen him only in the orange or blue jail uniform, and here he was wearing jeans, T-shirt, and a black leather jacket. Bassam spent *twenty-four* months in immigration custody, at three different jails. He was finally released at midnight on a deserted street near the Coast Guard buildings on the Boston piers. He had no money besides a check for $300 that he could not cash until the next day. He walked into a bar looking for an Arab friend who worked there. The friend was not on duty at the time, but as luck would have it that day, Bassam saw another friend at a second bar, also a former detainee, who agreed to put him up.

Bassam's last six hours before freedom were marked by painful restraint. Shackled in the back of a van along with six other men—"Dominicans," he told me—as they traveled between New England cities picking up and dropping off detainee cargo, he had the feeling that he was being taken to another jail rather than being processed for release. Earlier that day, Bassam said that Miguel, who works for the INS at the prison, came to get him. Bassam thought he was being transferred to a different unit in the immigration detention system. He did not want to go, because he had friends in his detention cell unit. "Well, you really prefer detention over the street?" Miguel asked jokingly. Miguel, who was usually just as authoritarian as the other jailers, was, I imagine, glowing in that moment of absolute power when a man tells another he is to be set free, teasing him casually about the possibility of continued incarceration. Bassam probably said "wow" in response. He said "wow" about fourteen times as we sipped coffee at the college cafeteria, intensely aware of his four-day-old freedom. Frankly, Bassam had often annoyed me during our prison visits because he would ask me the same question ten times hoping I would give him a different answer; wishing that, with every passing minute, I had somehow gained insight into the government's plans for him. And the nausea I contain whenever I am visiting a jail would suddenly threaten to spill out in the form of a tantrum.

Bassam had been ordered deported by an immigration judge in the spring of 2001 and was waiting for travel documents from the Syrian consulate, but these documents had never arrived. Generally, a detainee cannot be deported without these documents. I called the Syrian consulate a dozen times to follow up, but the people I needed to speak with were never available.

The consulate took the position that because Bassam was born of Palestinian refugee parents in Syria he did not qualify for Syrian travel documents. If only they had put in writing that they would not issue him travel documents, Bassam could have been released earlier. At my wit's end, I had asked an immigration officer what I could do to facilitate the process of securing the necessary papers. He told me to try the Palestinian Authority if Syria was being uncooperative. But his response was really just a delay tactic, a way to reject yet another custody review. This would allow the immigration officer to say that they had requested travel documents from the Palestinian Authority and needed at least three months to hear back from them, further delaying Bassam's case. I mentioned this to Bassam. We agreed never to bring up Palestine again. Luckily, the officer I had spoken with had not made any notation about this in the computer, as far as I can tell.

Many detainees think that the INS cannot hold you for more than six months, according to the Supreme Court decision *Zadvydas v. Davis*.[21] They are wrong on the law, right on wishful thinking. It is true that the *Zadvydas* decision held that some immigrants have constitutional rights and that a statute that permits the indefinite detention of people raises serious constitutional questions. However, the ruling did not set a specific time limit. In grappling with what is a reasonable period of detention, the Supreme Court ruled that after the six-month period, once an "alien" provides evidence that his or her embassy is unwilling to issue travel documents, the government must furnish evidence sufficient to rebut that showing. The government could use this to indefinitely detain a person, and they do, citing that the detainee has not demonstrated that his removal is not likely, and at the same time citing numbers of successful deportations to a certain country.

In Bassam's case, after the reasonable period of six months was over at the end of 2001, the government denied his release, stating that they had successfully deported many Syrians in the past and that Syria was taking people back. The written decisions denying Bassam release after his last two custody reviews did not offer so much as a single statement about why Syria was not taking *him* back. Bassam did not have a record of violence. His crime was having written a few bad checks. He was not a flight risk. If released on U.S. soil, he would be on an order of supervision. This meant he would report to the INS every month or so, and if he failed to show up even once, the government could revoke his order of supervision and rear-rest him, putting him back at the Bristol County Jail. Even by their hawk-ish reasoning, there seemed no legitimate reason to continue to detain him this long.

As we drank coffee together, Bassam told me that when he went to the bank to cash his $300 check, they would not do it because he had no pic-ture ID. He showed them his order of supervision, explaining that the INS gave it to him, but they still refused. He spoke to a manager, who Bassam told me was Pakistani. The manager cashed his check, shook hands with him, and said, "Al-ham-do lillah. Our people are in trouble. Best of luck."

Taking Risks for Change

The immigration service uses euphemisms such as "detention" and "de-tention center," but we should be calling it what it is: imprisonment and jail. And so we will not say Bassam spent two years in detention; we will say he was imprisoned at three different county jails in Massachusetts and Rhode Island. Michel was similarly shuttled from a jail in Massachusetts to a jail in Georgia. Shahid spent his last two months in the United States as a prisoner at Bristol—and jail has none of the extra privileges implied by the word *detention*. You get jail food. You wear jail clothes. You cannot take a walk when you want to. You may be locked down in a cell for up to eighteen hours a day. You cannot receive more visitors than other inmates do. You obey the rules of the jail. The jail guards treat you like any other prisoner. The administration gives you a number, a bed and a commode, and library hours just like any other prisoner. In fact, you are worse off be-cause you cannot participate in the educational programs county inmates can participate in.

Depending on the jail, you may or may not be mixed in with county in-mates. It always intrigues me when progressive lawyers focus on the issue of prisoners and immigration detainees intermingling. This implies that detainees are being contaminated through being held with people who have criminal convictions, and that separation from these people would be more humane. I do not necessarily disagree. Most immigration detainees are there for immigration violations or have criminal convictions for which they have long completed their sentences. In talking about their fellow in-mates, I have heard detainees themselves complain, "This guy is a mur-derer" or, "That guy is a drug dealer." But I have always felt they say this partly because immigration detention, in its elusive, arbitrary, and often indefinite nature, is so unbearable, that every little thing becomes a concern. From a strictly reformist standpoint, the government needs to stop renting bed space at county jails, because counties are administratively incapable of treating immigration detainees differently from their own inmates.

I despise jails. They are dehumanizing and degrading, and the staleness in the air is impossible to describe. It is intangible, yet real and sickening, like a viscous mixture of racism, xenophobia, and authority. You sense it when you are denied access because you do not have a proper ID, or your bar membership card has expired and the new card is in the mail, or you have a nose ring, or are made to wait four hours to get in because you came during headcount or feeding time. Correctional officers do not like being called "guards," we were told at Plymouth County Correctional Facility, because they are trained in administering correctional centers whereas guards could be security personnel at a restaurant. It is routine, however, to use disrespectful terms such as "aliens," "feeding," and "headcount" in relation to the detainees.

By shutting you out, or shutting you in, the legislators who made detention mandatory for many noncitizens with immigration violations knew what they were doing. By giving themselves so much control over someone's freedom and by controlling that person's access to lawyers and family members, they hope to silence protest from family members and lawyers, stifle resistance, and transform rage into subservient smiles.

Although I believe the ultimate struggle against discriminatory laws is in protest and advocacy outside the courtroom, lawyers and judges have a role to play as well by pushing for reform inside the courtrooms. Lawyers could creatively and constructively intervene in the racist justice system of the immigration courts. They could strategically call on government attorneys who make assumptions, perpetuate stereotypes, and engage in unethical practice. Immigration lawyers need to address this culture of racism and xenophobia surrounding Muslims that has permeated the immigration courtroom since 9/11 and existed well before that for blacks and Latinos. If government lawyers are able to use race, religion, and national origin as suggestions of criminality or connections with terrorist organizations, immigration lawyers could develop strategies to combat this. They could use information on racial profiling, criminalization of people of color, and police misconduct against minorities; they could use facts about terrorism that counter assumptions and stereotypes about who is likely to be a terrorist.

Also, immigration lawyers could document stereotypes that regularly pass as evidence in courtrooms and develop local and national strategies against this. Lawyers could also refuse to remain silent about such practices. Too often, we let these slip in the drive to win a case and maintain a judge's favor. It took one article in a Boston newspaper, initiated by a respondent's psychiatrist, about one of the immigration judges I have mentioned off and on in this article to get him suspended, while lawyers had for years maintained an eerie silence about his practices. The psychiatrist was an outsider—a witness in the judge's court—and he was appalled by the judge's blatantly sexist and racist remarks. Lawyers' silence makes us complicit in the government's attack on immigrants and their rights, liberty, and dignity.

Lawyers could also provide culturally specific information to counter biases any judges may have in interpreting a respondent's testimony. Too often, a client's inconsistent statements are used by judges to make a negative credibility finding—but one must develop tactics to show that the stress of testifying and the need to please someone in power explains much of the inconsistency. If one is representing a detained client and unable to show his positive qualities, one could present documentation on the rigors of jail life and how prolonged detention can make a client seem unpresentable and unworthy of discretionary relief. And this can be done without losing cases, sacrificing the profession, or appearing too adventurous.

Ultimately, however, immigration laws must change. In the meantime, lawyers strive to construct complex and creative legal arguments about how, for example, a crime does not constitute an aggravated felony or is not a crime of moral turpitude; they are taking risks for reform that highlight the indignities suffered by respondents. Many more should.

Immigration judges, too, should be critical of government practices. It is not acceptable that a Jamaican man was imprisoned for two weeks more than he should have been because the ICE could and did ignore the immigration judge's order. How would a government trial attorney feel about having to spend two weeks in Bristol County Jail because an official failed to follow a judge's order?

It is not acceptable that a detainee should wait for twenty-four months in jail to get a travel document to go home. A federal court judge in 2003 dismissed Bassam's poorly researched, untidily formatted, handwritten habeas petition requesting release because Bassam had confused the issues. In one desperate breath he asked for release from detention and asylum in the United States, complained about the treatment of Muslim detainees, and professed his deep ties to the country. The judge dismissed the asylum claim, but Bassam had explicitly told the judge earlier that he did not wish to pursue asylum. (You cannot normally ask for a form of relief in a federal court if you have been rejected in a lower court.) Ignoring Bassam's ties to family and friends in the United States and his complaints about the treatment he received in detention, the judge also dismissed the request for release, citing the government's contention that they have deported people to Syria in the past. It should not have to be this way.

Notes

1. *Immigration and Nationality Act,* § 244 (c)(2), 8 *U.S. Code* § 1254a(a)(1)(A); Immigration and Naturalization Service, *Regulations Concerning the Convention Against Torture,* interim rule, 8 *Code of Federal Regulations* §§ 244.1–244.4.

2. *Aliens and Nationality Act,* 8 *U.S. Code* § 1326.

3. Kearny Street is in downtown Boston. It is the location for courts that are holding removal hearings for nondetained persons.

4. Public Law 104-132, 110 *Stat.* 1214 (Apr. 24, 1996).

5. Public Law 104-208, 110 *Stat.* 3009 (Sept. 30, 1996).

6. *Immigration and Nationality Act,* § 240A(a), 8 *U.S. Code* § 1229b(a).

7. *Immigration and Nationality Act,* § 240B(a), 8 *U.S. Code* § 1229c.

8. A strong form of relief is generally regarded as legal status, which would allow a noncitizen to stay in the United States permanently and lawfully. A weak form of relief is one that does not grant permanent status and allows noncitizens the freedom to leave the United States at their choosing.

9. Immigration and Naturalization Service, *Regulations Concerning the Convention Against Torture,* § 208.18(a)(1).

10. U.S. Department of Justice, Executive Office for Immigration Review, *FY 2005, Statistical Year Book,* February 2006, M1, http://www.usdoj.gov/eoir/statspub/fy05syb.pdf (accessed November 6, 2007).

11. *Immigration and Nationality Act,* § 212(a)(9)(A)(ii), 8 *U.S. Code* § 1182 (a)(9)(A)(ii).

12. Immigration and Naturalization Service, *Regulations Concerning the Convention Against Torture,* § 208.18(a)(1).

13. Immigration and Naturalization Service, *Regulations Concerning the Convention Against Torture,* § 208.16 (c)(3).

14. *Child Citizenship Act of 2000,* Public Law 106-395, 114 *Stat.* 1631 (Oct. 30, 2000).

15. In re J-E-, 23 I & N Dec. 291 (Board of Immigration Appeals, 2002).

16. U.S. Department of Justice, *FY 2005, Statistical Year Book,* E1.

17. Ibid., E2.

18. *Immigration and Nationality Act,* § 240A(b), 8 *U.S. Code* § 1229a(b).

19. In re Andazola, 23 I & N Dec. 319 (Board of Immigration Appeals, 2002).

20. *St. Cyr v. Immigration and Naturalization Service,* 533 U.S. 289 (2001).

21. *Zadvydas v. Davis,* 533 U.S. 678 (2001).

CHAPTER 10

Why Black Immigrants Matter

Refocusing the Discussion on Racism and Immigration Enforcement

TAMARA K. NOPPER

SINCE SEPTEMBER 11, 2001, social justice activists and academics have emphasized how immigration enforcement has adversely affected South Asian, Arab, and Muslim immigrants.[1] Some have gone so far as to suggest that they are the primary targets of the Bush administration's "war on terror."[2] The recent political battle over illegal immigration, ushered in by various congressional bills, has also kept the discussion of immigrants' rights in the spotlight. While some activists have pointed out that anti-immigrant legislation proposals will adversely affect *all* immigrants, it is generally understood that debates about illegal immigration are really about Latinos, and specifically Mexicans. Taken together, activist conversations about immigrants' rights in the post–9/11 period have focused primarily on South Asians, Arab-Muslim groups, or Mexican-Latino groups.

The racist treatment of these groups merits attention, but the tendency to focus *only* on these groups limits our understanding of the scope of immigration enforcement today. As I explain in this chapter, recent trends in the policing, incarceration, and deportation of noncitizens cannot be explained simply by the post–9/11 "war on terror" or concerns about the rise of undocumented labor because there is a steadily increasing number of immigrants who enter the United States legally and are deported as a consequence of their encounters with the criminal justice system. I propose that the latter process, which is occurring most intensely for black immigrants, reflects the growing intersection between immigration enforcement and the forms of crime control to which black populations in the United States (both immigrant and native born) have been historically subjected.[3] This connection among the criminal justice system, immigration enforcement, and institutional racism is not as clearly apparent when our attention is focused only on the experiences of Asian/Arab-Muslim and Latino noncitizens. Thus, an exploration of black immigrants' experiences may help us trace the expansion of immigration enforcement and how it relates to the criminal justice system.

Immigrants' rights activists have generally neglected the experiences of black immigrants when it comes to making comparative claims about immigration enforcement and its impact on racialized communities. Nor do many engage data that is publicly available. Instead, much of the recent discussion focuses on enforcement actions and sting operations that are specific to particular regional and racial-ethnic groups. While these enforcement activities deserve activist attention, they do not necessarily speak to the broad continuities in patterns of enforcement across different groups.

A closer look at available data reveals that there are, indeed, trends in apprehension, incarceration, and deportation that span a number of groups and which precede 9/11. As I argue here, this data also suggests that we cannot understand the expansion of immigration enforcement without understanding what is happening to black immigrants. That is, it is important to consider how black immigrants experience enforcement— both to understand their experiences and to identify the myriad factors informing the expansion of immigration enforcement, a process that affects all immigrant groups. One such factor that will be emphasized here is the accelerated growth of the prison-industrial complex in the post–civil rights era.

In this chapter, I provide a selective review of government data on immigration enforcement and incarceration trends for a variety of immigrant groups. This review focuses on apprehensions by local police and federal agents, convictions and sentencing for immigration-related crimes, incarceration, and final removals (a form of deportation) for different immigrant groups. I also draw on some of the critical literature on race, citizenship, and incarceration to point out important continuities between the incarceration of black immigrants and native-born black Americans. In the conclusion, I show how an understanding of contemporary anti-crime measures and the growth of the prison-industrial complex, which has disproportionately incarcerated black populations, can expand our understanding of the factors driving the expansion of immigration enforcement today.

Apprehensions by Local Police and Federal Agencies

Data on apprehensions by local police and federal agents shows that Caribbean and African immigrants are among those identified as immigration violators, whether through arrests for criminal violations or strategies for locating immigration absconders that were originally developed as so-called antiterrorism measures. Although local police have been involved in the monitoring of immigrants for civil immigration violations for the past two decades,[4] they became even more involved in the process after September 11, 2001. Many local police departments and state governments have begun collaborating with the U.S. Department of Justice (DOJ) to enforce immigration laws and to supply information to the National Crime Information Center (NCIC) database. A Federal Bureau of Investigation (FBI) system, the NCIC keeps records of both citizens and noncitizens who have outstanding warrants and immigration violations, as well as of criminal history information. By involving local police in immigration enforcement, the DOJ was able to make more arrests of immigrants on the ground as well as increase the information entered into the NCIC and therefore accessible to police nationwide.

Before 2001, the inclusion of civil immigration records in the NCIC had not yet been approved by Congress. Less than a year after September 11, 2001, data on criminal and civil immigration violations began to be integrated into the NCIC system, culminating in the creation of the National Security Entry-Exit Registration System (NSEERS) in 2002. NSEERS is a database of registrations, fingerprints, and photographs of noncitizen men and boys from Arab and Muslim countries. The database now includes records of (1) those with convicted felonies who had been deported; (2) absconders, or those who remain in the country despite being subject to exclusion or orders of final deportation or removal; and (3) those who violate the NSEERS requirements. During routine police activity, such as traffic stops or arrests, police officers may arrest individuals whose names are in the NCIC as NSEERS violators, as well as any other noncitizen with an outstanding immigration violation.[5]

Although "anti-terrorism" was one of the main reasons cited by the DOJ and the Bush administration for including immigration violations in the NCIC, the process mainly affected Mexican and black immigrants. Indeed, immigrants from nations identified as possible "terrorist threats" (mostly Asian, Middle Eastern, and "Muslim" countries) compose only 4 percent of the total number of those who were accurately identified through the NCIC as immigration violators—and only a very small number of these persons were apprehended for reasons of "national security." In contrast, Mexican nationals alone made up 71 percent of the total group of immigration violators apprehended through the NCIC in 2004. Noncitizens from the Caribbean or Africa composed 8 percent of immigration violators during this same period.[6]

Compared with Mexican immigrants, the percentage of Caribbeans is relatively small. Nevertheless, the figure should give us pause, since it is over six times the representation of Caribbean immigrants in the national population.[7] It also indicates that there were twice as many black immigrants apprehended through the NCIC as noncitizens from Asian or Arab/Middle Eastern nations—despite the fact that post–9/11 national-security measures have focused primarily on Asian and Arab/Middle Eastern nationals.[8] While the latter groups have certainly been the victims of state violence since 9/11, black immigrants, with some exception, are rarely considered to be adversely affected by antiterrorism measures; hence the tendency among immigrants' rights activists to treat the post–9/11 period as the historical domain of South Asians, Arabs, and Muslims. Yet this data reveals that even when state measures are initiated to address terrorism, they have a negative impact on black immigrants. The massive scope of Mexican and Latin American apprehensions further underscores the relative insignificance of antiterrorism as the premise for these newly expanded enforcement practices.

Only a minority of immigrant apprehensions are actually conducted by state and local law enforcement agents. The bulk of immigrant apprehensions are conducted by federal agents attached to the Department of Homeland Security (DHS). In 2005 1,291,142 immigrant apprehensions were carried out by federal agencies. The DHS agencies primarily responsible for these apprehensions include Customs and Border Protection (CBP) and Immigration and Customs Enforcement (ICE).[9] This number included foreign nationals from 188 countries. About 85 percent of those apprehended were Mexican nationals.[10] These figures for 2005 are also consistent with trends for 2001–2004, when Mexican nationals were the overwhelming majority of immigration violators apprehended by the Federal government, with most of these apprehensions occurring at or near the U.S.–Mexico border.

TABLE 10.I

Alien Apprehensions (by nationality), October 1, 2001–September 30, 2004

Country	Total Alien Apprehensions	Percentage of Criminal Apprehensions
Canada	4,725	58
Colombia	33,540	15
Cuba	23,893	17
Dominican Republic	16,372	55
El Salvador	58,013	17
Guatemala	47,923	13
Honduras	65,313	13
Jamaica	7,734	74
Mexico	480,563	54
Nicaragua	5,227	25
Philippines	4,792	42

Source: Department of Homeland Security, "Detention and Removal of Illegal Aliens," April 2006, 8, http://www.dhs.gov/xoig/assets/mgmtrpts/OIG_06-33_Apr06.pdf (accessed November 18, 2007).

After Mexican nationals, nationals of Honduras, El Salvador, Guatemala, and Colombia were the most represented among total apprehensions for the same time period (see Table 10.I). However, the majority of apprehensions for nationals from these countries were *not* for reasons of criminal conduct. Conversely, immigrants from the Dominican Republic and Jamaica were apprehended more often for criminal offenses between 2001 and 2004. Out of 16,372 apprehensions of Dominican nationals, 55 percent were because of criminal conduct. During the same period, 74 percent of the apprehensions of Jamaican nationals were for criminal conduct. Despite not being the largest number of immigrants apprehended, both Dominicans and Jamaicans are nevertheless apprehended more because of criminal conduct than not, a dubious honor shared only with those from Canada and Mexico.[11]

Whereas criminal apprehension means becoming entangled in criminal justice proceedings, the option of voluntary departure allows many noncitizens to avoid this possibility. Almost a million of the noncitizens apprehended were given the option of voluntary departure , which allows a noncitizen to avoid a formal order of removal. In exchange for legally acknowledging "removability" and taking care of departure expenses, noncitizens granted voluntary departures are permitted to seek admission in the future. It is generally acknowledged that the vast majority of voluntary departures are issued to Latino noncitizens attempting to cross the U.S.–Mexico border without authorization.[12] This difference is important because it indicates that, even though Mexican-Latino noncitizens are deported in higher numbers, the terms of deportation and possibilities for reentry are more flexible than what is typically meted out to black immigrants. This issue is addressed in more detail in the next three sections.

Convictions and Sentencing for Immigration-Related Crimes

Immigrants who are not granted voluntary departures are much more likely to become entangled with the U.S. criminal justice system.[13] In 2005 there were 9,874 criminal arrests and 6,763 convictions for immigration-related violations, such as smuggling and trafficking and identity and benefit fraud. These individuals were routed into deportation proceedings as a result of these convictions but were not necessarily deported in the same year. Of the 208,521 individuals who were formally removed from the United States in 2005, about 43 percent, or 89,406, were deported as criminal aliens. Of those criminally removed, 77 percent were from Mexico.[14] It should be emphasized that although Mexican nationals made up a large share of criminal-related formal removals, this is completely separate from the number of Mexican nationals who were granted formal departures for unauthorized border crossing (which is a much larger number). In addition, data should not be misconstrued as involving the *same* immigrants for apprehensions, arrests, convictions, and deportations. This is because the DHS does not have a tracking system that monitors cases from apprehension to final disposition—a process that may last at least several months or, in some cases, several years.[15]

Nevertheless, data *is* available regarding the detention, conviction, and incarceration of immigrants. While definitive conclusions may not be easily drawn, patterns regarding immigration enforcement are identifiable and instructive. *These patterns show that incarceration trends, which are most intense for black immigrants, are also becoming a more pervasive feature of immigration enforcement in general, affecting a broad range of national-origin groups.* Further, this expansion in immigrant incarceration has been influenced by a growing intersection between federal enforcement activities—which have historically targeted black populations—and immigration enforcement. To this end, we need to consider how noncitizens are represented in both immigrant detention centers and other incarceration facilities, such as federal prisons and state and local jails.

Regarding the former, immigration detention centers are similar to jails in that they house people who are going through immigration court proceedings or are being processed for removal. Overall, the daily population in immigrant detention has steadily increased between 1994 and 2005, with the exception of the small decrease between the years 2001 and 2002 and a larger decrease between 2004 and 2005. While the average daily population in detention increased by over 200 percent in a decade, the average number of immigrants detained daily remains relatively low, with 19,619 immigrants detained in 2005.[16]

In 2005 the ICE detained a total of 237,667 immigrants. As reported by the Office of Immigration Statistics of the DHS, Mexican nationals made up 50 percent of all detainees but only 24 percent of detention bed days because of short stays.[17] In terms of bed days, nationals from Honduras, Guatemala, and El Salvador made up 9 percent, 8 percent, and 8 percent, respectively. Cuba and China made up 5 percent and 4 percent, respectively, of all bed days. And nationals from the Dominican Republic, Haiti, Jamaica, and Brazil each comprised 3 percent of all bed days in immigrant detention.[18] This distribution of nationalities in immigration detention centers has remained consistent for the past few years.[19]

Pertaining to immigrants in other incarceration facilities, the Bureau of Justice Statistics (BJS) reports that there were 91,117 noncitizens in either federal or state prisons by midyear 2005. Out of this number, 35,285 are in federal prison, making noncitizens about 19.3 percent of all federal inmates.[20] As Table 10.2 shows, this figure represents a steady increase in the overall number of noncitizens in prisons.

While the numbers of noncitizens in federal and state prisons has increased since September 11, 2001, the steady growth of this population may also be traced back to the 1996 Illegal Immigration Reform and Immigrant Responsibility Act (IIRAIRA). IIRAIRA increased spending for law enforcement efforts by the Immigration and Naturalization Service (INS).[21] After IIRAIRA, the number of INS law enforcement agents grew by 40 percent, with practically two-thirds of new officers hired by the CBP. This increase in spending also, predictably, produced an increase in

TABLE 10.2

Noncitizens Incarcerated (by type of prison), 1998–2005

Year	Total	Percentage in Federal Prison	Percentage in State Prison
2005	91,117	39	61
2004	91,815	37	63
2003	90,568	38	62
2002	88,677	38	62
2001	87,917	39	61
2000	89,676	40	60
1999	88,811	38	62
1998	77,099	36	64

Source: Bureau of Justice Statistics, Compendium of Federal Justice Statistics, 2004 (2006), 5.

immigration-related prosecutions. Between 1996 and 2000, the number of individuals prosecuted for immigration offenses increased by almost 150 percent from 6,607 to 15,613.[22] In 2004, immigration-related offenses became the largest group of all federal prosecutions (at 32 percent of all prosecutions), followed closely by drug-related offenses (at 27 percent). Thus, it appears that at this moment, issues of immigration enforcement, drug enforcement, and national security have become administratively co-ordinated to a degree previously unmatched. For example, the DHS has recently outpaced the FBI as the federal agency that conducts the most drug enforcement actions and has also become the fastest-growing employer of all federal law enforcement agents.[23]

With regard to demographics, prison data also shows that individuals categorized as Hispanic made up the overwhelming percentage (87 percent) of individuals charged with an immigration offense.[24] It is possible to see how the size of the incarcerated Hispanic population is tied to general increases in immigration-related prosecutions. Keep in mind that this increase is completely separate from border control practices that are geared toward apprehending unauthorized migrants. It is also significant that only legal immigrants can be jailed and deported because of criminal conduct, since unauthorized migrants are detained and deported solely on the basis of their "Improper Entry." This steady increase in Hispanic incarceration is best viewed in light of broader trends that are also having an impact on native-born blacks and black immigrants—and which are closely tied to the way that anticrime measures have begun to influence immigration enforcement.

For example, between 1985 and 2000, the incarceration rate for those convicted of immigration offenses increased from 57 percent to 91 percent. As John Scalia and Marika F.X. Litras explain, "These increases were due in part to changes in federal sentencing policy during the 1980s and 1990s, which increased the likelihood that immigration offenders would be sentenced to prison and that their sentences would be longer."[25] These changes in federal sentencing policy were built on legal precedents already established by the contemporary War on Drugs, which severely increased sentencing for drug-related crimes. As recounted by Eric Sterling of the Criminal Justice Policy Foundation, Democratic congressmen capitalized on the cocaine-related death of college basketball player Len Bias in 1986 to push a "tough on drugs" agenda to outmuscle their Republican counterparts.[26]

Subsequently, the Anti-Drug Abuse Act was passed by Congress in 1986, and mandatory minimums for drug offenses were introduced. A mandatory minimum sentence is a minimum number of years—generally five to ten—that must be served in prison as punishment for particular crimes. Sentencing for drug offenses is presumably calculated according to type and quantities. However, drug laws have translated into large numbers of people being sentenced under mandatory minimum laws even though many of them were purportedly not the original targets of anti-drug policies. As Sterling explains, "The idea behind mandatory minimum sentences was to encourage the government to prosecute high level drug offenders. However, the amounts that can trigger a substantial sentence are often lower than those a high level trafficker would be dealing in. . . . Most drug cases involve low level offenders."[27] As Marc Mauer explains, the "advent of a renewed generation of mandatory minimum sentencing statutes, now in place in all states and in the federal system, has led to dramatic increases in the number of incarcerated drug offenders."[28]

In 1988 another Anti-Drug Abuse Act was passed, this time introducing the category of aggravated felony. Over the years, the list of criminal offenses that are categorized as aggravated felonies has expanded to include crimes previously treated as misdemeanors. Today, aggravated felonies are determined by the length of sentences and the amount of money involved for various crimes.[29]

Both the 1986 and 1988 Anti-Drug Abuse Acts and subsequent modifications have had a profound impact on the growth of the prison-industrial complex—the incarcerated population grew dramatically after the late 1980s. Additionally, the building of more prisons since the passage of the Anti-Drug Abuse Acts has accelerated the growth of incarcerated individuals; 318 adult prisons were opened between 1989 and 1994.[30] Since 1991, despite a decreasing crime rate, the prison incarceration rate has increased by 50 percent.[31]

The passage of the Anti-Drug Abuse Acts also reinforced existing racial disparities in both arrests and sentencing. Drug arrests grew exponentially following the passage of the Anti-Drug Abuse Acts, increasing from 471,000 in 1980 to 1,247,000 by the end of the decade. African Americans bore the brunt of drug arrests, and by 1993 they made up 39 percent of all drug arrests, whereas in 1980 they accounted for 24 percent.[32] The pattern of blacks being overrepresented among those arrested for drug activity continues. Today, despite the lack of significant difference in illegal drug use for whites and blacks, the latter are arrested for drug activities at a number that is proportionally 150 percent more than the size of the black population. Conversely, whites are arrested for drug activities at a number commensurate with their population size.[33] In addition, blacks are much more likely to be convicted and to receive longer sentences than whites who are apprehended for similar drug-related violations.[34] The near-exclusive focus on low-level drug sellers, as opposed to users and big-time dealers, has also resulted in the targeted enforcement of blacks.[35] These trends have led some researchers to conclude that the primary aim of the War on Drugs has not been to curtail the illegal drug trade but to maintain existing racial hierarchies via incarceration and social control.[36]

The intersection of the War on Drugs and immigration enforcement is also apparent in increased prosecutions of immigrants for drug-related offenses. Between 1985 and 2000, prosecution of immigrants for drug-related offenses increased by almost 400 percent, from 1,799 to 7,803.[37] Subsequent amendments to the Anti-Drug Abuse Acts have intensified these trends by dictating tougher sentencing guidelines for repeat offenders, including those suspected of immigration violations committed in the United States following deportation for an aggravated felony conviction.[38]

This data indicates that more attention needs to be given to tracing the relationship between immigration enforcement and the growth of the prison-industrial complex. Such an investigation would take several angles that are outside the scope of this chapter. However, in the next section, I will pursue this line of inquiry by reviewing data regarding immigrant arrests and sentencing and consider how this data challenges activist discourse about immigration enforcement after September 11, 2001.

Particulars of Immigrant Arrests, Bookings, and Sentencing

In general, immigrants' rights activists have neglected some of the data relevant to a discussion about immigration enforcement and its relationship to the growth of the prison-industrial complex. This data may help trace how criminal justice proceedings inform the expansion of immigration enforcement vis-à-vis some of the anticrime policies addressed in the previous section. Data about the particulars of immigrant arrests, bookings, and sentencing is made available in the BJS's *Compendium of Federal Justice Statistics*, with the most recent edition reviewing the period from 2003 to 2004. In that year, there were 65 federal agencies that employed 105,000 full-time officers—an increase of almost 15 percent from 2003—who had the authority to carry arms and make arrests.[39]

The U.S. Marshals Service (USMS) is generally responsible for the booking, processing, and detention of all federal suspects, regardless of which agency makes the arrest. Out of the 140,755 suspects arrested for violating federal laws, the agencies the DHS comprises were responsible for a little over a third of all arrests and bookings. Out of 140,755 suspects transferred to the custody of the USMS, 40,000 came from CBP, 39,000 from the USMS, 12,000 from the Drug Enforcement Agency, 10,000 from ICE, and 9,700 from the FBI.[40] The majority booked by the USMS were processed for immigration violations (29 percent), followed by drug offenses (25 percent), supervision violations (17 percent), property offenses (12 percent), weapons offenses (7 percent), public-order offenses (7 percent), securing and safeguarding a material witness (4 percent), and violent offenses (4 percent).[41]

Noncitizens made up 43 percent of the total number of arrestees booked by the USMS. Not surprisingly, noncitizens accounted for the overwhelming majority (94 percent) of suspects booked for immigration violations.[42] Of the arrests and bookings for immigration offenses, 83 percent were for illegal entry, followed by 11 percent for smuggling, 4 percent for other immigration violations, and 3 percent for false claims of citizenship.[43]

In addition, noncitizens made up 29 percent of all suspects booked for drug-related offenses. Unfortunately, data showing the combination of the variables of race and citizenship status are not available, but in terms of racial background of offenders, whites (including white Hispanics) made up 72 percent of all arrestees, followed by blacks (24 percent), American Indians or Alaska Natives (1.7 percent), and Asian/Native Hawaiian or Pacific Islanders (1.6 percent). Out of these statistics, we see that only blacks and American Indians or Alaska Natives are represented in arrest figures at percentages double the size of their overall populations (see Table 10.3).[44]

Out of the 74,782 total offenders sentenced in 2004, 78 percent were sentenced to incarceration. Of those sentenced for felonies, about a third were for drug-related offenses and about a fifth for immigration violations. Those convicted of drug, violent, immigration, and weapons felonies tended to be imprisoned whereas probation rates were higher for those convicted of public-order offenses and property crimes. Among those felonies most likely to earn a prison sentence, immigration offenders were 90 percent likely and drug, violent, and weapons offenses were 93–94 percent likely.[45] The length of prison sentences varied depending on the felony (see Table 10.4).[46]

Unfortunately, data regarding the demographics of those sentenced in 2004 is not available in the compendium for that year, but it is for 2003. Noncitizens made up about a third of those convicted and sentenced to incarceration in 2003. Regardless of the offense, 77 percent of convicted U.S. citizens were incarcerated, whereas 85.5 percent of noncitizens were. When convictions were for violent, drug, or weapons offenses, the overwhelming majority of all those arrested were incarcerated, regardless of race.[47] Overall, average prison sentences were longest for males, blacks, non-Hispanics, and those with U.S. citizenship. Blacks were most likely, of all groups, to be incarcerated after being convicted of violent offenses, drug offenses, public-order offenses, and weapons offenses. Indeed, 72 percent of blacks who were convicted of immigration offenses were incarcerated, compared with 37 percent of Asian/Pacific Islanders who were convicted for the same offense (see Table 10.5).[48]

As Table 10.5 shows, there is more parity in the sentencing of blacks and Asians convicted of property crimes, particularly those categorized as "fraudulent." Fraudulence includes welfare fraud and forgery, both of which may be categorized as aggravated felonies.[49] Studies show that the welfare reform bill signed into law by President Bill Clinton in 1996 has had a grave impact on immigrant communities, including entangling them in the criminal justice system.[50] While all working-class and poor communities that received welfare money or services were adversely affected by changes in welfare policy, it is important to note that

TABLE 10.3

Federal Arrestees Booked by USMS, October 1, 2003–September 30, 2004

Percentage of Convicted Offenders Sentenced to Incarceration in Criminal Cases Terminated During 2003

	Total Number Arrested	All Offenses	Violent Offenses	Property Offenses		Drug Offenses	Public Order Offenses		Weapon Offenses	Immigration Offenses
				Fraudulent	Other		Regulatory	Other		
All Offenders	140,755	100.0	3.3	9.1	2.1	23.6	0.2	5.9	7.1	28.0
Race of Offender										
White	101,043	72.3	42.6	63.4	59.2	66.1	83.3	74.5	47.2	97.1
Black	34,024	24.4	41.0	31.6	34.1	31.0	7.6	20.3	50.6	2.2
American Indian or Alaska Native	2,398	1.7	15.0	0.6	4.6	0.9	7.9	2.4	1.3	0.1
Asian/ Pacific Islander	2,241	1.6	1.5	4.3	2.1	1.9	1.2	2.7	0.9	0.6
Citizenship										
U.S. Citizen	74,700	57.4	92.1	81.0	93.4	70.8	87.9	89.8	94.6	5.7
Not U.S. Citizen	55,504	42.6	7.9	19.0	6.6	29.2	12.1	10.2	5.4	94.3

Source: Bureau of Justice Statistics, *Compendium of Federal Justice Statistics, 2004* (2006) 19, http://www.ojp.usdoj.gov/bjs/pub/pdf/cfjs04.pdf (accessed November 18, 2007).

TABLE 10.4

Offenders Convicted and Sentenced to Prison and Time in Prison,
October 1, 2003–September 30, 2004

Category of Offense	Percentage of Convicted Defendants Sentenced to Prison	Average Months of Prison Sentence
Violent	94	96.2
Drug	93	83.6
Weapon	93	84.3
Immigration	90	26.9
Public-order	71	43.6
Property	60	27.4

Source: Bureau of Justice Statistics, *Compendium of Federal Justice Statistics, 2004* (2006) 69, http://www.ojp.usdoj.gov/bjs/pub/pdf/cfjs04.pdf (accessed November 18, 2007).

a historical feature of immigration policy is the fear that immigrants will become "public charges" and drain the state's resources.[51] This anxiety has continued to inform current debates about immigrants' and refugees' uses of welfare, as well as debates about the possibility of immigrants "importing" crime to the United States.[52] Indeed, embedded in celebrations of Asian refugees as hardworking and pro-American "model minorities" is an anxiety of their possible propensity to exploit the welfare system.[53]

Regardless of which immigrant or refugee group is being scrutinized, anxieties about the public coffer being drained are driven by the racist and sexist image of blacks as lazy and lacking ambition—except when it comes to exploiting the system. Because of this, the increasing criminalization of welfare use has been driven by specific attacks on African Americans and the deployment of antiblack imagery. While the most obvious example of these antiblack attacks is the stereotype of the black welfare queen, organized efforts to keep blacks from accessing welfare go back to the days of its establishment under the New Deal.[54] Contemporary concerns about immigrants' exploitation of the welfare system are informed, then, by the specter of immigrants "being like blacks." In this sense, antiblack rhetoric is employed in debates about welfare use and fraud, even when nonblack groups are being discussed.

TABLE 10.5

Convicted Offenders Sentenced to Incarceration by Demographics of Offender, October 1, 2002–September 30, 2003

Percentage of Convicted Offenders Sentenced to Incarceration in Criminal Cases Terminated During 2003

	Total Number of Convicted Offenders	All Offenses	Violent Offenses	Property Offenses		Drug Offenses	Public Order Offenses		Weapon Offenses	Immigration Offenses	Misdemeanors
				Fraudulent	Other		Regulatory	Other			
All Offenders	75,859	76	93	60	61	92	47	78	93	87	21
Race of Offender											
White	48,389	81	94	61	64	91	48	79	90	90	37
Black	16,840	81	95	59	52	95	59	86	95	72	19
American Indian or Alaska Native	1,023	75	93	45	69	88	—	73	95	54	18
Asian/Pacific Islander	1,489	60	82	53	59	86	51	61	93	37	9
Citizenship											
U.S. citizen	43,865	77.1	94.2	59.5	59.0	91.4	48.8	78.5	92.5	78.0	15.9
Not a U.S. citizen	24,596	85.5	83.3	60.8	81.8	94.3	51.4	83.5	91.2	88.9	64.3

Source: Bureau of Justice, *Compendium of Federal Justice Statistics, 2003* (2005) 76, http://www.ojp.usdoj.gov/bjs/pub/pdf/cfjs03.pdf (accessed November 18, 2007).

Convictions on fraud and other property-crime charges are partially responsible for the increased number of women, many of whom are black, in prisons nationally. In recent years, the majority of women in prison were incarcerated for either drug offenses or property offenses, including fraud. About 30 percent of the over 100,000 women currently incarcerated were receiving public assistance before they were arrested—compared with 8 percent of men—and over 35 percent earned incomes of less than $600 a month before their arrests.[55]

These patterns are found at the state level. In New York, for example, women are incarcerated mostly for nonviolent offenses, with 35 percent for drug offenses. Of imprisoned women, 60 percent do not have a high school diploma and 40 percent read at no higher than an eighth-grade level. And consistent with racial patterns of incarceration, almost 48 percent of the incarcerated population in New York state is black, and 24 percent is Latina.[56]

Some of these women must be noncitizens. Along with California and Texas, New York is one of the top three states with the highest numbers of noncitizens in its prison population.[57] The Women in Prison Project reports that, in 2004, the foreign born (many of whom were naturalized citizens) accounted for 12 percent of those in custody in the New York State corrections system.[58] This figure reflects a dramatic increase in foreign-born inmates, which grew 197 percent between 1985 and 2004. This spike is also connected to the general growth of the incarcerated population during the same period. The national origins of foreign-born persons held in custody are also telling. Although foreign-born inmates originate from 119 different countries, 71 percent during the period in question were from the Caribbean or South America. Three out of every five were from Colombia, Cuba, the Dominican Republic, Jamaica, or Mexico.[59]

These numbers suggest that despite their relative invisibility in immigrants' rights discourse, black and brown immigrants are nonetheless part of a growing trend of immigrant incarceration. A major factor contributing to this trend is the conviction of immigrants and other noncitizens for aggravated felonies. The use of aggravated felonies in immigration-removal proceedings is another example of the growing relationship between the prison-industrial complex and immigration enforcement. Moreover, it highlights the vulnerability of black immigrants in removal proceedings.

Aggravated Felonies and Immigrant Removals

The Anti-Drug Abuse Act of 1988 introduced the concept of the aggravated felony and made its use more specific in immigration proceedings. Specifically, the 1988 policy established a separate basis for deportation due to crimes such as murder, drug trafficking, or illegal trafficking of firearms or destructive devices.[60] Eight years later, the IIRAIRA amended the definition of an aggravated felony to be consistent with the provisions of the Antiterrorism and Effective Death Penalty Act, which was passed months before.[61] As many know, IIRAIRA was a draconian immigration policy that made aggravated felonies the basis of deportation and those convicted of them ineligible for relief from deportation. In addition, IIRAIRA was retroactive, meaning that immigrants convicted of crimes before 1996 are still subject to deportation, even if they have already served their sentences.[62] Since 1996, the category of aggravated felony has had an "evolving definition."[63] Today, aggravated felonies include crimes that formerly were considered misdemeanors. Thus, there are an increasing number of stories about immigrants being deported for crimes such as shoplifting or writing bad checks.[64]

As Bill Ong Hing points out, aggravated-felony provisions should not be underestimated in terms of their devastating impact on immigrants:

> Conviction of an aggravated felony results in harsh immigration consequences. For example, an aggravated felon is ineligible for release on bond, is ineligible for asylum, is ineligible for discretionary cancellation of removal, can be deported without a hearing before an immigration judge (if the person is not a permanent resident), and is not eligible for a waiver of moral turpitude offenses upon applying for re-admission. One of the worst consequences of aggravated felonies applies if the person returns to the United States illegally. A person who is convicted of an aggravated felony and removed, and then returns illegally to the United States can be sentenced up to twenty years in federal prisons just for the illegal re-entry.[65]

Unfortunately, data about the relationship between aggravated felony convictions and deportation data is not made readily available to the public by the U.S. government. Employing the Freedom of Information Act (FOIA), the research organization Transactional Records Access Clearinghouse was able to obtain data for 156,713 individuals who were in removal proceedings for aggravated felony charges between mid-1997 and May 2006.[66] Since aggravated felony policies do not apply to individuals who enter the United States without authorization, all these cases involve legal immigrants.

This data includes over two hundred nationalities. However, Latin American and Caribbean nations figured prominently in these numbers with Mexican nationals making up 43 percent in removal proceedings for aggravated felonies. Black immigrants, again a small part of the legal immigration flows, were well-represented among the larger shares of immigrants who had aggravated felony charges used during deportation proceedings; Dominicans made up 8 percent and Jamaicans 5.5 percent. *It is also significant that the majority of those charged were long-term residents, with the median length of residence in the United States being 14 years.* Indeed, 45 percent of those charged with aggravated felonies reported the language they spoke as English; almost 25 percent of Mexicans and Dominicans combined reported not Spanish but English as their primary language.

Of the total number of immigrants charged, almost 50 percent were charged only for being an aggravated felon—details of their particular offenses are not made available—and 33 percent were also charged as having been convicted for drug-related charges. Convictions for controlled substances range from drug trafficking or being in possession of a relatively small quantity of illegal drugs. Overall, the number of cases of aggravated felonies being utilized in immigration court proceedings has declined in recent years, a trend that noticeably emerges between 1999 and 2000. However, researchers suggest that this might be due to the greater jurisdiction of DHS to use administrative deportation orders against convicted aggravated felons as granted by the IIRAIRA.[67] Whatever the reason, these findings further demonstrate the growing relationship between immigration enforcement and criminal justice proceedings.

Some telling patterns are also revealed when looking at formal removals, more popularly referred to as deportations, which were introduced to U.S. immigration policy in 1891.[68] As already discussed, formal removals differ from voluntary departure in important ways. Those undergoing formal removals are processed through the immigration court system, which may result in rulings that often debar the deported individual from reentering the United States under any conditions. Conversely, voluntary departures usually leave the door open for the removed noncitizen to reenter the United States through legal channels and may be less stigmatizing for the individual. It also bears noting that most noncitizens granted voluntary departures

TABLE 10.6
Percentage of Total Formal Removals (by region), 1998–2005

Region	1998	1999	2000	2001	2002	2003	2004	2005
Africa	1.0	1.0	1.0	1.0	1.0	1.0	1.0	1.0
Asia	2.0	2.0	2.0	2.0	3.0	3.0	2.0	2.0
Caribbean	3.0	4.0	4.0	4.0	5.0	4.0	4.0	3.0
Central America	10.0	6.5	8.0	8.0	10.0	11.0	12.0	17.0
Mexico	81.0	83.0	81.0	80.0	73.0	74.0	73.0	69.0
South America	2.5	3.0	3.0	4.0	5.0	5.0	6.0	6.0

Source: Department of Homeland Security, "Table 41: Aliens Formally Removed by Criminal Status and Region and Country of Nationality: Fiscal Years 1998 to 2005," *2005 Yearbook of Immigration Statistics*, http://www.dhs.gov/xlibrary/assets/statistics/yearbook/2005/table41.xls (accessed November 18, 2007).

are unauthorized migrants, whereas most noncitizens who are put through the process of formal removal had some sort of legal status at one point in time (such as a temporary visa or legal permanent residency).

Not surprisingly, data shows that race plays an important role in formal removal proceedings. In 2005 Mexicans bore the brunt of formal removals (69 percent), followed by Central Americans (17 percent), and South Americans (6 percent) (see Table 10.6).[69]

This ranking of regions remained consistent between 1998 and 2005. However, differences between the regions become much more apparent when one looks at the percentage of immigrants deported because of criminal conduct. Specifically, black immigrants have high percentages of criminal deportations, even when their absolute numbers of deportations are relatively low. In 2005, criminal removals made up 74 percent of Caribbean removals and 48 percent for Mexico, 41 percent for Africa, and 35 percent for both Asia and Central America. Although Mexican nationals make up the highest absolute number of formal removals, the reasons for deportation remain fairly evenly divided between criminal and noncriminal offenses. Meanwhile, African migrants, who composed barely 1 percent of all formal removals, were much more likely to be removed for criminal

TABLE 10.7
Percentage of Criminal Formal Removals (by region), 1998–2005

Region	1998	1999	2000	2001	2002	2003	2004	2005
Africa	41	41	41	39	34	36	39	41
Asia	26	34	30	31	27	28	32	35
Caribbean	67	71	69	60	63	65	67	74
Central America	27	42	36	36	33	29	32	21
Mexico	34	37	38	41	52	46	47	48
South America	49	45	39	33	32	27	29	35

Source: Department of Homeland Security, "Table 41: Aliens Formally Removed by Criminal Status and Region and Country of Nationality: Fiscal Years 1998 to 2005," *2005 Yearbook of Immigration Statistics,* http://www.dhs.gov/xlibrary/assets/statistics/yearbook/2005/table41.xls (accessed November 18, 2007).

reasons than were Asian, South American, and Central American nationals (see Table 10.7).[70]

It is evident that deportation patterns for Caribbean nationals are distinct from those of all other regions. Between 1998 and 2005, more than 50 percent of the removals of Caribbeans each year were for criminal reasons, the *only* regional group for which this was the case. Between 2004 and 2005, the percentage of criminal removals increased from 67 percent to 74 percent. *Indeed, despite the emphasis on South Asians, Arabs, and Muslims after 9/11, Caribbean immigrants saw the biggest increase out of all of the regions in criminal deportations since 2001.*

The greatest disparity is evident when Caribbean and Asian nationals are compared. For example, a greater absolute number of Caribbeans are deported each year than Asian nationals, despite the fact that the U.S. Asian population is much larger than the U.S. Caribbean population.[71] Immigrants who are Asian nationals also are among the least likely to be removed for criminal reasons. It is significant, however, that Asian groups that have the highest removal rates—and the highest proportion of removals for criminal reasons—tend to be, but are not restricted to, the lowest-income Asian populations.[72] A similar pattern holds for Latin American nationals. Mexicans, who tend to be among the poorest segments of the U.S. Latino population, are more likely to be removed for criminal reasons than Central American and South American nationals (although there are individual nations within these regions whose criminal removal rates exceed that of Mexico). These trends suggest that for some groups, such as Latinos and Asians, nationality and its relationship to economic mobility is a factor in removal rates.

Yet when looking at Caribbean immigrants, we find no significant differences between nationalities in terms of criminal deportations. Or, at least, between 1998 and 2005, Caribbean immigrants are consistently deported at least 50 percent of the time for criminal reasons, regardless of nationality. With the exception of instances in which data was not available, there are only four instances in which criminal deportations fall below 50 percent for a Caribbean nationality (see Table 10.8).[73]

That Caribbeans, regardless of nationality, are deported so often for criminal reasons illustrates that their position in U.S. society is not as secure as it may otherwise appear. Although some have argued that Caribbeans are harder working, culturally superior, and more successful at addressing discrimination than African Americans,[74] it does not save Caribbeans from excessive incarceration. Even when looking at specific nationalities among Caribbeans, we see no major difference in terms of degrees of criminalization. That this dubious honor may not be claimed by any other regional group suggests that perhaps Caribbean immigrants and African Americans are similarly criminalized and that the former have, at best, a tenuous position in U.S. society.

Conclusion

The purpose of this discussion has not been to provide a definitive statement on race and immigration enforcement, but to discuss trends that complicate some of the existing narratives about the "post–9/11 immigrant." After September 11, 2001, much emphasis was placed on enforcement practices that specifically targeted South Asian/Middle Eastern or Mexican immigrants. Standing in for "types," the latter has become the face of the "illegal immigrant" while the former has become the face of those immigrants targeted as suspected "terrorists" and vaguely defined as "national security threats." At times, both the illegal immigrant and the terrorist have been conflated for ideological and policy purposes.[75] Whatever the case, the emphasis on these two sets of immigrant groups has translated into an implicit statement about racism and immigration enforcement. By focusing on groups who, for different reasons, are racialized as "brown" or "nonblack" some activists and scholars are contributing to a discourse that suggests that antiblack racism and anti-immigrant discrimination belong to two relatively distinct worlds. This dichotomization results in a tendency to treat the expansion of immigration enforcement and the expansion of the prison-industrial complex as two separate processes; the former pertaining to immigrants' rights issues and the latter pertaining to racial justice activism.[76]

This chapter has attempted to show that such distinctions are false, namely because the rise in immigrant incarceration in general, the rise in the number of immigrants being deported for criminal reasons (and specifically for drug offenses), and the leading role that federal immigration agencies are playing in coordinating drug and criminal prosecutions clearly points toward a growing connection between immigration enforcement and criminal law enforcement. While this point is acknowledged by different scholars and activists,[77] more attention needs to be given to how racism shapes this process.

As Aristide Zolberg reminds us, "from colonial times onward, Americans actively devised policies and laws that effectively shaped the country's population and hence its overall makeup."[78] The data reviewed here suggests that immigration policies are still being used to shape the U.S. population. However, this effort is currently being accomplished through strengthening the intersection of immigration enforcement and criminal enforcement, as opposed to explicit national-origins quotas. This is not to suggest that criminalization of immigrants is a new phenomenon, because it is not. However, although immigrants were criminalized during more restrictive periods of immigration, they did not necessarily face the same possibilities of punishment as post-1965 immigrants do. Nevertheless, even when nonwhite immigrants were able to enter the United States during restrictive periods, they were policed and at times punished more severely than their white counterparts. And as research shows, the technology and methods used to monitor all immigrants were developed primarily by monitoring nonwhite immigrants.[79] Because of this, immigration enforcement has always been characterized by a preoccupation with the nonwhite immigrant. And the total number of annual deportations and the percentage triggered by criminal convictions has increased steadily over the past four decades—precisely after the 1965 Immigration Act made

TABLE 10.8

Percentage of Criminal Formal Removals (by Caribbean country), 1998–2005

Country	1998	1999	2000	2001	2002	2003	2004	2005
Antigua-Barbuda	71	81	82	76	88	79	75	82
Aruba	100	—	—	100	—	—	—	100
Bahamas	83	73	87	84	76	80	81	90
Barbados	88	93	83	71	88	83	96	—
Bermuda	50	100	—	—	—	—	79	—
British Virgin Islands	—	—	100	—	—	100	—	—
Cayman Islands	—	—	—	—	—	—	—	—
Cuba	79	87	82	92	85	66	85	55
Dominica	67	78	69	61	83	85	37	71
Dominican Republic	68	73	66	54	57	65	72	79
Grenada	68	75	71	52	77	68	83	71

Guadeloupe	—	—	—	—	—	100	—	—
Haiti	61	65	81	77	62	50	27	54
Jamaica	66	68	70	65	72	74	73	83
Martinique	—	—	—	—	—	—	—	—
Montserrat	—	—	100	—	100	—	—	—
Netherlands Antilles	—	100	—	100	—	100	—	—
Puerto Rico	75	—	—	—	—	—	—	—
Saint Kitts–Nevis	81	—	—	100	89	—	60	—
Saint Lucia	59	74	67	57	63	71	42	63
Saint Vincent and the Grenadines	72	66	62	51	67	70	78	79
Trinidad and Tobago	—	69	59	51	48	53	65	77

Source: Department of Homeland Security, "Table 41: Aliens Formally Removed by Criminal Status and Region and Country of Nationality: Fiscal Years 1998 to 2005," 2005 *Yearbook of Immigration Statistics,* http://www.dhs.gov/xlibrary/assets/statistics/yearbook/2005/table41.xls (accessed November 18, 2007).

it possible for more nonwhites to be legally admitted and as more illegal nonwhite immigrants from countries affected by foreign policies and capitalist globalization sought entry.[80]

Also relevant to this chapter is that practices of immigration enforcement have been developed in response to antiblack anxieties regarding African Americans. As Vilna Bashi points out, immigration policies of many Western countries, including the United States, have been especially restrictive toward black immigrants because of the fear that they will import problems associated with African Americans, such as racial conflict, protest, and "social unrest."[81] While Bashi does not focus on the current period, methods of control used on black immigrants nevertheless have implications for contemporary immigration enforcement. For example, before the 1980s, the INS tended to detain immigrants it determined to be a security risk or likely to flee. But during Ronald Reagan's presidency, the INS began to use detention as a means of deterring illegal immigration—a gesture spurred by the arrival of Haitians and Mariel Cubans.[82] In 1987 a group of the latter, who could not be returned to Cuba, rioted in a Louisiana prison built specifically to hold them. In response, officials dispersed groups of Mariel Cubans to local jails—one of the first times immigration enforcement relied on local facilities to hold immigrants.[83] Finally, the expansion of immigration enforcement is informed by the exponential growth of the imprisoned population and the racist policies that are responsible for it.[84]

As already described, these anticrime initiatives have adversely affected everyone, including immigrants of all races. However, sentencing policies, while used against all racial-ethnic populations, affect black immigrants to a greater degree than other groups. Most activist challenges to immigrant criminalization do not seriously address the relationship between the growth of the prison-industrial complex and immigration enforcement and the role of antiblack racism in the expansion of both. Yet the data presented in this chapter certainly suggests that there is such a relationship.

Thus, there is a need for more comparative research that documents both differences and similarities in the way that native-born and immigrant racial minorities encounter the criminal justice system. This would also require some acknowledgement, as noted in the introduction, that the targeted enforcement of South Asians, Middle Easterners, and Arab/Muslim immigrants, while certainly racist, repressive, and condemnable, does not tell the entire story of what is happening with immigration enforcement today. In this regard, the roundups, sting operations, and violations of civil liberties that have been widely documented by activists and scholars since September 11, 2001, should not be confused with the more sustained and broad-based trends of immigration enforcement.[85]

South Asian and Arab/Muslim immigrant communities have been targeted based on race and, in some cases, religion—by both citizens and the state—as purported terrorists, a practice that preceded 9/11.[86] Yet South Asian and Arab/Muslim immigrants are not incarcerated, detained, and deported as *regularly* as black Americans or Caribbean, South American, Central American, or Mexican immigrants. Moreover, there has been relatively little change in U.S. immigration flows, from September 11, 2001, to the present—even for nationalities that have been the target of post–9/11 "security" measures.[87]

Following these trends, Mexicans are still a major share of U.S. immigration flows, both in terms of those admitted legally and those who enter without authorization.[88] There are also many similarities in terms of trends in immigrant incarceration for black immigrants and Mexicans (and Latinos more generally). However, deportations for criminal convictions still tend to be proportionally higher for black immigrants than for Mexicans. Further, since most black immigrants are deported through formal removal proceedings, rather than the voluntary departures offered to many of the unauthorized Mexican migrants, the outcome of deportation is often more final and severe and, in turn, potentially more stigmatizing. The fact that 41 percent of Africans and 74 percent of Caribbean nationals are deported as "criminal aliens"—the highest proportion of any nationality—means that there are virtually no conditions under which they may lawfully reenter the United States.

Taken as a whole, these findings suggest that black immigrants, particularly those from the Caribbean, experience something in the United States that nonblack immigrant groups do not, or at least not to the same degree. Despite this empirical data, activists generally do not give attention to black immigrant groups except to absorb them into a broad category of immigrants "of color." Indeed, immigrants' rights activism actually focuses more on African Americans as necessary allies than on black immigrants as targets of enforcement.[89] Whatever the motives, such gestures serve to universalize issues of racism instead of dealing with antiblack racism as a major factor driving the expansion of immigration enforcement vis-à-vis the growth of the criminal justice system. The data reviewed here indicates that despite contemporary immigrants' rights discourse that marginalizes them, black immigrants matter in and of themselves and also because their experiences may provide valuable insights into the relationship between racism and the expansion of immigration enforcement. Overall, it would perhaps be more instructive to look at how black immigrants, like African Americans, are positioned as legitimate targets for law enforcement and, ostensibly, to consider how antiblack racism informs enforcement policies used, to varying degrees, against all immigrant communities.

Notes

I want to thank Philip Kretsedemas for soliciting this chapter and for providing valuable feedback and encouragement.

1. Louise Cainkar, "The Impact of the September 11 Attacks and Their Aftermath on Arab and Muslim Communities in the United States," *GSC Quarterly* 13 (Summer/Fall 2004); Louise Cainkar and Sunaina Maira, "Targeting Arab/Muslim/South Asian Americans: Criminalization and Cultural Citizenship," *Amerasia Journal* 31 (2005): 1–27; Human Rights Watch, "Presumption of Guilt: Human Rights Abuses of Post–September 11 Detainees, August 2002, http://www.hrw.org/reports/2002/us911/USA0802.pdf; Tram Nguyen, "Detained or Disappeared?" *Colorlines* 17 (Summer 2002); Behzad Yaghmaian, "Suspected and Feared: Muslim Migrants after 9/11," Motherjones.com (December 2005), http://www.motherjones.com/commentary/columns/2005/12/muslim_migrants_after_september_11.html.

2. Cainkar and Maira, "Targeting Arab/Muslim/South Asian Americans."

3. I use the term *black* here to refer to immigrants from Africa and the Caribbean. I realize that I am using race and national origins interchangeably and that there are some limitations to this approach. For one, many immigrants from both regional areas may not identify as black. This is especially the case for people from the Caribbean, given that census data and anecdotal evidence show that many deny being black. Second, some African countries (especially South Africa and Zimbabwe) and some Caribbean countries are multiracial, which may be reflected among the immigrating populations. Finally, black immigrants are not limited to Africa or the Caribbean but may also be among immigrants from other regions, including but not limited to Canada, Central America, Europe, Mexico, and South America. Despite these limitations, I find that my operationalization of *black* is nevertheless useful for several reasons. First, the Department of Homeland Security data provides figures on national origins but not on race. Second, we know that blacks are well-represented in, if not the numerical majorities in, most African and Caribbean countries. Indeed, Latin America is home to the largest concentration of African descendants outside the African continent. Third, immigrants from both regions, re-

gardless of how they identify, are interpreted through the prism of race in the United States, which is guided by the fundamental antagonism between black and white. In regard to the last point, immigrants from the Caribbean may be perceived as black even if they do not identify as such. Taken together, my operationalization of *black* uses the available data, recognizes the limitations, and still has something useful to say about how immigrants from countries with high concentrations of African descendants fare under U.S. immigration enforcement.

4. Julie Su, "The INS and the Criminalization of Immigrant Workers," in *States of Confinement: Policing, Detention, and Prisons*, ed. Joy James (New York: Palgrave, 2002), 245–257.

5. Hannah Gladstein, Annie Lai, Jennifer Wagner, and Michael Wishnie, "Blurring the Lines: A Profile of State and Local Police Enforcement of Immigration Law Using the National Crime Information Center Database, 2002–2004," Migration Policy Institute Occasional Paper, December 2005, 7.

6. Gladstein et al., "Blurring the Lines," 14.

7. Approximately 2.8 million first-generation Caribbean immigrants live in the United States, composing little more than 8 percent of the national black population and little more than 1.2 percent of the total U.S. population (Migration Policy Institute, Migration Information Source, "United States Stock of Foreign Country by Birth, 1995–2005," http://www.migrationinformation.org/GlobalData/coun trydata/country.cfm [accessed November 7, 2007]).

8. Gladstein et al., "Blurring the Lines," 13.

9. The Border Patrol has a jurisdiction of about 8,000 miles, which includes areas around the U.S.–Canada border. Mary Dougherty, Denise Wilson, and Amy Wu, "Immigration Enforcement Actions: 2005," Office of Immigration Statistics, November 2006, 1. Both Immigration and Customs Enforcement (ICE) and Customs and Border Protection have seen significant increases in their budgets over the last twenty years, especially after the 9/11 attacks (Migration Policy Institute, "Immigration Enforcement Spending Since IRCA," November 2005, 2, http://www.migrationpolicy. org/ITFIAF/FactSheet_Spending.pdf [accessed November 7, 2007]). In 2005 the Border Patrol made 92 percent of all apprehensions, 99 percent of them along the southwest border (Dougherty, Wilson, and Wu, "Immigration Enforcement Actions," 3). That the Border Patrol has made the overwhelming number of apprehensions has been a consistent feature of immigration enforcement for the past twenty years (Migration Policy Institute, "Immigration Enforcement Spending," 1). Whereas the Border Patrol's focus is to police the borders, ICE investigates how immigration laws are enforced in the interior, with an emphasis on immigrants involved in criminal activity (Dougherty, Wilson, and Wu, "Immigration Enforcement Actions," 1–2).

10. Dougherty, Wilson, and Wu, "Immigration Enforcement Actions," 3.

11. Department of Homeland Security, "Detention and Removal of Illegal Aliens," April 2006, http://www.dhs.gov/xoig/assets/mgmtrpts/OIG_06-33_Apr06 .pdf (accessed November 7, 2007).

12. Dougherty, Wilson, and Wu, "Immigration Enforcement Actions," 4.

13. And conversely, immigrants who are already detained, or who have been previously incarcerated, are often unable to make use of voluntary departure if it is offered to them. See chapter 9 for a discussion.

14. Dougherty, Wilson, and Wu, "Immigration Enforcement Actions," 1.

15. Ibid., 3.

16. As with immigrant detention, the average daily population in local jails has steadily increased between the years 1995 and 2005. The average daily population in jail has not increased as rapidly as the numbers of immigrants detained. Between 1995 and 2005, the average number of inmates held in jails has increased by around 50 percent, compared with the 200 percent increase in immigrant detentions during the same time period. However, the sheer number of people in jails is significantly higher than the number in immigrant detention. For example, in 2005 the average daily population of immigrants in detention was 19,619, compared with the 733,442 who were held in jail. Put another way, out of the total average daily populations for both jails and immigrant detention centers, 97 percent of the inmates are held in jail. It is important to remember that inmates in jail may also be immigrants but that the percentage of noncitizens in jail is relatively small compared with that of legal citizens. Moreover, racial groups are disproportionately represented in local jails: whites 44 percent, blacks 39 percent, Hispanics 15 percent, and "other" (which includes Asians and Pacific Islanders) 1.7 percent (Page Harrison and Allen Beck, "Prison and Jail Inmates at Midyear, 2005," Bureau of Justice Statistics, May 2006), http://www.ojp.usdoj.gov/bjs/pub/pdf/pjim05.pdf [accessed November 7, 2007].

17. Some immigrants may have more bed days in detention because their countries may have policies that either block or inhibit the return of immigrants from the United States. Some of the countries who refuse to accept repatriated nationals or who are slow to cooperate with the process include China, Cuba, Eritrea, Ethiopia, India, Iran, Jamaica, Laos, and Vietnam. Nationals representing these countries were detained for a total of 981,202 days in 2003. In that year, Chinese nationals used 366,540 detention days, Jamaican nationals 241,114 days, and Vietnamese 137,280. A large number of immigrants from these countries who have or are pending final orders of removal are eventually released into the public and, according to the DHS, are unlikely to ever be repatriated because the countries refuse to provide documents relevant to the repatriation process. As of 2004 133,662 immigrants had been released into the United States despite pending or final orders of removal, with the majority of this group being nationals of China, India, and Jamaica (Department of Homeland Security, "Detention and Removal of Illegal Aliens," 17–19).

18. Dougherty, Wilson, and Wu, "Immigration Enforcement Actions," 4.

19. Alison Siskin, "Immigration-Related Detention: Current Legislative Issues," Congressional Research Service Report for Congress, Library of Congress, April 28, 2004, 12, http://www.fas.org/irp/crs/RL32369.pdf (accessed November 7, 2007).

20. Harrison and Beck, "Prison and Jail Inmates at Midyear," 5.

21. The Immigration and Naturalization Service (INS) was disbanded and reincorporated into the new Department of Homeland Security in 2002.

22. John Scalia and Marika Litras, "Immigration Offenders in the Federal Criminal Justice System, 2000," Bureau of Justice Statistics, August 2002, 1, http://www.ojp.usdoj.gov/bjs/pub/pdf/iofcjs00.pdf (accessed November 7, 2007).

23. Transactional Records Access Clearinghouse (TRAC), "Prosecution of Immigration Cases Surge in U.S. 2005," http://trac.syr.edu/tracins/latest/131/ (accessed November 7, 2007).

24. Scalia and Litras, "Immigration Offenders in the Federal Criminal Justice System," 4. It is not clear whether race is self-reported during the criminal justice proceedings but this may have an impact on the numbers given here. More, if race is self-reported, many of the Hispanic immigrant prisoners may be phenotypically read as black but may not report themselves as such.

25. Scalia and Litras, "Immigration Offenders in the Federal Criminal Justice System," 2.

26. Eric Sterling, "Drug Laws and Snitching: A Primer," *PBS Frontline*, December 2006, http://www.pbs.org/wgbh/pages/frontline/shows/snitch/primer/ (accessed November 7, 2007).

27. Ibid.

28. Marc Mauer, "Young Black Americans and the Criminal Justice System," in James, *States of Confinement*, 75–93.

29. (TRAC), "Prosecution of Immigration Cases Surge in U.S. 2005." For a detailed description of the list of crimes labeled as aggravated felonies, see Bill Ong Hing, "Deporting Our Souls and Defending Our Immigrants," *Amerasia Journal* 31 (2005): xi–xxxii.

30. David Goldberg, "Surplus Value: The Political Economy of Prisons and Policing," in James, *States of Confinement*, 205–221.

31. Sentencing Project, "New Incarceration Figures: Thirty-Three Consecutive Years of Growth," May 2006, http://www.sentencingproject.org/pdfs/1044.pdf (accessed November 7, 2007).

32. Mauer, "Young Black Americans and the Criminal Justice System," 77.

33. Bureau of Justice, *Compendium of Federal Justice Statistics*, 2004 (2006), 19, http://www.ojp.usdoj.gov/bjs/pub/pdf/cfjs04.pdf (accessed November 7, 2007).

34. American Civil Liberties Union, "ACLU Releases Crack Cocaine Report, Anti–Drug Abuse Act of 1986 Deepened Racial Inequity in Sentencing," press release, October 2006, http://www.aclu.org/drugpolicy/gen/27194prs20061026.html (accessed November 7, 2007); Judith Scully, "Killing the Black Community: A Commentary on the United States War on Drugs," in *Policing the National Body: Race, Gender, and Criminalization*, ed. Anannya Bhattacharjee and Jael Silliman, 55–80 (Cambridge: South End Press, 2002).

35. Marc Mauer, *Race to Incarcerate* (New York: New Press, 1999).

36. ACLU, "ACLU Releases Crack Cocaine Report"; Mauer, "Young Black Americans and the Criminal Justice System"; Scully, "Killing the Black Community."

37. Scalia and Litras, "Immigration Offenders in the Federal Criminal Justice System," 1.

38. For example, after these amendments were passed, the months sentenced to prison for unlawfully reentering the United States after a previous conviction for an aggravated felony increased from 57 to 71 months (Scalia and Litras, "Immigration Offenders in the Federal Criminal Justice System," 5).

39. Bureau of Justice Statistics, *Compendium of Federal Justice Statistics, 2004*, 13; Bureau of Justice Statistics, *Compendium of Federal Justice Statistics, 2003* (2005), 1, http://www.ojp.usdoj.gov/bjs/pub/pdf/cfjs03.pdf (accessed November 7, 2007).

40. Bureau of Justice Statistics, *Compendium of Federal Justice Statistics, 2004*, 13.

41. Ibid., 1.

42. Ibid., 19.

43. Ibid., 13.

44. Ibid., 19.

45. Ibid., 73.

46. Ibid., 69.

47. Ibid., 70.

48. Ibid., 76.

49. Hing, "Deporting Our Souls and Defending Our Immigrants."

50. Randy Capps, "How Are Immigrants Faring After Welfare Reform? Preliminary Evidence from Los Angeles and New York City," Urban Institute Policy Report, 2002, http://www.urban.org/uploadedPDF/410426_final_report.pdf (accessed November 7, 2007); Amanda Levinson, "Immigrants and Welfare Use," Migration Information Source, August 2002, http://www.migrationinformation.org/USFocus/display.cfm?ID=45 (accessed November 7, 2007); Angela Oh and Karen Umemoto, "Asian Americans and Pacific Islanders: From Incarceration to Re-entry," *Amerasia Journal* 31 (2005): 45–59.

51. Eithne Luibheid, *Entry Denied: Controlling Sexuality at the Border* (Minneapolis: University of Minnesota Press, 2002).

52. Drake Bennett, "Good Waves," *Boston.com News*, January, 2006, http://www.boston.com/news/globe/ideas/articles/2006/01/01/good_waves/ (accessed November 7, 2007); Federation for American Immigration Reform, "Immigration and Welfare," December 2006, http://www.fairus.org/site/PageServer?pagename=iic_immigrationissuecenters7fd8 (accessed November 7, 2007); George Grayson, "Mexico Prefers to Export Its Poor, Not Uplift Them," *Christian Science Monitor*, March 2006; Syd Lindsley, "The Gendered Assault on Immigrants," in Bhattacharjee and Silliman, *Policing the National Body: Race, Gender, and Criminalization*, 175–196.

53. Yen Le Espiritu, "The 'We-Win-Even-When-We-Lose' Syndrome: U.S. Press Coverage of the Twenty-Fifth Anniversary of the 'Fall of Saigon,'" *American Quarterly* 58 (June 2006): 329–352; Eric Tang, "Collateral Damage: Southeast Asian Poverty in the United States," *Social Text* 18 (2000): 55–79.

54. Jill Quadagno, *The Color of Welfare: How Racism Undermined the War on Poverty* (Oxford: Oxford University Press, 1996); Dorothy Roberts, *Killing the Black Body: Race, Reproduction, and the Meaning of Liberty* (New York: Vintage, 1998).

55. Women in Prison Project, "Women in Prison Fact Sheet," December 2006, http://www.correctionalassociation.org/WIPP/publications/Women_in_Prison_Fact_Sheet_2006.pdf.

56. Ibid.

57. Harrison and Beck, "Prison and Jail Inmates at Midyear," 5.

58. Women in Prison Project, Immigration and the Criminal Justice System Fact Sheet, December 2006, http://www.correctionalassociation.org/WIPP/publications/Immigration_Fact_Sheet_2006.pdf (accessed November 7, 2007).

59. New York State counts foreign-born inmates versus noncitizens.

60. Socheat Chea, "The Evolving Definition of an Aggravated Felony," FindLaw .Com (1999), http://library.findlaw.com/1999/Jun/1/126967.html (accessed November 7, 2007).

61. Public Law 104-208, *Illegal Immigration Reform and Immigrant Responsibility Act of 1996*, http://www.uscis.gov/propub/ProPubVAP.jsp?dockey=2b289cf41d d6b70a61a078a9fbfbc379 (accessed November 7, 2007).

62. National Immigration Forum, "Due Process: Immigration Laws Deny Access to Justice," January 2007, http://www.immigrationforum.org/DesktopDefault .aspx?tabid=174 (accessed November 7, 2007).

63. Chea, "Evolving Definition of an Aggravated Felony."

64. Cara Feinberg, "Staying Here," *Boston College Magazine* (Spring 2006).

65. Hing, "Deporting Our Souls and Defending Our Immigrants," xvii.

66. TRAC, "Aggravated Felonies and Deportation," December 2006, http:// trac.syr.edu/immigration/reports/155/ (accessed November 7, 2007).

67. TRAC, "How Often Is the Aggravated Felony Statute Used?" December 2006, http://trac.syr.edu/immigration/reports/158/ (accessed November 7, 2007).

68. Luibheid, *Entry Denied*, 9.

69. Department of Homeland Security, "Table 41: Aliens Formally Removed by Criminal Status and Region and Country of Nationality: Fiscal Years 1998 to 2005," *2005 Yearbook of Immigration Statistics*, http://www.dhs.gov/xlibrary/assets/statistics/yearbook/2005/table41.xls (accessed November 7, 2007).

70. DHS, "Table 41."

71. Caribbean nationals constitute approximately 1.2 percent of the total U.S. population (see note 7), whereas Asian Americans constitute 4.3 percent of the U.S. population (U.S. Census Bureau, "Census 2000 Brief, Race and Hispanic

Origin," http://www.census.gov/prod/2001pubs/c2kbr01-1.pdf (accessed November 7, 2007).

72. Most notably, Cambodians, who have extremely small numbers of formal removals, tend to be removed for criminal reasons about 50 percent of the time.

73. DHS, "Table 41."

74. Jemima Pierre, "Black Immigrants in the United States and the 'Cultural Narratives' of Ethnicity," *Identities: Global Studies in Culture and Power* 11 (2004): 141–170; Stephen Steinberg, *The Ethnic Myth: Race, Ethnicity, and Class in America*, 3rd ed. (Boston: Beacon Press, 2003); Mary Waters, *Black Identities: West Indian Immigrant Dreams and American Realities* (Cambridge: Harvard University Press, 1999); Mary Waters, "Ethnic and Racial Identities of Second-Generation Black Immigrants in New York City," *International Migration Review* 28 (1994): 795–821.

75. Hing, "Misusing Immigration Policies in the Name of Homeland Security," *CR: The New Centennial Review* 6 (2006): 195–224.

76. Lisa Wong Macabasco, "We Are All Suspects Now: Exploring the Human Cost of the Post-9/11 Immigration Crackdown," *Mother Jones*, November 2005, http://www.motherjones.com/news/qa/2005/11/tram_nguyen.html (accessed November 7, 2007).

77. Deepa Fernandes, *Targeted: National Security and the Business of Immigration* (New York: Seven Stories Press, 2006); Michael Welch, *Detained: Immigration Laws and the Expanding I.N.S. Jail Complex* (Philadelphia: Temple University Press, 2002).

78. Aristide Zolberg, "Rethinking the Last 200 Years of U.S. Immigration Policy," Migration Policy Institute, Migration Information Source, June 1, 2006, http://www.migrationinformation.org/Feature/display.cfm?ID=401 (accessed November 7, 2007).

79. Mae Ngai, *Impossible Subjects: Illegal Aliens and the Making of Modern America* (Princeton: Princeton University Press, 2005); Anna Pegler-Gordon, "Chinese Exclusion, Photography, and the Development of U.S. Immigration Policy," *American Quarterly* 58 (2006): 51–77; Nayan Shah, "Between 'Oriental Depravity' and 'Natural Degenerates': Spatial Borderlands and the Making of Ordinary Americans," *American Quarterly* 57 (2005): 703–725.

80. Department of Homeland Security, "Table 42: Aliens Removed by Administrative Reason for Removal: Fiscal Years 1991 to 2004, *2004 Yearbook of Immigration Statistics*, http://www.dhs.gov/xlibrary/assets/statistics/yearbook/2004/Table42.xls; Department of Homeland Security, "Table 45: Aliens Deported by Administrative Reason for Removal: Fiscal Years 1908 to 1980," *2004 Yearbook of Immigration Statistics*, http://www.dhs.gov/xlibrary/assets/statistics/yearbook/2004/Table45.xls (accessed November 7, 2007); Department of Homeland Security, "Table 46: Aliens Deported by Administrative Reason for Removal: Fiscal Years 1981

to 1990, 2004 *Yearbook of Immigration Statistics,* http://www.dhs.gov/xlibrary/ assets/statistics/yearbook/2004/Table46.xls (accessed November 7, 2007).

81. Vilna Bashi, "Globalized Anti-blackness: Transnationalizing Western Immigration Law, Policy, and Practice," *Ethnic and Racial Studies* 27 (2004): 584–606.

82. Welch, *Detained,* 106.

83. Ibid., 159.

84. Sentencing Project, "New Incarceration Figures."

85. Cainkar, "Impact of the September 11 Attacks"; Cainkar and Maira, "Targeting Arab/Muslim/South Asian Americans"; Human Rights Watch, "Presumption of Guilt"; Nguyen, "Detained or Disappeared?"; Yaghmaian, "Suspected and Feared."

86. Hussein Ibish, "At the Constitution's Edge: Arab Americans and Civil Liberties," in James, *States of Confinement,* 287–302.

87. Randa Kayyali, "The People Perceived as a Threat to Security: Arab Americans Since September 11," Migration Policy Institute, Migration Information Source, July 2006, http://www.migrationinformation.org/Feature/display.cfm?ID=409 (accessed November 7, 2007); Migration Policy Institute, "Legal Immigration to United States Increased Substantially in FY 2005," October 2006, http://www .migrationpolicy.org/pubs/FS13_immigration_US_2006.pdf (accessed November 7, 2007); Migration Policy Institute, "Immigration Enforcement Spending Since IRCA," November 2005, http://www.migrationpolicy.org/ITFIAF/FactSheet_ Spending.pdf (accessed November 7, 2007); Migration Policy Institute, "Legal Immigration to United States Up from Last Year," November 2005, http://www .migrationpolicy.org/pubs/FS12_immigration_US_2005.pdf (accessed November 7, 2007).

88. Jeffrey Passel, *The Size and Characteristics of the Unauthorized Migrant Population in the U.S.: Estimates Based on the March 2005 Current Population Survey,* Pew Hispanic Center, March 2006, http://pewhispanic.org/files/reports/61.pdf (accessed November 7, 2007).

89. David Bacon, "Looking for Common Ground," *Colorlines* 32 (Spring 2006); Macabasco, "We Are All Suspects Now"; Julie Quiroz-Martinez, "Missing Link," *Colorlines* 13 (Summer 2001); Evalyn Tennant, "Dismantling U.S.-Style Apartheid," *Colorlines* 24 (Spring 2004).

PART IV

Inside the Immigration Prison System: Activist Perspectives

CHAPTER 11

Rafiu's Story
An American Immigrant Nightmare

MALIK NDAULA WITH DEBBIE SATYAL

IT SEEMS IRONIC THAT THE PERCEIVED BEAUTY of the American Dream is that it allows freedom and opportunity to all. The American Dream supports the belief that through hard work and determination, any immigrant can achieve a better life, usually in terms of financial prosperity and enhanced freedom of choice. The concept is that anybody can get a share of the country's wealth if he or she is willing to work hard. It sounds good, but really what America does is it decides who is going to be allowed the freedom and opportunity to live the American Dream.

First of all, let me say I am not an immigration expert. It is true I know the system intimately, probably better than some lawyers, but I do not have a law degree. What I am an expert in is detention: cold, stale, worn-down prison and its decaying effect on people. Arriving in rough New York City in my early teenage years, I was undocumented and without much guidance, having come to the United States to escape the political situation in Uganda. I entered the United States on a Zaire passport (now Democratic Republic of Congo). Once here, I lived with friends of family for a short while before I was left to fend for myself. My parents had died in North Uganda before I came to the United States, and I did not have the resources or support structure to tell me that I could apply for political asylum. I did not even know how to go about the process. I am not sure of the exact type of visa I used to come to the United States, but I do remember that I lost my passport at the house of a woman who hosted me in my early days as a street hustler. She was a struggling heroin addict.

I ended up in prison when I was seventeen going on eighteen, for a two-year sentence. You can say I got myself caught in the crossfire of American street life. All this did not seem so bad at first. After all, it was a phase in the American way of things. Like many black males in this country, my options for higher education were very narrow, and being undocumented only made things much harder. I could not enroll in an educational institution even though I wanted to. I had to settle for working for day-labor agencies because other employers usually let me go after they learned about my legal status. I resorted to life in the streets, because in the streets no one cared if I was undocumented or where I came from. I was willing to learn, and they put me to work: it is that simple. But like the saying goes, "Crime pays." I soon learned that my life as I was living it would take me into another type of institution—prison—and it was in prison that my immigration status threw me into the legal matrix that is the crux of my story.

I will explain how I went from life on the streets to being locked up in immigration prison, to becoming an activist and so-called jailhouse lawyer on the "inside," and, finally, how I managed to win my case and become a legal advocate for detainees and immigrants' rights on the "outside." Although my story is exceptional in some respects, in many other ways it is no different from the stories of tens of thousands of noncitizens who are imprisoned and deported on an annual basis. This is why I have interwoven my story with those of the other detainees who mentored me and stood alongside me as we fought for our rights. One of the main points of my discussion is that change is possible and that even the most abusive prison conditions can be challenged by people who appear to have no standing in U.S. society. But my personal story also draws attention to systemic problems that are tied to the way the entire immigration system operates, and especially to its growing intersection with the prison-industrial complex. These problems cannot be fixed once and for all by isolated protests or even by class-action lawsuits. They require an across-the-board change in the way the system is run and the priorities guiding U.S. immigration policy. I do not promise to provide a clear solution to all these issues, but you will see that I do provide some suggestions about what works and what some beginning steps should be.

Entering the System

I did not know exactly what was in store for me after I finished serving time for my criminal offense. Like most incarcerated persons, I did time in a local facility, and most important, there were clear guidelines that defined the length of my sentence, the reasons I was being held, and the conditions that could either lengthen or shorten my sentence. But after my criminal incarceration, I entered a very different and very ambiguous world where I was kept in the dark about how long I was going to be held or even *where* I was going to be held.

After serving my sentence, I was transferred to immigration custody deep in the rural South. There I was placed in a one-thousand-man prison complex housing mostly West Indians, Africans, Cambodians, Vietnamese, and South Americans. The planes and buses are loaded up with immigrant detainees every day, and we are shipped from New York to the South like cargo. Men fight for their right to stay in the country with their family members, mothers, and children. They cry at night in the darkness when no one can see their emotional self, hiding the fact that they are hurt because the system has condemned them to mandatory exile without considering their ties to this nation. They are treated as if their families do not mean anything. The representatives of the immigration system tear you apart, telling your family you stand no chance of being allowed to remain in the country.

But why should you have to be *allowed* to remain here if your social support and family networks are right here in America? You were not born here, but you were raised here and it is the only thing you know. Your life is here. When you experience things from this perspective, the U.S. immigration system resembles an imperial regime that distributes rights and benefits based on citizen status. One associates this kind of system with ancient and medieval times, but it is happening today in the United States, which is arguably the single most advanced nation, in terms of civil and political rights, since the beginning of time.

In the summer of 2004, after I had spent five years in the immigration system, the government finally released me under the federal equivalent of parole and probation, known as supervised release. By the end of my experience in immigration prison, I had become very close with one of the most amazing characters I have ever known. His name is Rafiu Abimbola, and quite frankly I did not even like him when we first met. It was not anything personal, but I was young and thought the world of myself. Rafiu was the type of detainee who is standoffish and spends most of his time in the law library. Back then, that was not the type of thing I knew to respect. Once Rafiu found out that I, too, was African, he went out of his way to check up on me. My friendship with Rafiu turned out to be one of the only pleasures I had during my five years in the federal immigration system.

His story is not unlike that of many men and women, all chasing a shattered American Dream, but he was an inspiration for me. For three years, we shared the same life: the same pain, disappointments, harassment, shelter, food, and love of the law.

Rafiu was born in Nigeria and was about thirty-five years old when we were together; he is now thirty-nine. He speaks with a thick Nigerian accent and is a short, dark skinned man. He entered the United States by way of California on a visitor's visa in 1991 and lived there for two years before moving to New York City. He later on met a woman whom he fell in love with and married. They had a son, and in 1994 he adjusted his status to that of a legal permanent resident based on his marriage.

During his detainment, his family—wife and child—were in New York. He had nothing waiting for him in Nigeria, no way to make a living and no way to see his child. I believe that his perseverance came from wanting to stick around for his child. I, being the militant age of twenty-one and without children, was less cautious and diplomatic than Rafiu. Maybe it was the age, maybe it was his family, but despite our differences, there we were, locked up together.

I suppose that we are not unique, Rafiu and myself—both black as ebony. I sat in detention watching the myriad faces that passed by, that inspired such hatred from the guards. The politics of race are blatant in immigration prison if you are not in denial. Since the 1960s, most of the immigrants coming to America have been from Asia, Africa, and Latin America—very different from the Western European immigrants who had been the previous immigrant group to flock to the United States.

It seems to me that as the faces arriving in the United States have become increasingly dark, the backlash has become more fierce. I always thought that America was proud to be made up of the hardworking sons and daughters of immigrants, but the consequences of being a noncitizen have also increased in recent years, contrary to the politically correct images that Americans like to conjure up about their great-grandparents from abroad.

In 1996 the Immigration and Nationality Act (INA) underwent a major revamping that affected anyone who is not a citizen, legal permanent residents and undocumented aliens alike. This resulted in the enactment of the Illegal Immigration Reform and Immigrant Responsibility Act (IIRAIRA).[1] These changes in the INA have contributed to the government's goal of ridding the country of illegal immigrants, but at the expense of what? Due process concerns abound in the system, and it is mostly the poorest and least educated who are the victims. Plus, the law's retroactivity is unnecessarily harsh. A legal permanent resident can now be deported for a crime that he or she committed when it was not a deportable crime. Sounds unfair? Contrary to any concept of legality you knew in America? It does not matter.

Before IIRAIRA, immediate deportation was triggered only for offenses that could lead to five years or more in jail. After IIRAIRA, even minor offenses like shoplifting, which might be punished with just a probationary sentence, are enough for deportation. IIRAIRA even applies to legal permanent residents and naturalized citizens who have married American citizens and had American-born children.

The final upshot of this is that the 1996 "reforms" made deportation a mandatory punishment for a wide range of noncitizens, including some who have lived here for decades. When punishment is mandatory, this means judges do not have a say in deciding if deportation is fair; the court proceedings are merely ceremonial. It also means that noncitizens and their families are robbed of a fair day in court and of a chance to show how permanent exile from the United States would impact their families. The result? Every year, nearly 200,000 noncitizens are deported—a total of over 1 million since 1996.[2] They are torn apart from their families even when an immigration judge believes they deserve to stay in the United States to help raise their children and support their families. This means that families have to choose between either separating, which results in more single-parent households and the psychological and financial hardship that brings, or forcing their U.S.-citizen spouses and children into deportation with them in order to stay together. This also means that U.S.-born children may have to start over in a country with a new language and an uncertain future. In addition, the U.S.-born children may never be able to reestablish ties with their extended family in the United States.

Even though IIRAIRA was a bad development for noncitizens, it only reinforced a get-tough enforcement trend that had been gathering steam for the past few decades. The climate of post–9/11 America intensified this, making it possible for all these prosecutions—whether they are for mail fraud, drug possession, or shoplifting—to be lumped together with activities that are deemed to threaten national security, further justifying the speedy deportation of noncitizens who violate any variety of civil or criminal laws. This is all part of the backstory of why so many noncitizens are currently being held in immigration prison, with no end in sight, even though they have already served time for their original criminal or civil violation.

Fighting for Freedom in the Immigration Prison System

The context of the current immigration climate in the United States also pertains directly to me and Rafiu. We were both in prison awaiting the same fate, it seemed. Like most other detainees, we both were swept up through the criminal system. He came into the system in 1998 for a state charge and a federal charge, so he stayed in a state prison, Bridgeport Correctional Center in Connecticut, for two years and then was charged as being deportable for the state charge in 1999 based on his federal offense. The federal offense, fraud, however, was on appeal. Meanwhile, I was charged with a misdemeanor in 1999 that landed me in the system, and once I served my criminal sentence, I also was sent into immigration detention.

Now, do not be fooled by thinking that the immigration system puts people awaiting deportation into some special place. In fact, just the opposite is true. I have seen many people serve a light sentence for a criminal conviction with other offenders of the same security risk. After they finish doing prison time for their original offense, they get "picked up" by the immigration authorities (since they are now eligible for deportation because of their criminal offense), and the only thing that happens is that they are transferred into a different cell in the same prison. They are still in prison, in a cell. What this often means is that immigration detainees who have not committed serious offenses (and those who have not committed offenses beyond their immigration indiscretions) are often mixed up with those who have committed very dangerous crimes.

This did not actually happen with us. Worse by far, we were transferred from New York, where we had served our time for our criminal convictions, and sent to an immigration prison in Oakdale, Louisiana, until the federal authorities made a final decision about our legal status. It was difficult being held in a facility so far from the Northeast—the only region that Rafiu or I really knew in the United States. There is no jurisdictional problem with this. The immigration system is federal and has the authority to send detainees to any federal detention facility in the country where beds are available—without regard to family or where the person was originally sentenced. If this does not seem unfair to you, I suppose I can understand that and maybe there's no reason to expect that you would see this as un-fair. But remember this, immigration detainees are picked up by immigra-tion authorities, appear in court, have hearings, serve time before deportation, and are deported every day, all without the assistance of legal counsel. Because legal counsel is not provided for people in immigration detention, and most of them do not have much money, they must seek out nonprofits and pro bono and "low-bono" attorneys who might help them. So, few immigrants actually get an attorney, and even those who have an attorney have a hard time providing them with useful information and documents while they are being bounced from prison to prison around the country. Beyond the sentimental consequences of not seeing family nearby, being transferred to another jurisdiction has very tangible effects on a de-tainee's legal case.

Oakdale, Louisiana, is quite a place to be transferred to. It seemed to me that it was all just swampland. Rafiu was transferred to Oakdale in 2000, but he successfully argued that the government had instituted proceed-ings prematurely since the federal case against him had not been resolved. Under normal circumstances, the government should have released Rafiu until his appeal was exhausted. But he was not released. Instead, the gov-ernment introduced new charges of deportation, citing a state misde-meanor larceny offense from Connecticut. It has been argued that once a final decision has been reached in a civil suit, the issue should not be al-lowed for new litigation based on the same facts. This standard was obvi-ously not applied to Rafiu.

Rafiu was impressive, really. All he did in prison was read, write to orga-nizations for case law, and learn. He learned all about how to help immi-gration detainees file their appeals, apply for relief, and argue cases. You could say he learned by teaching himself how to be a lawyer. We were the lucky ones there. We both knew how to speak, read, and write English. Rafiu was actually enrolled at Long Island University pursuing a liberal arts bachelor's degree before being detained. I did not have that type of for-mal education, but I did earn my GED in my first few months at Oakdale. Education is invaluable in immigration detention, since most people do not get an attorney.

In 2002 the government tried to deport Rafiu for the first time. They sent him away to Batavia, in upstate New York, a federal prison that holds immigration detainees. This is the place many Africans who are being de-ported leave from with a U.S. Marshal. But this was not to be Rafiu's fate, even though he had received an order of deportation. Rafiu received a stay order from a federal court, allowing his deportation to be halted until the final disposition was given. Rafiu joined me once again in Oakdale.

Rafiu came back and continued his legal work. He worked day and night, reading, writing, and researching. The facilities in Oakdale were decent, probably because it was a federal prison, and Rafiu had the information he needed at the law library. What the law library lacked, he retrieved from nonprofits that would mail him the appropriate information.

He was frequently harassed by the prison guards for being a "writ writer." They would always use other excuses, but the truth was that Rafiu was a risk. A black man in prison doing nothing but reading made them nervous. They punished him for it. The guards would say things like "Your bed is not made right" or "Why are you holding other people's materials" when they knew that Rafiu had the material with permission from other inmates. The truth or falsity of their claims never mattered. They still used those flimsy charges to throw Rafiu into segregation.

Thought segregation was over? Not in prison. It is also known as "solitary" or "the hole." Let me tell you something: in prison, you have so little, but what little you do have is taken away in segregation. You are cut off from everything. The only time you leave the cell that you alone are confined to is for a shower three times a week and an extremely minimal form of "recreation." There is no human interaction in segregation, only the guard who hands you food through a slot in a little door to your cell. You are not allowed to bring anything into the cell with you. For Rafiu, that meant pictures of his wife and son or any letters from his wife. It also meant all the materials he had accumulated and all the cases he was working on. Beyond that, you are deprived of the simple things: any food that you have bought, any clothing, all access to your personal property is gone. The little freedom you had to walk around is not available to you. There is no natural light, because the window you have is made out of a material that does not let you see out. Furthermore, you are deprived of visits to the law library and contact with other inmates. This is how they tried to shut Rafiu down from helping other detainees on a day-to-day basis. They would place him in administrative detention for up to ninety days at a time. I would say this happened to Rafiu at least ten different times.

Later, in my work, I would encounter many stories about the things the officers or supervisors would do to detainees held in segregation, such as spit or pass gas in their food, or trashing their living space when they were in the shower or when they went outside for their one hour of recreation. For a detainee being held in segregation, recreation is only a tiny cage big enough to stand in, and that is all. A detainee who told me his cell was trashed said most of the time he refused to go out for recreation or take a shower because of what they would do. I knew of a detainee who was in segregation for ten months because the facility just kept adding to his "sentence" as a result of things he did while in segregation. But generally speaking, a detainee who has endured some of what I have mentioned is not encouraged to engage in civil disobedience.

We stayed in Oakdale for another two years—Rafiu being thrown into segregation, helping people, being harassed, and fighting our own cases. In the meantime, I had learned a thing or two myself about the system and the intricacies of immigration law. This would prove useful to us in our next prison.

We were transferred then to Concordia Parish Prison Facility in Louisiana. It was what you would expect from a county prison, and coming from a federal institution, we found it really bad. Arguably, we were transferred to rural county facilities because they had bed space that was badly needed. It seems however, that we were being used for commercial purposes.

I learned more about this after I finally got out. It turns out that Concordia was not an exceptional case. Politicians advocated for increased spending on prison expansion all the way through the 1990s. But as rural America invested in prison expansion, people began to notice that there were not enough prisoners to go around.

In fact, so many prisons being built increased pressures to expand the prison population just to offset the cost of construction. The targets of prison expansion have been racial minority youths, but many community-based organizations have been successful in developing programs that lower incarceration rates for native-born minorities in urban areas. As a result, there has been mounting pressure to find a new target for incarceration, which is where immigrants come in (and on top of this, the recent increase in spending for immigration enforcement makes immigration detainees a more lucrative client base than "regular" prisoners for both public and private prisons).[3]

So it is no surprise that jail officials liked to house immigrant detainees, especially when we spent long periods in their facilities. We were told by jail officers and Louisiana state prisoners that while the state of Louisiana paid on average $21 for a state prisoner, U.S. Immigration paid anywhere from $75 to $145 a day, depending on the facility and contract. It is ironic, then, that the same jails, in order to cut costs, often refuse to meet detainees' basic needs but will provide more help to state prisoners whom they get less money to keep.

Before 1996, what was then the Immigration and Naturalization Service had fewer than 5,000 detainees in its immigration prisons. Since 1996, the government has maintained an average of 23,000 immigrants in prison on any given day and wants to further expand detention bed space.[4] They call immigration detention civil confinement, but prison is prison no matter what label you use, and prison breaks people's souls, hearts, and even minds. The private companies that run a lot of the jails contracted by immigration authorities are in it for the money and only the money. They do not care whether people go untreated for medical complications, whether law libraries are equipped and staffed, whether food service is nutritious, and so on.

Most of the people transferred with Rafiu and me were from Connecticut, New York, and Massachusetts. Most of them had cases pending in federal court challenging their orders of deportation on constitutional grounds or on the statutory framework. They sent us to Concordia, I suspect, to frustrate us in our litigation.

Now, the government indicates that immigration detainees are being held for administrative purposes and are not treated as criminals. Yet in many ways they are treated worse than criminal detainees because they are not allowed the assistance of a public defender or any legal assistance— a right that is guaranteed to criminal defendants. Immigration detainees are often fed worse than those serving out their criminal sentences, are given only one hour a day of fresh air, are allowed to go to the law library for just five hours a week, and maybe visit with family and friends once a week for an hour. Knowing this still did not prepare us for Concordia.

Continuing the Struggle at Concordia

The things that we took for granted on the outside were at their worst in Concordia. The living conditions at the Concordia Parish Prison were so bad that it was possible for even the strongest of men to become frustrated, just from the horrific state of the facilities alone. Men who had been fighting their appeals for years considered giving up. Everything was dirty— *everything*. It was an in-living jail, which means that it was set up sort of like a dormitory situation. We stayed in there basically all day. Men were smoking constantly inside, and there was no ventilation, which made it hard to breathe. As far as the food goes—prison food is nothing to speak of to begin with, but there is a difference between not liking the food and just not having enough. We all used to say that even a ten-year-old would not be satisfied with the little food we were given.

The phones were really expensive. It would cost family members about $20 to accept phone calls from their loved ones, meaning that keeping in touch was unaffordable for some families. Rafiu's family, for one, could not afford it. To make it worse, the few legal providers and organizations that used to take our phone calls could no longer afford to give us the help we needed so badly. This had the desired effect of making our cases more difficult for us to handle.

In Concordia, we made sure we did not get hurt, because the medical services were horrible, involving days of waiting. Even a request for Tylenol was an ordeal. I remember when a diabetic was given half an orange as medication to stabilize his sugar levels instead of the insulin he required.

The guards in the Deep South were really racist. They would give non-Christians a hard time, for instance, if they were Muslim and wanted to pray. They did not allow them to keep Korans and generally were intolerant of anything that was different from what they were used to.

And we were really different. Besides Rafiu and me learning everything we could from law books, the group of guys who transferred with us were also very informed about what prison conditions were supposed to be like, being that we all had come from federal prison. I would say confidently that we were better educated than most prisoners and were especially more knowledgeable about the illegalities that these guards committed on a daily basis against us.

I have never been able to get over the maltreatment we endured at their hands. They handled us so much worse than they treated the noncitizens who were still serving time for criminal sentences, just on account of our status. But we weren't daunted. We had learned from other detainees in Oakdale who had the experience of serving long terms in federal prisons, guys who were like father figures to Rafiu and me. They showed us how to type up legal paperwork and gave us tips on filing documents. Because I did not have family to send me money, and Rafiu's family could not help him out either, these guys provided us with things we needed. And, finally, they taught us that by providing legal services to the people who were detained with us, we could help everyone and help ourselves. Because the laws have become so harsh, often there was no remedy for our fellow detainees. This is something that Rafiu or I would be able to spot almost immediately about someone's case—a helpful service to detainees whose families were not able to scrape together lawyers' fees.

At any rate, because the treatment was so inhumane, we started petitioning the warden with our grievances. We wanted him to address the horrific situation and the filthy conditions we were living in, which were starting to affect our strength and patience. Detainees had begun getting into fights with guards. I have to admit I was guilty of that as well. It was an all-around bad situation, but it was a perfect illustration of Rafiu's good influence on me. He never lashed out or became visibly angry. He would just write his complaints. On the other hand, I was militant and belligerent (I would take this opportunity to remind you that I was in my early twenties at the time and without much to lose), and there were plenty of others like me.

But to return to the matter of our prison conditions, we were especially deprived from a legal standpoint, since we could not reliably access the legal library. Also problematic was that the little room which served as a legal library had few materials relevant to immigration matters, and instead of a librarian, prison officials had two prisoners working in the library in exchange for benefits. Those of us coming in from Oakdale felt we could not trust those two guys—that they would leak the information we gave them and that they were too interested in being friendly with the guards.

So we all decided that we needed someone working in the library that we trusted, and after a discussion concluded that Rafiu, rather than I, should work there. We raised a petition, and believe it or not, our petition was granted and he was hired.

There was something satisfying about our victory. But being that we had been in prison for a while, our skepticism still ran high. We decided not to let on that there were two of us who were taking care of the legal needs of so many others. We figured if the guards knew that both of us worked on legal materials, they would weed both of us out, and the other detainees we helped would be left stranded. And so I relied on Rafiu to obtain the legal materials I needed. At this same time, we were corresponding with other detainees we had met in Oakdale, many of whom had been transferred to other prisons. Again, we had to devise a system for communication, because if the mail was going from one detention center to another, guards would confiscate the mail or delay it on purpose. What we had to do was ask people on the outside to mail the letters that they received from us to the detainees in other parish prisons, or we had family members of the detainees send their documents directly to Rafiu and to me. But Rafiu was fired from the law library after about a month, accused of something or other, and placed in segregation for a week. We guessed that the prison was not comfortable with the amount of mail he started sending out and receiving once he started working at the library. At this point, we were grateful we did not let on that I, too, was a jailhouse attorney. My fellow detainees urged me to take up where Rafiu had left off in the law library, but that did not interest me.

Around this time, Rafiu and I came across something of great interest to us. Rafiu had found an attorney to represent him in his immigration appeal in the Second Circuit Court. The attorney sent us Immigration and Customs Enforcement's detention standards from 2001. This was the first time we had seen anything like this. The problem with the standards is that they are only guidelines; there are no legal repercussions for violating them. But still, we were surprised. It seemed that not only were the folks at Concordia violating many of the guidelines, they did not even seem to know that they existed.

Since they were only guidelines, Rafiu began looking for an alternate source of legal authority. We needed to determine what the constitutional standard was for immigration detainees—particularly for those of us who were considered civil detainees because we had already served, or had never served, criminal sentences. What we learned was that the courts generally applied the standard of pretrial detainees to cases involving immigration detainees—meaning that there were due process clause considerations of the Fourteenth Amendment to be taken into account. According to what we were reading, Concordia Parish Prison was guilty of all kinds of due process violations.

We filed a class-action lawsuit against the jail. Rafiu wrote half of it, and I wrote the other half. We agreed what to sue on and what not to sue on. We collected signatures and submitted it to the court.

After Rafiu was fired from the law library, and after we put the lawsuit in motion, the expected happened: he was transferred to another parish prison with better conditions and a better law library. It seems that when the warden got wind of the class-action lawsuit, things started to change.

Computers were brought in to the law library, and immigration-related materials became available. We also started receiving more recreation time and prepaid phone calls so that we could better access our family. We also put in requests to use the phones for legal services. Obviously, the prison did not want to go through the expensive litigation and negative publicity that a lawsuit would entail, so they fixed things up. We changed things at Concordia within three months of being transferred there.

They started to treat us like humans instead of like animals. But it was frustrating how quickly they moved to transfer us out of there, just as conditions were improving. On Friday the prison heard of the lawsuit, and by Monday we were all being transferred to another parish prison.

This transfer was more taxing than the last. The ten-hour bus ride was horrible, and we all were handcuffed and shackled. We were on our way to Etowah County in Alabama. For some reason, all our colleagues from Oakdale were also being taken out of their parish prisons and transferred, including Rafiu. We all saw each other again on the bus.

At the Etowah County Jail, we were back to square one. Nothing worked! The only difference between this place and Concordia (when we had first arrived there) was that Etowah was a little cleaner. We all wondered how the place passed inspection, which it had just before we arrived. There was no real law library, access to phones was poor, and the guards were racist. We left Concordia in much better conditions than this. We heard a lot of the detainees there tell us that things would never change at Etowah. That was all right. We knew that change was possible because the same had been said about Concordia.

Prison Was Over, but Not the Fight

Fortunately for me, this is where my detention story ends. I had already been waiting in detention for ten months past the time I should have been. The attorney general finally had to answer for why I was still being detained, since I had already won my Board of Immigration Appeals case. The situation at Etowah had begun improving before I left. In the two weeks we had been there, we already effected change by our barking—we received computers with access to legal case summaries and better food.

When I left, I vowed to help the men who were still detained. I returned with the American Civil Liberties Union, and eventually turned this cause into my work. I became a Soros Justice Fellow with the National Immigration Project of the National Lawyers Guild in Boston and devoted my time to fighting prison abuses by the immigration system. I worked in Boston from 2005 to 2007. In fact, I believe that my detainees, support network, and friends were about six months ahead of the Office of Inspector General (OIG) in the Department of Homeland Security (DHS) when it first decided to monitor conditions in the detention system. We participated in this process, by sharing the information we had collected on conditions in detention centers across the country, with community and policy advocates, reporters, students, and even jail officials. I visited a few detention centers and set up meetings between immigration officers, prison wardens, and detainees who were seeking to improve conditions at least in the short term. I am thankful that there has been some genuine movement to improve conditions in immigration prisons and to set guidelines for what jails should provide when housing civil detainees. At the time of my exit from the National Immigration Project, the organization had petitioned the DHS to codify detention standards into regulations.

Meanwhile, Rafiu was still being held in the Etowah County Jail. I would receive mail from detainees telling me how much Rafiu was helping them, or had helped them receive relief from deportation. I was no longer allowed to dispense legal advice, since in the "real world" it matters that I am not bar certified, and I was now working for a nonprofit. But I would still help detainees by acting as a third party for their mailings. Rafiu would write me every week updating me on the cases he was working on.

Meanwhile, his own case was stalled in the Second Circuit Court while he helped everyone else. Rafiu's argument was that his theft offense should not be considered an aggravated felony under immigration law because of the way the statute could be construed. An aggravated felony is like a death sentence in immigration law. It means that almost any relief that might have been available to you is no longer available, and the 1996 laws (AEDPA and IIRAIRA) greatly expanded the list of aggravated felonies. To determine whether an offense is an aggravated felony, the court must look at the statute and the offense the detainee was convicted of by using the categorical approach. This approach does not, however, take into account the particulars of the case at hand but instead looks at the broad meaning of the offense.

In Rafiu's case, he was trying to argue that the statute under which he was convicted was divisible into two distinct categories: theft of service offenses and theft of property offenses. Rafiu further argued that it was the intent of Congress only to make theft of property offenses eligible for deportability. In 1995 Rafiu had been arrested for violating the relevant Connecticut General Statute; to wit, third-degree larceny. He argued, based on another case, that his conviction under Connecticut's third-degree larceny statute should not be construed as an aggravated felony.[5]

Rafiu was arguing that the court should apply this categorical approach because it was unclear whether he was convicted under theft of property or theft of services. The Second Circuit Court disagreed, stating that theft of services is still a deportable offense. He then took his appeal to the Supreme Court. He asked the Supreme Court to settle the matter because it was split among the federal circuit courts. The Seventh and Ninth Circuit Courts found that theft of services was not an aggravated felony because it did not involve a permanent deprivation. As a legal fiction, theft offenses are categorized in sets of offenses that involve one party taking another's property without permission with intent to permanently deprive the property owner. On that premise the argument can be made that an offense involving theft of services as opposed to theft of property does not involve the element of permanent deprivation, because services are not tangible things. The Supreme Court denied his certiorari request in December 2005. Rafiu was sent back to Nigeria, where he is now. During his six-year detention, his wife left him, unable to withstand the uncertainty and stress of being without him, and now he is without anything. He cannot see his son, although he communicates with his former wife and son via letters and phone conversations.

I feel bad for this man who helped so many people but was unable to win his own case. At one point, Rafiu was responsible for over three hundred detainees' cases in Etowah. He took over all the legal matters of the detainees, not just their immigration cases. Rafiu became an expert, and the detainees depended on him for a variety of matters; including petitioning prison wardens for redress of grievances, civil litigation to improve conditions, immigration legal assistance, postconviction relief for detainees with criminal offenses, and petitioning immigration officials.

Rafiu fought his case until every last option was unavailable to him. He finally could not fight anymore and went back to Nigeria. But Rafiu's legal argument was sound, and it is a bittersweet irony that the Supreme Court is supposed to hear a very similar argument once again soon.

Notes

1. Public Law 104-208, div. C. 110 *Stat.* 3009-546 (Sept. 30, 1996).
2. For a summary of recent trends see Department of Homeland Security, Office of Immigration Statistics, *2005 Yearbook of Immigration Statistics* (2006), 96.

3. For more information on the growing linkages between prison expansion in general, immigrant incarceration, and the privatization of the prison industry, see Meredith Kolodner, "Immigration Enforcement Benefits Prison Firms," *New York Times*, July 19, 2006; Andrew Stein, "Prison Stocks: A Secure Pick? Shares of the Top For-Profit Prison Operators Have Soared in the Past Year; Are They for You?" CNN/Money.com, April 30, 2004, http://money.cnn.com/2004/04/30/news/midcaps/prison_companies/index.htm (accessed November 14, 2007).

4. Page Harrison and Allen Beck, "Prison and Jail Inmates at Midyear, 2005," Bureau of Justice Statistics, May 2006, http://www.ojp.usdoj.gov/bjs/pub/pdf/pjim05.pdf (accessed November 14, 2007).

5. Kenneth Phillips; File No. A35-608-370, Board of Immigration Appeals, June 6, 2001.

CHAPTER 12

Families for Freedom
Against Deportation and Delegalization

SUBHASH KATEEL AND AARTI SHAHANI

AMERICA HAS MANY WORLDS, and the gap between two of them—between that of citizens and noncitizens—is deepening. Today, the United States is witnessing a major shift in the contours of membership, inequality, and control through the policing of noncitizens living on U.S. soil. We call this emerging system of inequality and punishment Immigrant Apartheid.

Immigrant Apartheid is a set of institutional and political processes leading to the creation of separate social, political, and economic spaces for citizens and noncitizens, derived from distinctions based on formal status. While the term *apartheid* typically has not been used to describe race and class in America, it is a familiar concept. U.S. history is rife with examples of second-class citizenship, and both formally and substantively, citizenship has been wedded to race historically. Jim Crow may be the clearest example.

Today, the United States cannot write race into the letter of law. That is, blacks cannot be three-fifths of a person *de jure*. But as migrants from Latin America, Asia, and Africa have replaced European flows, immigration status has been used as code for race.[1] While apartheid based on citizenship is not new, the breadth and scale of Immigrant Apartheid is historic. Local and federal governments are writing immigration status into law at an accelerating rate.[2] These laws, their enforcement, and the very culture of American politics have driven immigrants deeper underground. Whereas our parents' generation could open a bank account and buy a home while undocumented, today's green card holders are being deported en masse, and those without proper papers cannot even get a driver's license.[3] The fear immigrants have—of calling the police, of demanding pay for work, of putting a last name or valid address on a sign-in sheet—is no secret. The threat of being next for raids and deportation forms the very fabric of today's immigrant experience.

We have shared the thesis of Immigrant Apartheid with over a thousand quite diverse audiences. Some circles reject it—not for its validity as a description of our material reality, but because of the term's resonance and implications for strategy. Apartheid is clearly a racial concept, yet many colleagues in our movement are afraid to talk about immigrant rights as a racial issue. A handful have dismissed Immigrant Apartheid as extremist.[4] Yet in our community spaces—church basements, school classrooms, prison libraries—listeners consider the thesis obvious. No term besides *apartheid* quite fits what immigrants are experiencing on the ground.

We call the process that is institutionalizing Immigrant Apartheid *delegalization*. Delegalization is a sustained, state-sponsored movement to police populations through immigration status by: (1) coordinating resources from all levels of government and private actors to enforce existing sanctions against noncitizens and (2) making decisions in all branches of government to create new sanctions that would be considered unconstitutional if they were being endured by U.S. citizens. While delegalization is transforming what it means to be an immigrant, the process remains undertheorized. Our goal in this chapter is to illustrate where delegalization has developed most rapidly and its strategic implications for immigrants' rights organizing.

The authors of this chapter had the honor of becoming the first codirectors of Families for Freedom (FFF), a multiethnic defense network *by* and *for* immigrants facing deportation in New York. We write as organizers sharing lessons that cross issues and as participants in a historically specific immigrants' rights movement that we are committed to transforming as deeply as it has transformed us. Detention and deportation—the most severe punishments of delegalization—are the clearest examples of solidifying apartheid institutions. These civil policing systems increasingly resemble and depend on criminal policing agencies. Over the last seven years, we have struggled with families caught in these systems. Work and observations in the field have led us to this analytical framework.

Specifically, we will (1) describe how delegalization operates through the collaboration of local criminal institutions and federal civil immigration authorities; (2) trace how, locally and nationally, Families for Freedom has organized against deportation, despite it being considered by many veteran organizers to be an "unwinnable" fight; and (3) suggest how a successful immigrants' rights movement must recalibrate according to the realities of delegalization in order to combat the development of Immigrant Apartheid.

Legalization and Delegalization

If migration stopped flowing—if we were able to freeze the number of foreigners within our borders—the numbers subject to deportation would still climb, because the grounds for deportation are growing. Enforcement of the immigration laws is intensifying, too, and with it the raw numbers caught in the net. But this net is not cast evenly. The government does not (indeed, cannot) pick up every deportable immigrant,[5] so it has begun looking to the criminal justice system—a site that figures prominently in the lives of poor Americans—to increase the deportation rolls.

According to federal immigration authorities, deportations from 1981 to 1990 totaled 213,071, and 30,630 were of "criminal aliens." Fast-forward from 1996 to 2003 (a shorter period of time) and deportations total 1.2 million, with nearly half (517,861) for criminal violations.[6] "Criminal aliens" are people who have received convictions through the criminal courts of the judicial branch. They are growing in number, but not because immigrants are committing more crimes. Data suggests the opposite.[7] To understand the spike, we must investigate the growing link between immigration enforcement and the criminal justice system in the delegalization strategy.

The immigrants' rights movement is struggling ideologically with this material reality. The largest mass mobilizations in the nation's history were, ironically, driven by foreign nationals. Millions of them took to the streets in 2006—in towns big and small, red and blue. While debate nearly always outweighed consensus, the movement did name one central demand: legalization, the path to formal U.S. citizenship that begins with a green card.[8] But this demand for legalization was also accompanied by an insistence on separating out the Good (noncriminal) immigrants who "deserve" legalization from the Bad (incarcerated) immigrants who should be deported. This approach, however, highlights the major weak spot of the legalization movement, because enforcement practices are producing "Bad" immigrants and thereby eroding the central cry of legalization.

That one group demands rights *against* another less-deserving group is part and parcel of the politics of claims making.[9] That is, "Give us X because we are not Y." Often, claims makers create and deepen divisions that run contrary to self-interest or to strategy. Today, legalization is more limited than we imagine because: (1) the value of the green card is diminishing, (i.e., the legal/illegal divide is losing relevance); and (2) the risks associated with noncitizenship are increasing (i.e., the citizen/noncitizen divide is deepening).[10]

The immigrants' rights movement remains stuck in a paradigm that sees legalization or amnesty as the ultimate goal of any policy agenda. *Yet legalization does not solve delegalization.* Diverse evidence abounds to illustrate this claim.[11] The most ironic may be the growing number of green card holders who are being stripped of their "permanent residency" and deported for life. Green card holders are not among the 12 million people within the nation's borders who are still waiting for papers. They are those who already made it to the right side of the legal-illegal divide only to learn that they were still in a high-risk category. The rules of the game changed during their legal stays here. We turn to the stories of three families and one organization in New York City to illustrate how individuals are delegalized, and how one organized in response to delegalization.

A Prisoner's Daughter

My name is Aarti Shahani. Though I grew up surrounded by immigrants from different continents and my parents speak seven languages, I never planned to dive into the immigrants' rights movement. A simple event pushed me in and changed the way I see New York City.

The office building at 201 Varick Street in Lower Manhattan houses the Peace Corps, the Postal Service, and the Departments of Commerce and Defense. The address is far more New York than American. Just across the street from it is SOB's, which stands for Sounds of Brazil, one of the best clubs in the city. I started dancing there before I was legal, when Rudolph Giuliani was still mayor. In those late nights when I was still hustling into SOB's, I faintly remember noticing the office building across the street, but I never paid much attention. An unexpected phone call from my father one day, however, compelled me to bring the building into focus. He was crying, and through his tears I could just make out the words: they took him.

Dad was talking about my uncle, who had just become the special guest of another federal agency at 201 Varick, the Immigration and Naturalization Service. They were holding him and hundreds others as prisoners for deportation. My father ended up in the same place within a year's time, for a similar violation. This was all before the Towers a mile southeast of the building collapsed on September 11, 2001, before images of orange jumpsuits and camps saturated the American psyche, before the government gave immigration police a shot in the arm by adding "Department of Homeland Security" to their badges.

My family ran a wholesale electronics store on Broadway, selling watches and calculators in bulk, mostly to overseas buyers. We were all part of the store. My mother was among its founders and, in my estimation, the family's best business mind. An irresistible, pious guilt drove my brother, the eldest son, to work there after finishing school. My cousin had dropped out of school because he preferred the store life to an academic one. They said my sister and I had it easy. We would come by on weekends to redecorate the windows or cart merchandise on the streets of downtown.

We were not there that humiliating summer afternoon in 1996 when police officers entered with handcuffs and Miranda warnings, arresting both Dad and Uncle Ratan. We spent the next four years in a legal battle with the state that ended in both men pleading to improper cash transactions. Their crime was not properly reporting to the Internal Revenue Service their sales to foreigners.

In New York, fewer than 1 percent of misdemeanors and 5 percent of felonies go to trial.[12] The criminal courts rely on bargains: prosecutors present a list of charges in one indictment and offer to throw out the bigger ones if the defendant accepts guilt for the lesser. If the defendant exercises the right to trial and loses, the court promises to dole out the stiffest punishment possible. The public defender assigned to the case advises his or her client of this risk, and negotiates a deal.

Our attorneys never advised us that deportation would follow a plea. Deportation was not part of the sentence. The criminal judge never even brought it up. Instead, he gave my father a relatively painful slap on the wrist, though delivered it sympathetically. The judge said on the record that both men had "paid an exorbitant price in the infinite scheme of things" for their crime. He allowed their sentences to be served consecutively, so that one man could always be out running the business.

My uncle, who looked up to his brother as a father for much of his life, volunteered to go first. But New York made an error that resulted in him serving two years instead of eight months. After we cleared up the matter and thought he would finally come home, we learned the federal government planned to send him "back home" to India—a country in which he had not lived since the 1950s.

His deportation proceedings started in 201 Varick. Few people know that this office building contains prison cells. Some would take issue with the term *prison,* because it is legally incorrect in the eyes of the law. But the immigrant detainees are compelled to enter and stay. They sleep in dorms arranged body to body. They ask permission to go to the bathroom. Their hands, feet, and waists are shackled when they are moved from place to place. In other words, they are treated no differently than prisoners.

On the books, detention and deportation are civil—rather than criminal—*processes* run by the executive branch, not punishments given by the judiciary. For most detainees, it means that you are held like a prisoner without the niceties of the criminal justice system. In deportation cases, you get no free lawyer, no set sentence, no hearing with a jury of your peers.

My uncle's detention lasted only six months. It would have been shorter, but the immigration service twice failed to deliver him to the airport before his flight took off. His extended stays in state and federal custody were slowly acclimating him to being held longer than his due. Yet it did not blunt the rage. When I visited him in India years later, the wounds were still raw. He recounted for me the day when he was still being detained that he had a toothache so far gone and untreated, he yanked the molar from his mouth with the help of another inmate.

My dad had his dental work done before prison. Age and diabetes had advanced to his teeth, and they were all extracted just before he went inside. He was kept at Rikers Island, the largest jail in the country. A nice piece of property by LaGuardia Airport, it can house 20,000 but usually holds only half that. Employees call it an accidental city. It is the stuff of feature films and rap lyrics. Dad was too old to not stick out. Younger guys were always asking, "Poppy, why you here? Don't worry, poppy, I got you." Also, his gums shifted as they healed and pushed out his dentures, making the lines around his mouth deeper, his cheeks saggier, and leaving him without even fake teeth to chew. Dad served no more than his assigned term. Within eight months, he went from Rikers to 201 Varick. We got him out of there quickly, but his deportation case still persists six years later.

Shocking events can have the effect of skewing reality by traumatizing the witness. But in prison, certain shocks come from clarity. Before cool metal cuffed their wrists, my dad and uncle believed in law and order and America. That makes sense. They were two men running a business so successful that they could make the ultimate leap: a house in suburban New Jersey. After coming out, though, they recalled prison—both the criminal and civil—with the same bitterness that veterans remember Iraq. At first the stories would not stop, everything from strip searches in the middle of the night to fellow inmates bumming too many cigarettes.

I had my own stories from the visitation line. For instance, the prison always smelled bad to me, and there is no shortage of environmental surveys that show high toxin levels at these facilities. Also, I was surprised during my trips by how even veteran visitors showed disbelief at the very idea of prison. Perhaps a cage built by and for humans never loses its drama. The experience of visiting resembles the basic premise, architecture, and execution of the place itself. Prisons are made to be panoptic; that is, to see the population from one point at all times without being seen.[13] Inmates are controlled through their own imagination. Administrators marvel at the system when it works—when inmates and corrections officers do not beat up on each other too much, when programs are delivered, and when beds are filled.

America faces a prison crisis. Although over 2 million people are incarcerated, there remain too many empty facilities that were built throughout our War on Drugs.[14] Interestingly, cities and states that are losing big money for the lack of inmates are getting federal contracts to house civil detainees.[15] In New York, where the rich and poor often pay a couple of thousand dollars in monthly rent for cell-sized apartments, all the empty beds at Rikers must seem a tragedy to the government.

I let my imagination get the best of me during Dad's time locked up. I thought every day would be his last. Yet I hated to visit Dad because there was nothing to say. He wanted news of what we were doing to get him out sooner. I had to scavenge for things to do, if only to show effort.

The hunt for solutions turned me into a legal expert. Law is in my bones. I think about it all the time. Its linear structure and loopholes make sense to me. If my loved ones had never been arrested, I likely would have become a corporate lawyer or, worse yet, a civil libertarian. I fantasized about arguing before the Supreme Court, maybe even becoming a justice. But our legal case brought me so close to the law, I stopped believing in it. Or maybe something else in my bones took over. The shame I felt when my dad and uncle were first arrested turned into outrage. I began speaking out everywhere and became involved with a loose network of families nationwide whose loved ones were facing deportation for past crimes. It was a home of sorts, because it was the only space to embrace people like my dad and uncle, with rap sheets, the so-called Bad Immigrants.

But the immigrant families I worked with did not let go of the Good/Bad distinction. They just changed who fell where. Most championed our families' rights by highlighting the fact that we had green cards. We were not illegals. I was not comfortable with the lines drawn between legal and illegal. In the world of law, the distinction is losing relevance as the line between citizen and noncitizen deepens. Also, I grew up in Flushing, Queens, an immigrant metropolis. My family and our neighbors did not have papers for years. We did nothing in particular to deserve getting them. Morally speaking, it is hard to feel better about people having their parents or children deported just because they lack proper documents. On the visitation lines and in detention, it is all the same.

Still, this group fostered an activism born from direct experiences of deportation. With their help, my own family's story made it into the *Congressional Record*. Senator Edward Kennedy, today at the forefront of an effort called Comprehensive Immigration Reform, hailed my family as an example of why Congress needed to fix immigration laws passed in 1996.[16] These laws, passed under Democratic president Bill Clinton, made deportation and detention mandatory minimums. That is, they stripped judges of the power to assess the person locked up and facing exile. Judges can no longer grant bond, even if they believe an immigrant is not a threat to society or a flight risk. Judges cannot pardon an immigrant, even if deportation harms a family and community. Kennedy was at the forefront of a Fix '96 campaign.[17] On September 11, 2001, I was in the Capitol visiting other legislators to push his initiatives. But the campaign, and our efforts, collapsed with the Twin Towers.

The first protest I ever organized was in front of 201 Varick, on the Father's Day before September 11, 2001. My own dad had just been released from the facility. The weather was cruel. Rain beat against the concrete and our signs. Through running ink and torn corners, you could barely make out the demands, like "Give Back My Daddy." Through the thunder and downpour, we could hear those locked upstairs pounding against the fogged windows. In sorrow and solidarity, they saw us more clearly than we saw them. It was one of those rare moments when prisoners are unerased from society, if only for a moment. The protest made the evening news and the next day's papers. Most young organizers would have been proud.

But I was disappointed, especially by the turnout. The need to transform our private pain into public truth motivated me to organize an event. I truly believed we could stop the system "if only They knew." *They* referred to important people—like Oprah and the president. I had sent out e-mails urging the universe to come. But only thirty people showed up, almost entirely my own loved ones or folks I had met on the visitation line.

Today, in retrospect, this handful of people represented my first major success as an organizer: to draw the people personally affected by an issue into the struggle to change it. Few people think they have a place in politics. Deportation, a shocking event, radicalized each of us. That is, it planted a seed that could become consciousness, if nurtured.

Social Worker Turned Organizer

I was the only unexpected guest at the rally that Aarti's family organized, and I was fashionably late as always—call it the Midwest in me. My name is Subhash Kateel. I have been an antideportation organizer for the last seven years. Hundreds of people whom I have called friends have been deported and split far apart from their families. At least half a dozen of them have passed away. The first memorial I ever helped to organize was in the summer of 2006, for a close friend who died a few weeks after being deported to the Dominican Republic.

I did not grow up around many immigrants. I grew up in a small, segregated, working-class rust-belt town in Michigan. I come from Saginaw, the less-famous version of Flint. While we had no movies made about us, we did raise Stevie Wonder and had a tourist T-shirt with a smoking gun above the words "Come back to Saginaw. We missed you the first time." There is nothing especially interesting about my story: many people in my city saw the effects of more prisons and fewer jobs firsthand.

While prison was a familiar story, deportation was not. The first time I visited immigration prisoners was in 1999. I had moved to New York to get my degree in social work. The experience was culture shock. I came from Michigan State, a party school where smart people never knew they were smart. I went to Columbia University, where even dumb people carried themselves as if they were the guy who invented the artificial heart.

While at Columbia, I volunteered for an organization working with poor South Asians and helped them start a detention project. Shortly after graduation, I also became a caseworker at a Catholic agency in Newark. I was responsible for transitioning asylum seekers into life in the United States after their stay in a private prison now infamous for sex abuse and detainee suicides. The immigrants I visited came from all over the world: Sri Lanka, Pakistan, Nigeria, Haiti. It was like a United Nations, but without much of Europe.

People were locked in like cattle, held indefinitely, unable to access basics like fresh air and sunlight. When asylees were released from detention, I saw them take their first rays of natural sunlight after months or years of being locked up. As these folks became my friends, and their struggles became personal, my involvement in antideportation work grew. Deportation seemed even then the cruelest civil proceeding in America. Then September 11, 2001, gave this system—and the work against it—a meaning I could never have anticipated.

My colleagues and I immediately became regional leaders against the attacks on Arabs, South Asians, and Muslims. I was thrown into the position of organizing volunteers to visit detainees; pulling together marches and coalitions to fight abusive detention conditions; providing primary data to Amnesty International, Human Rights Watch, and major national and international media; and watching people I love and respect lose family members day in and day out. The work we did in one short year was historic, and the effects on me dramatic.

The effects on New York of the September 11 attacks were bizarre. I think of them in terms of two of my favorite blocks on Brooklyn: Coney Island Avenue (mostly Pakistani and Bangladeshi) and Flatbush (mostly Caribbean immigrants). They are parallel streets, living parallel realities as communities devastated by the deportation of breadwinners. Yet community leaders and members were neither speaking nor organizing together.[18] Black immigrants—disproportionately targeted by deportation, and being flagged through the criminal system—and South Asian immigrants shared bunks in detention centers post–9/11. But rarely did their respective community leaders on the outside fight with a unified voice.

After Aarti's family and I met, we joined with others to begin monthly "family meetings" for people being deported. These get-togethers for people facing deportation, people who needed support and wanted to give it, and/or people harmed by the law who wanted to change it was transformed into an organization open to anyone and everyone facing deportation.

FFF was born from impatience, and from the way that shocking events are radicalizing, so long as one remains hopeful. We had two basic goals: (1) to create a space for those facing deportation to join the fight to change the system, in order to infuse the political process with personal wisdom; and (2) to bridge New York's diverse communities, thereby building the institutional power needed to make change.

New York has the most diverse immigrant population in the country.[19] Community organizations exist in every zip code, for every nationality. Few are structured to mobilize constituents for change. Many provide a range of services: language access, education, housing, job placement, and HIV care.

Our project was more than services or self-interest. We thought big. The size of our vision was what first attracted people. Especially in the aftermath of 9/11, community leaders would often say that immigrants were too afraid to speak. While fear was high, the claim was a cop-out. Immigrants never stopped being engaged, some fiercely. Cabdrivers here in the United States run political parties back in the home country.[20] Nannies lead labor organizations.[21] Practically every immigrant belongs to some form of cultural association.

The challenge is in solutions. Traditional forms of engaging new immigrants, like voter mobilization, can be a dead end: noncitizens cannot vote, and getting the citizens we know to vote cannot be the primary solution when those who cast ballots have little access to lawmakers to begin with. Also, injustice has a strange ecology. To move the general public—that nebulous entity that pollsters cite but no one sees—the travesty must shock. But to move the survivors, it must look solvable. Like most poor people, immigrants are busy. When you work for pennies, minutes are as scarce as dollars. Our families were also accustomed to basic rights being violated. Deportation was not the first or last injustice. It was only the harshest. The denial of dignity provides a door, not a path, to reclaiming rights.

In forming the organization, we continually brainstormed: what makes it worthwhile for someone to come, and to stay? Our solution is an organizing method that we call ARM: Assist Ourselves, Raise Awareness, and Make 'em Bleed. The prongs refer to support, education, and action. We started as a support group on steroids, a kind of twelve-step meeting with a political vision. Family members would come together and share sorrow. At least one person, usually more, would cry inconsolably. We were not there to make it better, to make the pain go away. We thought in that pain was power, but first the pain needed to be acknowledged. After a few meetings, people would get frustrated. We started setting three-month plans for miniactions.

In community spaces, whenever you ask people what the solution is to any given problem—from gentrification to war—the word "education" rolls off people's tongues. The first action we agreed on was developing a newsletter. We needed a practical tool to teach others and recruit from the prison visitation lines. We included in that newsletter, and all our subsequent trainings, answers to one basic question: What is one thing you know now about the deportation system today that you wish you knew before it happened to you? Instead of the typical "know your rights" workshops, we took the "know how your rights will be violated" approach. We have taken these lessons to several thousand places by now, including street corners, neighborhood clubs, and Rikers Island.

FFF became one of the few organizations responding to the explosion in deportations. Deportation defies traditional legal models because most people have no meaningful hearing, no public defender or pro bono lawyer is assigned, and deportation and detention are mandatory minimums. It is commonplace for the judge, an attorney general appointee, to say on the record, "I wish I could help, but my hands are tied." Lawyers who do not have the heart to tell immigrants their case is hopeless send them our way. There is little formality in it. Our phone numbers are scribbled on prison walls. People call us nonstop in search of a lawyer. We have a rap explaining that we are not lawyers, we are a "human rights group"—another nebulous term.

We explain detention to parents who have no idea how to locate their children in the federal maze. We bring delegations of families to local congressional offices and the Capitol, consulates, and embassies, in search of support for last-ditch efforts. We help people gather the papers needed to analyze a case and assist the handful who have a chance in the courts to look for lawyers. Immigration is a lucrative industry. The poorest families pour their life savings into attorneys and *notarios,* who hustle them into believing the law can work. While we win cases, our contribution is sometimes more in damage control: saving people's money and delivering possibly the worst news of their life in the same breath.

Our group is now full of experts in what is probably the most sophisticated system of punishment and repression in the United States. Many of our detainee members did their own legal work, suffered through their own hunger strikes, and wrote petitions to everyone from the president to Al Sharpton. Our loved ones on the outside have sought help from any and every government agency, from child welfare to the foreign embassy.

Our biggest victories were initially in monitoring detention conditions. Families on the outside would tell us about abuses inside—from prisoners being denied fresh air or direct sunlight for months at a time, to guards beating people. If witnesses were willing to go on record, we would write a short letter to the prison warden and immigration authorities, laying out the situation as we understood it and our demands. We copied it to important people—like the ACLU or members of Congress. We threatened to go public, but did not jump to press. Each letter was an olive branch, giving authorities the opportunity to correct mistakes.

Fighting for Dignity: The Case of Richard Rust

There were times, however, when the press was key to monitoring prison conditions. By 2004 several women in FFF had a male loved one detained in Oakdale, Louisiana. Oakdale, the largest civil detention center in the country, is run by the Federal Bureau of Prisons. Started in 1991, during the first Gulf War, the town's Lebanese mayor lobbied hard for the contract to rescue the small town, which had a 31 percent rate of unemployment and an average annual salary of $7,000. Calling immigrant prisoners "a recession proof industry," he reasoned that when the world economy goes bad, and more immigrants come to the United States, Oakdale's business would go up.[22]

One day, a famous actor cut us a check for $5,000, no strings attached. We used the money to fly a dozen of us down to the prison town. Inspired by the Freedom Rides against segregation throughout the 1960s, we called our journey Freedom Flight. It was meant to reunite New Yorkers with their loved ones who were shipped from small detention facilities up North to this big one in the Deep South.

A recent death marred the reunion. We learned upon arrival that Richard Rust, a thirty-four-year-old man born in Jamaica and raised in Brooklyn, had collapsed on the floor of his cell in a detention facility the previous week. The ambulance took forty minutes to come. He arrived dead at the hospital. He left behind two children. Oakdale's warden, a native of Trinidad, restricted detainees from using the telephone and put them on lockdown following Richard's death. Maybe the situation shook him; maybe he did not want reports to escape.

The facts slipped out piecemeal. The grown men we visited whispered the news about the death to us. They passed handwritten notes to our consigliere, Benita Jain, an attorney who worked tirelessly to get legal information to the unrepresented prisoners. They recounted the death with amazing consistency. But we were not sure what to do with the information. It was a loaded gun whose trigger was not ours to pull.

We met Richard's family for the first time at his wake, which we heard about through the grapevine. It was an open casket. Through the makeup you could tell the corpse was young. But his face left no trace of where or why he died prematurely. A long line of loved ones passed him, some saying prayers and other grieving without words. Mourners talked about a man who worked as a technician, raised two young children, and smiled uncontrollably at times. No one mentioned Oakdale.

Those of us from the Freedom Flight did not have a connection to Richard in life. We attended because we needed to remember his death. When a person's life is taken prematurely, the cry for justice is a clear part of mourning. For Richard you could name a few people responsible, but mostly it was a process. He died on the floor of a prison a few thousand miles from home. He was taken there following a federal raid in 2004. Immigration agents came to his door at dawn, to begin deportation proceedings for a crime he had committed over a decade earlier and for which he had already served his sentence. They were resurrecting a past he never knew could haunt him.

We exchanged phone numbers with Richard's sister and stepmother at the wake and were surprised by how happy they were to meet us. Over the next few months, we would visit their homes and dig deeper into Richard's death. It turns out that Oakdale's warden informed the family by regular mail but addressed the notice incorrectly. They first heard the news through the wife of another detainee. The Jamaican consulate had been entrusted with the body.

We moved together, slowly. Months after the death, our loved ones in Oakdale were still under lockdown. The warden offered no official explanation, so Richard's family demanded answers in a short letter (see Figure 12.1).[23]

FIGURE 12.1

Letter of Inquiry from the Family of Richard Rust

Ms. Joyce Lewis
VIA REGULAR MAIL & FAX

October 4, 2004

J.P. Young, Warden
Oakdale Federal Detention Center
P.O. Box 5060
Oakdale, LA 71463

Re: Richard Rust

Dear Warden Young:

My name is Joyce Lewis. I have spent the summer mourning the loss of my son, Richard Rust. Richard was my husband's son, and I have raised him as my own since he was a teenager. We became especially close since his father died almost a decade ago. Richard died in your facility at age 34 on May 29, 2004. Your office informed me of his sudden death through a letter postmarked June 2, 2004, in an envelope incorrectly addressed to Mississippi rather than New York. I am writing now to express how upset I am at the way your office has treated our loss, and out of concern for the other prisoners at Oakdale.

I am a mother, and I can't be silent. America emphasizes the family. My question is: why is the government tearing apart families? Richard was the father of two young children, who truly needed his attention and guidance. I once read a survey that said that children who have two parent homes are more successful than those with just one parent. Evidently, only the Rich and Famous have the right to succeed, but not us poor Black people.

Richard was somebody's son, he was somebody's brother, he was an uncle, a friend, a grandson, a nephew. Richard belonged to someone. Most importantly, he belonged to his two young children. Richard's son saw his father in a casket. But he is so traumatized, whenever he sees a plane in the sky he says, "My daddy's coming home now." My son did not deserve to go to your prison to get killed.

FIGURE 12.1—CONTINUED

Richard made his mistakes, like most young people do—including the Rich and Famous. He also finished paying the price long ago. He was no nuisance to society. He supported his children, ensuring that they don't have to rely on welfare. Rest assured that now they will have to join the welfare rolls, as one parent alone can't support them in today's economic crisis. There was no reason to cut this young man's life short because the U.S. suddenly decides that they don't want people of certain colors and countries here.

Your office provided me with virtually no account of how Richard died. I understand from other families, however, that Oakdale F.D.C. employees did not help Richard when he collapsed. Some even made rude comments. At least one officer prevented detainees from giving Richard C.P.R. It took the ambulance at least 45 minutes to arrive. Why didn't they get to him faster? Why didn't any government employees come to my son's rescue? He was such a young man. Someone could have saved his life.

I also understand that following my son's death, dozens of young men were put into the hole for months. They were allowed one call per week. I even heard that you personally threatened inmates into being silent about Richard's death, and that you cut off their access to legal help. Why are other detainees being punished and threatened?

I ask your office to provide a full explanation as to how my son passed, specifically where he was when he first collapsed, whether any officers attempted to assist him immediately, and why fellow detainees were ordered to not provide him CPR. I also urge you to stop punishing other detainees. The friends he made on the inside, and those concerned about his passing, should not be put in isolation or denied access to legal help. We are all in mourning.

Answers are long overdue. My family deserves the truth. I look forward to hearing from you soon.

Yours truly, Joyce Lewis

cc: Craig Robinson, New Orleans Acting Field Office Director

Richard's family would not forget, and so the public came to know.

In 2005 National Public Radio investigative reporter Daniel Zwerdling had just finished covering detainee abuse in New Jersey jails. Guards in the facility widely hailed as the worst detention center set dogs on inmates. Guards in the "best facility" in Jersey beat an Egyptian man to a pulp.[24] FFF knew inmates at both facilities. One called us to report the beating hours after it happened. The man beaten was interviewed by telephone for our monthly radio show.[25] He explained that he had just had a growth removed from his knees and recounted for us in detail how officers, allegedly frustrated with the pace of his walk, bumped against his kneecaps while they were still recovering.

Zwerdling came to know us as a source for his reporting. The relationship between journalists and activists is always wrought with tension. They, unlike us, are not supposed to take sides. The majority do, shamelessly. But even among the handful with a sober approach, it is hard to stop being human. Zwerdling probably grew incensed with the stories of attack dogs and beatings. After exposing the New Jersey immigrant prison industry, he directed his microphone to the prison in the Deep South where a premature death still lay buried.

We had tried to get others to report on Richard's death, and faced a basic problem: our families are the Bad Immigrants. Following 9/11, journalists sympathetic to the plight of deportees did not want to endanger our struggle by highlighting imperfect families. They wanted to bleach reality, to focus on the most innocent victims—those deported for jumping a turnstile or filing the wrong documents.

Zwerdling did not let the conversation stop at the fact of a rap sheet. He spent nearly a year reconstructing Richard's death. He was so meticulous, it became annoying. He wanted fax confirmation reports to prove that letters we wrote to the prison and to immigration services were in fact delivered. He wanted eyewitnesses—several of them, on the record. These demands put people at risk. Detainees in Oakdale faced punishment for helping Richard's story make it out.

The result was the best eulogy Richard could have had. National Public Radio aired "The Death of Richard Rust," a detailed account mapping the likely cause of death as "negligent homicide."[26] It impressed FFF's most cynical members—like Aarti's father and the wife of another Jamaican at Oakdale who participated in the investigation. It even moved lawmakers. One congressman sponsored a bill demanding a report on all detainee deaths.[27] In a letter to the Government Accountability Office, eleven representatives demanded a full investigation into the health standards for immigrant prisoners and charged,

> We are equally troubled by the report that detention officials subsequently retaliated against a number of detainees who were friends of Mr. Rust or upset over his death by sending them to disciplinary segregation where some were forced to remain for three months. . . . Congress is currently considering legislation to significantly expand the numbers of and classes of aliens subject to mandatory detention in DHS custody. Before such expansion, we must be certain that DHS is capable of protecting detainees in its charge.[28]

American Children, Immigrant Families

This was not the only time FFF's commitments spiraled into congressional action.

The Halls of Congress are real. They exist physically. You can get to them from New York for $15 on a bus leaving from Chinatown. We chartered several Chinatown buses in 2006, on the ten-year anniversary of the laws responsible for our families' struggle.

Most Americans assume that deportation got tough after September 11, 2001, and the USA PATRIOT Act. But in fact current immigration laws are wedded to another act of terror. In April 1995, a white militiaman and veteran of the First Gulf War, Timothy McVeigh, bombed the Oklahoma City Federal Building. Exactly one year later, Congress passed the Antiterrorism and Effective Death Penalty Act.[29] A sister bill, the Illegal Immigration Reform and Immigrant Responsibility Act, was pushed through that October.[30] The 1996 immigration laws expanded the criminal grounds of deportation, stripped most noncitizens with past offenses even of the right to ask a judge for a pardon, and required that most remain locked up in civil detention as they fight their case.[31] That is, they transformed detention and deportation into mandatory minimums. It was easier to be an immigrant under Reagan than under Clinton. Another veteran from the First Gulf War, now detained under the 1996 laws for a drug addiction, remarked from his prison cell, "Now that's some irony."[32]

The year 1996 may also go down in American history as the birth of neoliberalism. Public housing programs were demolished. Welfare reform threw Americans off the rolls, and even furthered delegalization by cutting the benefits afforded green card holders for the first time in U.S. history.[33] Yet on the robust detention and deportation laws, Congress expressed regret in the immediate aftermath. Nancy Morawetz, a legal scholar who runs a clinic to help immigrant families and community groups, describes the chaotic process and flurry of activity leading to the legislation's passage and posits that the harshest provisions were accidental.[34] Although the United States has long expelled people for criminal convictions, detention and deportation as mandatory minimums is new.[35] September 11, 2001, did not change the legal framework so much as enhance the enforcement of the 1996 laws.

The laws run counter to American assumptions about the kind of justice that families deserve. Americans assume that immigrants who marry U.S. citizens and have American children are not often kicked out of the country. Immigrants (and the scholars who study them) assume that a green card, or lawful permanent residency, affords you the same rights as a citizen except for voting. And since most citizens do not vote, it is practically the same status.

The people who poured into our buses in 2006 were families who shared these assumptions, until they learned firsthand about deportation. They came to the nation's capital thinking, "If only *They* knew"—this time referring to lawmakers. Among them was Carol McDonald.

Carol fell in love with Linden Corrica in a farmers market in their home country of Guyana. She liked him from the beginning, played hard to get for a while, and said "I do" with a huge smile. She brought him from the countryside to Brooklyn in 1990, after her U.S.-citizen father legally brought her into the United States. In 1997 their daughter Natasha was born in Kings County Hospital. Now nine years old, she has Dad's ebony skin and Mom's cat eyes.

They were your standard working-class urban family. Carol was a home health aide and naturalized citizen. Linden took odd jobs and was Natasha's primary caretaker, toting her between public school, Burger King, and church. Carol and Linden's biggest difference was faith: Carol is a Pentecostal, one of the fastest-growing segments of global Christianity.[36] Linden is a Rastafarian, a religious movement prevalent in the Caribbean. Rastafarians grow dreadlocks, espouse vegetarianism, and often consider using marijuana a sacrament.[37] Linden followed all three tenets. Carol did not like his smoking.

Neither did the NYPD. In 2003 Linden was arrested in one of those stops and frisks that Giuliani made standard. In a city of 8 million, police stop and frisk over 500,000 people annually, and 85 percent of the targets are black or Latino.[38] Police found marijuana on Linden and took him to Rikers Island. Linden's immigration status, as a green card holder rather than a U.S. citizen, changed the basic consequence of being arrested. On his third day at Rikers, corrections officers entered his dorm and told him he had a "legal visit." He thought it was his public defender. Instead it was immigration. In a ten-minute interview, officers asked Corrica personal and legal questions and had him sign a paper before leaving. He told the truth and thought little of it. He was sent from New York to Oakdale after serving a week at Rikers.[39]

Carol and Natasha participated in the Freedom Flight. Natasha was seven at the time. Her cat eyes opened wide at the thought of seeing her father again. She was not prepared to be reunited in the same room in which detainees whispered details of a death to the rest of us. She tried to filter it all, so their words would not distract her joy. But tears streamed from her eyes the minute her father was out of view. She asked hesitantly, "Will the same thing happen to my daddy?" We worry in America about our children growing up too quickly. The trip to Oakdale either took years off Natasha's childhood or stripped it of the carelessness those years ought to have.

In the Capitol, Natasha stood pressed against her mother's chest in the office of Congressman Ed Towns, a black democrat who governs a district of African Americans and black immigrants. Carol was the fourth mother to speak. Her eyes staring out blankly, her summary turned into a plea:

> I am not even middle class, to be honest. My family is poor. And since my husband got taken, I've been struggling. My daughter misses her daddy. She tries to hide it with two faces—one for me, and one for everyone else. People tell me she's hurting. When school gets out, she watches the other children getting picked up by their daddies. . . . I'm struggling. I have diabetes. I take two insulin injections and three types of pills every day. My eyes are going bad. I need my husband.

Her eyes welled up with small droplets of tears, the type you get when you are tired of crying but cannot stop hurting. Natasha fixed her eyes on the floor. She probably did not know whether to be ashamed or proud.

A month earlier, we had moved a congressman to sponsor a bill that would recognize Natasha and other American children confronting a parent's deportation. José Serrano, a Puerto Rican from the Bronx, introduced the Child Citizen Protection Act, the only proposal in the immigration debate to explicitly write the interests of American citizens into immigration law.[40] It is not a legalization bill; rather, it is a response to de-legalization. It neither grants green cards nor removes anyone from the deportation rolls. It simply enables a judge to consider the well-being of American-born children before deporting a parent. Serrano introduced it because his office "was noticing so many issues concerning people being deported, and in the process their children were being hurt. We decided that one of the problems with immigration laws was that judges were not allowed to do what judges do—to judge and make sure that everyone's best interest is taken into account."[41]

Many of the same members of Congress who demanded an investigation into Richard Rust's death joined Serrano's effort. Following our families' testimony, Congressman Towns cosponsored the bill. He also gave a letter of support directly to Carol's family. So did New York City councilman Kendall Stewart. A child therapist also wrote to U.S. Citizenship and Immigration Services, warning that Linden's exile would "cause Natasha irreparable harm."[42] Newspapers, ethnic press, church leaders, and friends weighed in with their support.

Still, the support and pleas were not enough to save the family. After three years being detained and fighting his case, Linden was deported illegally to Guyana in October 2006. Natasha recounts getting the news from an unknown man on the phone, probably another detainee: "A Spanish guy called when mommy wasn't home and said they took daddy." After a judge ordered the deportation, Linden appealed to the federal courts with the help of jailhouse lawyers—fellow prisoners with self-taught legal expertise. They filed a habeas corpus petition to challenge the legality of his detention and deportation. The case faced setbacks in 2005, when Congress passed the REAL ID Act to strip immigrants of the constitutional right to habeas corpus. One court transferred his case to another. His appeal was still pending when authorities put him on a flight, despite a federal judge's explicit order that he not be deported.

Linden's deportation process did not end when the airplane wheels hit ground in Georgetown, Guyana. He was locked up in another prison for three days. As a deportee, he now must report to police monthly. Being without his own phone in rural Guyana, he used a neighbor's phone to tell a conference call of New York supporters, "I had no idea how long they would hold me. I prayed it wasn't as long as America did." Asked if he would fight to come back, he made Carol blush when he said without pause, "Anything for my beautiful wife."

Deportees are viewed as a national security threat throughout the Caribbean—the region that receives the highest concentration of U.S. "criminal aliens." Deportees are cited as the source of every problem from murder to national debt to hurricanes. The U.S. State Department, the same agency that pressures governments to take deportees, once tried to defuse the animosity against them by commissioning erudite Caribbean criminologist Bernard Headley to study deportee data and document that they were *not* a hazard. While the scholar uncovered in his research no connection between U.S. deportees and the Caribbean's purportedly rising crime rate, he did criticize the U.S. immigration laws leading to the deportees' expulsion in the first place.[43]

The foreign governments concerned with deportation—whether as a human rights or a national security issue—became the first clear target for our collective action. Deportation is one of the few forms of punishment that requires two state actors, the sending and the receiving country. More important, immigrants often have more pull with their home countries than they do with the United States. Immigrants here are part of political parties back home. In some countries, such as the Dominican Republic, a major receiver of deportees, they can still vote. In Jamaica, Haiti, and El Salvador, remittances from nationals in the United States represent upwards of 20 percent of the national income.

We started bringing delegations of families and supporters to visit consulates in New York and embassies in D.C., to push government officials to protect the rights of their nationals in U.S. jails, prisons, and detention centers. We have sent letters to the foreign ministries in receiving countries, with concrete policy recommendations to prevent illegal deportations like Linden's and inhumane treatment that can lead ultimately to deaths like Richard's. While domestically we are pushing legislative efforts that respect the right to family (like the Child Citizen Protection Act), we understand that the domestic immigration debate is ultimately transnational. State actors at all levels must speak on behalf of their base.

Mapping Delegalization and Fighting Immigrant Apartheid

FFF is attuned to delegalization because the people most dramatically affected by it—those physically caught in detention and deportation—constitute our base. Meanwhile the threat of deportation looms over our families and communities every single day.

If detention and deportation are the gravest sanctions of delegalization, then the Department of Homeland Security is its most dramatic symbol. In the largest reorganization of the federal government since Harry Truman's Defense Department in 1947, Congress thrust immigration functions into the newborn department. Immigration control, originally based in the Treasury Department, has been passed among many arms of the federal government. If its current home reveals something about America's character, then it is clear that the war on terror will be a protracted one.

When lawmakers put immigration oversight within the Department of Homeland Security, they also divided its functions among three agencies: Citizenship and Immigration and Services, the social workers who process immigration paperwork; Customs and Border Protection, the border police responsible for keeping aliens out; and Immigration and Customs Enforcement, the interior police charged with removing deportable aliens. This triumvirate was unequal. By 2005 the policing budget was fifty-two times greater than that of services, and surpassed other national security projects as well. In the same year that Hurricane Katrina ravaged New Orleans, the Federal Emergency Management Agency received only one-third the monies given to immigration police.[44]

The immigrants' rights movement has been caught between a rock and a hard place for years. Since 9/11 it has been berated with the question, How many immigrants are too many? What about the criminals and the terrorists? In this essay we pose another question: Is it worth pushing for legalization through campaigns that necessarily result in more delegalization? Or is the same political culture that railroaded through bad laws in 1996 railroading us into bad solutions a decade later?

The immigrants' rights movement has overlapping and separate leaders, only some of them bold enough to tread the issue of delegalization. But their tongues split in two, typically trying to parse the Good Immigrant from the Bad, to distinguish between the criminalization of civil immigration violators and real criminals. It is not that these leaders really believe that these distinctions should matter. If they did, Richard's death would have lain buried under the label of his crime; Aarti's family would never have made it into the *Congressional Record;* Linden would not have received public support from elected officials; and Congressman Serrano would not have introduced a bill that applies to immigrants both without *and* with criminal histories, so long as they have American children.

Rather, the ambivalence meeting delegalization reveals a deeper crisis of vision. Do immigrants deserve rights because we are Good, not Bad? Or are we demanding rights because Apartheid is wrong? Immigrants' rights organizers are burdened with making migration status less relevant, not more. Throwing people over the right side of the illegal-legal divide does not constitute victory when that divide is deepening.

The year 2006 saw immigrants rise up in protest, spontaneously but with conviction. This nonvoting bloc managed to defeat legislation that would have turned migration itself into a felony; and to spin America away from the assumption made only five years earlier, that immigration is purely a national security concern. The leaders today standing on the crest of that mass action need not fear the waves. Rather, we must dignify the action taken by these immigrant with demands equally daring in scale and clear in vision.

Notes

1. Over the course of the twentieth century, the demographics of immigration shifted dramatically, from a majority of white migrants—composing the last great wave of European migration in the 1920s—toward migration flows since 1965 that are predominantly composed of nonwhite Asian, Latino, African, and Caribbean nationals. In this context, it is difficult to avoid the conclusion that fears of the "browning of America" have informed the recent toughening of immigration laws—a concern that has been baldly stated by Patrick Buchanan in his latest book, *State of Emergency: The Third World Invasion and Conquest of America* (New York: Thomas Dunne Books, 2006).

2. Recent legislation (namely, AEDPA and IIRAIRA) and statements by the White House and the Department of Justice have expanded the "inherent authority" of local and state governments to collaborate with the Department of Homeland Security and take independent action to enforce federal immigration laws. See chapters 13 and 15 in this book for a more detailed discussion of these trends. For a discussion of policy developments such as the 2005 REAL ID Act and IIRAIRA which have dramatically curtailed the legal rights of noncitizens and even removed basic legal safeguards like the writ of habeas corpus, see chapter 4 in this book.

3. One study of immigration court cases from mid-1997 until May 2006 shows that individuals charged under the "aggravated felony" provisions of federal immigration law—all of whom entered the United States legally—lived in the United States for fifteen years on average. For 25 percent, the average time between their

original date of entry to this country and when deportation proceedings were started in immigration court is twenty years or longer, and for 10 percent it was more than twenty-seven years. The longest stay before being charged was fifty-four years. See Transactional Records Access Clearinghouse (TRAC), "How Often Is the Aggravated Felony Statute Used?" Table 1, http://trac.syr.edu/immigration/reports/158/ (accessed November 18, 2007). Against federalist respect for the sovereignty of individual states in the union, Congress enacted the REAL ID Act in 2005. Folded into the Emergency Supplemental Appropriations Act for Defense, the Global War on Terror, and Tsunami Relief, 2005, the bill places immigration status requirements on state motor vehicle departments, without funding the costs of meeting these requirements. See National Immigration Law Center, "Questions and Answers About Driver's Licenses Now that the REAL ID Act Has Become Law," June 2005, http://www.nilc.org/immspbs/DLs/q&a_dl_&_real_id_0605.pdf (accessed November 18, 2007).

4. Frank Sharry, the director of the National Immigration Forum, wrote, "Tolerate some restrictions on the same legalization program and some activist will accuse you of supporting an apartheid-like scheme destined to rip families apart." See Frank Sharry, "The Debate Right, Left and Center," *New American Media*, July 20, 2006.

5. DeGenova observes: "It is deportability, and not deportation as such, that has historically rendered Mexican labor to be a distinctly disposable commodity . . . in this way, migrant 'illegality' is a spatialized social condition that becomes inseparable from the particular ways that migrant workers from Mexico are racialized as 'illegal aliens' within the United States, and thus as 'Mexican' in relation to 'American'ness." Nicholas DeGenova, *Working the Boundaries: Race, Space and "Illegality" in Mexican Chicago* (Durham, N.C.: Duke University Press, 2005), 8. See also Nicholas DeGenova, "The Legal Production of Mexican/Migrant 'Illegality,'" *Latino Studies* 1, no. 2 (2004): 160–185.

6. See Immigration and Naturalization Service, "Table 69: Aliens Deported by Administrative Reason for Removal: Fiscal Years 1981–90," *Fiscal Year 1988 Statistical Yearbook*, http://www.dhs.gov/xlibrary/assets/statistics/yearbook/2000/Table69.xls (accessed November 18, 2007); Department of Homeland Security, "Table 43. Aliens Removed by Criminal Status and Region and Country of Nationality, 1993–2003," *Yearbook of Immigration Statistics 2003*, http://www.dhs.gov/xlibrary/assets/statistics/yearbook/2003/Table43D.xls (accessed November 18, 2007).

7. For recent comparisons of immigrant and citizen crime rates—showing that immigrants commit fewer or at least no more crimes than native-born persons—see Andrew Karmen, *New York Murder Mystery: The True Story Behind the Crime Crash of the 1990s* (New York: New York University Press, 2006); Ramiro Martinez Jr. and Abel Valenzuela Jr., eds., *Immigration and Crime: Race, Ethnicity and Violence* (New York: New York University Press, 2006); Robert J. Sampson, Jeffrey D.

Morenoff, and Stephen Raudenbush, "Social Anatomy of Racial and Ethnic Disparities in Violence," *American Journal of Public Health* 95 (2005): 224–232.

8. Historian Mai Ngai calls the illegal alien an "impossible subject" both because she is a "person who cannot be" and a "problem that cannot be solved." Mai Ngai, *Impossible Subjects: Illegal Aliens and the Making of Modern America* (Princeton, N.J.: Princeton University Press, 2005). In the policy world, advocates of all stripes know that it is politically infeasible to give everyone green cards or keep all immigrants out. While household consumption patterns and hemispheric globalization complicate the solutions, one problem is clear: there will always be illegal immigrants. Yet this essay argues that "illegality," which has become the defining motif of immigration discourse, loses or misnames the architecture of Immigrant Apartheid, which is based on a deepening distinction between citizens and noncitizens.

9. Sociologist Charles Tilly describes this dynamic as "contentious politics." Politics are contentious when modern social movements make collective claims "that, if realized, would conflict with someone else's interests." Charles Tilly, *Identities, Boundaries, and Social Ties* (Boulder, Colo.: Paradigm Publishers, 2005), 218.

10. For a treatment on how citizenship status and membership both are separate and converge as legal and sociological categories, see Linda S. Bosniak, "Membership, Equality, and the Difference that Alienage Makes," *New York University Law Review* 69 (1994): 1047. See also Linda Bosniak, "Citizenship Denationalized," *Indiana Journal of Global Legal Studies* 7 (2000): 447.

11. Six years after the enactment of IIRAIRA, the number of immigrants held in detention centers on an annual basis had more than quadrupled. Page Harrison and Allen Beck, "Prison and Jail Inmates at Midyear, 2005," Bureau of Justice Statistics, May 2006, http://www.ojp.usdoj.gov/bjs/pub/pdf/pjim05.pdf (accessed November 18, 2007). During a similar period of time (1996–2000), federal prosecutions of individuals for immigration violations more than doubled. Bureau of Justice Statistics, "Immigration Law Prosecutions Doubled During 1996–2002," U.S. Department of Justice, press release, August 6, 2002. And over the past two decades (1985–2002) federal spending on immigration enforcement almost quintupled. David Dixon and Julia Gelatt, "Immigration Enforcement Spending Since IRCA," Task Force Fact Sheet No. 10, Migration Policy Institute (November 2005), http://www.migration policy.org/ITFIAF/FactSheet_Spending.pdf (accessed November 18, 2007).

12. See New York State Division of Criminal Justice Services, "Disposition of Felony Arrests: New York State," 2004, http://criminaljustice.state.ny.us/crimnet/ojsa/dispos/nys.htm (accessed November 18, 2007).

13. Michel Foucault, *Discipline and Punish: The Birth of the Prison* (New York: Vintage, 1995).

14. See Bryan Gruley, "Mississippi's Prison-Building Spree Creates Glut of Lockups and Struggle for Convicts," *Wall Street Journal*, September 6, 2001; Dan Horn, "Lucasville Prison Riot: 10 Years Later Spending Cuts Endanger Reform, Advocates Say," *Cincinnati Enquirer*, April 6, 2003.

15. As of 2002, 68 percent of immigrant detainees were being held in either public/county jails or private prisons. It is also significant that whereas the inmate population in detention facilities run directly by the immigration system grew by 40 percent from 1994 to 2002, the population of detainees held in private facilities grew by ten times this rate during the same period. U.S. Department of Justice, Office of the Federal Detention Trustee, Detention Needs Assessment Baseline Report 2002: 14–15, http://www.usdoj.gov/ofdt/federal_detention_report_2002.pdf (accessed November 18, 2007).

16. *Congressional Record* (May 24, 2001): S 5633, wais.access.gpo.gov.

17. For an overview of the now-defunct Fix '96 immigration reform proposal, see "Fix '96: Restore Due Process to U.S. Immigration Law," American Immigration Law Association Issue Paper, March 14, 2001, http://www.immigrationlinks.com/news/news827.htm (accessed November 18, 2007).

18. While the relationship between different Latinos and the possibility of pan-Latino unity is being debated in the immigrant rights movement, and the mainstream is reporting heavily on the black/brown divide (referring to the tension between blacks and immigrants), the black immigrant identity itself is underscrutinized and the population undercounted. See chapter 10 in this book for more discussion on this issue.

19. For a demographic breakdown of the city's ethnic diversity, see New York City Department of City Planning, "Newest New Yorkers," January 2005. The city's foreign-born population rose from 28 percent of the total population in 1990 to 36 percent in 2000.

20. For an excellent account of efforts to organize the taxi industry in New York, see Biju Mathew, *Taxi! Cabs and Capitalism in New York City* (New York: New Press, 2006).

21. Conversation with Ida LeBlanc, general secretary of the National Union of Domestic Employees (N.U.D.E.). We had the pleasure of first meeting LeBlanc, a Trinidadian organizer, at a human rights hearing hosted by Domestic Workers United, a multiethnic coalition of domestic workers in New York.

22. See Mark Dow, *American Gulag: Inside U.S. Immigration Prisons* (Berkeley and Los Angeles: University of California Press, 2004).

23. Letter on file with authors.

24. Daniel Zwerdling, "Jailed Immigrants Allege Abuse: Immigrant Detainees Tell of Attack Dogs and Abuse," *All Things Considered*, National Public Radio, November 17, 2004.

25. The "War on Immigrants Report" is a monthly feature on *Global Movements, Urban Struggles* on WBAI, New York. Our cohost is Adem Carroll, a Muslim committed to his faith and community. Deepa Fernandes, the show's producer, recently completed her own vigorous reporting of the detention industry. Deepa Fernandes, *Targeted: National Security and the Business of Immigration* (New York: Seven Stories Press, 2006).

26. Daniel Zwerdling, "The Death of Richard Rust," *All Things Considered*, National Public Radio, December 5, 2005.

27. Amendment to HR 4437 (The Border Protection, Antiterrorism, and Illegal Immigration Control Act of 2005), offered by Representative Robert Scott (Democrat) of Virginia, December 7, 2005 (on file with authors).

28. House Judiciary Committee, letter to Government Accountability Office, December 14, 2005 (on file with authors).

29. Public Law 104-132, 110 *Stat.* 1214 (April 24, 1996).

30. Div. C of the Omnibus Appropriations Act of 1996, Public Law 104-208, 110 *Stat.* 3009 (Sept. 30, 1996).

31. We limit ourselves here to an *extremely* brief history of deportation and exclusion practices (renamed "removal" in 1996), at the expense of other issues and bigger pictures. For a discussion of the development of exclusion and deportation policies from the 1890s through the 1920s (in particular, cycles of nativism in U.S. history and highlighting the politics surrounding the advent of key moments such as the Chinese Exclusion Act, the Gentlemen's Agreement between the United States and Japan, and literacy tests in 1917), see John Higham, *Strangers in the Land: Patterns of American Nativism, 1860–1925* (New York: Rutgers University Press, 2002), and Matthew Jacobson, *Barbarian Virtues: The United States Encounters Foreign Peoples at Home and Abroad* (New York: Hill and Wang, 2001) (Jacobson links "immigration" powers to the development of the U.S. empire, especially under Theodore Roosevelt's administrations). For a discussion of exclusion and deportation with an emphasis on case law and extensive analysis of the Immigration and Nationality Act (as well as subsequent reforms to it), see Thomas Aleinikoff, David Martin, and Hiroshi Motomura, *Immigration and Nationality Laws of the United States: Selected Statutes, Regulations and Forms as Amended to 1998* (New York: Westlaw, 1998).

32. Conversation with Warren Joseph. Notes on file with author.

33. For a broad overview see Lisa Duggan, *The Twilight of Equality? Neoliberalism, Cultural Politics and the Attack on Democracy* (Boston: Beacon Press, 2004). For a critical overview of the impact of the 1996 reforms on immigrants, see Philip Kretsedemas and Ana Aparicio, eds., *Immigrants, Welfare Reform and the Poverty of Policy* (Westport, Conn.: Greenwood/Praeger, 2004).

34. See Nancy Morawetz, "Understanding the Impact of the 1996 Deportation Laws and the Limited Scope of Proposed Reforms," *Harvard Law Review* 113 (2000): 1936. See also Aarti Shahani, "Aggravated Felon Am I?" in *Deported: Removal and the Regulation of Human Mobility*, ed. Nicholas DeGenova and Nathalie Peutz (Durham, N.C.: Duke University Press, forthcoming).

35. In legal scholarship, the 1996 laws have generated many due process debates. Gerald Neuman, for example, argues that the laws raise the question of whether Congress can terminate the judiciary's traditional power to conduct habeas corpus review over the seizure, detention, and removal of aliens. Gerald L.

Neuman, "Habeas Corpus, Executive Detention, and the Removal of Aliens," *Columbia Law Review* 98 (1998): 961–988. Aliens facing removal historically have been entitled to judicial review of both the mandatory and discretionary aspects of the executive branch's removal determination, in accordance with the Administrative Procedure Act. After 1996, certain district courts, confusing the absence of the right to a judicial trial with the absence of the right to habeas review, are now mistakenly interpreting the immigration reforms as terminating judicial courts' power to review the constitutionality of executive deportation and detention orders. Neuman charges that this judicial deference is the "abandonment of the achievement of centuries of struggle against detention at the will of the executive" (Neuman, "Habeas Corpus," 970). Generally, due process debates meander between pity for persecuted alien masses and an aesthetic concern for our great institutions of law.

36. The Pew Forum on Religion and Public Life, "Spirit and Power: A 10-Country Survey of Pentecostals," Pew Research Center, October 2006.

37. See Horace Campbell, *Rasta and Resistance: From Marcus Garvey to Walter Rodney* (London: Hansib Publishing, 1997).

38. Nahal Toosi, "Vast Increase in Number of New York Police Stops Brings More Outrage at Sensitive Time," Associated Press, February 9, 2007.

39. In October 2004 the *New York Post* reported in alarming headlines, "Understaffed Feds Let Foreign Thugs Slip By" (Susan Edelman, October 24, 2004). The government was flagging only 300 foreign-born inmates weekly—40 percent of the total—"a failure that puts criminal aliens back on the streets."

40. Introduced to the U.S. Congress on March 28, 2006. José E. Serrano, "Serrano Introduces "Child Citizen Protection Act," press release, March 29, 2006, http://www.house.gov/list/press/ny16_serrano/060328ChildProtection.html (accessed November 18, 2007).

41. Interview by author, November 14, 2006.

42. Another mental health expert commented generally on the impact of deportation on children: "When children lose a family member this way, even though they may have a phone conversation with them, the physical separation feels like death." Nina Bernstein, "A Mother Deported, and a Child Left Behind," *New York Times,* November 24, 2004.

43. Headley traces the evolution of mandatory detention and deportation with the creation of mandatory minimums in the U.S. War on Drugs. As the former remained in full force, the repeal of the latter through early-release programs resulted in an accidental "two-tiered system": What has generated into a 'deportee problem' [is] rooted in the paradoxes of American immigration and criminal justice policies. . . . 'Aliens' [are now] in no position to make deals, to bargain, or to pursue more than marginal claims on the American political and judicial systems." Barnard Headley, *Deported*, Vol. 1: *Entry and Exit Findings, Jamaicans Returned Home from the U.S. Between 1997 and 2003* (Kingston, Jamaica: Stephenson's

Litho Press, 2005). See also Bernard Headley, "Giving Critical Context to the Deportee Phenomenon," *Social Justice* 33, no. 1 (2006): 40–56.

44. Office of Management and Budget, *Budget of the United States Government, Fiscal Year 2007*, http://www.whitehouse.gov/omb/budget/fy2007/dhs.html (accessed November 18, 2007).

PART V

Looking for "Illegals"

CHAPTER 13

Bordering the Other in the U.S. Southwest
El Pasoans Confront the Local Sheriff

KATHLEEN STAUDT

Cuando el dinero habla, todos callan
   —*Dicho*/Saying: "Money Talks"

THE U.S.–MEXICO BORDER has become a central focus in the recent immigration debates. Four southwestern states—California, Arizona, New Mexico, and Texas—once part of northern Mexico, have strong stakes in the outcomes of these debates. This chapter will focus on the immigration policy discourse and activism that has recently emerged in these states, with a special emphasis on Texas. This region is home to a large and growing Mexican heritage population, including citizens, permanent residents, and undocumented people. The border regions of these states are the site of numerous, interwoven political, economic, and cultural conflicts. These are also places of intense discursive contestation, which are continuously subjected to radically different ways of framing and interpreting cultural heritage, national identity, the significance of immigration, and the border's history, among other issues.

In the chapter's first section, I paint a picture of the border and southwestern region, its geography and diverse peoples. After that, I analyze public policies related to the border and immigrants, both at the state and local border levels. State politicians walk a fine line, appealing to nativist, anti-immigrant segments among conservative voters who differ considerably from most border people, including migrants from other parts of the United States. Then I focus on the 2-million-strong metropolitan area of the U.S.–Mexico border, El Paso, and Ciudad Juárez; the major historic gateway for Mexican migrants heading northward into the United States. This leads into (1) a detailed discussion of El Paso's immigration activism,

(2) responses to House Judiciary Committee Chair F. James Sensenbrenner's summer 2006 hearings held in El Paso, and (3) local challenges to the immigration checkpoints that were established in El Paso by the county sheriff's department (with financial support from the state and federal government).

My discussion will illustrate how government funding overwhelmed and outspent the alliance of El Pasoan human rights, students, and faith-based organizations that sought to defend the right of free movement and basic civil liberties for all immigrants. After the gubernatorial elections in late 2006, however, the politically influential business community joined the chorus of voices in praise of immigrants. Business is a constituency with material stakes in maintaining open doors to low-cost and plentiful labor. As the saying goes in Spanish and English, Money talks. The same has been acknowledged by sociologists like C. Wright Mills and G. William Domhoff.[1] However, the concept of "two-tiered pluralism" is also relevant.[2] That is, community activists enjoy formal rather than substantive equality in influencing the democratic process. Yet they used civic tools and access points in the border's feeble democracy to build a broader base for immigration reform.

Border Perspectives

The U.S.–Mexico borderline is two thousand miles long, stretching from the Gulf of Mexico to the Pacific Ocean. Mexico and the United States share the Rio Grande/Río Bravo river basin and have long cooperated in its management through binational institutions such as the International Boundary and Water Commission and the Comisión Internacional de Limites y Aguas. The terrain in much of the remaining border region is desert, with limited rainfall. It is treacherous territory over which immigrants pass in their northward trek. Currently, less than a hundred miles of the border is fenced, mainly in the limited urban areas.

Ten states form the border region, six of them in northern Mexico and four of them—Arizona, California, New Mexico, and Texas—in the U.S. Southwest. Together, over 80 million people live in the border states of both countries.[3] Mexico lost nearly half of its territory to the United States during mid-nineteenth-century occupation and war; thus the descriptor "southwest" seems like a misnomer in many local communities with generations of residents that—from their perspective—have only recently been designated as part of the United States. As some sociologists have pointed out, the Mexican migration flows that are now labeled "illegal" actually predate the existence of the U.S.–Mexico border as it is currently defined.[4] For almost two hundred years, these seasonal flows of labor have been an integral feature of the agricultural economy of the region. Hence, for decades, border crossing was informal and casual. However, more conservative regulatory approaches to managing cross-border migration flows became more prominent after the Mexican Revolution of 1910. Local officials (on the U.S. side of the border) also instituted degrading polices to disinfect crossers on public health grounds in 1917 and thereafter.[5] This was also accompanied by Jim Crow policies, which were used in many border states to segregate persons of Mexican heritage from the white-Anglo population.[6] Only in 1924 did the U.S. Congress establish the Border Patrol, but its early mission focused more on alcohol control than people. Since then, the extent of border control has waxed and waned with the demand for labor. There was a major crackdown in border control during the Depression era, leading to an increase in deportations. Shortly after this period, labor shortages led policymakers to recruit new flows of Mexican labor under the guest-worker arrangement known as the Bracero Program. Between 1942 and 1964, 4.6 million Mexicans were brought into the United States under this program, as temporary workers.[7] However, many braceros stayed in the United States, planting family and work roots.

The narrow border zone itself is worthy of focus, because it contains more people than many U.S. states. The border zone is officially defined as the land that runs twenty-five miles north and south of the border and is home to 14 million people, according to the 2000 censuses of both the United States and Mexico.[8] Border residents share the same air and water, and the economies of neighboring cities are closely connected. Businesses depend on shoppers crossing north and crossing south. According to the most recent annual figures, northbound crossers numbered 8,453 million pedestrians and 16,189 million vehicles that cross daily and legally.[9] Historian Oscar Martínez[10] classifies the U.S.–Mexico border region as interdependent, given the density of the political and economic networks that connect the cities in the Mexican and U.S. "sides." Of course, this is also an asymmetric relationship, given the vast differences in the power of these sovereign countries. Even so, Mexico is still the second-largest trading partner of the United States, after Canada, and the United States is Mexico's largest trading partner.

With the exception of San Diego, which is approximately 17 miles from the border, most of the U.S. border region is economically impoverished.

The three poorest counties in the United States are in Texas, immediately adjacent to Mexico.[11] Most residents on the U.S. side claim Hispanic heritage, which is the label that has appeared on the U.S. Census form since 1980. Six states draw two-thirds of the U.S. annual migration flow, with California and Texas at the lead, having the largest number of foreign-born residents in the United States. According to the census, 80 percent of El Pasoans are Hispanic (Mexican heritage) and 70 percent speak Spanish or Spanish and English. As many border theorists have explained, border zones are places of ongoing cultural and linguistic hybridity.[12]

With the exception of anti-Asian exclusions, the United States had an open door policy to all immigrants until the national-origin quotas introduced by the Immigration Act of 1924. Doors opened again in 1965, with a new emphasis on "human capital" and the principle of family reunification. Immigration laws, which are as complex and frequently reformed as tax laws, underwent major revisions in both 1986 and 1996. In 1986, the Immigration Reform and Control Act (IRCA)[13] established two new key principles, employer sanctions (for those who hired undocumented workers) and amnesty (for undocumented workers). Many undocumented persons who were working and living in the United States (most of Mexican heritage) took the opportunity to apply for citizenship under these new provisions. Under the 1996 immigration laws, however, policies toward both legal and undocumented immigrants became much more restrictive.[14]

For border residents, an even more significant change (for the worse) occurred after the attacks of September 11, 2001. The distant but national tragedy spawned a field of discourse that emphasized the threat of terrorism and was matched by policies that attempted to exert even tighter controls on all points of entry into the United States. The militarization of the border had already begun two decades earlier, with drug control policies that had attempted to stop the flow of illegal contraband into the United States from South America.[15]

However, the fearful climate created by this field of security-oriented policy discourse did not change many of the fundamentals of border life. The border region remained Janus-faced: on one side, the United States with remarkable records of public safety; on the other side, Mexico, with high homicide and femicide rates, given the long history of police impunity and complicity with the drug cartels.[16] El Paso, for example, has been ranked as the second safest big city in the United States over the last several years. A quarter of the city's population is foreign born, some of whom are undocumented, and many immigrants keep a low profile when it comes to matters of civic activism, law enforcement, and public safety.[17]

Meanwhile, the twenty-four county governments on the U.S.–Mexico border, fifteen of which are located in Texas, are responsible for processing those caught committing state felonies or multiple misdemeanors—a small proportion of whom are undocumented. The undocumented are not deported, but become part of the state-shaped, county criminal justice system paid for in large part by local taxpayers.[18] Thus, border residents face cross pressures. They live in a system that is relatively receptive to immigrants but also bear taxation burdens for state agencies that would appear to be a federal responsibility.

Each year, hundreds of *cruceros* (crossers) die making their way through unpopulated desert regions without adequate water, especially in Arizona.[19] These figures increased when the Border Patrol established blockades in major urban areas. Silvestre Reyes, a former Border Patrol Chief in El Paso and now its six-term congressional representative, established the 1993 blockade that was renamed Operation Hold the Line. Officers stationed in green vans positioned themselves near heavily populated areas of El Paso, forcing crossers into less-populated areas.

The U.S.–Mexico border region is a crossroads where many forces meet: the global economy, migration patterns, federal, state, and local public policies. Such complications would seem to merit extensive civic participation and activism, yet the population of the region is unorganized and has historically been marginalized from the political system. Only 5 to 20 percent of the population votes in local government elections, with this number doubling in state and national elections.[20]

In addition, anti-immigration sentiments articulated at the state and national level also resonate in the border zones. One reason for this is the compelling national discourse on security: who can be against security? Second, people express anxiety over immigrant cultural and linguistic assimilation. Witness the widespread influence of political scientist Samuel Huntington, who asserts that Spanish-speaking and Mexican immigrants are different from European immigrants.[21] Third, local county governments and their taxpayers reel under budgetary burdens attributable to immigrants.[22] County governments shoulder the costs of, for instance, law enforcement and emergency health care, only some of which are reimbursed by the federal government. County hospitals offer health care of last resort in the absence of a national U.S. health-care program. Currently, legislators in two border states (Arizona and Texas) have considered the imposition of a tax on immigrants' remittances to home countries to cover health-care costs.[23] Powerful voices in state government, even in border states, leaned away from policies that welcomed immigrant strangers in their midst—an area to which we will now turn.

State and Local Public Policies

The four southwestern U.S. border states are very different, politically and economically. Currently, there are two Republican governors (in California and Texas) and two Democratic governors (in Arizona and New Mexico). Let us consider just three out of many factors that explain variations in policy across these states. Some states exhibit one-party control of both the legislative and executive branches, such as Texas (which is Republican dominated) and New Mexico (which is Democrat dominated), freeing the party in power to pursue its agenda with minimal opposition. In some states, voters intervene directly on contentious public policy issues through referenda elections (as has occurred in Arizona and California). Some policies are made in relatively open public forums like legislative bodies, while other policies, born inside bureaucracies, are shielded from public oversight. Local politicians are subject to local electoral control in either partisan or nonpartisan elections. However, county governments generally serve as arms of the state, whereas city governments exercise more independence. All these access points present obstacles and opportunities for activists.

To understand the impact of public policy on immigrants, it is also necessary to look at the connections between a broad range of details, including issues that do not always appear to be directly related. For example, frontline workers (known as "street-level bureaucrats"[24]) make decisions about how policies are implemented that privilege or marginalize many categories of people, including immigrants. Health and welfare policies under federalism allow government workers to use legal status as a basis for determining who is eligible for these services. Nonprofit organizations that provide services for government reimbursement may ask noncitizens for Social Security numbers or other documents that verify citizenship. Another example is different states' requirements regulating the license to drive. These requirements stiffened after investigations revealed the ease with which the perpetrators of the attacks of September 11, 2001, obtained Virginia licenses. In most states, applicants must submit a Social Security card and, in some, must answer questions about citizenship before obtaining a driver's license. Among the four border states, only New Mexico allows all drivers—and not only those with legal documentation—to obtain authorization to drive.

Racial profiling has been a pattern throughout the United States. The litigation focus has been African Americans, later Mexican Americans, and only lately immigrants. It is not uncommon for drivers who are visible minorities to be subject to the practice at traffic checkpoints several times a year. However, weekly checkpoints are another matter. In El Paso County, Sheriff Leo Samaniego ordered deputies to conduct frequent checkpoints, with immigration consequences. This is analyzed in greater detail in the next section.

Education policies are another significant area of concern for immigrants. To be "born in the United States" confers immediate citizenship, but many citizen children live in immigrant households. The U.S. Supreme Court decision in *Plyler v. Doe* makes public education a right of residence, not citizenship.[25] In the Texas legislative session of 2007, House Representative Leo Berman (from the Dallas area) introduced an array of anti-immigrant legislation that would deny benefits to children of immigrant parents as well as denying automatic citizenship to those born in the United States (this standard of jus soli or "citizenship by birth" was conferred in the Fourteenth Amendment to the U.S. Constitution, to counter legislative developments in post–Civil War period that might have threatened the citizen rights of formerly enslaved African Americans and their children). One of Berman's goals was to challenge *Plyler v. Doe*, which grants children of all U.S. residents the right to public school education[26] and to the jus soli clause in the Fourteenth Amendment itself. These measures did not pass.

Public policies about bilingual or English-only education are important for Spanish-speaking immigrants in the southwest, having the power to undermine or enhance children's prospects for success. In *Lau v. Nichols* (1973),[27] the U.S. Supreme Court ruled that English-only classes denied access to students who spoke other languages, such as Spanish.[28] California and Arizona have used voter referenda to politicize measures for or against bilingual education. Recall the rhetorical flourish of a 1999 California referendum: "English for the Children" (an anti–bilingual education measure).

Education policymaking is also quite fragmented under the current system, with historically decentralized educational policy made at local school district levels, but increasingly at higher levels. Bilingual education is a case in point. In Texas, some of the 1,054 independent school districts opt for "early exit" provisions which fatally shorten and streamline bilingual education programs that, optimally, last five to seven years.[29] Southwestern states had opted for standardized testing prior to the No Child Left Behind law of 2001,[30] but since No Child Left Behind, these efforts to accelerate Spanish-speaking children into pass/fail English-only standardized tests has increased—and produced predictable failures. These outcomes have reduced high school graduation rates[31] and stigmatized public schools in Spanish-speaking areas by labeling them "low performing," either because of low test scores or the failure to meet Adequate Yearly Progress rates set in Washington, D.C.

A final public policy area to consider is the allocation and payment for state National Guard troops that have been provisionally deployed for border security until the number of federal Border Patrol agents is increased to meet the standards established by recent border control legislation. State National Guard units report to the governor, but drug enforcement and post–9/11 security measures entangle these units in federal laws and policies. In its "Secure Borders Initiative," the Department of Homeland Security reports that six thousand National Guard troops would work with Border Patrol officers in support functions.[32] Many units came from southwestern states, including 1,500 from Texas and only a few hundred from Arizona.[33] The fine line between federal and domestic law enforcement, under the Posse Comitatus Act of 1878,[34] has been blurred by the militarization of the border over the last two decades.[35] Although Texas governor Rick Perry advanced a fiscally conservative stance, his proposals for 2007 included the investment of considerable amounts of Texas revenue in border security using Texas National Guard troops.

Following this broad review of immigrant-relevant policies in four southwestern border states, we now move specifically to the Texas border region.

El Pasoans Confront the County Sheriff

El Paso is home to approximately 700,000 people, and like in other border cities and towns, a majority of the population is Spanish speaking. Some residents have deep roots in the region, and a local joke says that their ancestors' citizenship changed several times as borderlines were drawn and redrawn in the nineteenth century. Other residents arrived more recently, creating a diverse population of native-born, recent-immigrant, and first- and second-generation people with relatives in Mexico. Recall the earlier discussion that described the extensive border crossing which occurs daily, north to south and south to north.

THE POLITICAL CONTEXT: REPUBLICAN DIVISIONS

The debate over immigration and national security in El Paso must also be viewed in light of reports issued in 2005–2006 which asserted that the U.S. undocumented migrant population had doubled over the prior fifteen years, to reach a new high of approximately 12 million.[36] Alarmist interpretations of these reports claimed that the "floodgates" had broken as a new wave of "illegal aliens invaded" the U.S. desert borders.[37] This discourse emerged during a time when President George W. Bush's popularity was waning and the war in Iraq was increasingly viewed as a mistake in human and financial terms. From 2000 to 2006, Republicans dominated both the executive and legislative branches of government (and, some would argue, the judicial branch, given that seven of nine Supreme Court justices are Republican appointees). Party cohesion had long been questionable, given the conflicting agendas of the conservative right: one faction philosophically aligned with promarket, limited-government policies and the other, with socially conservative religious fundamentalists and nativist elements.

This divided Republican Party mobilized popular support around two approaches to immigration reform. The harsher approach would have criminalized not only immigrants, but also those who assisted immigrants, such as teachers, clergy, and nonprofit service staff, among others.[38] The softer approach would have established a temporary guest worker program and created a pathway toward legalization (albeit, penalty laden) for undocumented immigrants living in the United States.[39]

The figure of 12 million undocumented immigrants mobilized both Republican Party factions and mainstream Democrats around the need to "control" illegal immigration. However appealing, this term grossly oversimplified a process that would require the control of immigrants arriving by land, air, and sea; heightened enforcement and surveillance of visa overstays; investigations into bureaucratic backlogs that prevent citizenship applications from being processed in a timely manner; and the disastrous effects of free-trade agreements (such as NAFTA) on small-scale agriculture in Mexico that pushed migrants northward, among other factors.

However, the question remained, Given the growth of the undocumented population between the early 1990s and 2000, could the United States absorb yet another surge of 10–12 million undocumented immigrants over the next ten years? Put in these stark terms, to broad segments of the public, immigration control seemed essential.

BORDER PEOPLE REACT, IN MULTIPLE WAYS

In late 2005, when Representative Sensenbrenner's harsh bill HR 4437 passed in Congress, the measures came as a shock to many border people. They worried about personal ties, broken families, and tragic outcomes with deportation of their parents and grandparents. They wondered if their priests would be jailed. Nonprofit staff worried about putting themselves at risk with food and shelter programs. Although the civic involvement of border communities is weak, activism has grown among human and civil rights groups, faith-based groups that organize for social justice, clergy, and even local elected officials, Anglo and Hispanic alike.

Of course, the stakes for proimmigrant groups are very high at the U.S.–Mexico border. Virtually all U.S. citizens can trace their ancestry to immigrants, but the precarious nature of the immigrant experience remains a reality for most El Pasoans of Mexican heritage. Anxieties of a very personal nature began to emerge as people at the border began absorbing and discussing the harsh measures that were being proposed by immigration control advocates. What would happen if the government deported *abuelos y abuelas* (grandparents) or *tias y tios* (aunts and uncles)?

Border communities are predominantly Catholic. The Catholic faith tradition has been very supportive of immigrants' rights issues among its grassroots constituencies and within its institutional hierarchy. The U.S. Conference of Catholic Bishops issued a monograph, "Strangers no Longer: Together on the Journey of Hope," making their position on immigration clear.[40] In early 2006 a priest from a large Catholic church posted a big sign on a roof facing the Interstate 10 freeway which read, "Immigrants Welcome, No to House Bill 4437." University of Notre Dame professor and Catholic Priest Father Daniel Groody quoted the words of sociologist-theologian Lydio Tomasi at several academic conferences, stating, "It is not the church that saves the immigrant. Because of their faith, their dependence on God and their faithful witness amidst adversity, the immigrant saves the church."[41]

Meanwhile, opinion polls in El Paso consistently showed support for a softer approach to immigration reform, with as many as two-thirds being against a border wall.[42] At the national level, Hispanic public opinion also registered more support for softer reform measures than did mainstream, non-Hispanic opinion.[43] Although Mexican officials acknowledge the right of sovereign countries to make laws about entry, popular opinion in Cuidad Juárez and other areas was hostile about the *muro de odio,* or "wall of hate." El Paso youth, usually quiescent, walked out of schools in March and April 2006, spontaneously joining like-minded movements in other parts of the United States.

Although César Chávez Day (March 31) is an official holiday in the state of Texas, public school was in session. Traditionally, El Paso hosts a rally and a march on the holiday organized by Chicano activists (an aging crowd), at the downtown San Jacinto Plaza. But throughout the week, youth leaders communicated about walkouts with text messages, meetings, cell phones, and MySpace postings. On March 31, thousands of students walked out and joined the rally at the downtown plaza, waving Mexican and U.S. flags, as well as signs that affirmed immigrants' work ethics and denounced anti-immigrant racism. School administrators and local city police treated the walkouts as an act of civic expression but sought to control future activism with school lockdowns and veiled threats. Youth renamed San Jacinto Plaza (a name associated with the Texas independence struggle from Mexico during the creation of the Republic of Texas) the Plaza de los Lagartos (formerly the locale for an alligator pond and now statues), reclaiming it from official Texas history.

At the national level, human rights activists organized events on April 10 and on May 1, 2006—the traditional dates for celebrating Labor Day around the world. In El Paso, the Border Network for Human Rights mobilized its grassroots constituents for rallies and marches from all parts of the county, converging at the Plaza de los Lagartos on April 10. Activists called for work and consumer boycotts on May 1. At the border, Mexicans respected the event, and traffic at the international bridges and other points of entry was virtually nonexistent that day. Some El Pasoans took risks by staying away from work and school. The Paso del Norte Civil Rights Project (affiliated with the Texas Civil Rights Project) organized a teach-in at the Chamizal National Park, part of the U.S. Park Service. The Chamizal has special significance in El Paso–Cuidad Juárez. It commemorates the most recent exchange of land that transformed the Mexico-U.S. line—after a meandering river was fixed into a channel.

Youth activism was no longer visible after May. However, other groups emerged to contest the County Sheriff's checkpoint practices. These enforcement practices targeted the *colonias*—unplanned settlements outside the city limits where immigrant families establish initial footholds in their newly adopted homeland.

These checkpoint practices also highlighted differences of opinion within the growing Hispanic population on immigration issues. In 2006 Governor Perry initiated a new program that drew on funds from the U.S. Department of Justice (DOJ). These resources were made available to West Texas police and sheriffs' departments on the condition that they participate in enforcing border-security measures that target terrorists and drug trafficking. Although this project focused on criminal immigration offenses, it would also, inevitably, have required law enforcement officers to check suspects for civil immigration offenses (i.e., screening for legal status) as they conducted their investigations. The initiative, Operation Linebacker, drew on other clever sports metaphors that resonated with the mainstream population of Texas. Nevertheless, prominent members of the local law enforcement system, at both city and county levels, took different stances on Operation Linebacker—with some questioning the wisdom of involving the local sheriff's department in border security.

The city's police chief, Richard Wiles, ordered frontline police officers (street-level bureaucrats) to ask no questions about legal status. He took this stance because of his concern that if police become involved in asking these sorts of questions, noncitizen victims of crime would avoid talking to police out of fear that they could be detained for unrelated immigration violations. In contrast, County Sheriff Leo Samaniego, a Hispanic incumbent reelected as a Democrat in 2004, instituted new procedures during the spring of 2006 that allowed deputies to participate in the enforcement of federal immigration laws. The scope of these new enforcement powers includes the areas that deputies regularly patrol in their part of the county, areas outside the city's boundaries (in the *colonias*), and several small towns. The additional federal funds made available by Governor Perry may have been an incentive for County Sheriff Samaniego. Many law enforcement agencies are dependent on external funds for overtime pay and vehicles, and the El Paso County Sheriff's Office is no different. Even so, the El Paso City Police Department, which faces its own funding difficulties, has shunned incentive monies and will not participate in the enforcement of federal immigration laws unless ordered to comply.

Despite the lack of involvement from city police, the County Sheriff's Office went ahead with the new operation. Sheriff deputies staged checkpoints at various places around the county, asking drivers for not only their license and proof of insurance, but also for Social Security cards and immigration documents. When people could not produce these documents, deputies called the Border Patrol, who then placed the noncomplying individuals into deportation proceedings. Investigative journalists reported that 860 deportations occurred from April through June of 2006.[44] Later, investigative reporters analyzed six months of documents for the sixteen counties that participated in Operation Linebacker. The reporters found that for every *one* arrest made by the Sheriff's Office, "they reported seven undocumented immigrants to the Border Patrol."[45] During this time, El Paso deputies caught 1,076 undocumented immigrants, made 4 drug arrests, and confiscated 0.6 pounds of drugs.[46] If the reduction of "drug related and violent crime," as stipulated by the DOJ, was the true objective of Operation Linebacker, the initiative was a failure in El Paso County.

Human and civil rights organizations reacted to what they viewed as harassment and racial profiling. Harassment concerns also roused faith-based organizations, including two that were affiliated with the Industrial Areas Foundation (IAF).[47] Along with these community-based groups, residents reported that they were afraid to take children to school or go to work. Several priests reported that they stored food at the parish office for congregants who were fearful of leaving their houses to do their grocery shopping.

Community activists used a variety of tools available in a democracy, albeit a democracy that has always been relatively weak at the U.S.–Mexico border.[48] They met with the elected county attorney and state representatives. The Hispanic Caucus of the Texas state legislature sent a strongly worded letter to the governor, with widespread media publicity. Activists approached both the partisan County Commissioners' Court and the nonpartisan city council for what ultimately became successful resolutions demanding that local law enforcement maintain a hands-off approach to immigration enforcement. The resolutions also received wide media exposure. Sheriff's deputies stopped American Civil Liberties Union activist Carl Starr, who "looks Mexican," on a bus leaving El Paso. He filed a lawsuit charging harassment and racial profiling. The Paso del Norte Civil Rights Project joined the lawsuit. The Sheriff's Office settled out of court, promising to stop their local enforcement activities. Yet in the fall of 2006, Sheriff Samaniego revived checkpoints, with orders that deputies ask only for drivers' licenses and proof of insurance. Given that Texas laws have become increasingly harsh on document requirements for immigrant drivers, it is inevitable that deputies will find many "lawbreakers."

THE SENSENBRENNER HEARINGS, BORDER STYLE

U.S. Representative F. James Sensenbrenner, a Republican from Wisconsin and sponsor of HR 4437, used the summer of 2006 to hold hearings in various parts of the United States. A *New York Times* Opinion Editorial piece described them as "badly disguised campaign events" for the November midterm elections.[49] A member of the majority party in the Congress and chair of the House Judiciary Committee, Sensenbrenner and his staff had a domineering influence on the questions posed and in the selection of expert witnesses. However, the Democratic minority also had a voice in choosing some of the expert witnesses.

Sensenbrenner held hearings at the Chamizal National Memorial. Before the hearings, community activists and most of El Paso's state and local delegation held a press conference that registered their outrage about Sensenbrenner's decision to hold his immigration control forum in an overwhelmingly proimmigrant community. Human rights activists demonstrated outside the building, some dressed as *payasos* (clowns) to designate the circuslike atmosphere of the hearings. The public was allowed into the conference hall, which seated approximately four hundred. I estimated that the crowd was overwhelmingly against Sensenbrenner, given their reactions to his comments. He pounded the gravel, scolded, and threatened four times to have people removed from the room. One *payasa* who managed to sneak in with her clown mask on was captured in photographs that were widely circulated in the local media.

The question Sensenbrenner posed for the hearings bordered on ludicrous: "Should Mexico hold veto power over U.S. border security decisions?" Of course Mexico does not have veto power over U.S. immigration law, and there is no evidence that such power was being used directly or indirectly to influence the national immigration debate. Testimony was supposed to revolve around answers to this question.

The majority and minority parties used their official time in ways that were, predictably, for or against House bill 4437. The hearing organizers invited five experts to testify, each with written testimony and five minutes for verbal delivery. Two of the three experts chosen by the Republicans were Hispanics. These included Sheriff Samaniego, a House legislative analyst, and a Hispanic director of a support group for the Border Patrol. As their experts, the Democrats chose two Anglos: El Paso immigration lawyer Kathleen Walker and Chief Wiles. The three experts chosen by the Republicans spoke about the costs of immigrants, the dangers to the Border Patrol, and border terrorism. In the first two pages of his written and verbal testimony, Sheriff Samaniego used the words "terror" and "terrorism" no less than seventeen times. The lawyer chosen by the Democrats spoke about the long history of border cooperation between El Paso and Cuidad Juárez. Chief Wiles noted El Paso's designation as the second safest city in the United States, which was due in part to its community policing strategy and victim-friendly assistance; he also noted that it is on record as being in opposition to local police involvement in the enforcement of federal immigration laws.[50]

Sensenbrenner's hearing in El Paso was a brief fiasco, but Sheriff Samaniego's term of office is for a duration of four years, and his continuation of the checkpoints demonstrates his commitment to his department's involvement in border security. A broad alliance emerged to resist this. Border Interfaith—an IAF organization—used testimony from one of its members about the checkpoints in a public forum that included several politicians who were either running for office or incumbents facing reelection. The ensuing discussion revealed that the controversies surrounding the checkpoints are still alive for border residents, especially for *colonia* residents. More recently, a grocery store owner in a highly patrolled area posted signs in Spanish to warn his customers about checkpoints because he was losing business. Sheriff's deputies charged him with posting an unauthorized sign, which he decided to take to trial with support from civil rights organizations. County Attorney José Rodríguez dismissed the charges in January 2006 for lack of evidence.

Meanwhile, Washington Republicans found a compromise measure they hoped would control immigration at the border. Just before the November elections, the Secure Fence Act was signed into law. If fully funded, it will augment the existing fence (of less than one hundred miles) with seven hundred additional miles of fence along the southwestern border

THE TEXAS GUBERNATORIAL CAMPAIGN:
BUSINESS REACTS AND MONEY TALKS

The fall 2006 Texas gubernatorial race became a lurid example of immigrant bashing to build electoral support in nonborder areas. The Republican incumbent (Rick Perry), a Democrat, two independent candidates, and a Libertarian candidate ran for governor. This range of candidates was sure to divide the vote, given that all contestants were to be listed on the final ballot. And so a winner could emerge by carrying the largest minority of the voting public, rather than by winning a majority of the vote. One of the independent candidates, Carol Strayhorn, was also the elected state comptroller. All four of the major candidates used border security as their dominant campaign theme, playing far more to mainstream conservative Texans than to border people, who historically have low voter turnout rates. Meanwhile, business and corporate interests, which fund major parts of the campaign, complained about the impact of immigration control measures on their labor needs and costs.

Governor Rick Perry was reelected with 39 percent of the vote. Immediately after his electoral victory, he reached out to the business community at a state conference, complaining about "divisive" immigrant proposals and claiming to seek a temporary workforce immigration solution. He did not continue his $5 million Webcam operation so that Internet surfers can monitor how the state is policing the border, and his $100 million border security initiative, paid for with state money, will stretch out over two years.

President Bill Hammond of the Texas Association of Business, which cohosted the Texas Immigration Summit in December 2006, told the press that undocumented immigrants make an "incredible contribution" to the Texas economy.[51] Comptroller Strayhorn issued a lengthy and methodical report from her office demonstrating that immigrants were more "beneficial" than costly to the Texas economy.[52] Without the 1.4 million undocumented immigrants, her report concluded, the gross state product would have been $17.7 billion less in 2005. Ironically or not, this research was probably completed before she framed her campaign discourse, which had emphasized the need for better border control. State officials and the national Republican Party may also be calculating the impact that their position on immigration will have on future voter support, given that Hispanics are 35 percent of the Texas population and growing. As the case of Sheriff Samaniego illustrates, not all Hispanics think alike on immigration. Even so, the ensuing debates around immigration reform in Texas and other southwestern states have been tinged with more overtones of anti-immigrant racism. These tendencies may compel a larger number of Hispanics to join together to support a less punitive version of immigration reform.

Conclusion

This chapter analyzed the complexity of "keeping out the Others" as it applied to the struggle over immigration policy across several southwestern states, and specifically as it applied to the politics of the U.S.–Mexico border zone. As I have tried to demonstrate, border cities are indeed special places where sentiments about immigrants do not match the mainstream discourse on immigration reform.

The states of Arizona, California, New Mexico, and Texas have adopted different kinds of policies that benefit or burden immigrant populations in different ways. Their politicians often play to their constituents' anxieties about the seeming threats and costs of immigrants, both in terms of taxation and cultural assimilation. Apparently minor issues can also make a difference for immigrants, whether it is bilingual programming in education or licenses to drive vehicles.

El Paso, with its historically weak levels of civic participation, mounted a valiant effort to resist policies to "keep out the Other"—the "Other" in this case being, for the most part, Mexican immigrants. Both El Paso's social capital and its economy, which is part of the border zone, are thoroughly interdependent with those of Ciudad Juárez. Activists in faith-based, human, and civil rights organizations used a variety of strategies in El Paso's weak democracy to end the deportation of immigrants through Operation Linebacker. This included challenges to the sheriff's traffic checkpoints and challenges to the use of federal funds to support these state-level enforcement activities. Activists also used resolutions, public awareness campaigns, accountability sessions, and lawsuits to achieve their goals. They prevailed temporarily, but the sheriff reinstituted a large number of checkpoints and used existing state law, which mandated all vehicle operators to have valid drivers' licenses, as a rationale for traffic stops. These practices, in effect, turned many immigrants into lawbreakers. However, this sort of lawbreaking behavior contrasted greatly with the aims of Operation Linebacker to stop violent crime, drug trafficking, and terrorism.

My discussion has also shown that money talks. Federal and state monetary incentives changed street-level policing practices in the El Paso Sheriff's Office. However, the financial incentives that drew the County Sheriff's Office into border enforcement did not, perhaps, talk as loudly as the business community's ability to influence the state government's position on immigration after the gubernatorial elections. Businesses in Texas have money to invest not only in the economy but in campaign contributions. Their political capital is renowned in the one-party rule that Texas government has become.

Even so, the political influence of big business and other powerful actors does not diminish the efforts of community activists in resisting the anti-immigrant atmosphere that has been created in the outlying regions of El Paso County. Democracy in Texas and at the border seems to have two tiers, the more powerful of which is for those who have influence. However, those who belong to the "lower" tier—Mexican heritage and Anglo alike—demonstrate a civic capacity and political vision that anticipates the changing demographics of the state, which will become majority Mexican heritage in the next half century.

Stronger democracy at the border would strengthen the second of the two-tier system, giving the first tier a run for its money but probably not eliminating the hierarchy of privilege in U.S. democracy. Strong democracy would build on the temporary youth mobilization of 2006 and sustain and consolidate that cohort as they become adults in a wider space of political engagement. In 2006 marchers chanted in Spanish and in English: "Today we march, tomorrow we vote." Although voter turnout has not increased immediately in El Paso, coalitions are in place to mobilize interest. And if Sheriff Samaniego stands for reelection, he will surely face tough competition, not the least of which in the Democratic Primary election, for his partisan stance on immigration enforcement that never fit well with El Paso border communities. El Paso's majority Democratic locale has not been served well in the decade of Republican one-party rule statewide. But demographic tables are turning, and party majorities will likely change. Of course, caveats are in order about U.S. political parties, because the state's historically conservative Democratic Party routinely neglected the border as being less-organized or unorganized communities, except their chambers of commerce.

Border leaders have emerged in various grassroots, social justice, and faith-based organizations. They participate in IAF accountability sessions and quarterly meetings with elected officials who invariably promise "to work with them" once elected. They also work with immigration-rights advocates at the local, state, and national levels. Border voices are increasingly heard in the national immigration debates. Several delegations from border communities participated in immigration reform hearings that were held in Austin and Washington, D.C.—despite the fact that Congress failed to move on the 2007 Senate compromise bill.

Despite its many flaws, two-tiered democracy in the United States contains access points and opportunities for activists to target changes in policies and their political representatives. Again, few expect Sheriff Samaniego to survive reelection. And fatigue is setting in with a decade of conservative rule in Texas. In politics, some win today and lose tomorrow, but organized people talk and talk loudly through sustained activism. And it is only by struggling to hold the local and state government accountable for its enforcement practices that El Pasoans can hope to minimize the damage done by get-tough border control measures.

Notes

1. C. Wright Mills, *The Power Elite* (New York: Oxford University Press, 1956), G. William Domhoff, *Who Rules America? Power and Politics in the Year 2000*, 3rd ed. (Mountain View, Calif.: Mayfield Publishing, 1998).

2. Rodney Hero, *Latinos and the U.S. Political System: Two-Tiered Pluralism* (Philadelphia: Temple University Press, 1992). Hero revised the classic political debates between elite theorists who argue that elites control all decision making and pluralist theorists who argue that plural groups compete in a neutral process, with winners achieving decisions. Also see Susan Clarke, Rodney Hero, Mara Sydney, Luis Fraga, and Bari Erlichson, *Multiethnic Moments: The Politics of Urban Education Reform* (Philadelphia: Temple University Press, 2006).

3. Kathleen Staudt and Irasema Coronado, *Fronteras no Más: Toward Social Justice at the U.S.–Mexico Border* (New York: Palgrave USA, 2002), 15.

4. Immigration scholars have increasingly questioned "push-pull" dynamics and models that focus solely on economic incentives. Instead, they have explored how immigration flows can become self-sustaining forces that are propelled by social (and, in particular, familial) networks, the diplomatic history between host and sending nations, and a variety of formal and informal political forces that have an interest in sustaining immigration (see Saskia Sassen, *Globalization and Its Discontents: Essays on the New Mobility of People and Money* (New York: New Press, 1999). In this light, Mexican migration (both legal and illegal) is better understood as a sociocultural institution that has been enmeshed in both the politics and economy of the southwestern United States and northern Mexico since the mid-nineteenth century. For some additional context, see Douglas Massey, *Beyond Smoke and Mirrors: Mexican Immigration in an Era of Economic Integration* (New York: Russell Sage Foundation, 2003) and Mae Ngai, *Impossible Subjects: Illegal Aliens and the Making of Modern America* (Princeton, N.J.: Princeton University Press, 2005).

5. David Romo, *Ringside Seat to a Revolution: An Underground Cultural History of El Paso and Juárez: 1893–1923* (El Paso: Cinco Puntos Press, 2005), 233–243.

6. Ngai, *Impossible Subjects*.

7. Kitty Calavita, *Inside the State: The Bracero Program, Immigration, and the I.N.S.* (New York: Routledge, 1992).

8. Staudt and Coronado, *Fronteras no Más*, 11.

9. Thomas Fullerton and Roberto Tinajero, *Borderplex Economic Outlook: 2005–2007* (El Paso: UTEP Border Region Modeling Project), 14.

10. Oscar Martínez, *Border People* (Tucson: University of Arizona Press, 1996).

11. For other social and economic indicators, see John Sharp, *Bordering the Future: Challenge and Opportunity in the Texas Border Region* (Austin: State of Texas Comptroller of Public Accounts, 1998), also http://pie.tamucc.edu/strapln/bord-futur/chap01.pdf (accessed November 7, 2007).

12. Gloria Anzaldúa, *Borderlands/La Frontera: The New Mestiza* (San Francisco: Spinsters/Aunt Lute Press, 1987); Homi Bhabha, "Narrating the Nation," in *Nationalism*, ed. John Hutchison and Anthony D. Smith (New York: Oxford University Press, 1994), 306–312; Kathleen Staudt and David Spener, "The View from the Frontier: Theoretical Perspectives Undisciplined," in *The U.S.–Mexico Border: Contesting Identities, Transcending Divisions*, ed. David Spener and Kathleen Staudt (Boulder: Lynn Rienner, 1998), 3–34.

13. Public Law 99-603, 100, Stat. 3359 (Nov. 6, 1986).

14. See selections in Philip Kretsedemas and Ana Aparicio, eds., *Immigration Welfare Reform and the Poverty of Policy* (Westport, Conn.: Greenwood/Praeger, 2004).

15. Timothy Dunn, *The Militarization of the U.S.–Mexico Border, 1978–1992* (Austin: University of Texas, Center for Mexican American Studies, 1996).

16. Kathleen Staudt, *Violence and Activism at the Border: Gender, Fear and Everyday Life in Ciudad Juárez* (Austin: University of Texas Press, forthcoming).

17. Kathleen Staudt, *Free Trade? Informal Economies at the U.S.–Mexico Border* (Philadelphia: Temple University Press, 1998).

18. Tanis Salant, *Illegal Immigrants in U.S./Mexico Border Counties: The Costs of Law Enforcement, Criminal Justice, and Emergency Medical Services* (Tucson: University of Arizona, 2001), 8–11, 39.

19. Karl Eschbach, Jacqueline Hagan, Nestor Rodríguez, Rube Hernández-Leon, and Stanley Bailey, "Death at the Border," *International Migration Review* 33 (1999): 430–454; Staudt and Coronado, *Fronteras no Más*.

20. Staudt and Coronado, *Fronteras no Más*; Kathleen Staudt and Clarence N. Stone, "Division and Fragmentation: The El Paso Experience in Global-Local Perspective," in *Transforming the City: Community Organizing and the Challenge of Political Change* (Lawrence: University Press of Kansas, 2007), 84–108.

21. Samuel Huntington, *Who Are We? The Challenge to America's Identity* (New York: Simon and Schuster, 2004).

22. For the pioneering first of these commissioned studies, see Salant, *Illegal Immigrants in U.S./Mexico Border Counties;* also, Institute for Policy and Economic Development, *At the Cross Roads: U.S./Mexico Border Counties in Transition* (El Paso: University of Texas at El Paso, Institute for Policy and Economic Development, 2006).

23. Eliot Shapleigh, *Lifting the Lamp Beside Texas' Door: Addressing the Challenges and Opportunities of Immigration in Texas for the 2007–2009 Biennium* (Aus-

tin: State Senator Shapleigh's Office, December 14, 2006), 49–50. These measures failed in Texas (2007) and have not passed in Arizona.

24. Michael Lipsky, *Street-Level Bureaucracy: Dilemmas of the Individual in Public Services* (New York: Russell Sage, 1980).

25. 457 U.S. 202 (1982).

26. Kathleen Staudt and Randy Capps, "Con la Ayuda de Dios? El Pasoans Manage the 1996 Welfare and Immigration Law Reforms," in *Immigration Welfare Reform and the Poverty of Policy,* ed. Philip Kretsedemas and Ana Aparicio (Westport, Conn: Greenwood/Praeger, 2004).

27. 414 U.S. 563 (1973).

28. Susan Rippberger and Kathleen Staudt, *Pledging Allegiance: Learning Nationalism at the El Paso-Juárez Border* (New York: Falmer/Routledge, 2003), 97.

29. Wayne Thomas and Virginia Collier, *A National Study of School Effectiveness for Language Minority Students' Long-Term Academic Achievement,* Center for Research on Education, Diversity & Excellence, 2001, http://crede.berkeley.edu/research/llaa/1.1pdfs/1.1_1onorthwest.pdf (accessed November 7, 2007).

30. One example is the so-called Texas Miracle of the early 1990s. Standardized testing advocates claimed miracles in Texas school achievement, improving learning overall and reducing gaps between ethnic and economic groups. This formed some of the idea base for No Child Left Behind. Angela Valenzuela calls this supposed miracle a "mirage" in the introduction to her edited collection. "The Accountability Debate in Texas: Continuing the Conversation," in *Leaving Children Behind: How "Texas-Style" Accountability Fails Latino Youth,* ed. Angela Valenzuela (Albany: SUNY Press, 2005), 1.

31. See selections in Valenzuela, *Leaving Children Behind.*

32. See Department of Homeland Security, "Secure Border Initiative," October 12, 2006, http://www.dhs.gov/ximgtn/programs/editorial_0868.shtm (accessed November 7, 2007).

33. Arizona Governor Janet Napolitano's Web site asserts the need for more federal reimbursement for the use of state National Guard troops under Article 32. See State of Arizona Executive Office, "Gov. Napolitano Signs Agreement to Put National Guard on Border," press release, June 1, 2006, http://www.governor.state.az.us/dms/upload/NR_060206_Guard%20MOA%20Release.pdf (accessed November 7, 2007).

34. Shapleigh, *Lifting the Lamp Beside Texas' Door,* 31.

35. Dunn, Militarization, chap. 4.

36. See Jeffrey Passel, *The Size and Characteristics of the Unauthorized Migrant Population in the U.S.: Estimates Based on the March 2005 Current Population Survey,* Pew Hispanic Center, March 2006, http://pewhispanic.org/files/reports/61.pdf (accessed November 7, 2007). According to Passel's report, this population almost doubled between the early 1990s and the present.

37. It has been estimated that there are approximately 12 million undocumented persons in the United States, but 35–40 percent of these persons are non-Mexican, and 25–40 percent initially entered the United States legally, with temporary visas. Thus, it is not possible to categorize all undocumented migrants as "Mexican" or as illegal border crossers. The rise of the undocumented population should also be viewed in light of increased demands for low-wage labor, which draws on preexisting channels of U.S.–Mexican migration and changes in U.S. immigration policy that have made it more difficult for migrant workers to enter the United States with the option to become legal permanent residents. For more details, see Passel, *Size and Characteristics of the Unauthorized Migrant Population*.

38. The most extreme example being the REAL GUEST Act, developed by Colorado Representative Tom Tancredo. For details on these and other proposals, see Eliot Turner and Marc R. Rosenblum, *Solving the Unauthorized Migrant Problem: Proposed Legislation in the US* (Washington, D.C.: Migration Policy Institute, September 1, 2005), http://www.migrationinformation.org/Feature/display.cfm?ID=333 (accessed November 7, 2007).

39. A prominent example is the bipartisan Secure America and Orderly Immigration Act that was proposed by Senators Ted Kennedy and John McCain. For a review, see Turner and Rosenblum, *Solving the Unauthorized Migrant Problem*.

40. U.S. Conference of Catholic Bishops, *Strangers No Longer: Together on the Journey of Hope* (Washington, D.C.: U.S. Conference of Catholic Bishops, 2003).

41. Two examples include Fr. Daniel Groody, Public Address, Lineae Terrarum Conference (El Paso/Ciudad Juárez, March 29, 2006); and Fr. Daniel Groody, Public Address, Borders Workshop, American Political Science Association Conference (Philadelphia, August 30, 2006).

42. This was before the border wall was renamed a "fence," after the 109th Congress approved the Secure Fence Act of 2006 before it adjourned in fall 2006. Louie Gilot, "Border Fence, Citizenship Denial Opposed," *El Paso Times*, February 23, 2006.

43. Roberto Suro and Gabriel Escobar, National Survey of Latinos: The Immigration Debate, Pew Hispanic Center, July 13, 2006.

44. Brandi Grissom, "Reports Find Linebacker Caught 860 Immigrants," *El Paso Times*, June 23, 2006.

45. Darren Meritz, "Border Group Fears for Rights," *El Paso Times*, December 10, 2006, B1.

46. Brandi Grissom, "Operation Linebacker Catches More Immigrants Than Criminals," *El Paso Times*, November 20, 2006.

47. The Industrial Areas Foundation is a national organization, with regional, state, and local groups, that "organizes the unorganized," mainly training leaders in faith-based organizations seeking social justice. The late Saul Alinsky is credited with this sometimes confrontational but essentially reformist approach to

gaining accountability from government. See Saul Alinsky, *Rules for Radicals: A Pragmatic Primer for Realistic Radicals* (New York: Vintage, 1971).

48. Staudt and Coronado, *Fronteras no Más.*

49. *New York Times*, "Immigration's Lost Year," Opinion Editorial, September 19, 2006.

50. Police Chief Wiles was referring to an official resolution from the Major City Chiefs (composed of U.S. police chiefs from 57 major cities, including El Paso) which registered their opposition to the local enforcement of federal immigration laws.

51. Steve Taylor, "Hammond: Strayhorn Report Shows Incredible Contribution Undocumented Workers Are Making," *Rio Grande Guardian*, December 7, 2005.

52. Carole Keeton Strayhorn, *Undocumented Immigrants in Texas: A Financial Analysis of the Impact to the State Budget and Economy* (Austin: Comptroller of Public Accounts, December, 2006), http://www.window.state.tx.us/specialrpt/undocumented/ (accessed November 7, 2007).

CHAPTER 14

Framing the Debate on Taxes and Undocumented Workers

A Critical Review of Texts Supporting Proenforcement Policies and Practices

JORGE CAPETILLO-PONCE

DURING THE PAST THREE DECADES, a combination of restrictive immigration policies and expanding migratory pressures has produced a rapid growth in the population of undocumented immigrants in the United States, which the latest Pew Hispanic Center reported as reaching 12 million as of March 2004.[1]

A question that was hotly debated during the 1990s and remains a topic of academic and public interest is that of whether undocumented immigrants cover the cost of the public services they use, be they schools, welfare, or health care. Media and public-opinion reports as well as scholarly literature on the costs/benefits of undocumented immigration have gradually been framed around its fiscal impacts, with the more pessimistic of the assessments pointing to a need for stricter enforcement policies.

A new interpretive framework—a new discourse—has also revealed itself in the past two decades via "the semantic shift from 'citizen' to 'taxpayer' as the central focus of civic life."[2] The alleged tax burden imposed upon the broader community by immigrants via their use of social services has been linked by some scholars to the emergence of a new nativism. Kitty Calavita, for instance, sees this as the result of ongoing economic transformations, the retrenchment of the welfare state, and what Sidney Plotkin and William Scheuerman call "balanced-budget conservatism."[3] Calavita describes this as a vision that elevates "protecting taxpayer interests to the highest priority of government, stigmatizing poor, property-less people as somehow less than fully citizens. And of course those who are not even citizens—not even legal residents—are the ideal target of blame, more undeserving than the traditional undeserving poor. As economic insecurity intensifies with the continued globalization of the economy and the displacement of domestic labor, 'nativist' or balanced-budget conservatism simultaneously channels that anger into anti-immigrant nativism and legitimates the backlash."[4]

Notes on Methodology: Structural versus Cultural Explanations

In order to shed further light on the problem that Calavita has limned for us, this chapter offers a critical review of texts that frame the immigration debate around tax issues as a way of justifying proenforcement policies. My review is not a conventional content analysis of common themes that are representative of a large number of cases. Instead, I provide an in-depth analysis of particular types of texts—produced by such distinct agencies as the mainstream media, political organizations, academic think tanks, and the blogosphere—and I explore the discursive-thematic connections among these types.

The decision to utilize this mix of texts was inspired by Edward Said's seminal work *Covering Islam,* in which he analyzes how the media and the experts determine how we see Islamic societies.[5] In a similar fashion, my research is based on the notion that these texts, although varying widely in their provenance, constitute an integrated field of discourse that is making claims about the harmful effect that undocumented immigrants, and especially undocumented workers, are having on the fiscal health of the United States. These arguments provide millions of individuals who are not acquainted with the many details of the debate over undocumented workers and taxes with an explanatory framework that transforms a complex problem into a simpler, coherent, and intelligible whole.

We can appreciate more clearly the emergence of this discourse when we observe the similar approaches that these different texts and agencies take in examining the fiscal effects of undocumented work in the United States, and how they reinforce each other's viewpoints. In this respect, Calavita's notion of balanced-budget conservatism is a key methodological element in my analysis, because it runs through and connects the different types of texts analyzed here.

Following Hans Vermeulen, we can place balanced-budget conservatism in the category of structural explanations as opposed to cultural explanations. Vermeulen considers that structural explanations are found in the realm of technology, the economy, and other material structures such as the stock market, the Supreme Court, or the fiscal sector of a government.

Structural explanations focus on the system, not on individuals or groups. In contrast, cultural explanations are found in the realm of beliefs, values, and ideas; for example, the damaging effects of immigration on the sense of community and nationality, or the "culture of poverty" that many Americans see in undocumented immigrants. In general, cultural explanations assign blame or praise to specific individuals or groups.[6]

Moreover, cultural and structural explanations are generally associated with different political ideologies. Conservative writers tend to stress cultural explanations, while liberal writers tend to stress structural explanations. But even within the conservative camp, which will be the focus of my analysis, those who utilize structural explanations such as balanced-budget conservatism or arguments that emphasize the illegal status of specific immigrants are seen as more moderate than those who rely on cultural explanations. The most notable examples of the former type include nativist arguments that stress race, ethnicity, morality, or language, which are situated in a more radicalized, right-wing political space.

It is clear that balanced-budget conservatism ultimately is used, in the selected texts, with nativist intentions; that is, to make sharp distinctions between Americans and "others." I will, however, not conflate the two terms—balanced-budget conservatism and nativism—as Calavita does, but will keep them apart for methodological purposes. Thus, balanced-budget conservatism will refer to structural explanations that focus on scientifically proving the negative effects of undocumented immigrants on the fiscal system of the country. Nativism will refer to cultural explanations based on anti-immigrant sentiments expressed in populist, racist, and/or xenophobic terms that target specific individuals or groups for exclusion because of the threats they are perceived to pose to U.S. national identity. While distinguishing cultural from structural explanations, my analysis also draws attention to the implicit connections between culturalist perspectives (i.e., nativism) and structural arguments (i.e., balanced budget conservatism). It is important to underline here, however, that my main focus is not on cultural explanations. I use this perspective to draw points of comparison with my main concern: the discursive construction of structural, proenforcement arguments and illustrating how these arguments deploy framing devices that resonate with both mainstream and right-wing perspectives on immigration.

It is also important to emphasize just how new this discourse that connects taxes to unauthorized migration really is. As recently as 1986, just after the enactment of the Immigration Reform and Control Act (IRCA), the debate over undocumented immigrants was centered not on taxes versus benefits but on the way that undocumented immigration was allegedly depressing wages and displacing American workers—hence the employer-sanctions centerpiece of IRCA. Indeed, immigrants' consumption of costly social services was rarely mentioned until the early 1990s, when we saw the passing of such proenforcement measures as Proposition 187 in California and PRWORA and IIRAIRA in Congress.[7] Then along came the tragic events of September 11, 2001, and with it a new discourse, colored by the theme of national security. We saw at that time the incorporation of such terms as "border control" and "securing our borders" into the immigration lexicon—thus making the link between undocumented immigration and the ongoing War on Terror. The attacks also provided conservative and even some moderate sectors of American society with a new justification to apply more pressure on lawmakers to pass new immigration laws that contained a heavy enforcement component and a get-tough approach toward immigration reform.

Media Coverage, Blogs, and Public Opinion

It is clear that the debate about undocumented immigrants is more and more being framed around the tax-burden argument. Cordell Whitlock's piece is typical of recent attempts to gain a seeming objectivity simply by contrasting the pros and cons of the issue:

> Valley Park's [Missouri] immigration ordinance has fueled local debate on the issue. Supporters of the law seem to echo sentiments expressed by Susan Brust after Tuesday night's vote: "If you're an illegal immigrant you're not paying taxes. You are using up our public funding and you're sending your kids to school for free," said Brust, who is a Valley Park resident. . . . "Undocumented immigrants do pay both federal and state income taxes," says Steven Legomsky, a professor of international law at Washington University. Legomsky says many illegal immigrants work for legitimate companies that deduct taxes from paychecks. "It is true that from time to time an undocumented worker will be paid cash under the table, but the same is true for U.S. citizens, and, on balance, the amount undocumented workers pay in the balance of taxes are equal to the amount they receive in government services."[8]

Such "objective" framings are, however, gradually being superseded by more aggressive presentations designed to influence the viewer/reader to support proenforcement policies and practices. These aggressive presentations may not be typical of the bulk of immigration reports appearing in the mainstream media. Even so, the reports being filed by the likes of CNN's Lou Dobbs and Fox News's Bill O'Reilly on undocumented immigrants and their purportedly negative impacts—cultural, economic and otherwise—lie at the heart of the conservative zeitgeist. Also typical of this right-wing discourse is the adoption of a seemingly populist stance partially informed by balanced-budget conservatism. This perspective is evinced by the following excerpt published by the *FreeRepublic,* a conservative news forum:

> Those in favor of foreign labor are corporations who are addicted to cheap labor. They are the ones who are benefiting. But their benefit comes at the American taxpayer's expense when you consider that the American taxpayer is virtually subsidizing the labor costs of the greedy corporations by supplying the illegal foreign workers and their families with welfare, free education, free medical, WICs, housing assistance, etc.—something the corporations won't. Most illegal aliens do not receive the typical paycheck with tax deductions—they are paid in cash and do not pay taxes.[9]

This populist stance is even more pronounced in blogs, a recent format that has become prominent in setting the online agenda. Mainstream-media journalists assume their role to be that of mediators between the powerful and the powerless (the top–bottom approach), and are more likely to use supposedly objective framing of multiple perspectives, cautious descriptions, and structural explanations to present their arguments to the public. In contrast, bloggers conduct their business at the grassroots level (the bottom–up approach), using ironic, edgy, and challenging explanations closer to the cultural camp, as well as decidedly partisan language.

The so-called blogosphere is populated by such right-wing sites as vdare.com, redstate.com, strata-sphere.com, and thinkprogress.org—among many others—which regularly discuss unauthorized immigration. In fact, it is in the blogosphere that we encounter the most radical proenforcement proposals, based mostly on cultural explanations that sometimes border on racism and xenophobia. Proposals run from building a wall that runs across the entire U.S.–Mexico border, including "razor wires and minefields put into place as well,"[10] to proposing mass deportation of all undocumented residents in the United States.

Another example is Edwin Rubenstein's critical examination of the only study of the costs of mass deportation. This study includes costs associated with apprehending (between $150 billion and $160 billion), detaining (between $33 billion and $37 billion), prosecuting (between $9 and $11 billion), and removing (between $8 and $9 billion) undocumented immigrants, for a grand total of around $206 billion over five years.[11] While Rubenstein considers $206 billion "an absurdly large figure," he estimates the total fiscal benefits of deportation at $51 billion per year—$25 billion in deficit reduction and $26 billion in forgone displacement losses. Those benefits, according to Rubenstein, will make mass deportation pay itself in about four years, and he adds the nativist slogan: "Plus, of course, we'd get America back."[12]

Mainstream-media icons such as Dobbs and O'Reilly, as well as less-known bloggers like Rubenstein have helped to fuel anti-immigrant sentiments among the general public and to provide ammunition to other proenforcement advocates. But the bigger picture, beyond the confines of punditry, is harder to elucidate, showing just how vulnerable the public's views are to influence by a host of variables. We can begin by noting, as Philip Martin does, that all the public-opinion surveys conducted between 1965 and 2006 have shown that most Americans want to see both legal and illegal immigration reduced.[13] Further, a 2002 study by the Chicago Council on Global Affairs revealed differences between elite and mass opinion: 55 percent of the public said legal immigration should be reduced, compared with 18 percent of opinion leaders—which suggests that support for immigration rises with income and education.[14]

Public opinion often changes according to changing economic circumstances. For example, a 1997 PBS poll showed that during the late 1990s, when the economy expanded and unemployment rates were low, public opinion became less restrictionist, with fewer than 50 percent of Americans wanting immigration reduced or stopped altogether.[15] The same poll showed, however, that 63 percent were concerned about immigrants taking jobs from Americans or causing racial conflict, and 79 percent were concerned that immigrants were overburdening the welfare system and pushing up taxes. Another example is provided in a January 1997 poll conducted by the Public Policy Institute of California, which also found opinion shifting as the economy boomed—52 percent considered Mexican immigrants a benefit to the state because of their hard work and job skills, while only 36 percent described them as a burden for their use of public services and schools.[16]

Terrorism and a weakening economy made Americans more restrictionist at the start of the twenty-first century. A Fox News opinion poll in November 2001 found that 65 percent of Americans favored stopping all immigration during the War on Terror, and a January 2002 Gallup Poll reported that 58 percent of Americans, up from 45 percent in January 2001, thought immigration levels should be decreased.[17] As for the present climate, a 2006 nationwide survey conducted by the Pew Hispanic Center revealed that 56 percent of the participants think most recent immigrants are not paying their fair share of taxes, while 33 percent believe they are doing so.[18]

In contrast to public opinion, scholarly research shows that over two-thirds of undocumented immigrants do, in fact, pay Medicare, Social Security, and personal income taxes.[19] However, this is rarely reported by the mass media. It is also rarely reported that the 1996 welfare reform bill has disqualified undocumented immigrants—and most legal immigrants with less than five years of residence—from nearly all government programs, including food stamps, housing assistance, Medicaid, and Medicare-funded hospitalization (the only services allowed to them are emergency medical care and K–12 education).[20]

The public more frequently hears about the efforts of conservative politicians such as Tom Tancredo (R-Colorado) who have attempted to push proenforcement bills through Congress that would criminalize the giving of aid to undocumented immigrants. In fact, the passage of nativist measures of this kind would only add to the already vast number of restrictions and penalties that undocumented immigrants find themselves confronted by in today's United States.[21]

Many organizations are attempting to draw public attention to what they see as the damage that undocumented workers are doing to the U.S. economy. Good examples are FAIR (the Federation for American Immigration Reform), the Council of Conservative Citizens, the Immigration Reform Caucus, the Minuteman Project, and ProjectUSA. FAIR, for instance, relies on a mostly nativist outlook, charging that immigrants, besides causing fiscal imbalance, contribute to population growth and environmental degradation, and weaken the cultural bonds that hold Americans together. In the 1990s FAIR's proenforcement efforts were focused on enacting strict immigration quotas, calling for a sharp reduction in immigration—from 1 million to perhaps 150,000 a year. More recently, however, the organization has reinforced its call for stricter enforcement by relying on the themes of balanced-budget conservatism. It has issued a report estimating that the current annual costs that undocumented immigration is imposing in just three areas (education, emergency-room medical services, and incarceration) amount to around $36 billion a year.[22]

FAIR's media director, Ira Mehlman, has declared that his organization does not believe in mass deportation: "It's the straw man that proponents of amnesty set out so they can set it on fire." Instead, FAIR's projection, according to Mehlman, is that if current laws protecting the borders and penalizing employers who hire undocumented workers are enforced, many undocumented immigrants will leave the country. "Once we get their numbers down, cut in half say, or three quarters, what you do with those that remain, that's something we can figure out. Three million is obviously better than 12 million."[23]

Negative Effects and Proenforcement Academic Studies

This new interest in the debate by the mainstream media, the blogosphere, and the American political establishment about taxes and undocumented workers has found both echo and support in academia, where discussion rages over the fiscal pros and cons of maintaining a large undocumented population within the U.S. borders. The con group has two basic subcomponents: the Negative Effects camp, which limits itself to studying the negative impact of undocumented immigration on different segments of the economy, and the Proenforcement camp, which is more concerned with proposing enforcement policies and practices to counter the negative fiscal effects.

The Negative Effects camp stands within a long tradition of scholarly research into the economic repercussions of immigration, both documented and undocumented. Some of these studies have argued, as Slobodan Djajic points out,[24] that undocumented foreign workers displace low-skilled natives, depress wages, and neutralize market pressures that otherwise would bring a rising trend in wages.[25] Other studies suggest that the availability of unskilled legal and illegal migrants lowers the pace of structural adjustment and technological progress, reducing the economy's competitiveness in the international market.[26] Still other studies say that when capital is mobile across sectors, illegal immigration draws capital to the underground economy, thereby depriving the rest of the economy of capital and causing it to stagnate.[27]

There is of course a connection between the larger and less politically charged camp of Negative Effects studies, and the smaller but much more vocal Proenforcement camp. Proenforcement studies contain many of the same themes as Negative Effects studies, but with a more pronounced emphasis on the shortfall between the contribution that undocumented workers make to the economy and the benefits they draw from the host country's social programs—and they use this to argue for stronger enforcement measures. These kinds of studies have seen a boom lately, owing to a general interest in the fiscal impact of immigrants in our time of economic insecurity and balanced-budget conservatism.

Whereas all the existing Proenforcement studies have been used to advance a conservative, immigration-control agenda, the same is not true for the Negative Effects literature. However, liberal or bipartisan Negative Effects studies have produced data that have been appropriated by conservative think tanks that support a Proenforcement agenda. One influential example is the 1998 report by Jeffrey Passel and Rebecca Clark on immigrants in New York state.[28] It stands as a milestone because it is one of the first academic efforts to provide estimates on population, incomes, and taxes by legal status. It gives separate estimates for naturalized citizens, legal permanent aliens (green card holders), refugees, legal nonimmigrants (diplomats, foreign students, and international business transfers), and undocumented immigrants.

The study shows that undocumented immigrants pay substantially less in taxes than documented immigrants: $2,400, versus $6,300. Legal immigrants pay on average between 28 and 31 percent of their income in taxes, while undocumented immigrants pay around 15 percent. This is the result of substantially lower annual incomes for undocumented immigrants ($12,100) when compared with legal immigrants, with an average income of $18,700. The authors underline the fact that due to their low income, undocumented workers are placed in lower tax brackets. Further, the authors assume that this group has lower compliance rates than other New York residents.

Passel and Clark make it clear, however, that the tax payments made by undocumented immigrants were by no means insubstantial: they brought in more than $1 billion a year in the late 1990s. That figure looms all the larger when it is juxtaposed with another fact provided by the study, which is that New York's undocumented immigrant population constitutes a smaller share of the state's total immigrant population (16 percent) than in any other state except New Jersey. The study also notes that the 1996 welfare reform laws (PRWORA) did reduce the use of welfare by undocumented immigrant households, exactly as intended.

A more recent study, by the Urban Institute, this time focusing on the immigrant population in metropolitan Washington, D.C., was issued in 2005. This study shows that while taxes paid by documented immigrants are on par with those paid by native-born Americans, households containing undocumented immigrants, and those with temporary protected status, paid in 1999–2000 less than 2 percent of that city's taxes even though they made up more than 4 percent of its households.[29]

Nonetheless, neither of the Urban Institute's studies supports a Proenforcement agenda, because neither makes the connection between undocumented workers paying fewer taxes and the idea that undocumented workers, as a whole, impose a net fiscal drain on the U.S. economy. However, it is possible to see how their findings could be incorporated by immigration control advocates into arguments which claim that undocumented workers are "not paying their fair share of taxes."

Probably the most influential studies in the area of the economic, demographic and fiscal effects of immigration during the 1990s were *The New Americans*[30] and *The Immigration Debate*,[31] which were derived from extensive research conducted in 1996 by the National Research Council (NRC). Like the Urban Institute studies, these reports provided data that contributed to the Negative Effects literature, but their mode of explanation and policy suggestions were not derivative of the Proenforcement camp. These studies found that immigrants' education level is a key determinant of their fiscal impact. According to the NRC studies, every immigrant—either documented or undocumented—who arrives with less than a high school education, imposes a net fiscal cost on the United States of $89,000 over a lifetime, whereas the immigrant with a high school education costs $31,000 over a lifetime. The adult immigrant who has more than twelve years of schooling, in contrast, provides the United States with a lifetime gain of $105,000.

The NRC studies reached the conclusion that an immigrant's fiscal balance—taxes paid minus cost of services consumed—hinges primarily on his or her earnings. In California, households headed by Latin American immigrants received in 1996 almost $5,000 more, on average, in federal, state, and local services than they paid in taxes, because they had below-average incomes and thus paid lower taxes—even though they had more children attending public schools than households headed by U.S.-born Californians. California households headed by U.S.-born persons paid, on average, $2,700 more in federal taxes than they received in federal benefits, while immigrants had exactly the opposite fiscal balance.

These studies do not recommend tougher enforcement measures, but they do call for more selective recruitment of immigrant workers, voicing their support for "immigration policies that would select more highly educated immigrants," because these "might serve to alleviate immigrant concentration as well as selective demographic displacement of the native born by immigrants that has been observed over the 1985–1995 period."[32] In other words, the proposals of the NRC studies are more focused on altering the mix of immigrants admitted to the United States and are less concerned with lowering immigration levels—an objective that is more typical of a proenforcement agenda.

Three vital facts must, however, be noted about those NRC studies. First, they did not draw a dividing line, as did the Urban Institute studies, between documented and undocumented immigrants. Second, they were elaborated, in part, to support suits being filed against the federal government by several states, including California, Florida, and Texas, seeking to recoup the cost of providing public services to undocumented migrants. And third, the NRC studies make no room in their calculations for the indirect benefits of immigration, for example that cheap immigrant labor significantly reduces production costs for many important industries. The most notable examples are construction industries in several states, agribusiness in California, and the garment industry in New York City and Los Angeles.

On the other hand, the NRC studies demand our attention if only because they were among the first to reveal an imbalance between the federal, state, and local government taxes paid by immigrants and the expenditures made for their benefit. The taxes paid by immigrants are mostly income taxes withheld by the federal government. These revenues pay for Social Security and health-care benefits. As for the state and local taxes paid by immigrants, these usually are low simply because the workers (especially undocumented ones) have low earnings. Little wonder, then, that many states are trying to set up some sort of revenue-sharing arrangement with the federal government, to help them cope with the negative fiscal impact of their immigrants.[33]

Perhaps the most influential think tank at the center of the proenforcement camp is the Center for Immigration Studies (CIS), with one of the most vocal scholars being its director of research, Steven Camarota. He has authored many articles demonstrating the link between undocumented workers and taxes. His writing also illustrates how the bipartisan discourse on Negative Effects has been translated into proenforcement arguments that are derivative of the balanced-budget conservatism noted earlier. His most recent study, which builds on findings in both the Urban Institute and the NRC studies, is based on data drawn from the Census Bureau's March 2003 current population survey.

This study offered the following five findings. First, households headed by undocumented workers (Camarota uses the term "illegal aliens") imposed more than $26.3 billion in costs on the federal government in 2002 and paid only $16 billion in taxes, creating a net fiscal deficit of almost $10.4 billion, or $2,700 per undocumented household. Second, among the largest costs are Medicaid ($2.5 billion), treatment for the uninsured ($2.2 billion), food-assistance programs such as food stamps, WIC, and free school lunches ($1.9 billion), and federal aid to schools ($1.4 billion). Third, nearly two-thirds of undocumented workers do not possess a high school degree. Thus, the chief reason they create a fiscal deficit is their low education level and resulting low incomes and tax payments. Fourth, although on average undocumented workers impose a drain on federal coffers that is less than half that of other households, their tax payments are only one-fourth that of other households. And fifth and last, many of the costs associated with undocumented workers arise as a result of their American children, who are awarded U.S. citizenship upon their birth here.

Camarota sees three options: (1) to allow undocumented workers to remain in the country but to reduce the costs they impose—something he considers a very difficult task; (2) to grant them legal status, as a way of increasing the taxes they pay; but such a measure, according to Camarota, would increase the estimated annual net fiscal deficit from $2,700 per household to nearly $7,700, to produce a total net cost of $20 billion a year; and (3) to enforce the law and reduce the size of the undocumented population, thereby also bringing down the costs of undocumented immigration. That last option is the one Camarota and his colleagues at CIS see as our best hope of reducing the cost of unauthorized immigration. Camarota believes that significant resources could be devoted to enforcement efforts while still leaving taxpayers with a significant net savings.[34]

In line with the position taken by FAIR, Camarota and his colleagues at CIS do not consider mass deportation a viable option, but consider that if current laws protecting the borders and penalizing employers who hire undocumented workers are enforced, many undocumented immigrants will leave the country. That is, CIS's proenforcement strategy is not mass raids of 12 million people but what they call "mass self-deportations of all undocumented immigrants." They call this strategy "attrition," the act of weakening or exhausting undocumented immigrants' will to stay in the United States by constant harassment and "cutting them off from American jobs and society."[35]

Concluding Remarks

This chapter has examined aspects of the discourse on undocumented workers that use tax burden–based arguments to justify get-tough enforcement measures. As noted earlier, some of these proenforcement arguments are informed by nativist sentiments—grounded in cultural explanations of the "immigrant problem"—which tend to call for the harshest enforcement measures, such as mass deportations and a U.S.–Mexico border wall. However, other proenforcement arguments deploy structural explanations that draw on arguments based in balanced-budget conservatism. As I explained in this review, this latter type of proenforcement argument has been especially effective because it is able to appropriate data from mainstream sources while advancing the arguments of far-right anti-immigration groups.

It is important, however, to underline that other voices are disrupting this field of discourse. Positive pieces about the plight of undocumented workers and their economic contributions appear here and there in the mainstream media and even in the blogosphere.[36] And just as there is an extensive Negative Effects literature, there is also a growing Positive Effects literature, showing that undocumented workers contribute their share and more to the public coffers, and pushing for the legalization of undocumented immigrants by arguing that low-skilled foreign workers are needed and that their presence benefits the economy.[37]

Debate also is growing as to the education level of recent immigrants,[38] as well as about the different costs to city, state, and federal governments for the services utilized by undocumented residents.[39] At least one study argues that if we really wanted to protect our domestic market, we should shift away from immigration quotas and toward tariffs, because the imposition of an optimal tariff assures that each immigrant makes a net positive contribution to the public coffers.[40] In short, there is a competing proimmigrant discourse trying to emerge, but only in a rather defensive form, and as of yet not strongly enough to break up the consolidated power of the prevailing proenforcement one, or to turn around this nation's present anti-immigrant trend.

On the other hand, while there is a rich body of scholarship in such areas as the economic and demographic impacts of immigration, when it comes to fiscal impact, one finds only a handful of empirical studies (both pro- and antienforcement). The problem with most of these studies is twofold. First, it is common for the conceptual foundation to go unstated, making it possible to tilt one's research toward a desired result. And second, due to the complexity of the subject, most studies in this field either provide an incomplete accounting of taxpayer costs and benefits, by ignoring some programs and taxes while making much of others, or fail to acknowledge indirect benefits of immigration, such as the effect of cheap undocumented labor on many industries.

Given that many of the scholars discussed in the present paper are periodically being cited in newspaper pieces, television programs, and even in the blogosphere, it is not surprising to see lacunae in their research contributing to the polarization of public opinion on this issue. My research suggests that much of the blame for the distorted framing of the debate over the connection between taxes, undocumented workers, and proenforcement policies and practices is located right within that research-media/public opinion intersection.

Those in the proenforcement camp, for instance, are sure to see Positive Effects studies as nothing more than a smokescreen, behind which lurks advocacy of open borders and full amnesty. And those on the other end of the spectrum will see the position taken by Dobbs, O'Reilly, Rubenstein, Melhman, and Camarota as merely a stalking horse for their own nativist, proquota, and proattrition agenda. Again, such polarized reactions are to be expected, given that this field is not only logistically difficult, but also one riddled with gaps caused by the scarcity of sound data. Such gaps all but ask this and that analyst or media pundit to fill them in with her or his own hopes or dogmas.

Immigration control advocates have filled this gap by arguing for stronger enforcement measures. Conservative politicians, anti-immigrant icons in the mainstream media, and organizations and think tanks like FAIR and CIS have produced a politically correct discourse on immigration enforcement that emphasizes compliance with current laws, negative fiscal effects, and the implementation of anti-immigrant laws designed to encourage undocumented immigrants to leave the United States of their own accord (the "attrition" model). On the other hand, populist bloggers that cater to right-wing or even white supremacist groups have also connected the debate over taxes and undocumented workers to their own radical stance, but in ways that are deemed to be outside mainstream political discourse.

Both camps appropriate the discourse on balanced-budget conservatism. However, this discourse is put to its best use by Camarota's attrition model, which uses structural arguments to reduce a complex socioeconomic problem to a simple arithmetic equation: more immigrants equals more fiscal damage. Precisely because of its seemingly moderate stance, it is a more effective proenforcement argument than the overtly nativist sort that we find in the blogosphere, because it emerges from between the lines of mostly mainstream media outlets, popular political leaders, and renowned scholars and organizations, thus acquiring an aura of respectability among the general public.

Notes

1. Jeffrey Passel, *The Size and Characteristics of the Unauthorized Migrant Population in the U.S.: Estimates Based on the March 2005 Current Population Survey*, Pew Hispanic Center, March 2006, http://pewhispanic.org/files/reports/61.pdf (accessed November 10, 2007). This report also estimated that as of March 2004, the number of persons living in families in which the head of the household, or the spouse, was an unauthorized immigrant was 13.9 million; 4.7 million of those were children, out of which 3.2 million were U.S. citizens by birth but living in "mixed status" families.

2. Kitty Calavita, "The New Politics of Immigration: 'Balanced-Budget Conservatism' and the Symbolism of Proposition 187," *Social Problems* 43, no. 3 (1996): 283.

3. Sidney Plotkin and William Scheuerman, *Private Interest, Public Spending: Balanced-Budget Conservatism and Fiscal Crisis* (Boston: South End Press, 1994).

4. Calavita, "New Politics of Immigration," 284, 300.

5. Edward Said, *Covering Islam* (New York: Pantheon Books, 1981).

6. Hans Vermeulen, *Culture and Inequality* (Amsterdam: Institute for Migration and Ethnic Studies, 2001).

7. Belinda Reyes, *Dynamics of Immigration: Return to Western Mexico* (San Francisco: Public Policy Institute of California, January 1997).

8. Cordell Whitlock, "Immigration Debate: Illegal Immigrants and Taxes," KDSK NewsChannel 5, http://www.ksdk.com/news/news_article.aspx?storyid=104531 (accessed November 10, 2007).

9. The FreeRepublic, "Myths and Half-Truths About Illegal Immigration," June 20, 2001, http://www.freerepublic.com/forum/a3b30c0535a05.htm (accessed November 10, 2007).

10. Thinkprogress Entry #58, http://www.thinkprogress.org/2006/03/27/buchanan-deport-immigrants/ (accessed November 10, 2007).

11. Rajeev Goyle and David Jaeger, *Deporting the Undocumented: A Cost Assessment* (Washington, D.C.: Center for American Progress, 2005), http://www.americanprogress.org/kf/deporting_the_undocumented.pdf (accessed November 10, 2007).

12. Edwin Rubenstein, "National Data: No-one's Suggesting Mass Deportation, but It Would Pay for Itself," V.DARE.com, January 26, 2006, http://www.vdare.com/rubenstein/060126_nd.htm (accessed November 10, 2007).

13. Philip Martin, "Immigration Shaping and Reshaping America," June 2003, http://www.npc.umich.edu/news/events/PRB-Monograph-Final.pdf (accessed November 10, 2007). In his study, Martin mentions a book by Julian Simon in which he states that in 1953, for the only time in the past seventy years, more than 10 percent of the public favored increasing immigration (Julian Simon, *The Economic Consequences of Immigration* [New York: Blackwell, 1989]).

14. World Views 2002, "The Global Economy: Immigration," chap. 5 in *American Public Opinion and Foreign Policy* (Chicago: Chicago Council on Global Affairs and German Marshall Fund of the United States, October 2002), http://www.worldviews.org/detailreports/usreport/html/ch5s5.html (accessed November 10, 2007).

15. This poll of 800 adults, conducted July 31–August 17, 1997, for the PBS program *State of the Union* was reported in Susan Page, "Fear of Immigration Eases," *USA Today*, October 13, 1997.

16. Reyes, *Dynamics of Immigration: Return to Western Mexico*.

17. Philip Martin, "Immigration Shaping and Reshaping America," June 2003, 13, http://www.npc.umich.edu/news/events/PRB-Monograph-Final.pdf. Martin underlines, drawing on an article in the *Los Angeles Times*, that "the most significant development in the national immigration debate is what hasn't happened: No lawmaker of influence has moved to reverse the country's generous immigration policy, which for more than three decades has facilitated the largest sustained wave of immigration in U.S. history." (Patrick J. McDonnell, "Wave of U.S. Immigration Likely to Survive Sept. 11," *Los Angeles Times*, January 10, 2002).

18. Passel, *Size and Characteristics of the Unauthorized Migrant Population in the U.S.*

19. For a thorough overview of recent data, see Francine Lippman, "Taxing Undocumented Immigrants: Separate, Unequal and Without Representation," *Harvard Latino Law Review* 9 (2006): 1–58.

20. Referring to the Personal Responsibility and Work Opportunity Reconciliation Act of 1996, Pub.L 104-193, 110 *Stat.* 2105 (Aug. 22, 1996).

21. The Immigration Reform and Control Act of 1986 set penalties for employers who knowingly hire undocumented workers at the same time that it legalized 2.7 million unauthorized immigrants. In 1996 Congress approved three major

immigration-related laws: (1) The Anti-Terrorism and Effective Death Penalty Act, which morphed into the PATRIOT Act after 9/11; (2) The Personal Responsibility and Work Opportunity Reconciliation Act, which made most legal immigrants who entered the United States after August 22, 1996, ineligible for federal means-tested welfare benefits; and (3) the Illegal Immigration Reform and Immigrant Responsibility Act, which, in order to reduce undocumented immigration included such measures as adding 1,000 more Border Patrol agents each year for five years (boosting the total from 5,175 in 1996 to almost 10,000 by 2000), setting up a pilot telephone-verification program to enable employers to verify the status of newly hired workers, and demanding that social-service agencies ascertain the legal status of applicants before granting benefits.

22. FAIR, "The Costs to Local Taxpayers for Illegal or 'Guest' Workers," January 2007, http://www.fairus.org/site/PageServer?pagename=research_localcosts (accessed November 10, 2007).

23. KFWB News 980, "Cost of Removing 12 Million Illegal Immigrants Would Be Immense," April 7, 2006, http://www.kfwb.com/pages/23066.php? (accessed November 10, 2007).

24. Slobodan Djajic, "Illegal Immigration and Resource Allocation," *International Economic Review* 38, no. 1 (1997): 97–117, esp. pp. 98–99.

25. Michael Greenwood and John McDowell, "The Factor Market Consequences of U.S. Immigration." *Journal of Economic Literature* 24 (1986): 1738–1772.

26. Lawrence Harrison, "Those Huddled, Unskilled Masses: Is Our Immigration Policy Contributing to Our Economic Undoing?" *Washington Post*, January 12, 1992, 22.

27. Andrea Ichino, *The Economic Impact of Immigration on the Host Country* (Bocconi University, 1992).

28. Jeffrey Passel and Rebecca Clark, *Immigrants in New York: Their Legal Status, Incomes, and Taxes* (Washington, D.C.: Urban Institute, 1998).

29. Randy Capps, Errol Henderson, Jeffrey Passel, and Michael Fix, *Civic Contributions: Taxes Paid by Immigrants in the Washington Metropolitan Area* (Washington, D.C.: Urban Institute, 2005).

30. James Smith and Barry Edmonston, eds., *The New Americans: Economic Demographic and Fiscal Effects of Immigration* (Washington, D.C.: National Research Council/National Academy Press, 1997).

31. Ibid.

32. National Research Council, *The Immigration Debate: Studies on the Economic, Demographic, and Fiscal Effects of Immigration* (Washington, D.C.: National Academy of Sciences, 1998), 425.

33. Steven Camarota, *The High Cost of Cheap Labor: Illegal Immigration and the Federal Budget* (Washington, D.C.: Center for Immigration Studies, 2004).

34. Francine Lipman. "Taxing Undocumented Immigrants: Separate, Unequal and Without Representation," *Harvard Latino Review* 9 (2006).

35. See the analysis in http://www.bluelatinos.org/node/372 (accessed November 10, 2007). This blog piece is based on a July 19, 2006, article by Julia Preston in the *New York Times* about the conservative enforcement proposals (including Camarota's) in Congress.

36. For example, in a 2005 story focusing on the funds undocumented workers bring into the U.S. Social Security Administration, Eduardo Porter of the *New York Times* said that they thereby contribute "more than most Americans to the solvency of the nation's public retirement system" (Eduardo Porter, "Illegal Immigrants Are Bolstering Social Security with Billions," *New York Times*, April 5, 2005). Then, too, the *Wall Street Journal* for many years has advocated high levels of immigration and open borders, and for a simple economic reason: because more people means more consumers and more workers, those being the twin engines of economic growth. The first *Wall Street Journal* editorial that made this proposal appeared in the July 3, 1986, issue. This proposal was repeated in another editorial on July 3, 1990. After that, the *Wall Street Journal* advocated open borders in several articles and editorials, especially after the NAFTA debate took center stage in its pages during the early 1990s. A number of blogs, such as bluelatinos.org (http://www.bluelatinos.org/node/372, accessed November 10, 2007), take a more positive stance vis-à-vis undocumented immigrants.

37. Julian Simon has written extensively about immigrants' contribution to the fiscal well-being of the United States. Julian Simon, "Immigrants, Taxes and Welfare in the United States," *Population and Development Review* 10, no. 1 (1984): 55–69; Julian Simon, *The Economic Consequences of Immigration* (New York: Blackwell, 1989); Julian Simon, "Public Expenditures and Immigrants to the United States, Past and Present," *Population and Development Review* 22, no. 1 (1996): 99–109. Other Urban Institute studies paint a more positive picture of undocumented immigrants, stating that they pay the same real estate taxes and the same sales and other consumption taxes as everyone else. See Randy Capps and Michael Fix, *Undocumented Immigrants: Myths and Realities* (Washington, D.C.: Urban Institute, 2005); Randy Capps, Michael Fix, Jeffrey Passel, *A Profile of the Low-Wage Immigrant Force* (Washington, D.C.: Urban Institute, 2003); Jeffrey Passel, Randy Capps, and Michael Fix, *Undocumented Immigrants: Facts and Figures* (Washington, D.C.: Urban Institute, 2004). (All available at http://www.urban.org.) In a seminal 1950s study, Bernard showed that foreign workers, in the role of consumers, contribute to an expansion of the market, stimulate investment spending, and further the process of employment creation (William Bernard, "Economic Effects of Immigration," in *Immigration: An American Dilemma*, ed. Benjamin Ziegler [Boston: D.C. Heath, 1953], 50–70). Abrams argues that in the United States, inflows of illegal foreign workers often meet labor shortages that even the Labor Department considers genuine (Elliott Abrams, "Immigration Policy: Who Gets In and Why?" *The Public Interest* 38 [1975]: 3–29). Piore considers that if the domestic labor market is sufficiently segmented, native workers are largely insulated from

the direct employment effects of illegal immigration (Michael Piore, *Birds of Passage: Migrant Labor and Industrial Societies* [Cambridge: Cambridge University Press, 1979]). According to Djajic, for some sectors of the economy—agriculture in the southern regions of California and Texas or the garment industry in large cities such as New York and Los Angeles—the availability of cheap, clandestine foreign labor is essential to the survival of a large number of enterprises. This means that goods and services produced by the migrants are likely to cost less, benefiting the nation's consumers (Slobodan Djajic, "Illegal Immigration and Resource Allocation," *International Economic Review* 38, 1 [1997]: 97–117). George Borjas considers that modern econometrics cannot detect a single shred of evidence that immigrants have a sizable adverse impact on the earnings and employment opportunities of natives of the United States (George Borjas, *Friends of Strangers: The Impact of Immigrants on the US Economy* [New York: Basic Books, 1990]). David Card's econometric study concluded that the 1980 influx of Cuban immigrants to Miami in the Mariel boatlift had no measurable negative effect on local wages and employment (David Card, "The Impact of the Mariel Boatlift on the Miami Labor Market," *Industrial and Labor Relations Review* 43 [1990]: 245–257).

38. Enrico Marcelli and Wayne Cornelius, "The Changing Profile of Mexican Immigrants to the United States," *Latin American Research Review* 36, no. 3 (2001): 105–131. In their study, Marcelli and Cornelius show that the more recent cohorts of immigrants from Mexico are more likely to settle permanently in the United States, to be younger, to have a greater proportion of females, and to have higher levels of education. In the area of education it is important to note that the proenforcement camp places education at the center of this debate, pointing to a connection between level of education and earnings, and thereby tax contributions. And yet most experts agree that the net fiscal cost, or benefit, of immigration depends on the extent to which the existing fiscal imbalance will be borne by future generations. But given that most of the studies reviewed in this paper offer their readers little more than snapshots of taxes paid and costs of services provided at particular points in time, the static and stereotypical image now held by most of the population of an undocumented immigrant who is inevitably uneducated as well, will persist.

39. Sydney Weintraub, "Illegal Immigrants in Texas: Impact on Social Services and Related Considerations," *International Migration Review* 18, no. 3 (Autumn 1984): 733–747. One argument in Weintraub's study of the state of Texas in *Plyler v. Doe* was that since the federal government is responsible for immigration legislation and control, it and not the state should be responsible for meeting the cost to educate undocumented children. The Supreme Court, although ruling against Texas on the main issue of the obligation of the state to provide this education, did indicate its agreement that the federal government had a financial obligation to compensate Texas. These imbalances could be corrected by the federal govern-

ment's providing financial aid to those schools and health providers in recognition of the "profit" that the federal government earns from illegal immigrants' exclusion from receiving federal benefits. The National Research Council reports and Weintraub's study suggest that the costs imposed by undocumented immigration fall with disproportionate severity upon local governmental structures. We know that on the macro level, many federal fiscal institutions are enriched by undocumented immigration because most immigrants pay Social Security taxes while remaining ineligible for Social Security or Medicare benefits, and that consumers as a whole benefit from the lower labor costs made possible, in part, by the vast labor pool of undocumented immigrants. But because it is unconstitutional to deny emergency medical care and free public schooling to the children of undocumented immigrants, local school systems, hospitals, and other local-government service providers incur additional costs as a result of undocumented immigration that they do not recover in taxes. Thus, it is only when we in the academic community have begun to zero in more closely on that important macro/micro discrepancy that we will then also be able to make some sense of the other potent dichotomies related to this issue: the social costs versus benefits of undocumented work, and the pro and con reactions to enforcement policies and practices that crop up in different parts of this nation.

40. Lipman, "Taxing Undocumented Immigrants." Lipman asserts that most unauthorized workers pay a higher effective tax rate than similarly situated documented immigrants or U.S. citizens. According to Lipman, if the government were simply to remove the quotas, undocumented immigrants and their employees could move out of the black market and the public coffers would benefit via reduced expenditures and increased revenues.

CHAPTER 15

What Does an Undocumented Immigrant Look Like?

Local Enforcement and the New Immigrant Profiling

PHILIP KRETSEDEMAS

In January 2002 two men walking down the street in western Maine were stopped and asked for identification. They were both Hondurans and had Temporary Protected Status, although one was carrying what looked like an expired Employment Authorization Document because the immigration service had not processed his renewal yet. The police officer took the men to the local immigration office and dropped them off. Immigration agents held the men for three days before releasing them.[1]

In what experts said was a first for the Chicago area, two Carpentersville trustees have proposed that the village punish landlords and businesses that "aid and abet" illegal immigrants. . . . "If I sit back and continue to ignore this issue [and] it hits us in the face and the pocketbook, costing millions and millions of dollars, then I don't deserve to sit in this seat," said [one of the trustees] at a special meeting of Carpentersville's Audit and Finance Commission.[2]

Alongside the national debate over immigration reform has emerged a relatively new debate over the role that local governments should play in enforcing federal immigration laws. A staple feature of all these local-enforcement proposals are screening practices that allow law enforcement officers, other government workers, and some private citizens to identify and detain undocumented migrants.

Local enforcement is undeniably controversial[3] but it is also, in some respects, peripheral to the trends that are defining immigration enforcement at the national level. Some variant of local enforcement has been adopted by police departments in every state, but federal enforcement agencies are still responsible for the vast majority of deportations.[4] Local enforcement has also proved to be a nonstarter at the level of federal policy. Although local-enforcement legislation has been approved by the House of Representatives, it has yet to be endorsed by the Senate.[5]

These developments have done little, however, to dampen enthusiasm for local enforcement among state and municipal lawmakers. In the space of less than six months, in 2006 alone, over one hundred municipal governments drafted laws that targeted undocumented immigrants.[6] There is also a growing movement toward enacting similar laws at the level of state government.[7] Along with authorizing local police to partner with federal immigration agents,[8] many of these laws levy fines against landlords and business owners for contracting services with undocumented persons. Some also require service providers to check the legal status of their clients.[9]

All these laws and proposals rely on a commonsense appeal, as I explain in this chapter, what is most compelling about local-enforcement proposals is the information it distorts and conceals. Most local-enforcement proposals have been couched in a discourse of economic nationalism, suggesting that aggressive enforcement is used to reduce the fiscal burden of unauthorized migrants for taxpayers and local governments. However, there are also elements within the anti-immigrant movement that are not simply concerned about illegal immigration, but about the long-term impact of legal immigration on the "traditional" culture of the United States.[10] These sorts of concerns have surfaced in municipalities that have enacted English-only ordinances alongside their illegal immigrant laws.[11] In this case, it is clear that the goal of the immigration control movement is not simply to capture "illegals" but to impose an enforceable standard of cultural assimilation for all U.S. residents, regardless of legal status. Recent developments within the Department of Justice (DOJ) and Department of Homeland Security (DHS) have also made it possible for local-enforcement measures to target noncitizens who entered the United States legally but who have criminal convictions—drawing attention to a connection between local enforcement, immigration enforcement in general, and the expanding prison-industrial complex.[12]

These examples provide a cursory illustration of the issues that are rumbling just below the movement to expand local enforcement. In the remainder of this chapter, I explore the connections between these disparate factors and explain how they have intensified (and normalized) a form of racial-ethnic profiling that is being used to make distinctions between "Americans" and "alien others." On one hand, this requires an understanding of the racialized subtext of the discourse on illegal immigration and immigration enforcement. On the other hand, the expansion of immigrant profiling is also being shaped by tensions that are only incidentally tied to questions of race and racialization. For example, it is possible to see how local enforcement has been used to mollify fiscal tensions between federal and local governments that have been created by the past two decades of neoliberal economic restructuring. It is also important to account for the political struggles over immigration reform that have shaped the form and direction that local enforcement has taken in recent years. In this regard, local enforcement should be viewed not just as an organic expression of the immigration control movement, but as an array of enforcement practices that have been defined by the conflicts—and backroom negotiations—of both pro- and anti-immigrant forces.

In the following discussion I elaborate on this context; first by mapping the political context which has given rise to local enforcement. This is followed by a more detailed discussion of the legal history of local enforcement that explains how the proliferation of these measures at the state and municipal level has been made possible by federal policy developments. In the final section, I explain how these policy statements and legal precedents set the stage for the forms of immigrant profiling that are "required" by local-enforcement practices.

Local Enforcement as a Solution to the So-Called Immigration Problem

It is important to acknowledge the broader context in which local enforcement of immigration has taken shape. It is significant, for example, that local-enforcement measures are being expanded during a time when the social services and public amenities of local governments across the United States are facing mounting demands. One reason for these mounting demands is the growth of the low-income population, which is being fueled, in part, by new immigration flows.[13] However, this resource scarcity has also been affected by over a decade of reforms that have reduced federal funding for a range of state and municipal services.[14] Meanwhile, the growth of the low-income population is not simply a product of immigration, but of three decades of neoliberal economic restructuring that has dismantled the safety nets of the Keynesian welfare state, increased the gap between the rich and the poor, and produced a labor market that is composed of a much larger share of lower-paying, impermanent positions.[15] This transformation—which explains why many native-born persons cannot afford to buy homes in the same neighborhoods in which they were raised[16] and why they need much higher levels of education to compete for jobs that barely allow them to maintain a middle-class lifestyle—is not a direct outcome of the economic aftershocks of immigration. Instead, the post–cold war surge in U.S. immigration is better understood as a parallel development, facilitated by the same policies that were used throughout the 1980s to deregulate and restructure the U.S. economy.

There is a great deal of debate over the extent to which new immigrants take jobs from native born persons.[17] However, the only area where there is a general consensus on the displacement argument involves labor positions that are usually filled by low-skilled individuals who have no more than a high school education. Further, the persons most at risk of displacement are younger racial minorities whose limited job options have been conditioned by forms of institutional discrimination that are "indigenous" to U.S. labor markets.[18] It should also be noted that these trends are occurring during a period of time when national unemployment rates are at a five-year low.[19] In this regard, the primary problem facing many native-born workers is not the absence of jobs, but a dearth of quality jobs; ones that are permanent and that offer middle-class wages and benefits.

In a similar vein, the fiscal hardships that are being experienced by municipal governments are not simply a product of increased immigrant flows. Immigration tends to place more strain on local governments than it does on federal agencies and the business sector, because federal policies have been structured in such a way that the costs of immigration are unequally distributed among these sectors (with local governments bearing a greater part of the fiscal burden). However, it is possible to see why immigration has become a convenient target for municipal governments and segments of the U.S. middle class, which have become frustrated with the resource scarcity produced by the past several decades of economic restructuring. The anti-immigrant agenda reduces the complexities of regulating labor markets and crafting and implementing socioeconomic policy to a very simple solution: reduce the number of foreigners among us. This approach also allows for a very straightforward us/them dichotomy that places the blame for the economic woes of the U.S. middle class on individuals who are perceived as being foreign to American national culture.

These sentiments helped to pave the way for policy solutions—such as local enforcement—that use immigration enforcement as a strategy for reducing the fiscal burden of unauthorized migration on middle-class taxpayers.[20] However, this effort to correct the unequal distribution of the economic costs of immigration by policing immigrant bodies is also, in large part, an exercise in futility. Precisely because local enforcement *is* local, it does not guarantee any consistency in the way that it is implemented from place to place. Although a growing number of municipalities are considering these laws, a much larger number are not, and some municipal governments have signed resolutions that explicitly reject the practice of local enforcement.[21] This indicates that it is highly unlikely that local enforcement will be effective as a strategy for reducing the national population of undocumented immigrants.

Instead, it sets the stage for the uneven enforcement of immigration laws in particular localities—and within particular zones in these localities. For example, local enforcement practices cannot guarantee that every "illegal" in a given township will be identified and deported, but they can ensure that unauthorized migrants who attempt to access government services or to rent housing in certain parts of town will be screened for legal status. These practices will probably result in more deportations of unauthorized migrants. However, it is also likely that these measures will simply force undocumented persons to relocate to other communities where local-enforcement measures are not being deployed or not being deployed as extensively.

Local-enforcement measures are also likely to have a chilling effect on the legal immigrant population. Many local-enforcement measures allow government workers the discretion to selectively screen individuals who they believe are likely to be undocumented. Thus, any person, regardless of their legal status, who exhibits "suspicious behavior" and emits signs of "foreign culture" could be targeted if he or she enters a zone where these enforcement practices are in effect.

Moreover, restrictions on immigrants' rights affect not only the individual immigrants but their households and family networks.[22] The primary reason for this domino effect is that most immigrants live in mixed-status families composed of U.S. citizens, legal permanent residents, persons with temporary legal status, and/or undocumented persons.[23] The legal-status concerns of one member of the household often have an impact on the other members. A typical example is the U.S. citizen children of undocumented parents who are not enrolled in health-care plans because their parents are afraid that they will be deported if they attempt to access these services for their children.[24]

In the years immediately following passage of the Personal Responsibility Work Opportunity Reconciliation Act of 1996, community-based agencies worked in partnership with federally funded health-service providers to convince immigrant communities that these were "unreasonable fears."[25] In the climate created by local enforcement, however, these are very reasonable fears. Outreach efforts that were conducted in the late 1990s emphasized that the frontline staff of health and welfare programs were not authorized to share information about legal status with immigration authorities, but local-enforcement measures being incorporated into state and municipal legislation are directed precisely toward increasing this sort of information sharing between government agencies. Under these laws, immigrant parents who apply for health care for their children through a provider that receives government funds are likely to be screened for legal status. If they are undocumented, this information will most certainly be passed on to the local police or immigration authorities.

Local-enforcement practices that ban undocumented persons from renting in certain parts of town are also likely to intensify the residential segregation of the mixed-status households that include these persons. It is possible that these practices will reinforce forms of spatial segregation that correspond with the ambiguous dividing line that separates the formal and the informal economy, with low-income immigrants (both legal and undocumented) being overconcentrated in the latter.

These observations are premised on the understanding that policies can produce outcomes that extend far beyond their formal objectives. Local-enforcement practices are especially vulnerable to these blind spots because of the wide-ranging and often unrealistic objectives that they are being used to achieve. In addition to the fiscal burdens of local governments, these measures have been touted as a solution to the employment woes of native-born persons, fears of immigrant crime, and general concerns about quality-of-life issues (such as overcrowded housing, loitering, and drunk-driving fatalities) that are associated with unauthorized migration. Regardless of the validity of these claims, it is significant that a growing number of local governments—and their constituents—feel that unauthorized migrants are the cause of so many social problems. This perception, combined with mounting pressure to do something about these issues, is precisely the context in which immigrant profiling can become a normal feature of the bureaucratic practice of government workers.

I explore this further in the next two sections, beginning with a discussion of the legal history of local enforcement, and followed by a discussion of immigrant profiling. I should emphasize that the purpose of this discussion is not to highlight the most egregious cases of immigrant profiling that have occurred in recent years, but to describe practices that have become fairly routine, including those that have received some validation from the federal courts.

Local Enforcement and the National Policy Context

It would appear self-evident that local-enforcement measures are being driven by a political process that is occurring at the local level. However, the local spread of these measures is a fairly recent development within a policy debate that for the past several years was confined largely to the federal level. Most important, state and municipal governments would have no authority to take action on undocumented migration if it were not for policy statements issued by the federal government. One of the most important features of these federal developments is the expanded discretion they give local law enforcement officers to apprehend persons who are suspected of being illegal migrants. The language of these developments makes no reference to race or ethnicity, but the expanded discretion they provide opens the door for a variety of screening practices that can incorporate racial-ethnic profiles.

It is only within the last ten years that the federal government has begun to affirm the inherent authority of local governments to participate in the enforcement of federal immigration laws. The 1952 Immigration and Nationality Act was the first piece of legislation that provided guidelines for the role of local police in enforcing federal immigration laws. However, the language in the act did not specifically discuss the role of local police, and it explicitly described immigration enforcement as the province of federal immigration agents.[26] For the following three decades, this was interpreted as meaning that local police were not responsible for enforcing immigration laws, but with the tacit understanding that the local enforcement of such laws was viable if directly pertinent to an ongoing criminal investigation. The 1983 *Gonzales v. City of Peoria* decision has been widely credited with establishing the legal precedent for this interpretation, which allows local police limited authority to enforce criminal immigration laws.[27] Although arguably setting a precedent for the expansion of local enforcement, this decision also reinforced the understanding that enforcement of civil immigration violations (which includes screening people for legal status) was beyond the authority of local police if it was not pertinent to an ongoing criminal investigation.

In recent years, however, federal policymakers have begun to depart significantly from this interpretation of the law. These changes were presaged by the 1996 Immigration Reform (IIRAIRA) and Anti-Terrorism (AEDPA) Acts, which included some provisions under which local police could enforce civil immigration laws.[28] None of these provisions, however, granted local police continuous authority to enforce civil immigration laws and, in most cases, this authority was still closely tied to criminal law enforcement. During this period of time, the legal opinions of the Department of Justice continued to affirm the precedent stemming from *Gonzales v. City of Peoria.*

In 2002 the Office of Legal Counsel within the Department of Justice made an about-face on this matter. It published an opinion which stated that local police have the inherent authority to enforce civil and criminal immigration laws. It is also significant that this opinion was not made public until 2004, when the Department of Justice was forced to disclose it as the result of a lawsuit filed under the Freedom of Information Act. This was accompanied by a number of complementary developments. As of 2001, the Department of Justice had already authorized the practice of placing immigrants with outstanding deportation orders into the National Crime Information Center (NCIC) database.[29] This practice was expanded by subsequent decisions to include noncitizens in the NCIC who were suspected of being national security risks but who did not necessarily have a criminal violation, as well as noncitizens who had violated the terms of their student visas. A March 2003 decision by the Department of Justice relaxed criteria for the accuracy of information entered into the NCIC and exempted this information from the standards of the Privacy Act.[30] In 2002 White House counsel also produced a written statement which confirmed that local police have inherent authority to arrest all persons whose names are placed in the NCIC database.[31]

The cumulative effect of these decisions has been the creation of a national database that includes both civil immigration violators and criminal violators. It also includes a large number of cases that straddle these two categories—namely, individuals with outstanding orders of deportation because of prior criminal convictions. It bears emphasizing that these are persons who have become "deportable" because they have been incarcerated—not because they have entered the United States illegally.

During this same period of time, there was a sustained effort to pass local-enforcement legislation at the federal level. For example, the Clear Law Enforcement for Criminal Alien Removal Act (CLEAR) and the Homeland Security and Enforcement Act (HSEA) were both local enforcement bills which were introduced to Congress in 2003 and defeated the following year.[32] Both bills were oriented toward crime control of some sort but relied on an expanded definition that included antiterrorism measures, immigration enforcement, and conventional crime control. They also required local police departments across the United States to enforce civil and criminal immigration laws and threatened to sanction local police departments that refused to comply.

The policy debate over CLEAR and HSEA revealed the vulnerability of local-enforcement proposals that call for the mandatory involvement of local police. Many local police departments saw these proposals as jeopardizing their community policing programs and unfairly increasingly their workload without a corresponding increase in federal funding.[33] Libertarians and conservative think tanks worried about the creation of a national police force and the corresponding dangers this would pose to states' rights and the civil liberties of all U.S. residents.[34] Immigrants' rights activists were concerned about the obvious dangers this legislation posed to the civil, legal, and human rights of noncitizens.[35] Because of its diverse, bipartisan composition, this coalition was able to capture the "reasonable center" of the debate around local enforcement.

These unlikely alliances occurred in the context of a widening rift between proimmigration Republicans and anti-immigration Republicans who were largely concentrated in the House of Representatives. While the anti-immigrant right were praising the actions of the Minutemen, the Bush administration was characterizing these same groups as vigilantes;[36] and while the anti-immigrant right saw get-tough enforcement practices as a step toward the goal of restricting immigration, proimmigration Republicans saw these enforcement measures as acceptable only insofar as they supported a free-trade agenda that relied on a continuous stream of immigrant labor.[37]

The unauthorized migrant is, ironically, a direct product of the unfettered economic forces that are idealized by this free trade agenda—where the flow of labor is determined entirely by market demands, without respect to the "artificial" controls imposed by immigration quotas or, for that matter, minimum-wage laws. It is also telling that these free trade policies (the North American Free Trade Agreement [NAFTA] being the primary case in point) have reinforced precisely the sort of push-pull dynamics that encourage unauthorized migration. As recent studies have shown, Mexican wages have fallen steadily since the enactment of NAFTA, at the same time that U.S. wage levels, relative to Mexican wages, have steadily increased.[38] It should also not be surprising that, during this same period, the size of the U.S. unauthorized migrant population has more than doubled.[39]

These issues are rarely addressed by proimmigration forces in Congress, but they do appear—albeit in very different form—in the discourse of the anti-immigrant right, which has been fairly successful in linking its agenda to concerns about immigration that are shared by a broad cross section of the U.S. population. As some researchers have noted, the U.S. public has tended to be more supportive of restricting immigration than the public- and private-sector elites who have crafted U.S. immigration policy since the mid-twentieth century.[40] This fluctuating support for immigration restrictions does not necessarily translate into support for restrictions on immigrants' rights or get-tough enforcement practices.[41] However, conservative populists have mobilized a relatively small but influential constituency which believes that restrictions on immigration flows, restrictions on immigrants' rights, and tougher immigration enforcement all go hand in hand.[42] The popular slogans of this movement have positioned the immigrant—and especially the undocumented migrant—as the symbol of everything that is wrong with free trade and globalization. As a consequence, the goal of restricting immigration has become equated with the idea of defending an embattled American middle class. This economic nationalism also tends to rely on a racialized interpretation of territory and culture, where the goal of "taking back America" is accomplished by the removal of unassimilated alien bodies.[43] This movement is also taking shape alongside the expansion of immigration enforcement and a rise in immigrant incarceration. As a result, there is growing pressure for immigrants to assimilate but, for many, this is a very coercive and unegalitarian process that bears a much closer resemblance to Portes and Zhou's segmented assimilation than the integrationist ideals of the Great Society or even, for that matter, the nineteenth-century melting pot.[44]

Not surprisingly, these get-tough sentiments influenced the stance on immigration taken by the Republican-dominated 109th Congress, which convened in 2005 and 2006. They are reflected in calls for a new Operation Wetback, an initiative that the federal government used to deport over

800,000 Mexican nationals in the early 1950s.[45] They are also reflected in the staunch resistance of House Republicans (and the reticence, more recently, of the Democrat majority) to endorse any version of a guest worker program that would offer temporary legal status to unauthorized migrants.[46] The House Republicans who are most sympathetic to the anti-immigrant movement have issued proposals that call for significant expansions in border control (including the deployment of military troops) and local enforcement as a precondition for accepting a new guest worker program.[47]

In contrast, the original guest worker proposal issued by the White House contained no additional immigration enforcement provisions.[48] Since this time, President George W. Bush has made statements indicating that he is willing to include more enforcement measures in the White House proposals—including expanded local-enforcement provisions—as a precondition for passing a new guest worker program.[49] It is significant that this openness to local enforcement in the Executive Office occurred only after the White House encountered sustained resistance to any form of a guest worker program in the House of Representatives. Other guest worker proposals that have staked out a middle ground on this issue have also incorporated measures that require some expansion in the screening of legal status. Some examples include the Secure America and Orderly Immigration Act (introduced by Senators Kennedy and McCain), the Comprehensive Enforcement and Immigration Reform Act (introduced by Senators Cornyn and Kyle), and the STRIVE Act (introduced by Representatives Gutierrez and Flake).[50] Although differing in their degree of support for new enforcement measures, these bills all include additional increases in border control and some form of mandatory workplace inspection requiring employers to check the legal status of their workers.

Similar enforcement provisions were included within the immigration bill that was approved by the Senate in Spring 2006 but that was prevented from being passed into law because of opposition in the House.[51] There was some expectation that the results of the fall 2006 midterm elections, which resulted in a new Democratic majority in the House, might give new life to this bill, but its most recent incarnation (in the form of the Senate Comprehensive Immigration Reform Bill) also fell through in June 2007.[52] Despite its failure, the debate over the 2007 Senate bill demonstrated that, if adopted, any version of a guest worker program will be accompanied by an intensification of immigration enforcement. So whether or not tougher enforcement is viewed by moderates as something that is logistically necessary for the implementation of a guest worker program, it is undoubtedly viewed as something that is politically necessary for securing popular support for the program.

This situation provides some insight into the middle ground that has begun to emerge around the question of local enforcement. On one hand, supporters of proimmigration policies in Congress, the federal courts, and the Executive Office have resisted the implementation of local enforcement as a matter of federal mandate.[53] On the other hand, there has been a tacit acceptance that a guest worker program will require new strategies for verifying the legal status of temporary workers which, at the very least, would require the cooperation of local employers. Furthermore, the changing opinions of the Department of Justice have sent a clear signal to local governments that they have the authority and the means (via the expanded NCIC database) to begin experimenting with local-enforcement practices.

These developments indicate that the failure to pass local enforcement legislation at the federal level has not stopped the spread of local enforcement laws; it has only shifted the policymaking process downward to state and municipal governments. The recent expansion of state and municipal laws that contain local-enforcement measures are the most apparent evidence of this "local turn" in the struggle over local enforcement. Some municipal ordinances have been successfully challenged by groups that have appealed them to the federal courts.[54] Even so, the publicity surrounding these ordinances has been sufficient to drive large sections of the Hispanic community out of some townships, regardless of whether the laws were formally enacted.[55] This reaction is reminiscent of the immigrant response to the welfare restrictions included in the Personal Responsibility Work Opportunity Reconciliation Act of 1996. The publicity surrounding these restrictions drove over half of the immigrant caseload from the welfare rolls, leading to significant levels of underenrollment for eligible persons in many low-income, immigrant communities.[56]

These sorts of anxieties are typical of the climate created by legislation that singles out immigrants. Regardless of their official intent, many immigrants tend to read these laws through the nativist undertones that resonate through national and local debates over immigration reform. This is why the impact of local enforcement is likely to extend far beyond the confines of the unauthorized migrant population, leading legal immigrants to also alter their behavior in anticipation of the racial-ethnic profiles that, they believe, will be used to determine who will be screened as a suspected "illegal," who is most deserving of access to state services, or who is preferred as a renter or homeowner in certain residential areas.

Local Enforcement and Immigrant Profiling

In the previous section, I noted that immigration enforcement has become an important bargaining chip for proimmigration conservatives and moderates who are looking to sweeten their guest worker proposals for members of Congress who favor stronger immigration and border controls.[57] Given this context, it is almost assured that spending on immigration enforcement will be increased as a precondition for implementing a new guest worker program. If this were to occur, it would merely be an extension of already-existing trends.

From the early 1990s to the present, unprecedented spending increases on immigration enforcement have occurred alongside the growth of the noncitizen workforce (including legal immigrants, undocumented persons, and temporary workers), which is now responsible for a major portion of population and workforce replenishment throughout the United States. Nationally, immigration has been responsible for over 40 percent of population growth from the late 1980s to the present.[58] The absolute number of immigrants entering the United States during this time has been on par with the peak decades of European migration and probably exceeds these levels if one accounts for unauthorized migration.[59] During this same period (between 1985 and 2002), spending on immigration enforcement more than quadrupled, from $1 billion to $4.9 billion.[60]

It also bears noting that even if the unauthorized migrant population were converted into guest workers, these individuals would still be subjected to enforcement practices that were originally put in place to capture "illegals."[61] It has been estimated, for example, that between 25 to 40 percent of the current unauthorized migrant population entered the United States legally with some form of temporary legal status.[62] So, although a new guest worker program could be effective in reducing unauthorized border crossing, it would also shift the emphasis of immigration enforcement toward the surveillance of temporary workers and the deportation of noncitizens who overstay their visas. It is possible to see how local-enforcement measures could support federal enforcement efforts, by creating an intricate web of screening practices at the local level, designed to capture individuals with expired work visas. This solution might satisfy some proimmigration policymakers, but the climate created by these practices would be hardly different from the climate that is being created by the illegal-immigrant laws that are currently being enacted throughout the United States.

These examples illustrate how increases in the noncitizen work force—which take place in a climate of aggressive enforcement—can create new demands to find more effective ways, including immigrant profiling, of filtering undocumented persons out of the legal resident population. Local-enforcement measures in particular are geared toward identifying undocumented persons after they have entered the nation, or after their temporary status has expired. Because it is not possible, legally or logistically, to screen every resident in a township, it becomes necessary to develop targeted screening practices. These screening practices rely on the discretion of frontline workers, who may ask to see a person's legal papers based on whether the suspect fits a behavioral, physical, or cultural profile of someone who is likely to be undocumented.

For example, it is not very difficult for local police—who are "looking for illegals"—to target areas where they expect to find undocumented persons. In this context, "foreign appearance" can easily be used as a pretext for screening some individuals more closely than others. One monitoring study by a legal services organization noted that "Fairfax County police often harass immigrant day laborers and their contracting employers at a site in Annandale, Virginia. Certain officers look for any reason to stop and question a worker, as a pretense to ask for documentation and see if it appears fraudulent."[63] A community-based organization in North Florida noted that "in Jacksonville/Duval County, [police] were parking in front of Latino grocery stores, in front of mobile homes, and at the bus stations to pick up undocumented individuals."[64] News reports have illustrated how violations, such as riding a bicycle on the wrong side of the road, can provide opportunities for local police to question individuals about their legal status.[65]

The most significant case in recent history that addressed the matter of racial-ethnic profiling and local enforcement was *Muehler v. Mena,* which was decided by the Supreme Court in 2004.[66] Iris Mena is a naturalized citizen who was detained and questioned at her place of residence along with several other renters. The police entered her residence because they suspected that two murder suspects might have been renting rooms in the same apartment. The police were accompanied by Immigration and Naturalization Service (INS) officers, because the suspects were believed to belong to a gang that was composed of unauthorized migrants. As it turned out, Iris Mena had no knowledge of the suspects and had no connection to the crime being investigated. Even so, she was detained for two to three hours, and at gunpoint for a period of time. The officers admitted that Mena's ethnic appearance and other circumstantial factors caused them to assume she and the other renters were undocumented. Her legal status was not determined until the very end of the detainment. On reviewing the case, the Supreme Court found that the circumstances of Iris Mena's detainment were within the limits of reasonable search and entry.

Some policy papers have interpreted this as a lukewarm decision for immigrants' rights because it did not attempt to expand existing legal precedent on the role of police in enforcing immigration laws.[67] On the other hand, the Mena decision provides a rather disturbing glimpse into the kinds of enforcement practices that are already authorized under existing law. In this case, the Supreme Court sent the signal that judges should give police the benefit of the doubt when racial-ethnic profiles are used by investigating officers to determine who is, or is not, undocumented. It is also significant that although the federal courts have rejected some forms of local enforcement, none of these objections has specifically challenged the use of racial-ethnic profiles as the basis for identifying a suspected unauthorized migrant.[68]

While these decisions do not explicitly authorize racial-ethnic profiling, they also do not acknowledge the racialized subtext that is woven through the popular discourse on illegal immigration. It appears to be beyond the scope of these court decisions to consider that native-born persons and naturalized citizens who "look like" illegal immigrants might be regularly subjected to invasive searches and other forms of discriminatory treatment on the basis of little more than their ethnic appearance. These court decisions take the racialized construction of the illegal alien (as a brown/Mexican) as a reasonable generalization rather than as the product of a policy history that has been systemically biased against nonwhite, non-European migrant groups.

As Mae Ngai has noted, this racialized subtext was enmeshed in the legal construct of the "illegal alien" from its inception in the 1920s.[69] The illegal alien category was not linked to a particular national-origin group. In this regard, it differed from most of the immigration laws of the Jim Crow era, including the Asian exclusion acts,[70] the national-origins quotas introduced by the Immigration Act of 1924, and the policies that were used to segregate Mexican Americans and Mexican nationals in some southwestern states.[71]

Instead, the illegal alien designation allowed for a relatively loose articulation of race and legal status which presaged the forms of institutional discrimination and coded racial discourse that emerged in the post–civil rights era.[72] For example, all foreign nationals who entered the United States in excess of the newly established quotas could, potentially, be categorized as illegal aliens. In this regard, the designation was race-neutral. However, the quotas that were established for different national-origin groups insured that some groups (namely African and Latin American nationals) would exceed their quotas much faster—and hence become "illegal" much faster—than others. Further, policies that were used to regularize "deserving immigrants" who had entered the United States without authorization were guided by unquestioned assumptions about the desirability of European versus non-European immigrants.[73] In this context, it was not a contradiction that the legalization programs of the 1930s and 1940s provided amnesty to European "illegals" whereas Mexican seasonal laborers (regardless of whether they were defined as "illegals" or temporary workers) were seen as a population that required constant policing.

A similar bias appears to be at work in the street-level implementation of local-enforcement practices. The only national study of local enforcement has shown, for example, that these practices have predominantly focused on Mexican nationals.[74] Mexican persons constitute little more than 7 percent of the total U.S. population and approximately 56 percent of the unauthorized migrant population (see Table 15.1). However, between 2002 and 2004 they composed 71 percent of all individuals who were identified as immigration violators by police departments, nationwide, that were using the NCIC database.

It bears emphasizing that this figure only accounts for individuals who were *successfully* identified as immigration violators. Over 40 percent of the persons who police identified as immigration violators, using the NCIC database between 2002 and 2004, turned out to be false leads.[75] Data was not collected on the national origins of these persons who were falsely identified. However, this high error rate indicates that the total percentage of Mexican persons who were detained for suspected immigration violations was probably higher than 71 percent. In contrast, European and Canadian nationals were only 1 percent of the immigration violators identified by local police, even though they compose 6 percent of the U.S. undocumented population. It is also striking that Asian nationals and Pacific Islanders compose 13 percent of the undocumented population, but are no more than

TABLE 15.1

Local Enforcement Apprehensions of Immigration Violators (by national origin)

	Identified as Immigration Violators by Local Police, 2002–2004 (in percent)[1]	Unlawfully Residing in the U.S., 2000–2006 (in percent)[2]
Mexican	71	56
Latin American (other than Mexican)	14	22
Asian and Pacific Islander	2	13
European and Canadian	1	6
African	1	
Caribbean	7	3[3]
Middle Eastern (and nationals of predominantly Muslim nations)	2	

[1] *Source:* Hannah Gladstein, Annie Lai, Jennifer Wagner, and Michael Wishnie, "Blurring the Lines: A Profile of State and Local Police Enforcement of Immigration Law Using the National Crime Information Center Database, 2002–2004," Migration Policy Institute Occasional Paper (December 2005).

[2] *Source:* Jeffrey Passel, *The Size and Characteristics of the Unauthorized Migrant Population in the U.S.: Estimates Based on the March 2005 Current Population Survey,* Pew Hispanic Center, March 7, 2006, http://pewhispanic.org/files/reports/61.pdf.

[3] In the report from which this figure was taken (Passel, *Population in the U.S.*), this category was originally designated "African and Other Migrant Groups." For the purposes of this table, this figure of 3 percent should be read as including African undocumented migrants, Caribbean undocumented migrants, Middle Eastern undocumented migrants, and all other nationalities not included in the national-origins categories listed in the far left-hand column.

2 percent of the immigration violators identified by local police. Indeed—with the exception of Caribbean migrants[76]—the rate of apprehension for all other national-origin groups was lower than their presence in the undocumented population.

These disproportionate apprehension rates for Mexican and Caribbean nationals bring to mind the forms of selective enforcement that have been documented by critical studies of the incarceration of African American youth.[77]

It is also important to consider the selectivity of the data included in the National Crime Information Center (NCIC) database. Approximately 90 percent of the persons identified as immigration violators through the database, between 2002 and 2004, were persons with outstanding orders of deportation due to prior felonies for which they had already served time.[78] Although the contents of the NCIC database are classified, this statistic indicates that persons with prior felonies probably compose a large majority of the case files.

The vast majority of persons with prior felonies have held some form of legal status at some point in time. In many cases, these persons have only lost their legal status, thereby becoming deportable, because of their prior convictions.[79] As a result, the immigration violators who are being apprehended by local police—under the aegis of local enforcement—seem to be very different from the unauthorized border crossers that these laws were originally designed to capture. This is yet another piece of the puzzle that, typical of most things to do with local enforcement, further complicates its officially stated objectives.

Conclusion

Because local enforcement is still in its nascent stages, it is not possible to make a definitive statement on its future trajectory. For example, will local enforcement be a short-lived and largely symbolic gesture made by local governments seeking to appease angry constituents during a time of economic restructuring and cultural-demographic change? Will local enforcement become an institutionalized feature of virtually all aspects of U.S. public life, exhibiting a scope and range that has not been seen since the racial exclusions of Jim Crow? Or, will local enforcement be defined by the role it is beginning to play in an expanding immigration and prison-industrial complex?

These are not mutually exclusive possibilities. However, the connection between local enforcement and the prison-industrial complex is the most firmly supported by available data. It is rather ironic that this connection is the least apparent, if one is judging the goals of local enforcement by the official rationale of the illegal-immigration laws that are currently sweeping the nation.

It is not clear how the arrest and deportation of immigrants with prior felonies reduces the fiscal burden imposed on local governments by the undocumented population. However, it does illustrate how local enforcement is being used as a mechanism for integrating local policing practices within an expanding, immigration-oriented prison system.[80] Moreover, this is occurring during a time when immigration violators are becoming the fastest growing segment of the federal prison population, despite the fact that crime rates attributable to the immigrant population are, at worst, no higher than crime rates for the general population.[81]

The racialized undertones of the illegal-immigration debate (and the racial-ethnic profiles used to apprehend "illegals") play into this issue in at least two ways: this racialized discourse normalizes the policing and legal-juridical practices that allow for the disproportionate incarceration and deportation of black and brown noncitizens, and—and just as important—the racialized discourse on the "illegal immigrant problem" distracts attention from the possibility that local enforcement is being used to address issues that have very little to do with unauthorized migration.

To obfuscate matters further, the controversies surrounding local enforcement are routinely sidelined by the national debate over immigration reform, which has been largely unconcerned with immigrant profiling or immigrant incarceration. As I noted earlier, the proimmigrant forces leading this debate are willing to consider some increase in immigration enforcement as a practical concession to adopting a new guest worker program. This does not mean that proimmigrant Republicans and Democrats necessarily favor local enforcement (in fact, most have voted against federal local-enforcement legislation), but it does indicate that there is a general openness to a variety of enforcement practices, so long as they do not interfere with labor market demands for noncitizen workers. It is also likely that the national policy debate and federal court decisions will continue to play a critical role in defining acceptable versus unacceptable local-enforcement practices, as they have for the past several years. However, these decisions have largely focused on questions of implementation; they have yet to challenge the inherent authority to enforce federal immigration laws on which all forms of local enforcement rest. It also bears noting that local governments clearly are aware of, and are making use of, this inherent authority. The failure of the Congress to ratify a new immigration bill in 2007 has already begun to spur a new wave of county-level illegal-immigration ordinances, as local governments feel pressured to come up with their own solutions to the "immigration problem."[82]

There is also much that is not known about local enforcement. For example, there is very little data available—and certainly no national data—

on the number of undocumented persons who are apprehended by police without the assistance of the NCIC database. This would include individuals who are apprehended during routine traffic stops and individuals who are screened after being jailed for minor violations or because they have participated in a police investigation. It is not possible to say how representative prior felons are of the total population of noncitizens who are arrested and deported as a result of local enforcement. There is even less known about the numbers of noncitizens who are being tracked into the immigration system by government workers other than the police, or by private citizens who have been authorized to screen for legal status.

Meanwhile, there are no signs that the passage of illegal-immigration laws at the level of local government will slow down any time soon. And although there may be a complex array of factors driving this process, they all point toward the increased use of immigrant profiling as an expedient screening practice. The very nature and objectives of local enforcement requires local police, health-care workers, educators, social workers, employers, and landlords, among others, to answer the question posed by this chapter's title: What does an undocumented immigrant look like?

Notes

I want to express my appreciation to Lois Rudnick and Panayota Gounari for their comments and patient advice on the early drafts of this chapter.

1. As reported by the Immigrant Legal Advocacy Project, Portland, Maine. Excerpted from the National Immigration Forum, "State and Local Police Enforcing Immigration Laws: Stories from Around the Nation," December 2003.

2. Excerpted from John Keilman and George Houde, "Illegal Immigrant Residents Targeted: Crackdown Weighed in Carpentersville," *Chicago Tribune*, September 29, 2006.

3. For an introduction to the current debate, see National Immigration Forum, "Backgrounder: Immigration Law Enforcement by State and Local Police," May 2004, http://www.immigrationforum.org/PrintFriendly.aspx?tabid=572 (accessed November 10, 2007).

4. For example, over 1.2 million apprehensions of immigration violators were carried out by federal agents in 2005, compared to a total of little more than 20,000 immigration violators apprehended by local police (through the use of the National Crime Information Center database) between 2002 and 2004. Mary Dougherty, Denise Wilson, and Amy Wu, "Immigration Enforcement Actions: 2005," Office of

Immigration Statistics, November 2006, 1, http://www.dhs.gov/xlibrary/assets/ statistics/yearbook/2005/Enforcement_AR_05.pdf (accessed November 10, 2007); Hannah Gladstein, Annie Lai, Jennifer Wagner, and Michael Wishnie, "Blurring the Lines: A Profile of State and Local Police Enforcement of Immigration Law Using the National Crime Information Center Database, 2002–2004," Migration Policy Institute Occasional Paper, December 2005, 13, http://www.migration policy.org/pubs/MPI_report_Blurring_the_Lines_120805.pdf (accessed November 10, 2007).

5. For an overview, see National Immigration Forum, "Issue in Brief: Immigration Law Enforcement by State and Local Police," January 31, 2006, http://www .immigrationforum.org/documents/PolicyWire/Legislation/SLE-IssueinBrief.pdf (accessed November 10, 2007).

6. This surge took place between the summer of 2006 and winter 2007 and was initiated, in large part, by a highly publicized ordinance adopted by the mayor of Hazelton, Pennsylvania. Michael Rubinkam, "Illegal Immigrant Laws Face Setbacks," Associated Press, January 20, 2007. See also Edwin Garcia, "State Republicans' Forum Focuses on Illegal Immigrants: Effort Meant to Help Build Legislative Package," *San Jose Mercury News*, September 28, 2006; Summer Harlow, "Small Towns Play Big Role on Immigration: Fear of Persecution Forces Many to Move," *News Journal,* October 15, 2006; John Keilman and George Houde, "Illegal Immigrant Residents Targeted"; John Wagner, "Ehrlich Seeks Driver's License Limits," *Washington Post,* October 3, 2006.

7. Developments at this level are happening almost as fast as the spread of local enforcement measures through municipal governments. At this writing, ten or more states are considering some variant of local enforcement legislation. See Jacques Billeaud, "States Seek to Punish Companies for Illegal Immigration," Associated Press, March 21, 2007; Associated Press, "A Look at Illegal Immigration Proposals Filed by Texas Lawmakers," January 28, 2007; Roger Brokaw, "States Can Deter Illegal Immigration," *Marion Ledger,* February 9, 2007; Eliot Shapleigh, *Lifting the Lamp Beside Texas' Door: Addressing the Challenges and Opportunities of Immigration in Texas for the 2007–2009 Biennium* (Austin: State Senator Shapleigh's Office, December 14, 2006), 49–50; Oregonian Politics Team, "Flores, Thatcher Unleash Anti-Illegal Immigration Proposals," *Oregonian,* February 9, 2007. Other states have already implemented these laws (see chapter 13 of this book for a discussion of how this has taken shape in New Mexico). For example, the Colorado state legislature passed a series of immigration bills that did not explicitly mandate local enforcement but which—according to Hispanic community organizations—resulted in police officers screening for legal status during routine traffic stops. John Ensslin, "Speaker: Immigration Laws Have Had 'Unintended Consequences,' Lawmaker Says Legislation May Need Reworking," *Rocky Mountain News,* January 29, 2007.

8. In addition to municipal local enforcement laws, two state governments have signed memorandums of understanding (MOUs) with the Department of Homeland Security allowing their local and state police to collaborate with federal agents in the enforcement of federal immigration laws. These states include Alabama and Florida. More recently, L.A. County has become the first municipal government to enter into a similar MOU with federal immigration authorities. See National Immigration Law Center, "L.A. County to Enter Limited MOU with ICE to permit Immigration Enforcement at County Jail," *Immigrant Rights Update* 19, no. 1 (2005), http://www.nilc.org/immlawpolicy/arrestdet/ad085.htm (accessed November 10, 2007).

9. See notes 6 and 7.

10. For several illustrations of the rhetoric of far-right, anti-immigrant groups, see David Holthouse, "Ruckus on the Right: Angry Former Supporters of the Minutemen Civil Defense Corps Are Questioning Group Founder Chris Simox's Accounting," *Intelligence Report* 123 (2006): 62–67; Susy Buchanan, "Deadly Force: Brandishing Insults and a Gun, Roy Warden Routinely Threatens Latinos with Death," *Intelligence Report* 123 (2006): 13–17.

11. Rubinkam, "Illegal Immigrant Laws Face Setbacks." For more on the English-only movement, see James Crawford, "Anatomy of the English-Only Movement," in *Language Legislation and Linguistic Rights,* ed. Doublas A. Kibbee (Philadelphia: John Benjamins, 1998).

12. The most significant developments are the 2002–2003 legal opinions issued by the Department of Justice and the White House. These are discussed in greater detail in the section titled "Local Enforcement and the National Policy Context."

13. One of the more widely publicized examples of this trend was the dispute over allocation of municipal welfare services in Lewiston, Maine, after the town experienced an unexpected surge in its Somali refugee population. Although the event was instigated by tensions and disconnects between federal policies and local resources, it was often framed as a controversy pitting (African) noncitizens versus (white) citizens. For an example of this conservative framing of the issue, see Roger McGrath, "The Great Somali Welfare Hunt: The Refugee Act of 1980 Has Turned Thousands of Somali Bantu into American Dependents," Somalia Watch/The American Conservative, November 24, 2002, http://www .somaliawatch.org/archivejuno2/021124201.htm (accessed November 10, 2007). For an alternative perspective, see Maggie Jones, "The New Yankees," *Mother Jones,*March/April2004,http://www.motherjones.com/news/feature/2004/03/02_ 401.html?welcome=true (accessed November 10, 2007).

14. For a review, see Audrey Singer, "Welfare Reform and Immigrants: A Policy Review," in *Immigrants, Welfare Reform and the Poverty of Policy,* ed. Philip Kretsedemas and Ana Aparicio (Westport, Conn.: Greenwood/Praeger, 2004), 21–34.

15. An exorbitant amount of literature has been written on this topic. For a very good selection of essays on this subject, see Stanley Eitzen and Maxine Baca Zinn, eds., *The Reshaping of America: The Social Consequences of a Changing Economy* (Englewood Cliffs, N.J.: Prentice Hall, 1989). Also, Lisa Duggan, *The Twilight of Equality? Neoliberalism, Cultural Politics, and the Attack on Democracy* (Boston: Beacon Press, 2004). It should be noted that these are criticisms of the neoliberal policies that have been used to restructure the economy in which immigrants are being "integrated"—but they are not denunciations of immigration in general, or of any particular immigrant population. Conservative populists, however, have made this connection. For an example, see Patrick Buchanan, *The Death of the West: How Dying Populations and Immigrant Invasions Imperil Our Country and Civilization* (New York: St. Martin's Griffin, 2002).

16. For one account, see Katherine Neuman, *Declining Fortunes: The Withering of the American Dream* (New York: Basic Books, 1994).

17. For a recent overview that centers on the question of labor markets, social welfare, and other economic impacts, see Nicolaus Mills, ed., Arguing Immigration: The Controversy and Crisis over the Future of Immigration in America (New York: Touchstone, 2006).

18. This has been acknowledged by researchers in both the proimmigration and immigration-control camps. See Nelson Lim, "On the Backs of Blacks? Immigrants and the Fortunes of African Americans," in *Strangers at the Gates: New Immigrants in Urban America*, ed. Roger Waldinger, 186–227 (Berkeley: University of California Press, 2001); Andrew Sum, Paul Harrington, and Ishwar Khatiwada, "The Impact of New Immigrants on Young, Native-Born Workers, 2000–2005," Center for Immigration Studies, September 2006, http://www.cis.org/articles/2006/back806.html (accessed November 10, 2007).

19. Associated Press, "Unemployment Rate Approaches 5-Year Low," September 2, 2006. It also bears noting that unemployment rates since the late 1990s have been at historic lows. The current employment rate (as of fourth-quarter 2006) is 4.6 percent. In 1997 the U.S. unemployment rate was 4.9 percent, which at the time was a twenty-seven-year low.

20. This is reflected in the recent emphasis on forcing employers, landlords, and service providers to screen for legal status—an effort to limit the participation of unauthorized migrants in local labor markets (reducing job competition with "natives") and their use of publicly funded medical and educational services. For examples, see Joel Currier, "Valley Park Reconsiders Immigration Ordinance," *St. Louis Post-Dispatch*, February 5, 2007; Mary Mogan Edwards, "Immigrant's Arrest, Pending Expulsion Cause Civil-Rights Fight," *Columbus Dispatch*, January 9, 2003; Harlow, "Small Towns Play Big Role on Immigration"; Keilman and Houde, "Illegal Immigrant Residents Targeted."

21. For a list of local governments, police departments, nonprofits, and community-based organizations that oppose local enforcement measures, see Na-

tional Immigration Forum, "Proposals to Expand the Immigration Authority of State and Local Police," September 2006, http://www.immigrationforum.org/documents/TheDebate/EnforcementLocalPolice/CLEARHSEAQuotes.pdf (accessed November 10, 2007).

22. Several examples of case studies illustrating this dynamic can be found in Kretsedemas and Aparicio, *Immigrants, Welfare Reform, and the Poverty of Policy.* For a statistical description of this phenomena using national data, see Jennifer Van Hook, Jennifer E. Glick, and Frank D. Bean, "Public Assistance Receipt Among Immigrants and Natives: How the Unit of Analysis Affects Research Findings," *Demography* 36, no. 1 (1999): 111–120.

23. It has been estimated that one in ten U.S. families with children are mixed-status families, meaning that they contain citizens and noncitizens. Within immigrant populations specifically, this figure increases to 85 percent. Since mixed-status families can contain a mixture of citizens, legal permanent residents, asylees, and unauthorized migrants, among others—it is not possible to account for the precise proportion of mixed-status families that count unauthorized migrants among their members. However, the prevalence of these families indicates that it is possible for unauthorized migrants to be widely dispersed among them. Michael Fix and Wendy Zimmerman, "All Under One Roof: Mixed-Status Families in an Era of Reform," Urban Institute, October 6, 1999.

24. See Families USA Foundation, "One Step Forward, One Step Back: Children's Health Coverage After CHIP and Welfare Reform" (October 1999).

25. See Families USA, "One Step Forward, One Step Back"; Lisa Carcari Stone and Anna Quiroz-Gibson, "Puerta Abierta o Puerta Cerrada? Citizenship, Health Care and Welfare Reform in New Mexico," in Kretsedemas and Aparicio, *Immigrants, Welfare Reform, and the Poverty of Policy,* 63–88.

26. Also known as the McCarran-Walter Act of 1952. *Immigration and Nationality Act* (Public Law 82–414, 66 Stat. 163).

27. Appleseed, "Forcing Our Blues into Gray Areas," http://www.appleseeds.net/Portals/0/Documents/Publications/forcingourbluesintograysweb.pdf (accessed November 10, 2007).

28. This also allowed for the crafting of memorandums of understanding (MOUs) between the immigration system and state/local police agencies. Although these agreements limit federal/local cooperation to the specific terms and time frame of the MOU, they are also rather flexible documents. For example, the Florida MOU allows all police agencies—statewide—to collaborate with federal immigration officers as they see fit and has no expiration date. For a general discussion of these MOUs and the significance of IIRAIRA and AEDPA for local enforcement, see Appleseed, "Forcing Our Blues into Gray Areas"; National Immigration Forum, "Backgrounder"

29. Appleseed, "Forcing Our Blues into Gray Areas," 15–18.

30. National Immigration Forum, "Backgrounder."

31. Ibid.

32. For an overview of both proposed bills see National Immigration Forum, "Proposals to Expand the Immigration Authority of State and Local Police."

33. See the statements against local enforcement made by police departments in ibid.

34. National Immigration Forum, "Conservatives and Cops Agree: The CLEAR Act and Its Senate Companion Are Bad Public Policy," April 30, 2004, http://www .immigrationforum.org/DesktopDefault.aspx?tabid=587 (accessed November 10, 2007).

35. Michele Waslin, "Immigration Enforcement by Local Police: The Impact on Latinos. National Council of La Raza," February 20, 2003.

36. Carla Marinucci and Mark Martin, "Governor Endorses Minutemen on Border: He Parts with Bush on Armed Volunteers Stopping Illegal Immigrants in Arizona," *San Francisco Chronicle*, Friday, April 29, 2005.

37. This is best illustrated by the different priorities and emphases of the immigration reform proposals that were forwarded by proimmigrant and anti-immigrant Republicans in the 108th Congress. See the review provided in Eliot Turner and Marc R. Rosenblum, "Solving the Unauthorized Migrant Problem: Proposed Legislation in the US. Migration Policy Institute," September 1, 2005, http://www.migrationinformation.org/Feature/display.cfm?ID=333 (accessed November 10, 2007). For an overview of proimmigration perspectives among Republican voters, also see Manhattan Institute, "Earned Legalization and Increased Border Security Is Key to Immigration Reform According to Republican Voters: New Poll," October 17, 2005, http://www.manhattan-institute.org/html/immigration_pol_pr.htm (accessed November 10, 2007).

38. For a concise overview, see Douglas Massey, "March of Folly: U.S. Immigration Policy After NAFTA," *American Prospect* 3, no. 1 (1998).

39. See Jeffrey Passel, *The Size and Characteristics of the Unauthorized Migrant Population in the U.S.: Estimates Based on the March 2005 Current Population Survey*, Pew Hispanic Center, March 2006, http://pewhispanic.org/files/reports/61 .pdf (accessed November 10, 2007).

40. This divide between elite and popular opinion actually predates the mid-twentieth century. However, the changes in U.S. policy, marked by the 1965 Immigration Act, set the tone for the most recent incarnation of these tensions. Daniel Tichenor has noted that, between 1977 and 1996, popular support for some decrease in immigration has varied from a low of 42 percent to a high of 66 percent (terminating at 58 percent support for immigration controls in 1996). See Daniel Tichenor, *Dividing Lines: The Politics of Immigration Control in America* (Princeton, N.J.: Princeton University Press, 2002), 19. For a more wide-ranging discussion, see Justin Chacón and Mike Davis, *No One Is Illegal* (Chicago: Haymarket, 2006), and Aristide Zolberg, *A Nation by Design: Immigration Policy in the Fashioning of America* (Cambridge: Harvard University Press, 2006).

41. For example, although immigrant public opinion tends to be only moderately more critical of immigration controls than that of the native born, immigrant communities have been adamantly critical of policies that reduce immigrants to second-class citizens. Notable examples include restrictions on immigrants' social rights (via the Personal Responsibility Work Opportunity Reconciliation Act of 1996; Public Law 104–193, 110 Stat. 2105, Aug. 22, 1996) expedited deportation procedures (introduced by the Illegal Immigration Reform and Immigrant Responsibility Act of 1996; Public Law 104–208, 100 Stat. 3009–546, Sept. 30, 1996), and the restrictions on immigrant legal and civil rights advanced through a variety of post–9/11 "security" measures. See Roger Daniels, *Guarding the Golden Door* (New York: Hill and Wang, 2004); Jonathan Reider, "Getting a Fix on Fragmentation," in *The Fractious Nation?* ed. Jonathan Reider (Berkeley and Los Angeles: University of California Press, 2003), 13–15.

42. Tamar Jacoby has estimated the constituency for the anti-immigrant movement to be approximately 20 to 25 percent of the national population, being composed mostly of white males with lower levels of education. Tamar Jacoby, "Immigration Nation," *Foreign Affairs,* November/December 2006, http://www .foreignaffairs.org/20061101faessay85606/tamar-jacoby/immigration-nation .html. However, it is also important to note that support for immigration control can take many forms that are not necessarily reducible to the rhetoric of the anti-immigrant right—and that as recently as 1996, 58 percent of the U.S. population favored some decrease in immigration. See note 40.

43. For definitive examples of this policy and cultural agenda, see Patrick Buchanan, *Death of the West* (New York: St. Martin's/Griffin, 2002), and Samuel Huntington, *Who Are We? The Challenges to America's National Identity* (New York: Simon & Schuster, 2004).

44. Alejandro Portes and Min Zhou, "Segmented Assimilation and Its Variants," *Annals of the American Academy of Political and Social Sciences* 530 (1993): 74–96.

45. Sarah Lynch, "Pearce Calls on 'Operation Wetback' for Illegals," (Scottsdale/Mesa, Ariz.) *East Valley Tribune,* September 29, 2006. Statistics on deportations under Operation Wetback are from 1953 to 1955 as reported in Mae Ngai, *Impossible Subjects: Illegal Aliens and the Making of Modern America* (Princeton, N.J.: Princeton University Press, 2005), 155–156.

46. Although a guest worker program was incorporated within an immigration reform bill, approved by the Senate in Spring 2006, its companion bill did not pass in the House. This was largely due to the resistance of the anti-immigrant, Republican right which had a much stronger hold on the House, at the time. Bloomberg News Service, "Business Group Seeks Senate Immigration Win After House Defeat," March 16, 2006. For an account of emerging conflicts between the Democrats on this matter, see Nicole Gaouette, "Democrats Clash on Immigration Policy: Tensions in Party Rise to the Surface," *Los Angeles Times,* November 24, 2006.

47. Turner and Rosenblum, "Solving the Unauthorized Migrant Problem."

48. The President's proposal couches the new guest worker program in the context of the immigration enforcement and security measures that were intensified after September 11, 2001. However, no new enforcement or security measures are proposed within the context of the guest worker program itself. See White House, Office of the Press Secretary, "President Bush Proposes New Temporary Worker Program" January 7, 2004, http://www.whitehouse.gov/news/releases/2004/01/20040107-3.html (accessed November 10, 2007).

49. White House, Office of the Press Secretary, "President Bush Addresses the Nation on Immigration Reform," May 15, 2006, http://www.whitehouse.gov/news/releases/2006/05/20060515-8.html (accessed November 10, 2007).

50. For a review of the first two bills, see Turner and Rosenblum, "Solving the Unauthorized Migrant Problem." For a review of the STRIVE bill, see NAFSA Association of International Educators, "Summary of STRIVE Act 2007," March 2007, http://www.nafsa.org/_/File/_/strive_summary.pdf (accessed November 10, 2007).

51. Bloomberg News Service, "Business Group Seeks Senate Immigration Win After House Defeat," March 16, 2006; Donna Smith, "Senators Near Compromise on Immigration," Reuters, March 16, 2006.

52. Jake Tapper, "Immigration Reform Bill Dies in Senate," ABC News Online, June 28, 2007, http://abcnews.go.com/Politics/story?id=3326113&page=1&CMP=OTC-RSSFeeds0312 (accessed November 10, 2007).

53. The most recent effort at passing federal-level local enforcement legislation before the Republicans lost control of the Congress was the 2005 Illegal Immigration Enforcement and Empowerment Act (S 1823), which took the inherent authority of local governments several steps further than the proposed Homeland Security Enhancement Act. The bill was never passed into law, but efforts were made to incorporate elements of it into subsequent legislation (such as the 2006 Secure Fence Act that was signed into law on October 26, 2005). Although unsuccessful, these and other efforts did play a role in keeping immigration and border control arguments on the table. See National Immigration Law Center, "Bill Authorizing Enforcement of Immigration Law by State and Local Authorities Introduced in Senate," *Immigrant Rights Update* 19, no. 8 (2005), http://www.nilc.org/immlawpolicy/LocalLaw/locallaw001.htm (accessed November 10, 2007). In early 2007 Representative Elton Gallegly (Republican, Simi Valley, California) also proposed new federal laws that would use IRS individual tax identification numbers as a basis for identifying (and deporting) unauthorized migrants. These proposals, however, do not contain any local enforcement measures, as conventionally defined, and are not expected to survive in the Democrat-controlled Congress. Michael Collins, "Gallegly Introduces Numerous Immigration Bills," *Ventura County Star,* February 9, 2007.

54. Pam Belluck, "Towns Lose Tool Against Illegal Immigrants," *New York Times,* August 13, 2005; Rubinkam, "Illegal Immigrant Laws Face Setbacks"; *El Diario/La Prensa,* "Hazleton Anti-Immigrant Law Declared Unconstitutional," July 26, 2007.

55. Harlow, "Small Towns Play Big Role on Immigration"; Rubinkam, "Illegal Immigrant Laws Face Setbacks."

56. For an example of how this played out in the South Florida Haitian immigrant population, see Philip Kretsedemas, "Avoiding the State: Haitian Immigrants and Welfare Services in Miami-Dade County," in *Immigrants, Welfare Reform and the Poverty of Policy*, ed. Kretsedemas and Aparicio (Westport, Conn.: Greenwood/Praeger, 2004), 107–136.

57. For a recent example, see the negotiations between proimmigration and proenforcement Republicans over the enforcement measures (and funding for these measures) that were to be included in the 2006 Secure Fence Act. Nicole Gaouette, "Bush Signs Fence Bill, Pushes Back," *Los Angeles Times*, October 27, 2006.

58. Andrew Sum, Johan Uvin, Ishwar Khatiwada, and Dana Ansel, *The Changing Face of Massachusetts* (Boston: Mass Inc. and Northeastern University Center for Labor Market Studies, 2005); Andrew Sum et. al., *Immigrant Workers in the New England Labor Market: Implications for Workforce Development Policy* (Boston: New England Regional Office Employment and Training Administration, U.S. Department of Labor, 2002).

59. Immigration peaks in the early 1900s approached 1.3 million per annum. In contrast, immigration peaks in the late 1980s and early 1990s remained just under 1.1 million. See Ruth Ellen Wasem, "Immigration and Naturalization Fundamentals—Report for Congress," Congressional Research Service, Library of Congress, May 20, 2003, http://fpc.state.gov/documents/organization/34520.pdf (accessed November 10, 2007). However, it is likely that total annual migration in the 1990s was higher by a few hundred thousand persons per annum if one accounts for the undocumented population, which increased from between 5 and 6 million in the early 1990s to between 11 and 12 million by 2003. See Jeffrey Passel, *Size and Characteristics of the Unauthorized Migrant Population in the U.S.* Estimates based on the March 2005 Current Population Survey, Pew Hispanic Center, March 7, 2006, http://pewhispanic.org/files/reports/61.pdf (accessed November 10, 2007).

60. Migration Policy Institute, Immigration Enforcement Spending Since IRCA, November 2005, http://www.migrationpolicy.org/ITFIAF/FactSheet_Spending.pdf (accessed November 10, 2007).

61. Government data show that over 800,000 temporary workers are admitted to the United States each year, but this only accounts for those entering with I-94 forms, or for less than 20 percent of the nonimmigrant flow (in 2005 the total flow of nonimmigrants into the United States totaled over 175 million, while nonimmigrants with I-94 forms totaled only 32 million). Since a large portion of nonimmigrants who enter without I-94 forms are individuals crossing the U.S.–Mexico border for short visits (easily numbering in the tens of millions per annum), it is very likely that the total number of temporary workers each year is at least double

the number admitted with I-94 forms. For details on the I-94 population, see Department of Homeland Security, "Temporary Admissions of Nonimmigrants to the United States: 2005," July 2006. See also Department of Homeland Security, "Table 26: Nonimmigrant Admissions (I-94 Only) by Class of Admission: Fiscal Years 1996 to 2005" 2006, http://www.dhs.gov/xlibrary/assets/statistics/yearbook/2005/Table26D.xls (accessed November 10, 2007).

62. Passel, *Size and Characteristics of the Unauthorized Migrant Population in the U.S.*

63. As reported by the Virginia Justice Center, Fairfax, Virginia. Excerpted from the National Immigration Forum, "State and Local Police Enforcing Immigration Laws."

64. As reported by the Hispanic Organization of North Florida. Excerpted from the National Immigration Forum, "State and Local Police Enforcing Immigration Laws."

65. See Lornet Turnbull, "Deportation in the Rise in Central Ohio; Minor Traffic Violations Earn Illegal Immigrants a Quick Ticket Home," *Columbus Dispatch,* May 5, 2003.

66. *Muehler et al. v. Mena,* 544 U.S. 93 (2005); see also *Mena v. City of Simi Valley,* 226 F.3d 1031 (9th Cir., 2000).

67. Appleseed, "Forcing Our Blues into Gray Areas."

68. See note 53 for citations of news stories that discuss the basis for federal court challenges to local enforcement measures.

69. Mae Ngai, *Impossible Subjects.*

70. Bill Hing, *Defining America Through Immigration Policy (Mapping Racisms)* (Philadelphia: Temple University Press, 2004).

71. Ngai, *Impossible Subjects,* 147–152.

72. See Paul Gilroy, *There Ain't No Black in the Union Jack: The Cultural Politics of Race and Nation* (Chicago: University of Chicago Press, 1991); Michael Omi and Howard Winant, *Racial Formation in the United States: From the 1960s to the 1980s* (New York: Routledge, 1986).

73. Ngai, *Impossible Subjects,* 84–88.

74. Hannah Gladstein, Annie Lai, Jennifer Wagner, and Michael Wishnie, "Blurring the Lines: A Profile of State and Local Police Enforcement of Immigration Law Using the National Crime Information Center Database," 2002–2004, Migration Policy Institute Occasional Paper, December 13, 2005, http://www.migrationpolicy.org/pubs/MPI_report_Blurring_the_Lines_120805.pdf (accessed November 10, 2007).

75. This figure averaged 42 percent for all three years. The proportion of false leads decreased gradually each year, but as of 2004 (the last year included in the study) it was still fairly high, at 35 percent. Gladstein et al., "Blurring the Lines."

76. The apprehension rate for Caribbean immigrants was approximately five to six times their representation in both the unauthorized and legal immigrant popula-

tion. Caribbean immigrants composed 7 percent of those apprehended through the NCIC (see Table 15.1) but, conservatively estimated, were little more than 1 percent of the undocumented population. Because the data for undocumented migrants was not thoroughly disaggregated, Caribbean migrants were included within a group totaling 3 percent of the national undocumented population along with several other national origin groups, including Africans, Middle Eastern persons and all others not included in the list of nationalities shown for Table 15.1. It also bears noting that, at 2.8 million, the Caribbean population of legal immigrants is little more than 1.2 percent of the U.S. population. Migration Policy Institute. Migration Information Source. United States Stock of Foreign Country by Birth 1995–2005, http://www.migrationinformation.org/GlobalData/countrydata/ country.cfm (accessed November 10, 2007).

77. Michael Tonry, *Malign Neglect: Race, Crime, and Punishment in America* (New York: Oxford University Press, 1996).

78. Gladstein et al., "Blurring the Lines."

79. It is very telling, for example, that the majority of noncitizens in deportation proceedings for aggravated felonies in 2005 are legal residents with a median length of fourteen years' residence in the United States. See chapter 10 for a more detailed discussion of these statistics. Also see Transactional Records Access Clearinghouse (TRAC), "Aggravated Felonies and Deportation, December 2006, http://trac.syr.edu/immigration/reports/155/ (accessed November 10, 2007).

80. From its inception in November 2002, federal drug and crime enforcement became incorporated within the Department of Homeland Security. Since this time, criminal prosecutions of immigrants have been the fastest growing sector of federal prosecutions. Immigration-related offenses have now become the largest group of federal prosecutions (at 32 percent of all prosecutions), overshadowing the former dominance of the War on Drugs (drug enforcement prosecutions unrelated to immigration make up only 27 percent of the national prosecution caseload). What is significant in this change is not just that immigration matters have outpaced other forms of federal law enforcement, but that immigration has become the dominant paradigm through which all other forms of federal law enforcement are being reoriented. For example, the Department of Homeland Security has now become the primary drug enforcement agency and has become the fastest growing employer of federal law enforcement agents. See Transactional Records Access Clearinghouse, "Prosecution of Immigration Cases Surge in U.S. 2005," http://trac.syr.edu/tracins/latest/131/ (accessed November 10, 2007).

81. For a recent discussion, see Eyal Press, "Do Immigrants Make Us Safer?" *New York Times*, December 3, 2006. It is notable that even analysts who are generally unsympathetic to immigrants' rights issues (and support some form of immigration control) have acknowledged that there is some basis to these statistics. Carl Horowitz, for example, acknowledges that the vast majority of government data and independent academic studies of U.S. crime rates from the early 1900s to the present

show that the number of crimes committed by immigrants has been consistently lower than or at the very least no greater than the native-born crime rate. To advance his argument for the "hidden statistics" on immigrant crime, Horowitz resorts to speculations of unreported crimes within immigrant communities, for which he provides no concrete data. Horowitz acknowledges that the evidence that does exist of higher immigrant crime rates appears to (1) be limited to Hispanic immigrants and (2) concern crimes in which Hispanics victimize other Hispanics. Carl Horowitz, "An Examination of U.S. Immigration Policy and Serious Crime," Center for Immigration Studies, April 2001, http://www.cis.org/articles/2001/crime/toc .html#fear (accessed November 10, 2007). It is also ironic that these trends in the under-reporting of immigrant victimization would likely increase if local enforcement measures (supported by pro-enforcement advocates) were to be expanded.

82. Zoe Tillman, "More Communities Use Local Police to Enforce U.S. Immigration Law," *Christian Science Monitor,* July 17, 2007.

Immigration Reform at a Crossroads

PHILIP KRETSEDEMAS AND DAVID C. BROTHERTON

WHEN THE DEMOCRATS WON THE MAJORITY in the House and Senate in the 2005 midterm elections, there was some anticipation that things would finally begin to move on the question of immigration reform. Two years later, however, it became apparent that the Democrats were just as concerned as the Republicans about being the party to usher in a very unpopular immigration reform bill. At the time of this writing, the most recent immigration reform proposal was Senate bill 1639, which received a fair measure of bipartisan support (most notably from Senator Ted Kennedy and President George W. Bush), but not enough to overcome objections within both major parties.[1] It can be argued that the bill failed because it tried to accommodate too many agendas and as a consequence contained just enough objectionable measures to alienate people on all sides of the immigration debate. However, it is also a fairly safe assumption that if the bill had catered solely to immigrants' rights constituencies or solely to immigration restrictionists, it would not have passed. This indicates that the bill's failure was not merely a product of inept framing or poor strategic decisions but that it reflects a genuine moment of indecision on the part of U.S. policymakers that reveals a deeper ambivalence on the question of immigration. Once again it draws attention to unresolved tensions within the past several decades of U.S. immigration policy—in which the drive to expand the recruitment of immigrant workers and to celebrate the United States as a nation of immigrants conflicts with growing pressure to treat immigration as a security issue.

As a result, federal policy on the regulation of immigrant labor markets is currently in limbo, leaving these labor markets—and especially the segments that employ unauthorized migrants—to their own devices. Consider the example of the immigration raid in New Bedford, Massachusetts, that we referenced in chapter 1. Despite the fact that many of the workers were deported and that some members of upper management were arrested, the factory was shut down for little more than a day and continues to produce materials for the U.S. military while the owners await their trial date.[2] And although this type of high-profile raid may have intimidated some employers, there still is no viable alternative to unauthorized migrant labor for many others. Throughout the Southwest, farmers are dramatically reducing their crop-yield projections because intensified border enforcement is limiting their access to unauthorized migrant labor.[3] But it is also evident that many farmers still seek out this labor and will make use of these workers if they present themselves, while others try to apply for guest workers or turn to prison labor.[4] Undoubtedly, similar scenarios are playing out in the food services industry, the construction industry, and other sectors that pay under-the-table wages.

These developments underscore the hegemonic position that immigration enforcement occupies within the ongoing immigration debate. As noted earlier, immigration reform has been derailed for the foreseeable future and policymakers are being unusually ambivalent about accommodating the immigrant labor needs of the business lobby. However, there is absolutely no ambivalence on the part of either immigration restrictionists or proimmigration moderates about the need to intensify immigration enforcement. The former are adamant about the need for get-tough enforcement measures, and the latter have supported stronger enforcement as a necessary precondition for expanding immigrant labor markets.

The confluence of these tendencies is likely to fuel a continuing push in immigration enforcement, regardless of whether the United States adopts a new guest worker program, though a new guest worker program would likely intensify enforcement measures. Future increases in immigration seem inevitable if one balances the aging and relatively low birthrate of the U.S. population against workforce replenishment needs.[5] But as things stand now, there are no signs that policymakers are willing to publicly acknowledge, much less plan for, these contingencies. Meanwhile, get-tough enforcement measures continue to be attractive to politicians and other public officials who want to demonstrate that they have the "immigration problem" under control.

But the trends documented in this book should not be treated simply as the product of a cyclical, nativist reaction to new immigration flows. It is just as likely that they mark the beginning of a paradigm shift in the way immigrants are being incorporated into the U.S. economy and society. To grasp the full scope of this paradigm shift, however, it is necessary to consider the total climate created by intensified enforcement measures, and not simply the impact on the groups and individuals directly targeted. And so not only must the impact of deportation be assessed in terms of the damage done to the deportee and his or her immediate family, it is also important to consider the disciplinary effect that deportations, immigration raids, and antiterrorist dragnets have on the entire immigrant population.

As David Brotherton observed, these developments should challenge scholars and researchers to develop a more intensive understanding of how globalized techniques of social control are mediating the segmented assimilation of the new immigrant cohort.[6] But this cannot be done without students of immigration engaging the literature in criminology (particularly its critical schools) and vice versa. It is instructive to consider that the Chicago-school approach to social control theory had three basic tenets regarding societal value commitment (coming as it did in reaction to earlier European authoritarianism): (1) the reduction of coercion, (2) the elimination of human misery, and (3) the elevation of the role of rationality in social organization and interactions. Unfortunately, none of these tenets figures into the priorities guiding immigration policy—and immigration enforcement—today. It is a comment on how far theory and practice have diverged in the U.S. treatment of the immigrant when the mainstream Chicago-school paradigm looks positively radical compared with policy-makers' adaptation to the new normal of the wartime security state.

A telling sign of this new normal is the growing intersection between the immigration system and the criminal justice system. Several of the contributors drew attention to the role that the criminal justice system is playing as an entry point into the immigration system. Malik Ndaula and Debbie Satyal discussed the economic agenda that has been driving the expansion of the prison industry, and how it has spilled over into the expansion and privatization of immigration detention centers. Tamara Nopper situated immigrant incarceration in the context of social control strategies that have historically targeted black populations. Similarly to Nopper, Subhash Kateel and Aarti Shahani explained how immigrant incarceration challenges the blind spots of mainstream immigrants' rights activism. But instead of criticizing immigrants' rights activists for reifying the differences between blacks and immigrants, as Nopper does, Kateel and Shahani criticized them for making false distinctions between the social justice demands of "good" versus "bad" (incarcerated) immigrants. Most important, Kateel and Shahani explained how virtually any conviction renders an immigrant vulnerable to deportation and to being detained under conditions that would probably be considered illegal if they were imposed on persons incarcerated within the criminal justice system.

Another theme that emerged from the chapters was the tendency of enforcement measures to blur the lines between immigration violations, crime control, and matters of national security. For example, Kathleen Staudt pointed out that local enforcement measures that are ostensibly geared toward apprehending unauthorized migrants are being framed simultaneously as border control and crime control measures. Philip Kretsedemas also noted the nationwide patterns indicate that local enforcement agencies appear to be more successful at apprehending noncitizens who have prior felony convictions than arresting unauthorized border crossers. At the same time, the recent increase in municipal-level illegal-immigration laws has been informed by broadly defined concerns about immigration and national security.

In a similar vein, Irum Sheikh explained how post–9/11 antiterrorist operations deliberately conflated immigration law violators (primarily unauthorized migrants) with possible terrorism suspects. Once again, this blurring of categories has been facilitated by the current security-oriented policy climate. Abira Ashfaq explained how this broad-brush-stroke approach can play out in immigration court proceedings. The assumption that any Middle Eastern noncitizen may be a terrorist, regardless of the violation that brought the person before the immigration court, can play a decisive role in the way immigration judges exercise their discretion.

It is also important to consider how the mass media has helped to set the tone for this enforcement climate. Several of the contributors—in particular, Ira Kurzban, Jorge Capetillo-Ponce, and Michael Welch and Liz Schuster—explored this subject. Kurzban traced connections between growing class inequalities and concentrations in media ownership and how this has set the context for the media discourse on immigration policy. Capetillo-Ponce mapped a rather expansive field of anti-immigrant discourse that includes far-right blogs, mainstream editorials, and more sober policy analyses. In the process, he demonstrated how these diverse elements tend to reinforce a common set of themes that equated the so-called immigration problem with unauthorized migration in particular.

Michael Welch and Liza Schuster provided a similarly detailed analysis of media constructions of asylum seekers and other "deportable aliens" in the United States and the UK. Their investigation indicates that an analysis of the institutional factors driving immigration enforcement should be accompanied by an analysis of media constructions of "deportable aliens," especially of the ways that these Others are positioned as "anonymous, or 'nameless,' folk devils."

These media constructions take on a special significance because they legitimize enforcement measures that often stretch the boundaries of the law. The current administration has justified these enforcement practices, nonetheless, as being warranted by emergency conditions necessitated by a fear of future terrorist strikes, general concerns about border control, and so forth. As a result, the media often obscures the fact that some enforcement measures which are depicted as practical and desirable are actually highly contested and radical departures from what is considered accepted legal procedure.

Several of the contributors examined these kinds of practices, and as philosopher and political theorist Giorgio Agamben has noted, the unique thing about them is that they operate by suspending the law rather than by introducing new laws.[7] At the same time, these emergency measures are often justified as being in the spirit of the law, and are guided by legal precedent. Mark Dow and Dan Malone explained how this process unfolded in the treatment of Guantánamo detainees and within the U.S. system of secret prisons. In both cases, the imperatives of national security allowed the government to act in the manner it deemed necessary without regard to legal standards or, rather, by selectively ignoring or abiding by these standards. And by this means, as Malone pointed out, it becomes possible to apprehend people on the basis of concealed evidence and to hold them in secret prisons. Dow also noted that government officials stopped just short of granting themselves the right to dispose of the lives of Mariel detainees.

Nevertheless, immigrant detainees do often die within the immigration prison system, even if these deaths are not explicitly premeditated on the part of government workers. The case of Richard Rust, discussed by Kateel and Shahani, illustrates how the untimely death of immigrant detainees may be brought about by gross neglect, which stems from the immigration system's insulation from public oversight as compared with the criminal justice system. The few checks and balances that do exist have been further weakened by get-tough enforcement measures. These measures—whether they take the form of stepped-up border control, dragnet operations, or laws on illegal immigration—are, in their own way, expressions of an undeclared state of emergency which is precipitated by anxieties about immigration in general. Unlike the secret prisons discussed by Dan Malone, these enforcement measures are not guided by statements from the executive branch that officially suspend the law to create an entirely new carceral space. Instead, a diverse assortment of executive statements, federal guidelines, and court decisions have been used to expand the discretionary power of enforcement officers to apply the law (or not) as they see fit.

As Ira Kurzban explained, the elimination of habeas corpus for immigration detainees by the REAL ID Act is a very significant—and alarming—legal precedent. It is especially significant that, historically, habeas corpus has been suspended when martial law has been imposed. In the case of the REAL ID Act, however, habeas corpus has not been temporarily suspended, it has been permanently eliminated. The result is that court officials have been granted expanded powers for processing immigration violators not unlike those that governments grant themselves in times of emergency—except that, in this case, the emergency is deemed permanent and limited to a specific category of persons.

Philip Kretsedemas noted, for example, that statements from the White House and the Department of Justice have affirmed the inherent authority of local governments to enforce federal immigration laws, despite the fact that this inherent authority is not explicitly articulated in existing federal immigration laws and despite the fact that these local enforcement measures are still being contested in the federal courts.

Another example is provided by Arsalan Iftikhar's discussion of the U.S. Army's case against Captain James Yee, which was originally pursued as an antiterror investigation but devolved into a criminal case and eventually noncriminal charges that were dropped, just as all previous charges had been. Captain Yee was being held under conditions that violated federal law and Yee's constitutional rights. But the charges against Yee were being pursued in the context of post–9/11 emergency measures—initiated by officials in the executive branch—that authorized the suspension of normal legal standards for the purpose of apprehending terror suspects. It can be argued that the primary reason for Yee's acquittal was the lack of credible evidence of his being a terrorist, and not that his legal rights had been violated. If the government had been able to make a stronger case, it is not likely that these breaches of legal procedure would have prevented Yee from being detained as an enemy combatant. The issue at stake here is not merely that due process and other legal rights were violated in the course of the prosecution, but whether the government, and the army in particular, had the legitimate authority to suspend these rights and procedures. This is a particularly vexing question, because once it is accepted that government has the authority to suspend basic legal and civil rights, these diminished legal standards then make it more difficult to assess the severity of the violations that occur in their absence.

Captain Yee's case opened the door to a number of other questions that are beyond the scope of this volume. But it is worth asking why it is that immigration enforcement, out of all the functions that fall within the government's purview, has provided such an uncontroversial rationale for policies and executive decisions that have been able to expand this discretionary authority. Why is it that immigration enforcement has provided the context for the government to suspend or ignore basic legal rights and that these developments have been tolerated, even lauded, by many U.S. citizens? This book provides one, provisional answer to this question by explaining that policy and media discourse over the past two decades have been very persistent about connecting immigration issues to purported issues of national security. But it bears emphasizing that these connections were being made many years before September 11, 2001. Even during the 1990s, when domestic terrorism—mythologized in the figure of Timothy McVeigh—had much greater public visibility than Osama Bin Laden and al-Qaeda, the immigration policy climate that we are living in now was already beginning to take shape. This indicates that the official state of emergency declared after 9/11 was merely an intensification of a more general set of anxieties concerning immigration and security that had been building for several years prior.

Any possibility of breaking from the current state of immigration policy requires a thorough interrogation of the immigration-security nexus and requires scholars and practitioners to look beyond the apparent form of immigration policy debates and the goal of advocating for "better laws" and toward a critical analysis of the assumptions that have guided immigration policy trends for the past decade. The challenge is not merely to strengthen legal and civil rights, but to question the unquestionable imperatives that have justified the suspension and removal of these rights for noncitizens.

It is also important to consider how the Otherness of the noncitizen obfuscates the broader significance of recent developments in immigration policy and enforcement. One of the great illusions of Otherness is the idea of an impermeable, ontological divide that separates "us" from "them." It is this illusion that makes it possible to tolerate dramatic curtailments in the rights afforded to noncitizens since, it is thought, this could not possibly have any bearing on legal protections for citizens. Worth remembering, however, is that former Captain James Yee and attorney Brandon Mayfield are both U.S. citizens. Even so, they were subjected to aggressive enforcement practices that were informed—and authorized—by the very same exceptional measures that allowed federal agents to arrest and deport unauthorized Muslim noncitizens as likely terrorist threats. It is also possible to trace continuities between the priorities guiding these enforcement practices and the vacuum of accountability that surrounds the death of Richard Rust—which, as Kateel and Shahani argued, is a structural feature of the immigration system's treatment of detainees. If we are to fully acknowledge these continuities, however, we need to acknowledge the social, political, economic, and cultural threads that crosscut the lifeworlds of citizens and noncitizens. Although these worlds have become more separate over the past two decades, they are not wholly separable—and it is not possible to gain an accurate understanding of the current state of U.S. democracy or the future prospects for U.S. society in general, without considering how these worlds intersect and inform each other.

Notes

1. Jake Tapper, "Immigration Reform Bill Dies in Senate," *ABC News,* June 28, 2007, http://abcnews.go.com/Politics/story?id=3326113&page=1&CMP=OTC-RSSFeeds0312 (accessed November 6, 2007).

2. Maria Sacchetti and Yvonne Abraham, "Fear Grips Kin After Immigration Raid," *Boston Globe,* March 8, 2007.

3. Julia Preston, "Farmers Call Crackdown on Illegal Workers Unfair," *New York Times,* August 11, 2007.

4. Nicole Hill, "U.S. Farmers Using Prison Labor: With Tightening Restrictions on Migrant Workers, Some Farmers Are Turning to the Incarcerated," *Christian Science Monitor,* August 22, 2007.

5. The U.S. population is not aging as fast as that of other industrialized nations, but it is—as in these other nations—aging faster than in the developing world. It is expected that the percentage of persons in the United States who are sixty-five and older will increase from 13 to 20 percent between 2000 and 2050. See Kevin Kinsella and Victoria Velkoff, *An Aging World: 2001* (Washington, D.C.: U.S. Department of Health and Human Services and U.S. Department of Commerce, 2001). This will intensify the already existing age disparities between immigrants and the native born, given that immigrants are younger on average and have higher birthrates than the native-born population. See Laura Beavers and Jean D'Amico, *Children in Immigrant Families: U.S. and State-Level Findings from the 2000 Census* (Baltimore, Md., and Washington, D.C.: Annie E Casey Foundation and Population Reference Bureau, 2005); Margie Shields and Richard E. Behrman, "Children of Immigrant Families: Analysis and Recommendations," *The Future of Children* 14, no. 2 (2003): 4–15. As a result, it is likely that younger immigrant workers will play an increasingly critical role in paying into the Social Security and health-care system to support a growing cohort of aging native-born persons. Scholars have noted that these factors are responsible for the rise of immigration in Japan, Italy, and Spain, which have been historically "reluctant" immigration nations. See Wayne Cornelius, Takeyuki Tsuda, Phillip Martin, and James Hollifield, eds., *Controlling Immigration: A Global Perspective* (Stanford, Calif.: Stanford University Press, 2004).

6. Sociologists have used the term "segmented assimilation" to refer to the process where minorities (including immigrants) are unequally integrated into a given society. This can involve being tracked into job sectors, residential communities, and services that are substandard to, and segregated from, those of the middle and upper middle class. See Alejandro Portes and Min Zhou, "The New Second Generation: Segmented Assimilation and Its Variants," *Annals of the American Academy of Political and Social Science* 530 (1993): 82.

7. Giorgio Agamben, *State of Exception* (Chicago: University of Chicago Press, 2005).

An Annotated List of Immigration Laws

This annotated list provides a very brief overview of the major immigration-control and security-oriented laws that have been passed in the last twenty years, offering a glimpse of the progression of restrictions on immigrants' rights and of immigration-control measures, as well as of measures that have expanded immigration levels. It should be emphasized, however, that this is a partial list that focuses on watershed moments in immigration law. For the sake of simplicity, we have not included federal court decisions or drug-enforcement and anticrime bills that have implications for immigration enforcement. The reader is also advised to look to the index for where these laws are discussed in the book in conjunction with other policies and practices.

Immigration Reform and Control Act of 1986

The Immigration Reform and Control Act of 1986 (IRCA) was the first attempt to substantively amend the Immigration and Nationality Act of 1952 for the purpose of enhancing immigration control (the last prior amendment was the Hart-Cellar Immigration Act of 1965, which famously removed racial/national quotas from U.S. immigration policy). One of the main features of IRCA was its emphasis on controlling illegal immigration. Toward this end, it increased funding for the enforcement arm of the Immigration and Naturalization Service and introduced a new set of sanctions, both legal and financial, against employers who fail to comply with screening guidelines designed to identify unauthorized migrants. The act also expanded the U.S. temporary worker program and introduced a new legalization, or amnesty, program for unauthorized migrants currently working in the United States. As a consequence of these measures, and of the legalization program in particular, IRCA actually facilitated a significant spike in immigration levels not matched until the immigration flows of the early 1990s.

Immigration Reform Act of 1990

The Immigration Reform Act of 1990 continued the increase in spending for immigration enforcement inaugurated by the Immigration Reform and Control Act of 1986, with an emphasis on border control. However, it also laid the foundation for the immigration boom of the 1990s (which matched the size and scope of the "great migration" period of the late nineteenth century and which continues, at a slightly diminished rate, today). The act increased annual immigration quotas by almost 50 percent and dramatically expanded the temporary visa program. Following the passage of the 1990 act, nonimmigrants with temporary visas became the fastest-growing segment of the annual flows of noncitizens entering the United States.

Personal Responsibility and Work Opportunity Reconciliation Act of 1996

The Personal Responsibility and Work Opportunity Reconciliation Act of 1996 is also referred to as the Welfare Reform Act of 1996. It contained unprecedented new measures restricting immigrant access to federal means-tested social programs, primarily including welfare-cash assistance, Social Security disability benefits, food stamps, and public housing and rent vouchers. As a result, most immigrants who entered the United States after August 1996 and who have fewer than five years of legal residence (measured in terms of full-time work quarters) are ineligible for most federal services. This act also granted state legislatures more flexibility and authority to design their own state-level welfare programs using federal funds (disbursed as block grants). As a consequence, some states elected to extend the ban on immigrant welfare use beyond five years. The Personal Responsibility and Work Opportunity Reconciliation Act did not, however, apply to state-funded social services, since state legislatures had complete freedom to determine immigrant eligibility for these programs. Nevertheless, immigrant welfare use dropped dramatically shortly after the law was enacted, accounting for more than half of the welfare savings that accrued during the first year of implementation. Immigrant welfare rates have increased moderately since that time but still do not approach pre-1996 levels.

Antiterrorism and Effective Death Penalty Act of 1996

The Antiterrorism and Effective Death Penalty Act of 1996 limited the application of habeas corpus for federal prisoners, foreshadowing the broader habeas corpus restrictions introduced by the REAL ID Act (see below). The act also contained several measures oriented toward the surveillance and sanctioning of groups providing financial and material support for terrorist operatives in the United States and abroad. As it concerns immigration, the act included new measures to expedite the removal of noncitizen terror suspects from the United States and to bar entry of these persons into the United States.

Illegal Immigration Reform and Immigrant Responsibility Act of 1996

The Illegal Immigration Reform and Immigrant Responsibility Act of 1996 (IIRAIRA) introduced the most sweeping changes to immigration enforcement since the 1952 Immigration and Naturalization Act, far outpacing the Immigration Reform and Control Act and the Immigration Reform Act of 1990. Like prior immigration laws, it increased funding for border control as well internal enforcement activities. However, it also contained provisions that reinforced the immigration-related antiterrorism measures in the Antiterrorism and Effective Death Penalty Act (AEDPA). It expedited removals of unauthorized migrants and increased the bar on reentry as well as limiting legal options for noncitizens charged with an immigration violation. It expanded the range of offenses that count as aggravated felonies for immigration/deportation purposes and made a number of immigration offenses prosecutable under the federal antiracketeering act (Racketeer Influenced and Corrupt Organizations [RICO]), inaugurating a new point of intersection for immigration enforcement and federal law enforcement efforts. IIRAIRA expanded the grounds for exclusion for legal immigrants deemed to be a public charge, reinforcing the signals sent by the immigrant welfare restrictions contained in the Personal Responsibility and Work Opportunity Reconciliation Act of 1996. It also gave immigration officers a greater degree of discretion in barring the entry of noncitizens and authorized memorandums of agreement allowing state law enforcement to partner with federal agencies in immigration enforcement, The latter introduced a legal precedent that supports present-day local enforcement practices, and the act in general promotes more rigorous and restrictive admissions criteria for asylum seekers and noncitizens entering with temporary visas—primarily students and professional workers.

Enhanced Border Security and Visa Entry Reform Act of 2001

The Enhanced Border Security and Visa Entry Reform Act of 2001 continued the increase in spending on the immigration enforcement arm of the Department of Homeland Security (DHS, formerly the Immigration and Naturalization Service) that was initiated by the Immigration Reform and Control Act (but was increased most dramatically by the Illegal Immigration Reform and Immigrant Responsibility

Act [IIRAIRA]). It also attempted to integrate the objectives of the Antiterrorism and Effective Death Penalty Act and IIRAIRA, effectively tightening the connection between antiterrorism activities and immigration enforcement. It authorized increases in government spending on technologies that would enhance border control, such as the implementation of surveillance measures in U.S. ports of entry, and technology that would the augment the ability of government agencies to monitor terrorist suspects. It also authorized new forms of information sharing and joint planning between the DHS, the State Department, and the FBI. Finally, it bears emphasizing that in order to achieve the goal of identifying terrorism suspects the act introduced surveillance strategies geared toward the near-comprehensive tracking and screening of all foreign nationals as they enter and leave the United States.

USA PATRIOT Act of 2001

The USA PATRIOT Act did not contain any significant immigration-related provisions. However, its antiterrorism measures reinforced many of the same priorities introduced by the Antiterrorism and Effective Death Penalty Act and greatly expanded the ability of the government to monitor all U.S. residents, including noncitizens. Among other things, the USA PATRIOT Act greatly expanded and expedited the government's authority to wiretap and to trace patterns of Internet use and other information trails without having to abide by prior standards for disclosure. At the same time, the act allowed for much greater information sharing between different government sectors, for the purpose of investigating and prosecuting terrorism suspects.

REAL ID Act of 2005

The REAL ID Act intensified many of the measures that were introduced by the Illegal Immigration Reform and Immigrant Responsibility Act (IIRAIRA). Unlike IIRAIRA, however, it focused primarily on restricting legal options for noncitizens in the immigration court and criminal court systems. Among other things, it further limited judicial review options for noncitizens facing deportation (in particular, for noncitizens being deported because of criminal convictions), expanded the grounds of inadmissibility and deportability for terrorism-related charges, and introduced even more rigorous criteria for asylum claims.

Secure Fence Act of 2006

The Secure Fence Act continues the increase in spending on border control that can be traced to the Immigration Reform and Control Act and, more recently, to the Enhanced Border Security Act. It expanded the application of border control technology, increased the number of border control agents, and authorized the construction of additional fencing along the U.S.–Mexico border. The additional fencing, which totals over $1 billion, is the most expensive provision of the act, and it has been criticized because it only secures approximately one-third of the U.S.–Mexico border. It bears noting that the intensified border control activities set in motion by this act are partly responsible for the shortage of unauthorized migrant workers experienced by the U.S. agricultural industry in 2007.

ABSCONDER: A noncitizen who remains in the United States after an immigration judge has issued an order of deportation/removal.

AGGRAVATED FELONY: A category that covers a diverse range of violent and nonviolent offenses, including but not limited to murder, rape, drug trafficking, perjury, theft, fraud, or failure to appear before a court of law for an offense punishable by a term of five or more years. For the purpose of immigration law, an aggravated felony committed by a noncitizen is sufficient cause for the issuance of an order of deportation/removal. Recent immigration laws (notably the 1996 Illegal Immigration Reform and Immigrant Responsibility Act) have broadened the range of offenses deemed aggravated felonies for noncitizens who face the prospect of deportation/removal.

ASYLUM SEEKER: A noncitizen who applies for asylum. Noncitizens granted asylum are officially designated as refugees by the U.S. government and are usually granted a broader range of social rights than noncitizens admitted as immigrants or nonimmigrants under temporary visas. Asylum relief is granted to noncitizens who have suffered persecution in their home country or country of last habitual residence. It can also be granted to noncitizens who have a well-founded fear of future persecution in their home country or country of last habitual residence if such persecution is based on race, religion, nationality, political opinion, or membership in a particular social group. *See also* Refugee

BOND HEARING: A court hearing that is used to determine whether a criminal defendant is eligible to be released on bond before his or her trial. A bondsman pays the bail fee for defendants who cannot afford the fee, allowing the defendant to be released from jail until his or her trial commences.

BORDER CONTROL: Immigration enforcement practices that focus on apprehending unauthorized migrants. This includes practices that aim to prevent unauthorized migration at the U.S. border and internal checkpoints and policing designed to apprehend unauthorized migrants after they have entered the United States.

CANCELLATION OF REMOVAL: A form of immigration relief that dismisses the deportation/removal proceedings being issued against a noncitizen, allowing the noncitizen to remain in the United States for a limited period of time (usually no more than ten years), during which he or she has the option of applying for more secure legal status. *See also* Deferred Action/Stay of Removal; Withholding of Removal

CIRCUIT COURT: A federal court of appeals, or appellate court, that hears cases that have been appealed from lower courts (i.e., district, state, or county courts). There are thirteen U.S. circuit courts, each of which handles cases in a specific regional jurisdiction.

DEFERRED ACTION/STAY OF REMOVAL: Similar to cancellation of removal, this is a determination that stays the order of deportation/removal being issued against a noncitizen, though usually for a shorter period of time than a cancellation of removal determination. A deferred action effectively grants the noncitizen temporary legal status and the option of adjusting to permanent legal status, although it is possible that the option to adjust will be denied, routing the noncitizen back into deportation/removal proceedings.

DEPORTATION: Also called formal deportation. An order issued by an immigration court requiring a noncitizen to be returned to his or her home country or country of most recent habitual residence. With the passage of the 1996 Illegal Immigration Reform and Immigrant Responsibility Act, the term *deportation* was replaced by the term *removal*.

DETENTION: The policy of holding noncitizens of indeterminate legal status in government facilities—either prisons, county jails, or other, similar facilities—until the immigration courts have made a final determination as to whether they will be allowed to remain in the United States or be removed/deported. Among the persons who may be detained are unauthorized migrants; persons who entered the United States seeking asylum; and persons with legal status (including naturalized citizens) who have become "deportable" because of a prior felony conviction, a civil immigration violation, or the expiration of his or her temporary legal status.

DISTRICT COURT: A court that hears cases in a particular portion (or the entirety) of a state. District courts may be part of the federal or local/state court system.

ENTERED WITHOUT INSPECTION: *See* Illegal Entry/Illegal Reentrant

EXCLUSION: A determination which rules that a noncitizen residing on U.S. soil may be excluded from being granted legal status and, hence, not be considered to be an individual who is legally present in the United States. Although excludable persons may still apply for legal status, they also face the prospect of being deported or being indefinitely detained until a final determination on their legal status is made. Under the 1996 Illegal Immigration Reform and Immigrant Responsibility Act, orders of deportation and exclusion have been consolidated under the term *removal*.

GUEST WORKER: A category of nonimmigrant who has been admitted to the United States on a temporary visa that authorizes that person to work in a particular occupational sector. Guest workers are granted very limited legal and social rights and are usually authorized to work only in occupational sectors or for employers specifically identified under the terms of the worker's temporary visa. *See* Temporary Visa

HABEAS CORPUS: An order (which can be requested by a prisoner or detainee) requiring law enforcement officials to appear in court to help a judge determine whether an individual is being lawfully imprisoned or detained. Habeas corpus is a safeguard against illegal confinement and has been used to contest deportation/removal proceedings.

ILLEGAL ENTRY/ILLEGAL REENTRANT: A noncitizen who enters the United States without authorization. Illegal reentry is considered an aggravated felony in most cases, especially if the noncitizen was originally expelled from the United States because of a felony conviction. *See also* Aggravated Felony; Unauthorized, Undocumented, or Illegal Migrant

IMMIGRANT: In legal terms, an immigrant is a noncitizen who has been admitted to the United States with the option of adjusting to permanent status (i.e., applying for a green card and eventually becoming a naturalized citizen). The term *immigrant*, as a legal status, can be distinguished from the more generic term *migrant*, which refers to any individual who enters the United States (with or without authorization) for the purpose of habitation of either permanent or temporary duration. A migrant can, in turn, be distinguished from a nonimmigrant who enters the United States without the intent of becoming a permanent or temporary inhabitant, as in the case of a tourist or visitor. *See also* Asylum Seeker; Nonimmigrant

IMMIGRATION COURT: A court that is part of the federal immigration system, which can be distinguished from courts that are part of the federal criminal and civil justice system. The highest level of the immigration court system is the Board of Immigration Appeals (part of the Executive Office for Immigration Review, which is a branch within the Department of Justice). The primary purpose of immigration court hearings is to make a final determination on the legal status of a noncitizen, which will result either in the person's deportation/removal or the granting of permanent or temporary legal status. Immigration court judges are appointed by officials within the immigration system, whereas judges in the federal or local/state criminal system are either elected by popular vote or appointed by federal officers in the executive branch, contingent on approval from other elected officials.

IMMIGRATION PRISON: *See* Detention

IMMIGRATION SYSTEM: A term that refers to the totality of federal agencies that have primary responsibility for enforcing all aspects of immigration policy. As of 2002 all federal agencies responsible for immigration services and enforcement (formerly agencies of the Immigration and Naturalization Service) were incorporated into the Department of Homeland Security, which is managed by a cabinet secretary who reports directly to the president. This system is separate, however, from the immigration court system, which falls under the Department of Justice. *See also* Immigration Court

LEGAL PERMANENT RESIDENT: A noncitizen who has been granted legal status that allows permanent residency in the United States. Legal permanent residents hold green cards. Legal permanent residents do not have the same scope of legal and social rights as naturalized citizens.

LOCAL ENFORCEMENT: Policies and practices (issued by federal, state, or municipal government agencies) that authorize local or state police to enforce federal immigration laws, typically allowing police to screen individuals for legal status.

NATIVE-BORN CITIZEN: A term that distinguishes citizens born on U.S. soil from naturalized citizens. Native-born citizens are immune to all forms of immigration enforcement. A naturalized citizen, however, still faces the prospect of deportation/removal if they commit what has been deemed a "deportable" offense (although the conditions that render naturalized citizens "deportable" are much more limited than the conditions that apply to noncitizens without permanent legal status).

NATURALIZED CITIZEN: An immigrant who has had their legal status adjusted, allowing them to access all of the legal and social rights of a native born citizen (except for the option of running for U.S. president). *See also* Native-Born Citizen

NONCITIZEN: A term that applies to all persons residing in the United States who are neither native-born nor naturalized citizens, including immigrants, nonimmigrants, refugees, persons with temporary protected status, and unauthorized migrants.

NONIMMIGRANT: A term that describes all noncitizens who have been authorized to enter the United States without the option of becoming permanent residents. Tourists and other visitors as well as students and workers/businesspersons admitted under temporary visas fall into this category.

NOTICE TO APPEAR: A legal term that refers to an issuance by a court demanding that a person who is in violation of a city or county ordinance, but who is not immediately present before the court, must appear forthwith. In the context of immigration law, a notice to appear is often issued when a noncitizen has been deemed deportable because of a change in his or her legal status, often because of a prior felony conviction.

PRIOR FELON: Within the context of immigration law, a prior felon is a noncitizen who is facing the prospect of deportation/removal because of a prior felony conviction. *See also* Aggravated Felony

PRISON-INDUSTRIAL COMPLEX: A term referring to the collection of private- and public-sector organizations that are involved in the management of the federal and local prison system and in lobbying for funding and legislation that supports the expansion and entrenchment of the national prison system.

REFUGEE: The legal status conferred on a noncitizen who is granted asylum by the U.S. government. A refugee is generally understood to be a noncitizen who applies for refugee status from outside the United States, whereas an asylee is an individual within the United States who has been officially recognized as an asylum seeker but has not been granted refugee status. A further distinction is noncitizens who are seeking asylum but have not been recognized by the U.S. government as asylees. Refugees are often granted more social rights than noncitizens who are admitted as immigrants—especially after the 1996 Illegal Immigration Reform and Immigrant Responsibility Act—but refugee status is not a permanent legal status. Refugees must apply for permanent residence (i.e., for a green card) if they wish to reside permanently in the United States. *See also* Asylum Seeker

RELIEF: Any legal remedy that grants a noncitizen legal status and/or dispels an order of deportation/removal.

REMOVAL: *See* Deportation

STAY OF REMOVAL: *See* Deferred Action/Stay of Removal.

TEMPORARY PROTECTED STATUS: Temporary legal status granted to noncitizens of designated nations, for reasons broadly consistent with the criteria used for asylum/refugee determinations. Temporary protected status is granted to noncitizens who are temporarily unable to safely return to their home country because of ongoing armed conflict, an environmental disaster, or other extraordinary and temporary conditions. Temporary protected status is generally of a shorter duration than refugee status, although it may be renewed.

TEMPORARY VISA: A document that confers temporary legal status, of varying length, upon a noncitizen. In most cases, the length of a temporary visa cannot be extended and a noncitizen cannot obtain a new temporary visa without leaving the country, although guest worker programs have allowed some noncitizens with temporary visas to renew while residing in the United States. There are several different categories of temporary visas, including but not limited to visas granted to business visitors, tourists, investors, students, fiancés, athletes, entertainers, and religious workers. Additionally, several nations are part of the U.S. government's visa waiver program, which allows citizens of those countries to visit the United States for ninety days for vacation or business purposes without the issuance of a visa.

TEMPORARY WORKER: *See* Guest Worker

UNAUTHORIZED, UNDOCUMENTED, OR ILLEGAL MIGRANT: A noncitizen who has entered the United States without authorization. Also referred to as an illegal alien. It should be noted that unauthorized or undocumented persons are not immigrants; that designation is granted to noncitizens who have been formally admitted to the United States with the option of becoming legal permanent residents or naturalized citizens.

VISA OVERSTAY: A noncitizen admitted to the United States under a temporary visa who has remained in the United States, without authorization, beyond the time period stipulated by that visa.

VOLUNTARY DEPARTURE: A determination which requires a noncitizen—usually an individual who has entered the United States without authorization and who has not been convicted for a criminal violation—to leave the United States on his or her own accord within a specified period of time. Voluntary departure is different from a formal deportation/removal proceeding, because it does not require the noncitizen to be placed in immigration detention (until he or she is required to leave the United States) and it usually does not prohibit the noncitizen from applying for reentry to the United States through legal means.

WITHHOLDING OF REMOVAL: Relief from deportation, used to prevent removal to a country where the noncitizen will very likely face persecution based on race, religion, nationality, political opinion, or membership in a particular social group.

Abira Ashfaq practiced as an immigration attorney between 1999 and 2003 as a Soros Justice Fellow and then as a detention attorney at Boston College Law School for the Catholic Legal Immigration Network (CLINIC). From 2004 through 2007, she worked as an immigration attorney. She has also periodically worked on social justice issues in South Asia, including research projects on women in jails in Pakistan and fish workers detained at the India-Pakistan sea border. She has published several articles in academic and popular journals on her experiences defending immigrants in the U.S. courts.

David C. Brotherton is a professor and chair of the Department of Sociology at John Jay College of Criminal Justice/CUNY and a member of Ph.D. faculties in criminal justice, sociology, and urban education at the Graduate Center/CUNY. He is the author of *Gangs and Society: Alternative Perspectives* (coedited with Louis Kontos and Luis Barrios, 2003), *The Almighty Latin King and Queen Nation: Street Politics and the Transformation of a New York City Gang* (with Luis Barrios, 2004), and *Globalizing the Streets* (coedited with Michael Flynn, 2007), all published by Columbia University Press. He is currently completing a manuscript on Dominican deportees with Luis Barrios titled "Back to the Homeland: Processes and Consequences of Criminal Deportation for Dominican Immigrants." He has also written numerous journal articles on immigration and criminal justice issues.

Jorge Capetillo-Ponce is an associate professor of sociology and a research associate at the Mauricio Gastón Institute at University of Massachusetts–Boston. He has published in the areas of social theory, race and ethnic relations, media studies, Latino Studies, and U.S.–Latin American relations. He is the editor of *Images of Mexico in the U.S. News Media* (2000). His latest publications are *Deciphering the Labyrinth: The Influence of Georg Simmel on the Sociology of Octavio Paz; Politics,*

Ethnicity, and Bilingual Education in Massachusetts; From 'A Clash of Civilizations' to 'Internal Colonialism': Reactions to the Theoretical Bases of Samuel Huntington's 'The Hispanic Challenge'; and *The Search for Consensus amid Conflict by Boston's Latino and Black Communities: The New Majority and Whittier Street Health Center Trends* (forthcoming).

David Cole is a professor of law at Georgetown University and has extensive experience working on precedent-setting federal and Supreme Court cases concerning the civil liberties of noncitizens and other issues pertaining to First Amendment and constitutional rights. He is the legal affairs correspondent for *The Nation* and a commentator on National Public Radio's *All Things Considered*. His recent publications include *Enemy Aliens: Double Standards and Constitutional Freedoms in the War on Terrorism* (2nd edition, 2005) and *Terrorism and the Constitution: Sacrificing Civil Liberties for National Security* (3rd edition, 2005, with James X. Dempsey).

Mark Dow began writing about detention in the early 1990s after briefly teaching English at Miami's Krome detention center, and then working for about two years on the staff of Miami's Haitian Refugee Center. He is the author of *American Gulag: Inside U.S. Immigration Prisons* (2004) and coeditor with David R. Dow of *Machinery of Death: The Reality of America's Death Penalty Regime* (2002). His essays, poems, and reviews have appeared in the *Boston Review, Miami Herald, Los Angeles Times, Threepenny Review, Pequod, Conjunctions, Green Integer Review, nthposition, New Politics, Prison Legal News,* and many other publications. He currently teaches English at Hunter College in New York City.

Arsalan Iftikhar is contributing director and editor for *Islamica* magazine. Until 2007, he served as the first-ever National Legal Director for the Council on American-Islamic Relations (CAIR) in Washington, D.C. His interviews and commentaries have appeared in international media outlets such as CNN and BBC World Service, as well as the *Washington Post, New York Times, San Francisco Chronicle, Dallas Morning News, Miami Herald, Detroit Free Press, Rolling Stone* and *Newsweek* magazine. He is a contributing author to *Taking Back Islam* (2003), winner of the 2003 Wilbur Award for Religion Book of the Year.

Subhash Kateel is a cofounder and codirector of Families for Freedom. Previously, he worked at Jesuit Refugee Services and American Friends Service Committee (Wayfarer House) as a caseworker for formerly detained asylum seekers. He also cofounded and coordinated the Detention Project for Desis Rising Up and Moving. Subhash has received various honors for his organizing work, including a Soros New York Community Fellowship and the Volunteer of the Year Award from the Detention Watch Network. Additionally, he is on the grantmaking board for the Funding Exchange's Saguaro Fund, and he coproduces and cohosts a monthly radio show, *The War on Immigrants Report,* on WBAI NYC.

Philip Kretsedemas is an assistant professor of sociology at the University of Massachusetts–Boston. His research and academic publications have examined the changing discourse of race in North America and the impact of social welfare and immigration policy on Afro-Caribbean and Latino communities in both the United States and Canada. His recent work has appeared in *Current Sociology, Stanford Law and Policy Review,* and the *Journal of Sociology and Social Welfare.* He is also a coeditor (with Ana Aparicio) of *Immigrants, Welfare Reform, and the Poverty of Policy* (2004).

Ira J. Kurzban is past president and general counsel of the American Immigration Lawyers Association. He has litigated over fifty cases concerning the civil liberties of noncitizens. His cases have set a number of critical legal precedents for U.S. immigration law and international human rights, including a $500 million judgment against Jean-Claude Duvalier, former dictator of Haiti. He has published in several highly regarded law journals and is the author of the widely acclaimed *Kurzban's Immigration Law Sourcebook* (currently in its 9th edition).

Dan Malone is a writer and a journalism instructor at Tarleton State University in Stephenville, Texas. Articles he wrote about foreigners in U.S. prisons won the 2002 National Media Award from the Detention Watch Network, and news stories he coauthored about civil rights violations for *Dallas Morning News* were recognized with the 1992 Pulitzer Prize for investigative reporting. He also is coauthor of *America's Condemned: Death Row Inmates in Their Own Words* (1999).

Malik Ndaula is a former jailhouse lawyer who spent three years detained in immigration custody, securing his release as a pro se litigant in 2004. From 2004 to 2006, he was a legal worker for the National Immigration Project of the National Lawyers Guild, with support from a Soros Justice Fellowship. During this time, he coordinated Keeping Hope Alive, an outreach program that provided advocacy and litigation support for detainees and their families. He is currently working as a community organizer and legal worker for Families for Freedom, an immigrant rights collective based in New York City.

Tamara K. Nopper is a Ph.D. candidate in Temple University's Department of Sociology. She also serves as an adjunct faculty member in the Sociology Department and in the American Studies program and is a researcher for the Institute of Global Management Studies. Her research interests are race science and theory as informed by gender, sexuality, capitalism, immigration, citizenship, globalization, and Asian American communities. She is in the process of completing a dissertation on how government institutions and ethnic banks make capital and resources available to Korean immigrant entrepreneurs to open and expand businesses in the United States. Her writings have appeared in both popular and academic publications.

Debbie Satyal is a student at Boston College Law School and an immigrant rights advocate. Her interest in immigrant rights stems from her experience migrating to the United States, at a young age, with her parents from Kathmandu, Nepal. She is involved with Boston College's Immigration and Asylum Project, the Ruby Slippers Post Deportation Human Rights Project, and other clinical and extracurricular experiences relevant to immigration law.

Liza Schuster is a senior lecturer in the Department of Sociology at City University, London. Formerly she served as a senior researcher at the Centre on Migration, Policy and Society at the University of Oxford. Her work focuses on migration and asylum in particular. She is the author of *The Use and Abuse of Political Asylum in Britain and Germany* (2003) as well as a number of articles on the treatment of asylum seekers, the rights of migrants, and the link between migration and racism in Europe. She is currently completing *States, Citizens and Migrants: Rights and Racism in Europe.*

Aarti Shahani is a cofounder and codirector of Families for Freedom, a multiethnic defense network for immigrants facing deportation. She became an organizer after her uncle was deported and her father placed in deportation proceedings. She received a New Voices Fellowship to work with the National Immigration Project of the National Lawyers Guild and the Charles H. Revson Fellowship at Columbia University. She writes and speaks regularly on immigrant and prisoner issues.

Irum Sheikh is a filmmaker and an ethnic studies scholar who has been researching the topics of the September 11 attacks, representations of race and gender, and the internment of Japanese and Latin Americans through art and writing over the last ten years. Her dissertation, "September 11 Detentions: Racial Formation and a Hegemonic Discourse of Muslim Terrorist," uses theories of racial formation and hegemony to illustrate the racialization of Muslims before and after 9/11. Her latest documentary about the Japanese–Latin American internment during World War II, *Hidden Internment: The Art Shibayama Story,* has been widely shown at film festivals and conferences. Currently, she is writing a book that includes oral histories of people detained after 9/11 and confined at the Metropolitan Detention Center in New York City.

Kathleen Staudt is a professor of political science and director of the Center for Civic Engagement at the University of Texas at El Paso. She received her Ph.D. in political science from the University of Wisconsin in 1976 and has published a dozen books, among them *Fronteras No Mas: Toward Social Justice at the U.S.–Mexico Border* (2002, with Irasema Coronado) and *Pledging Allegiance: Learning Nationalism at the El Paso–Juarez Border* (2003, with Susan Rippberger). Her book *Voilence and Activism at the Border: Gender, Fear, and Everyday Life in Cuidad Juarez* is forthcoming.

Michael Welch is a professor in the Criminal Justice program at Rutgers University–New Brunswick. He also is a visiting fellow at the Centre for the Study of Human Rights at the London School of Economics. He is the author of several books on prisons and social control, *Detained: Immigration Laws and the Expanding I.N.S. Jail Complex* (2002), *Ironies of Imprisonment* (2005), and *Scapegoats of September 11th: Hate Crimes and State Crimes in the War on Terror* (2006).

Anti-Drug Abuse Act (1988), 212–213; aggregated felony and, 220

Antidrug and anticrime rhetoric: anti-immigrant sentiment in, 63–65; due process rights and, 66

Anti-Haitian policies at Guantánamo Bay, Cuba, 29, 30–32, 35

Anti-immigrant sentiment, 335, 337–338; constituency for, 359n42; economic struggle of middle class and, 67–68; effects on economy, 73; effort to ramp up, 73; elimination of current, 74; emergence of new enforcement legislation, 73; growth of, 63; media coverage of, 76n14; roots of, 63–64; scope of global, 2

Antiterrorism and Effective Death Penalty Act (AEDPA) (1996), 8, 94, 179, 183, 220, 255, 275, 281n2, 330n21, 376–377, 377, 378

AOL-Time Warner, 71

Apartheid, 258; immigrant, 258–259, 279–281

Appleby, Scott, 127–128

Arab-Muslims, 24n30; hate speech and, 11; immigration flows of, 1; openness of United States to, 20n4; racialization of, 82–89; racial profiling of, 87–88; relaxation of criteria for registration of, 11; September 11, 2001 terrorist attacks and, 108–137; stereotypes of, 11, 82–89; sympathizing with al-Qaeda, 88; targeting of communities of, 229; treatment of, after 9/11, 10–11

Aristide, Jean Bertrand, 31, 34

Arizona, immigration policies in, 291

Article 32 hearing, 116

Ashcroft, John, 34, 124, 148; power of, 108, 109–114; success of

government's intelligence process and, 85; under USA PATRIOT Act, 108; war on terror and, 143

Ashfaq, Abira, 14, 368

Asian exclusion acts, 348

Asian nationals, identification of, as immigration violators, 349–350

Assembly-line removals, 182–184

Asylum seekers, 33–35; containing, 141–146; criteria for admitting, 20; detaining of, 51; hostility toward in Europe, 154n9; invention and dramatization of bogus, 146; in secret prisons, 45; societal reaction to, 146

Atkins, Clyde, 30–31

Atlantic Records, 71

Azmath, Mohammad, 83–85, 92–93

Azmath, Tasleem, 84

Bad Immigrants, 264

Baghram, 149

Bail for Immigration Detainees, 146

Balanced-budget conservatism, 314, 315–316, 318, 328

Barbed wire, 146

Barr, Bob, 118

Barry, Kevin, 118

Bashi, Vilna, 228

Bergeron, Russ, 49

Berman, Leo, 297

Bilingual education, 298; public policies about, 297

Bin Laden, Osama, 53, 54, 371

Black Entertainment Television, 71

Black immigrants, 204–237, 267; as aggravated felonies, 220–224; apprehensions by local police and federal agencies, 206–209; arrests, bookings, and sentencing of, 214–219; convictions for immigration-related crimes, 209–214; racist treatment of, 204–205

Blanket Detention Order (2003), 142–143

Blogosphere, 318–319

Bond grant, 188

Bond hearing, 188; changed circumstances and, 188

Border crossing, impact of guest worker program on reducing unauthorized, 346

Border Interfaith, 305

Border Network for Human Rights, 301

Border Patrol, 295, 303, 304; establishment of, 293; jurisdiction of, 231n9

Border Protection, Antiterrorism, and Illegal Immigration Control Act (2005), 78n51, 285n27

Border residents, impact of 9/11 on, 294

Border terrorism, 304

Border zone, 293

Bralo, Zrinka, 141

Bregman, Martin, 39

Brotherton, David, 13–14, 153

Burundi, Temporary Protected Status (TPS) and, 181

Bush, George W., 299; anti-Haitian policies of, 34, 35; creation of Office of Homeland Security, 25n40; immigration policy under, 30, 344, 365; patriotism and, 87; proposal for guest worker program, 360n48; success of government intelligence process and, 85

Business-friendly immigration policy, 3

Byers, Stephen, 148

Calavita, Kitty, 314, 316

California, immigration policies in, 291

Camarota, Steven, 325, 327, 328

Camp Delta, 55

Campus Watch, 127

Camp X-ray, 44, 55, 115

Canadian nationals, identification of, as immigration violators, 349–350

Cancellation of removal, 179, 193–196

Cancellation waivers, 185

Capetillo-Ponce, Jorge, 16–17, 368–369

Carballo v. Luttrell, 42n48

Caribbean immigrants: apprehension rate for, 362–363n76; criminal deportations of, 224, 226–227

Caroll, Adem, 98, 284n25

Carter, Jimmy, policy toward Mariel Cubans, 37

Castlebury, James, 46

Castro, Fidel, 36; political prisoners of, 38–39

Catholic faith as supportive of immigrants' rights, 300

Center for American-Islamic Relations (CAIR), 11

Center for Constitutional Rights, 103, 111

Center for Immigration Studies (Commonwealth of Independent States [CIS]), 324–325

Center for National Security Studies, 149

César Chávez Day (March 31), 301

Chahal, Karamjit Singh, 145

Chamizal National Memorial, Sensenbrenner hearings at, 204–205

Chamizal National Park, 301

Change, taking risks for, 199–202

Cheney, Richard B., 34, 69; Scalia's insistence on ruling on court case involving, 72

Chicago Council on Global Affairs, 319

Immigration and Nationality Act
(1952), 244, 340, 375
Immigration and Nationality Technical
Corrections Act (1994), 75n7
Immigration and Naturalization Act
(1965), 75n2
Immigration and Naturalization
Service (INS), dismantling of, 19
Immigration control advocates,
327–328
Immigration control movements, goal
of, 335
Immigration courtroom, description
of, following 9/11, 90
The Immigration Debate, 323
Immigration detention centers, daily
population in, 210
Immigration enforcement, 1–25; before
and after 9/11, 8–12; expansion of,
15; mapping terrain, 7–8; media
coverage of, 6; money spent on,
346; in regulating labor flows, 3;
War on Drugs and, 213–214
Immigration flows: cyclical, nativist
reaction to new, 366–367; growth of
low-income population and, 336
Immigration laws: aggravated felony
provisions of federal, 281–282n3;
creation of tiered system of rights,
13; uneven enforcement of, 338. See
also specific law
Immigration minutemen, 69
Immigration officers: expansion of
powers, 65–66; protection of,
against legal proceedings, 65
Immigration prisons: abuses in, 15–16;
fighting for freedom in, 246–250;
visiting in, 266
Immigration problem: local enforcement as solution to so-called, 336–
340; needs and addressing, 74–75

Immigration raids, 7, 18
Immigration reform: at crossroads,
365–373; national debate over, 334
Immigration Reform Act (1990), 376
Immigration Reform and Control Act
(1986), 3, 6, 25n38, 294, 316–317,
329–330n21, 375
Immigration Reform Caucus, 320
Immigration-related crimes, convic-
tions and sentencing for, 209–214
Immigration restrictionist movement, 2
Immigration violators: apprehension
of, 353–354n4; drug convictions
and, 22–23n18; local enforcement
apprehensions of, by national
origin, 350
Inadmissible aliens, 36
Incarcerated immigrants, rights of, 12
Indefinite detention, 47, 197–199
Industrial Areas Foundation (IAF),
303, 312–313n47
Inspector General, Office of (OIG)
2003 report: of rights violations of
detainees, 91–92, 106n37
Institutional discrimination, 8
INS v. St. Cyr, 194
International Boundary and Water
Commission, 292
International Committee of the Red
Cross, 55–56, 56–57
Investigative reporting, rarity of, 70
Iraqi asylum seekers: obligation of
United States to resettle, 20n4;
refusal of, 1
Islam, Yusuf, 10, 11, 108, 128–130
Islamic Circle of North America
(ICNA), 98

Jailhouse lawyers, 242, 278
Japanese American Citizens League
(JACL), 96–97, 113

Japanese Americans: FBI raids on, 104*n*16; FBI raids on, during World War II, 86, 104*n*16; internment of, 103; shame and guilt felt by, in World War II, 97; treatment of, during World War II, 95, 97
Al-Jihad, 99, 100
Jim Crow policies, 293
Johnson, Jimmy, 51
Johnson, Sterling, 32
Joseph, David, 34, 143
Juárez, Ciudad, 16, 291
Judicial discretion, forms of, 14
Judicial review, diminution of, 72
Judicial system: democracy and, 72; politicized and polarized, 72
Jus soli, standard of, 297
Justice, U. S. Department of (DOJ): immigration reform and, 335; misuse of material witness statute, 124–125; Office of Legal Counsel within, 341
Justice Statistics, Bureau of, 61*n*15

Kamel, Abdullah, 57–58
Kamel, Mansour, 57–58
Kanj, Bassam, 53
Kateel, Subhash, 16, 266–267
Kaye, Ron, 140–141
Kennedy, Edward M., 119, 129, 265, 344, 365
Keynesian welfare state, dismantling of safety nets, 336–337
Khalifa, Ahmed, 86
Khan, Ayub, 83–85, 92–93
Klein, Jerry, 88
Kleinschmidt, Gerhard, 54
Kneedler, Edwin S., 39, 40
Know-Nothings, 63
Koresh, David, 32
Kretsedemas, Philip, 17, 153, 370

Kroc Institute, 127–128
Kurnaz, Murat, 57
Kurnaz, Rabiye, 57
Kurzban, Ira, 9–10, 34–35, 368–369

Labor flows, immigration enforcement in regulating, 3
Labor markets, role of immigrants in, 3
Labor movement, support for legalizing migrant workers, 3
Land, Mitch, 56, 58
Lau v. *Nichols*, 297
Law enforcement departments, immigration enforcement by, 5–6
Lawful permanent residents (LPRs), 179
Lawless enclave, 32
Lawyers: jailhouse, 242, 278; pro-bono, 247
LeBlanc, Ida, 284*n*21
Lee, United States v., 72
Legal immigrations, long-term impact of, on traditional culture of, 335
Legalization, delegalization and, 260–261
Letter of law, race and, 258–259
Levin, Carl, 119
Lewiston, Maine, dispute over allocation of municipal welfare services in, 355*n*13
Liberia, Temporary Protected Status (TPS) and, 181
Life magazine, 71
List of Five Thousand, 110–111
Little, Brown and Co., 71
Lledo, Pedro, 122–123
Local enforcement, 16; connection between prison industrial complex and, 351; as controversial, 334–336; economic nationalism and, 335;

Middle class: decline of, 67–68; disintegration of, 69–70; economic struggle of, 67–68, 337

Middle Eastern asylum seekers, refusal of, 1

Middle Eastern noncitizens, assumption of, as terrorists, 368

Migration flows, openness to, 1

Military Commissions Act (2006), 67

Miller, Geoffrey, 117

Minimum wage, 74

Minuteman Project, 5, 320

Mixed status families, 357*n*23

Mohammad, Azmath, 100–101

Moral panic, 138–141; sociology of, 139; theory of, 11

Morawetz, Nancy, 276

Muehler v. *Mena*, 347–348

Murkowski, Lisa, 114

Muslim factor, 125

Nagata, Donna, 96

Napolitano, Janet, 311*n*33

National Association for the Advancement of Colored People, 113

National Coalition for Anti-Deportation Campaigns, 146

National Crime Information Center (NCIC): black immigrants apprehended through, 207; including immigration violations in, 206–207

National Crime Information Center (NCIC) database, 206, 349; creation of, containing civil immigration violators and criminal violators, 341; placement of immigrants with outstanding deportation orders on, 341; selectivity of data included in, 351

National Guard troops, allocation and payment for, 298

National Immigration Forum, 282*n*4

National Immigration Project of National Lawyers Guild, 75*n*8, 254

Nationalist Egalitarian, 20*n*7

National League of Cities, 113

National Origins Quota System, 1, 63, 294; elimination of, 64

National policy context, local enforcement and, 340–346

National Public Radio investigation, 274

National Security Entry-Exit Registration System (NSEERS), 11, 111–112; creation of, 206

National Union of Domestic Employees (N.U.D.E.), 284*n*21

Native-born workers, dearth of quality jobs for, 337

Nativism, 10, 17, 316

Ndaula, Malik, 15

The New Americans, 323

New Bedford, Massachusetts: immigration raid in, 18, 366

Newburn, Tim, 153

New Line Cinema, 71

New Mexico, immigration policies in, 291

New York, diverse immigrant population in, 268

Ngai, Mai, 283*n*8

Nicaraguans, granting Temporary Protected Status (TPS) to Hondurans and, 35

Nicholas, Sandra, 90

9/11, racializing, criminalizing, and silencing, 81–107

Nisei (first generation), lack of intergenerational dialogue between *sansei* (second generation) and, 96

Nixon, Richard M., civil liberties under, 72